The New Zealand Bed & Breakfast Book

2010

Published by...

Moonshine Press

P.O. Box 6843
Wellington
New Zealand
Tel: +64 4 385-2615
Fax: +64 4 385-2694
Web: www.bnb.co.nz
Email: info@bnb.co.nz

ISBN 978-0-9582569-5-7

Cover illustration *Arrowtown,* an acrylic on canvas by Susie Stone courtesy of Millwood Gallery, Wellington
www.millwoodgallery.co.nz

Welcome to this edition of The Bed & Breakfast Book. Bed & Breakfast in New Zealand means a warm welcome and a unique holiday experience. Most B&B accommodation is in private homes with a sprinkling of guesthouses and small hotels. Each listing in the guide has been written by the host themselves and you will discover their warmth and personality through their writing. The New Zealand Bed & Breakfast Book is not just an accommodation guide – it is an introduction to a uniquely New Zealand holiday experience. The best holidays are often remembered by the friends one makes. How many of us have loved a country because of one or two memorable individuals we encountered? For the traveller who wants to experience the real New Zealand and get to know its people, bed and breakfast offers an opportunity to do just that. We recommend you don't try to travel too far in one day. Take time to enjoy the company of your hosts and other local people. You will find New Zealand hosts friendly and generous, and eager to share their local knowledge with you.

We have carefully inspected every property;

B&B Approved **B&B Approved;** All B&Bs in The Bed & Breakfast Book have been inspected on joining. They conform to the Schedule of Standards following. As important as the requirement of meeting a physical standard, we expect that all of our properties will offer excellent hospitality. Some hosts who are members of associations or marketing groups, which also undertake inspections, have chosen to display the logos below.

@ home NEW ZEALAND **The @home NEW ZEALAND** logo represents the largest organisation of hosted accommodation providers in New Zealand. It assures you of a warm welcome from friendly, helpful hosts. Accommodations displaying this logo are regularly assessed every two years and have met the quality standards set by the Association.

qualmark ★★★★★ guest & hosted **Qualmark™** is New Zealand tourism's official mark of quality. All Qualmark™ licenced accommodation listed in this directory means they have been independently assessed as professional and trustworthy, so you can book and buy with confidence. They will meet your essential requirements of cleanliness, safety, security and comfort; and offer a range and quality of services appropriate to their star grade.

Heritage Inns; A collection of luxury historic hosted character bed and breakfast lodges across NZ, are superior and often recommended by tourists. Our B&Bs have knowledgeable and friendly hosts. Our luxury accommodation ranges from the quiet honeymoon lodge in boutique romantic locations to central city accommodation - rivaling superior apartments, hotels or motels. Alternatively, enjoy the genuine NZ experience of an idyllic farmstay, lodge or luxury country B&B.

Superior Inns; Superior Inns of New Zealand properties are specially selected. All offer a true bed and breakfast experience, highlights of your visit to New Zealand. The specially selected bed and breakfast properties offer spacious bedrooms with bathrooms, luxury fittings, private guest lounges, fabulous delectable breakfasts and a chance to meet other visitors or be on your own. Our hosts can organise airport pickups, rental cars, restaurant bookings, honeymoon packages and short stay options.

Finding your way around

We travel from north to south listing the towns as we come to them. In addition, we've divided New Zealand into geographical regions, a map of which is included at the start of each chapter. In some regions, such as Southland, our listings take a detour off the north to south route, and follow their nose - it will soon become obvious.

Happy Travelling
The B&B Book Team

Our Guarantee

Hosts in The New Zealand Bed & Breakfast Book are committed to offering quality hospitality. If you receive hospitality which is less than you expected please discuss your concerns with your hosts at the time. If you are not satisfied you should contact the publishers who will take up the matter with the hosts. If you are still not satisfied the publishers will refund their assessment of a fair proportion of the tariff you paid.

Your comments

We welcome your views on The Bed & Breakfast Book and the hosts you meet.
Please visit our website **www.bnb.co.nz** or write to us at,
PO Box 6843, Wellington, New Zealand.

Comment Forms

Please help us to maintain our high standards by sending us comments about where you stayed. Guest Comments forms are available from your hosts.

- You may submit your comment on our website **www.bnb.co.nz**
- Or your hosts will give you a comment form.
- Or simply cut one from the back of the book.
- Each comment returned will be in our ongoing monthly draw for a free night's B&B.
- Each person staying can submit a comment for an increased chance of success.
- Guest comments are displayed on the hosts' pages at **www.bnb.co.nz**

About Bed & Breakfast

Our B&Bs range from homely to luxurious, but you can always be assured of generous hospitality.

Types of accommodation

Traditional B&B

Generally small owner-occupied home accommodation usually with private guest living and dining areas.

Homestay

A homestay is a B&B where you share the family's living area.

Farmstay

Country accommodation, usually on a working farm.

Self-contained

Separate self-contained accommodation, with kitchen and living/dining room. Breakfast provisions usually provided at least for the first night.

Separate/suite

Similar to self-contained but without kitchen facilities. Living/dining facilities may be limited.

Bathrooms

Ensuite and private bathrooms are for your use exclusively.
Guests share bathroom means you will be sharing with other guests.
Family share means you will be sharing with the family.

Tariff

The prices listed are in New Zealand dollars and include GST. Prices listed are subject to change, and any change to listed prices will be stated at time of booking. Some hosts offer a discount for children - this applies to age 12 or under unless otherwise stated. Most of our B&Bs will accept credit cards.

Reservations

We recommend you contact your hosts well in advance to be sure of confirming your accommodation. Most hosts require a deposit so make sure you understand their cancellation policy. Please let your hosts know if you have to cancel, they will have spent time preparing for you. You may also book accommodation through some travel agents or via specialised B&B reservation services.

Breakfast & Dinner

Breakfast is included in the tariff, with each host offering their own menu. You'll be surprised at the range of delicious breakfasts available, many using local produce. If you would like dinner most hosts require 24 hours notice.

Smoking

Most of our B&Bs are non-smoking, but smoking is permitted outside. Listings displaying the no smoking logo do not permit smoking anywhere on the property. B&Bs which have a smoking area inside mention this in their text.

Accessibility

♿ Certified as being wheelchair accessible.

Schedule of Standards

General

Friendly, warm greeting at door by host
Local tourism and transport information available to guests
Property appearance neat and tidy, internally and externally
Absolute cleanliness of the home in all areas used by the guests
Absolute cleanliness of kitchen, refrigerator and food storage areas
Gate or roadside identification of property
Protective clothing and footwear available for farmstay guests
Hosts accept responsibility to comply with local body bylaws
Host will be present to welcome and farewell guests
Hosts' pets and young children mentioned in listing
Smoke alarms in each guest bedroom and above each landing
Evacuation advice card displayed in each bedroom (recommended)
Working torch beside every bed
Suitable fire extinguisher in kitchen and on landing of each upper floor (recommended)
Fire blanket in kitchen (recommended)

Hosts accept responsibility to comply with applicable laws and regulations

Fire safety laws and requirements
Insurances
Swimming and spa pool regulations
Other laws impacting on operation of a B&B

Bedrooms

Each bedroom solely dedicated to guests with...
Bed heating
Heating
Light controlled from the bed
Wardrobe space with variety of hangers
Drawers
Good quality floor covering
Mirror
Power point near a mirror
Waste paper basket
Drinking glasses
Clean pillows with additional available
No Host family items stored in the room
Night light for guidance to w.c. if not adjacent to bedroom
Blinds or curtains on all windows where appropriate
Good quality mattresses in sound condition on a sound base
Clean bedding appropriate to the climate, with extra availabl

Bathroom & toilet facilities

At least one bathroom adequately ventilated and equipped with...
Bath or shower
Wash handbasin and mirror
Covered wastebasket in bathroom
Extra toilet roll
Lock on bathroom and toilet doors
Electric razor point if bedrooms are without a suitable power point
Soap, towels, bathmat, facecloths, fresh for each new guest
Towels changed or dried daily for guests staying more than one night
Sufficient bathroom and toilet facilities to serve family and guests

New Zealand and Regions

Contents

Introduction ______ 2
New Zealand Regions Map ______ 6

North Island
Northland ______ 8
Auckland ______ 43
Waikato, King Country ______ 81
Coromandel ______ 96
Bay of Plenty ______ 116
Gisborne, East Coast ______ 159
Taranaki, Wanganui, Ruapehu, Rangitikei ______ 163
Hawkes Bay ______ 178
Manawatu, Horowhenua ______ 200
Wairarapa ______ 208
Wellington ______ 215

South Island
Marlborough ______ 250
Nelson, Golden Bay ______ 268
West Coast ______ 296
Canterbury ______ 314
South Canterbury, North Otago ______ 365
Otago, North Catlins ______ 381
Southland, South Catlins ______ 422

Index ______ 441

Northland
Houhora
Cape Karikari
Coopers Beach
Kaitaia
Ahipara
Kerikeri
Okaihau
Paihia
Russell
Opua
Pakaraka
Opononi
Omapere
Whangarei
Taiharuru
Whangarei Heads
Ruakaka
Dargaville
Waipu
Waipu Cove
Paparoa
Matakohe
Kaiwaka
Te Hana
Wellsford
Warkworth
Sandspit
Puhoi
Orewa
Kaukapakapa
Silverdale
Helensville
Albany
Auckland
1
10
12
14
0 Kilometres 45
0 Miles 27

Houhora *44 km N of Kaitaia*

Houhora Lodge & Homestay Homestay

B&B Approved

Jacqui & Bruce Malcolm
3994 Far North Road,
Houhora, RD 4, Kaitaia

Tel (09) 409 7884
or 021 926 992
Fax (09) 409 7801
houhora.homestay@xtra.co.nz
www.topstay.co.nz

Double/Twin $130-$195
Single $100-$130
(Full breakfast)
Children $30.00
Dinner $45 by arrangement
Visa MC accepted
Children welcome
3 King/Twin 3 Single (3 bdrm)
Bathrooms: 2 Ensuite 1 Private

We have fled our largest city with Max our Hunterway cross dog to live on the shores of Houhora Harbour, and look forward to sharing this special part of New Zealand with you. Come and enjoy remote coastal walks, shell-collecting, Cape Reinga, 90 Mile Beach and other attractions. We can arrange 4x4 trips, sport or game fishing and provide relaxed and quality accommodation on your return. Home-made bread, home-grown fruit, home-pressed olive oil, vegetables and eggs. Wireless internet, fax and laundry facilities available.

~

Coopers Beach *4 km N of Mangonui*

Doubtless Bay Lodge *B&B*

B&B Approved

Barbara & Ian Easterbrook
33 Cable Bay Block Road,
Coopers Beach, Mangonui

Tel (09) 406 1661
or 021 824 571
Fax (09) 406 1662
enquiries@doubtlessbaylodge.co.nz
www.doubtlessbaylodge.co.nz

Double/Twin $98-$120
Single $75-$85 (Full breakfast)
Children $25
Visa MC Eftpos accepted
Children welcome
3 Queen 1 Twin (4 bdrm)
Own kitchenettes - no cooking
Queens with table and chairs
Bathrooms: 4 Ensuite

Friendly New Zealand hosts. Breakfast on the balcony or in the dining room with panoramic views over Doubtless Bay and surrounding countryside. Short walk to the golden sands of Coopers Beach and local shops. Each room has own ensuite, Sky TV, fridge, tea/coffee making facilities. Guest laundry and barbeque available. Cape Reinga tours, fishing trips and golf games can be arranged. Visit the many historic places, isolated beaches and local wineries in the area. Let us help you make this the perfect holiday destination.

Kaitaia - Pamapuria *10 km S of Kaitaia*

Plane Tree Lodge *B&B Homestay Cottage with Kitchen*

Rosemary & Mike Wright
Pamapuria, RD2,
Kaitaia, Northland

Tel (09) 408 0995
or 0274 338 859
Fax (09) 408 0959
reservationsplanetreelodge@xtra.co.nz
www.plane-tree-lodge.net.nz

Double/Twin $150-$185
Single $100-$125
(Special breakfast)
S/C cottage sleeps 4 $180-$220
Visa MC Eftpos accepted
Children welcome
3 Queen 1 Twin 1 Single (5 bdrm)
3 in B&B 2 in cottage
Bathrooms: 3 Ensuite 1 Private

Rosemary, Mike, Polly & Jenna, (their golden retrievers), welcome you to Northland, where summer lingers longer. Experience the beauty & tranquility of subtropical N.Z. Enjoy the difference of receiving great hospitality in a quiet, peaceful rural setting with large relaxing gardens.Your friendly knowledgable hosts love helping to plan your activities or adventures from their architectually designed home. Relax in the evening with a spa & complementary glass of wine, & wake each morning to birdsong & the aroma of a delicious breakfast.

Kaitaia *15 km S of Kaitaia*

Bush Walk B&B/Homestay *B&B Homestay*

Sandra
42 Te Rore Road,
RD 1, Kaitaia 0481

Tel (09) 408 4959
or 021 182 7553
Fax (09) 408 4009
sandra21madhousefarm@xtra.co.nz

Double/Twin $90
Single $70
(Full breakfast)
Children 3-12 yrs half price,
Under 3 free
Visa MC Eftpos accepted
Pet free home
Children welcome
1 Queen 1 Single (2 bdrm)
Bathrooms: 1 Family share

Enjoy a relaxing sojourn in a peaceful bush setting and experience all Northland has to offer. A warm welcome awaits guests who come to stay at this unusual 'A' frame, timber interior home situated on 6 acres of garden and native bush. Wake up to birdsong and at the end of the day relax and watch the sun set behind the hills. BBQ facilities are available.

Ahipara *15 km W of Kaitaia*

Beachfront *Luxury Apartment with Kitchen Self contained and serviced*

Paul and Jenny Steele
14 Kotare Street,
Ahipara, 0551

Tel 09 409 4007
or 021 227 3376
Fax 09 409 4007
pauljenny@beachfront.net.nz
www.beachfront.net.nz

Double/Twin $150-$350
Single $120-$300
(Full breakfast extra)
Dinner $60 pp by arrangement
Visa MC Eftpos accepted
Children and pets welcome
4 King 2 Double (4 bdrm)
4 Super King Double or 8 single
Bathrooms: 4 Ensuite
All bedrooms ensuite

Upmarket absolute water front self-contained seviced, private apartments. A studio covered patio with a 2nd bedroom option. A two bedroom apartment with balconies. All bedrooms ensuite - wireless broadband -surf views from every pillow Paul and Jenny are 5th generatiion New Zealanders and have a cat called Sunshine who is not allowed in the apartments.

Ahipara - Ninety Mile Beach *8 km N of AHIPARA*

Taharangi Marie Lodge *Luxury Homestay*

B&B Approved

Ron and Connie Adams
PO Box 59,
Kaitaia, 0441

Tel (09) 406 7462
or 021 926 949
taharangi@xtra.co.nz
www.90mile.co.nz

Double/Twin $300-$400
(Continental breakfast)
4 course dinners with fresh seafood
Visa MC accepted
Children welcome
2 King/Twin (2 bdrm)
Guestsuites
Bathrooms: 2 Ensuite

Built 1997 the Lodge is set in the dunes of Ninety Mile beach. Absolute Beachfront with no neighbours for 7 km.Ron 5th generation Kiwi Connie Maori have intimate knowledge to make your stay in the North special Fresh seafood features in the New Zealand cuisine of the Lodge. Come as a stranger leave as a friend.

Bay of Islands - Kerikeri *10 km N of Kerikeri Central*

Kerikeri Inlet View *B&B Homestay Farmstay*

Trish & Ryan Daniells
99C Furness Road,
RD 3, Kerikeri

Tel (09) 407 7477
or 027 567 4477
or (09) 407 7478
Fax (09) 407 7478
kerikeri_inlet_view@hotmail.com

Double/Twin $95
Single $50 (Full breakfast)
Children $15
Dinner $20 by arrangement
Visa MC accepted
Children and pets welcome
1 Queen 2 Double 2 Single (3 bdrm)
Bathrooms: 1 Ensuite 1 Private
1 Guest share

We welcome you to our spacious home on top of our 1100 acre beef and sheep farm. Enjoy the panoramic views from the Kerikeri Inlet to the Bay of Islands while you relax in our spa pool. Join us for breakfast consisting of seasonal fruit, homemade bread and butter, free-range chook eggs, and our own sausages, before exploring the many attractions around Kerikeri. We have avocado and olive orchards and free farm tours. Note: Please phone first for detailed directions. We can speak some Japanese.

Bay of Islands - Kerikeri *2 km W of Kerikeri*

Palm View House *Luxury B&B*

Judy & Tony Pratt
8 Kotare Heights,
Kerikeri, Bay of Islands

Tel (09) 407 6883
or 021 024 50615
palmview@xtra.co.nz
www.palmview.co.nz

Double/Twin $180-$270
Single $170-$260
(Full breakfast)
Children not suitable
Dinner by arrangement
Visa MC accepted
Not suitable for children
1 King/Twin 2 King (3 bdrm)
all ensuite bedrooms
Bathrooms: 3 Ensuite

If you are looking for luxury holiday accommodation, with stunning views, peace and tranquility, then you have found Palm View House, set in 1 acre of beautiful gardens, which was built in 2007, and was awarded bronze for House of the Year 2008. We have 3 luxury suites, with ensuites,bathrobes, fluffy towels and many toiletries.All suites have fridges,TV,DVD,CD electric blankets, iron and ironing board, coffee/tea making facilities,also spectacular inlet views .We are 2 ks from Kerikeri village.Judy and Tony offer you a warm welcome.

Bay of Islands - Kerikeri *20 km N of Paihia*

B&B Approved

Glenfalloch *B&B Homestay*

Keith
48 Landing Road,
Kerikeri

Tel (09) 407 5471
Fax (09) 407 5473
glenfall@ihug.co.nz
www.kerikeri-accommodation.co.nz

Double/Twin $90-$115
Single $80-$90
(Full breakfast)
Children $25
Dinner $30pp by arrangement
Visa MC accepted
Children welcome
1 King 1 Queen 1 Double
1 Single (3 bdrm)
Bathrooms: 2 Ensuite 1 Private

Venture down Glenfalloch's driveway to our secluded bed and breakfast, nestled in a garden paradise. Enjoy the hospitality of Keith. Relax in the spa and swimming pool and on teh decks, or for the energetic there is lawn tennis. Glenfalloch is just 500 metres from Kerikeri's Stone Store and Kemp Mission House, and adjacent to the lovely Rainbow Falls walking track. Kerikeri is unique and offers some good golf courses within short distances, lovely shops and excellent restaurants.

Kerikeri-Waipapa *5 km N of Waipapa*

B&B Approved

Ipipiri Lodge *Luxury B&B Lodge*

Elaine and Graham Belben
216 Ness Road,
Waipapa,
Kerikeri, 0295

Tel 09 407 4159
or 0800 407 4159
Mobile 0272 12 4159
info@ipipirilodge.co.nz
www.ipipirilodge.co.nz

Double/Twin $180-$250
(Full breakfast)
Dinner by arrangement, extra cost
Seasonal local produce and goods
Visa MC Eftpos accepted
Not suitable for children
1 King/Twin 2 King (3 bdrm)
2 king and one king single twin
Bathrooms: 3 Ensuite

Welcome to Ipipiri Lodge a great holiday destination set within rural farmland. Each suite has luxurious towels, hair dryer, bathrobe/slippers, and complimentary toiletries, fridge, tea/coffee making facilities, tv/stereo/alarm clock, iron and ironing board and own patio. Elaine has retired after 27 years in the Navy. She has a huge passion in wine, arts and crafts and local history.Graham has also retired after 30 years in the navy and his interests are wine, rugby, and gardening.We share our house with our elderly dog Jeddah, and Reilly the cat.

Bay of Islands - Paihia *7 km N of Paihia*

Lily Pond Estate B&B (Est 1989) *B&B*
Allwyn & Graeme Sutherland
725B Puketona Road
Paihia 0204
Lily Pond Estate sign at gate

Tel (09) 402 7041

Double/Twin $105
Single $60
(Continental breakfast)
1 Double 1 Twin 1 Single (3 bdrm)
Bathrooms: 1 Private 1 Guest share

Drive in through an avenue of mature Liquid Amber trees to our comfortable timber home on our 5 acre country estate growing citrus and pip fruit. The guest wing has views of the fountain, bird aviary, small lake and black swan with the double and twin rooms having private verandah access. Fresh orange juice, fruit and home-made jams are served at breakfast. We are born New Zealanders, and will gladly share our Bay of Island knowledge to make your visit most memorable.

Bay of Islands - Paihia *0.5 km SE of Wharf*

Craicor Accommodation *Luxury B&B Apartment with Kitchen*
Garth Craig & Anne Corbett
49 Kings Road Paihia,
PO Box 15 Paihia 0247

Tel (09) 402 7882
Fax (09) 402 7883
craicor@actrix.gen.nz
www.craicor-accom.co.nz

Double/Twin $160
Single $120
(Breakfast by arrangement)
Continental breakfast optional $7.50pp
Visa MC Amex accepted
Not suitable for children
2 King 2 Single (2 bdrm)
King size beds luxury
100% cotton linen, own comforters
Bathrooms: 2 Ensuite

The perfect spot for those seeking a quiet, sunny and central location. Discover the Garden Suite and Tree House. Self-contained modern apartments nestled in a garden setting with trees that almost hug you, native birds and sea views. Each apartment has ensuite bathroom, fully equipped kitchen for self-catering, super king bed, TV, insect screens and is tastefully decorated to reflect the natural colours of the surroundings. Safe off-street parking, all within a 5 minute stroll to the waterfront, restaurants and town centre.

Bay of Islands - Paihia *0.5 km NW of Paihia*

Windermere *B&B Apartment with Kitchen*

Richard & Jill Burrows
168 Marsden Road,
Paihia,
Bay of Islands

Tel (09) 402 8696
or 021 115 7436
Fax (09) 402 5095
windermere@igrin.co.nz
www.windermere.co.nz

Double/Twin $120-$220
Single $100-$180
(Continental breakfast provisions)
Children $25
Extra adult $50
Visa MC accepted
2 Queen 2 Single (2 bdrm)
Very large studio units
Bathrooms: 2 Ensuite

If you want a holiday in a secluded bush-clad setting with sea views and be only across the road from Paihia's main swimming beach, then this is your ideal location. Windermere is a leisurely stroll along the waterfront to Paihia village, restaurants and shops. Superior ensuited accommodation is provided. For longer stays one suite has its own laundry, and full kitchen. The other suite has microwave and fridge. Each suite has its own decks where you can view the spectacular sunsets. Sky TV. Outdoor Spa.

Bay of Islands - Paihia *6 km W of Paihia*

Appledore Lodge *Luxury B&B*
Separate Suite Cottage with Kitchen

Janet & Jim Pugh
624, Puketona Road,
Paihia, Bay of Islands

Tel (09) 402 8007
or 021 165 0072
Fax (09) 402 8007
appledorelodge@xtra.co.nz
www.appledorelodge.co.nz

Double/Twin $170-$260
Single $140-$190
(Continental breakfast)
Unsuitable for children under 12
Minimum 2 nights occupancy
Visa MC Amex accepted
Pet free home
2 King/Twin 1 Queen 1 Double (4 bdrm)
River views from every pillow
Bathrooms: 4 Ensuite - Large ensuites in all accommodation.

Miniature waterfalls and rapids await your discovery as the Waitangi River gently tumbles past your bedroom window. Tranquillity & peace is here to rediscover with our spellbinding riverside setting where. Fish for trout, stroll the riverbank or swim in our new 10mtr pool. Set in two acres all our accommodation have magnificent views up & down the river, are self-contained with ensuite & private decks. Janet's special home made breakfast basket is provided to take at your leisure. We look forward to meeting you.

Bay of Islands - Paihia *0.2 km S of wharf*

Chalet Romantica *B&B Apartment with Kitchen*

Ed & Inge Amsler
Bedggood Close, Paihia/Bay of Islands, 0200
Tel (09) 402 8270
|or 027 226 6400
Fax (09) 402 8270
info-chalet@xtra.co.nz
www.chaletromantica.homestead.com/accom1.html

Double/Twin $135-$225
Single $125-$210 (Full breakfast)
Children $15 when sharing room with parents
Apartments $ 155 - $ 255
Breakfast $15 p.p.
Visa MC Eftpos accepted
Children welcome
2 King/Twin 1 Queen (3 bdrm)
Bathrooms: 2 Ensuite 1 Private

Spoil yourself and experience the magic of Chalet Romantica. Each room has its own balcony with superb seaviews, quality furnishings and fittings, wireless internet, crisp linen and extra comfy beds. Central town location within a stroll to shops, wharf and excellent restaurants.In house pool, spa, gym and laundry facilities.

For our B&B guests a gourmet breakfast is served in stunning conservatory overlooking the Bay.

We'd love to welcome you and to share our slice of paradise with you!

Bay of Islands - Paihia *0.2 km N of Paihia-Central*

Allegra House *B&B Apartment with Kitchen*

B&B Approved

Heinz & Brita Marti
39 Bayview Road,
Paihia,
Bay of Islands

Tel (09) 402 7932
or 027 470 1137
Skype allegra1957
Fax (09) 402 7930
allegrahouse@xtra.co.nz
www.allegra.co.nz

Double/Twin $135-$220
Single $135-$220
(Continental breakfast)
Children negotiable
Apartment $175-$255
Visa MC accepted
2 King/Twin 1 King 1 Queen (4 bdrm)
Bathrooms: 4 Ensuite

Allegra House, our spacious, modern home is centrally located, just up the hill from Paihia's wharf, shops and restaurants. Spectacular views from all rooms. B&B rooms have ensuite bathroom, tea/coffee making facilities, fridge, TV and balcony. Self catering apartment with separate bedroom, large bathroom, fully equipped kitchen and spacious lounge opening onto a large balcony. Each room has its own air conditioning and the whole house is smokefree. BBQ, laundry facilities and internet access. Plenty of good local information.

Bay of Islands - Paihia *7 km N of Paihia*

Quilters Rest *B&B Separate Suite*

Sue & Andy Brown
41 Retreat Road,
Paihia,
Bay of Islands

Tel (09) 402 6047
or 021 164 7483
a.s.brown@xtra.co.nz

Double/Twin $120-$180
(Special breakfast)
Visa MC accepted
Pet free home
Not suitable for children
1 Queen (1 bdrm)
Bathrooms: 1 Ensuite

Enjoy the peace and tranquility at our private located home. Set in 3 acres of English style gardens. Minutes from Paihia waterfront and within easy reach of all the Bay of Islands offers. Relax by the pool and spa, for your exclusive use or sit above the valley and watch the sunset. A slice of paradise in your private suite with husband and wife hosts discretely on hand, devoted to making your stay completely memorable.Remember that during your stay you are our sole guests.

Bay of Islands - Paihia *0.5 km SW of Post Office*

Decks of Paihia *Luxury B&B*
Philip & Wendy Hopkinson
69 School Road,
Paihia, Bay of Islands

Tel (09) 402 6146
or 021 278 7558
Fax (09) 402 6147
info@decksofpaihia.com
www.decksofpaihia.com

Double/Twin $165-$220
(Continental breakfast)
Visa MC accepted
Not suitable for children
3 King/Twin (3 bdrm)
Stylishly furnished, ensuite, aircon & heating, TV/DVD
Bathrooms: 3 Ensuite
Stylish tile & granite bathrooms

Recently constructed contemporary home incorporating 3 guest suites with private ensuite bathrooms. Quiet peaceful central Paihia location. Stylish modern furnishings provide a very comfortable interior with generous living spaces. All guest suites open onto secluded deck areas overlooking the swimming pool offering ample sun drenched outdoor living space. Philip and Wendy are experienced operators in the hospitality industry, and offer an extensive knowledge of Northland. Philip has strong links to the area - his great grandfather Patrick McGovern was Russell's police constable during the 1880s.

Bay of Islands - Paihia *1 km N of Paihia Central*

Admiral's View Lodge *B&B Separate Suite Apartment with Kitchen*
Deb & Mark Yarrall
2 MacMurray Road,
Paihia, Bay of Islands

Tel (09) 402 6236
Fax (09) 402 6237
admiralsviewlodge@ihug.co.nz
www.admiralsviewlodge.co.nz

Double/Twin $95-$225
(Breakfast by arrangement)
Children welcome in apartments and twin studios
Apartments $175-$275
Visa MC Diners Amex
Eftpos accepted
Children welcome
4 King 6 Queen 2 Double
6 Twin 11 Single (11 bdrm)
Bathrooms: 11 Ensuite

Relax at our Qualmark rated 4+ star lodge in a quiet location.Sea views (many units), sunny terraces. 2 spacious Apartments, 7 Luxury studios, 2 with spa baths, plus our popular Garden studios. Meander along to the beach, restaurants/cafes & activities, take the ferry to Romantic Russell or soak up historic Waitangi. Meet our children - Guy and Anna - and our friendly cat, Eva. Sky TV; airconditioning (most units); high speed internet; Dvd players, activity booking service; Free bikes & tennis; Guest BBQs; Filtered water.

Paihia *1 km S of Paihia Central*

All View Lodge *B&B*

Robyn & Peter Rhodes
30 H Sullivans Road, Paihia, Bay of Islands
Tel (09) 402 8606
Fax (09) 402 8607
allviewlodge@xtra.co.nz
www.allviewlodge.co.nz

Double/Twin $225-$250 (Full breakfast)
2 day min stay may apply during peak season
Visa MC accepted
3 Queen 2 Single (3 bdrm)
Bathrooms: 1 Ensuite 1 Private
Island View Suite has large 2 person bath

Opened October 2008 Paihia's most unique beachfront location, stroll along beach to cafes and tourist pier.

We have 2 suites, 1x1 bedroom and a 1x2 bedroom, 1 private bathroom, 1 ensuite with 2 person bath, both suites have lg walk-in showers, toiletries, hairdriers, bathrobes.

Spacious lounge/dining areas and private patios. Guests full laundry and kitchenette adjacent to both suites. Private entry to suites by external stairway or internal lift. Private beach access. Superb uninterrupted sea and island views, complimentary kayaks, start of coastal walking track. No traffic noise.

Warm friendly local hosts of 35yrs are committed to bringing you the best the Bay of Islands has to offer. Generous full breakfast included in tariff and evening meals available. We have 2 friendly toy poodles. WIFI access. Courtesy pickup from Kerikeri airport or bus depot.

Bay of Islands - Paihia *3 km N of Paihia Central*

Fallsview B&B *B&B Homestay*
Midge & Bob Turner
4 Fallsview Road,
Haruru,
Paihia 0204

Tel (09) 402 7871
or 027 200 9523
turnerfallsview@xtra.co.nz

Double/Twin $130
Single $70
(Full breakfast)
1 Double 1 Single (2 bdrm)
Double bed settee avlb if req
Bathrooms: 1 Guest share
Separate toilet

Ground floor accommodation with access to pretty garden. Comfortable beds and large lounge with fridge, microwave, tv, coffee/tea facilities. Off street parking. Breakfast upstairs with glorious country views and glimpse of the Haruru Falls and Waitangi river.

Paihia *8 km NW of Paihia*

Morepork Riverside Lodge *B&B Homestay*
Paul & Barbara
846 Puketona Road,
Paihia, Bay of Islands

Tel (09) 402 5577
or 021 986 687
Fax (09) 402 5575
enquiries@moreporklodge.co.nz
www.moreporklodge.co.nz

Double/Twin $135-$190
Single $130-$145 (Full breakfast)
May not suit younger children, please enquire before booking
Gourmet evening meals b/a
Visa MC accepted
2 King 1 Single (2 bdrm)
2xKing + single folding slat bed available
Bathrooms: 2 Ensuite

We offer friendly B&B/Homestay accommodation set in four acres on the Waitangi River. Stroll through our native bush & gardens, home to many NZ birds including Moreporks. Feed our tame goats & sheep. Meet our two friendly cats. We'll happily advise you on local attractions and places to dine. We provide full breakfast and offer gourmet meals. Rain-water from our reservoir is UV sterilized/filtered. We are both "Kiwi" born & bred. Rooms have: Private Deck, Ensuite (one with Spabath), TV/DVDs, Sofa, Tea/Coffee, Refrigerator, Wireless Broadband.

Bay of Islands - Paihia - Opua *5 km S of Paihia*

Rose Cottage *B&B Separate Suite*

Pat & Don Jansen
37A Oromahoe Road,
Opua 0200,
Bay of Islands

Tel (09) 402 8099
or 027 605 9560
Fax (09) 402 8096
pdjansen@xtra.co.nz
www.bnb.co.nz/rosecottageopua.html

Double/Twin $100-$130
Single $100
(Full breakfast)
Minimum bookings two nights
Pet free home
Not suitable for children
1 Queen 1 Double (2 bdrm)
Bathrooms: 1 Private

Welcome to our peaceful hilltop home.Sunny guest rooms open onto a private deck overlooking panoramic upper harbour,bush and rural views.Guest wing has private entrance,tea/coffee and fridge facilities,also T.V. Hosting one party at a time is ideal for 2,3 or 4 guests.Close to coastal and bush walks,also wineries.Pat is a retired nurse and Don a retired carpenter.Interests include hosting guests,local history,gardening,reading and fishing. We look forward to sharing this beautiful and historic area with you.

Bay of Islands - Paihia - Opua *5 km S of Paihia*

Seascape *B&B Homestay Self-contained Flat*

Vanessa & Frank Leadley
17 English Bay Road,
Opua,
Bay of Islands

Tel (09) 402 7650
or 027 475 6793
Fax (09) 402 7650
frankandvanessa@leadley.co.nz

Double/Twin $140-$160
Single $100-$120
(Special breakfast)
Self-contained flat $140-$160
Visa MC accepted
1 Queen (1 bdrm)
Bathrooms: 1 Ensuite

Photo taken from the house

Seascape is on a tranquil bush-clad ridge. Enjoy spectacular views, stroll through bush to the coastal walk-way, enjoy our beautifully landscaped garden, experience the many activities in the Bay, or relax on your deck. We are keen NZ and international travellers. Other interests include music, art, gardening, boating, and Rotary. Our fully self-contained flat has queen bed, TV, laundry, kitchen, BBQ, own entrance and deck. You are welcome to join us for breakfast or to look after yourselves. 2 night minimum preferred.

Bay of Islands - Paihia - Opua *5 km S of Paihia*

Pt Veronica Lodge *B&B Homestay*

Audrey & John McKiernan
39 Point Veronica Drive,
Opua,
Bay of Islands
Tel (09) 402 5579
or 021 182 0697
Fax (09) 402 5579
stay@ptveronicalodge.co.nz
www.ptveronicalodge.co.nz

Double/Twin $160-$220
Single $160-$200
(Full breakfast)
Visa MC accepted
Not suitable for children
1 King/Twin 1 Queen (2 bdrm)
Bathrooms: 2 Ensuite

On the coast between Paihia and Opua located above the coastal track with views towards Paihia and Russell. A special place, peaceful, romantic,restful, with bush and coastal walks. We invite you to soak in the spa or rest on the decks. Bedrooms are air conditioned with views over an inlet. Shops, Cafe's and restaurants are within 10 minutes drive. An ideal base to explore the Bay of Islands and Northland. Audrey, John and our friendly dogs, Bonnie & Clyde, welcome you.

~

Bay of Islands - Russell *0.1 km W of Russell Central*

Te Manaaki *Apartment with Kitchen Cottage with Kitchen*

Sharyn & Dudley Smith
2 Robertson Road,
PO Box 203,
Russell 0242
Tel (09) 403 7200
or (021) 972 171
Fax (09) 403 7537
info@temanaaki.co.nz
www.temanaaki.co.nz

Double/Twin $150-$280
Single $150-$280
(Breakfast by arrangement)
Children $20
Visa MC accepted
Children welcome
2 King 1 Twin (2 bdrm)
Bathrooms: 2 Ensuite

Te Manaaki overlooks the picturesque harbour and village of historic Russell with its delightful seaside restaurants, shops and wharf a gentle stroll away. Magnificent harbour, bush and village views are a feature of guests private accommodation. The Villa is an attractively appointed sunny spacious deluxe unit set in its own grounds and adjacent to the main house. The Studio is a self-contained suite-styled apartment on the ground floor of our new modern home. Both units have mini-kitchen facilities, Sky TV & off-street parking.

Bay of Islands - Russell *1 km NW of Russell Central*

B&B Approved

Arapohue House *B&B*

Bradley & Vivienne Morrison
9 Wellington Street,
Russell,
Bay of Islands

Tel (09) 403 8109
or 027 272 8881
021 943 484
Fax (09) 403 8107
arapohuehouse@xtra.co.nz
www.arapohuehouse.com

Double/Twin $160-$220
Single $150-$165 (Full breakfast)
Visa MC Eftpos accepted
Pet free home
Not suitable for children
2 Queen (2 bdrm)
Comfortable beds, robes, tea & coffee
Bathrooms: 2 Ensuite

This beautiful old bungalow has been rebuilt recently. Only 200 metres from Russell Beach, it is an easy leisurely, level walk to all the fine restaurants and coffee houses. Historic Russell, with it's museum and craft shops, offers natural history with nature walks, and beautiful beaches. We can organise any trips you wish, and you are welcome to spend time in our beautiful garden. All bedrooms have tea & coffee facilities, digital radio clocks, hair dryers & colour TV. Free wireless internet available.

~

Bay of Islands - Russell - Okiato *9 km S of Russell*

B&B Approved

Aimeo Cottage *B&B Cottage with Kitchen Studio unit with mini-kitchen*

Annie Hormann
26 Okiato Point Road,
Russell

Tel (09) 403 7494
or 027 27 22 393
aimeo@xtra.co.nz
www.bay-of-islands.co.nz/aimeo

Double/Twin $160-$180
Single $150-$170
(Special breakfast)
Children $25
Visa MC accepted
Children welcome
2 King/Twin 1 King 1 Single (2 bdrm)
1 Self-contained Studio,
1 Balcony King Room
Bathrooms: 1 Ensuite 1 Private

A quiet place to relax. We have sailed half way around the world to find this beautiful quiet place in the heart of the Bay of Islands and would be happy to share this with you for a while. Aimeo is built on the hill of Okiato Point, which is the site of NZ's first capital. 8 km to Russell, once known as the hell hole of the Pacific, now home to an international comunity, with many historic buildings, an interesting museum and art galleries.

Bay of Islands - Russell - Matauwhi Bay *1 km E of Russell*

@ home NEW ZEALAND

Ounuwhao B&B *B&B Cottage with Kitchen Seperate Suite*

Marilyn Nicklin
16 Hope Avenue, Matauwhi Bay, Russell,
The Heart of the Bay of Islands

Tel (09) 403 7310 or 027 414 1310 Fax (09) 403 8310
thenicklins@xtra.co.nz www.bedandbreakfastbayofislands.co.nz

Double/Twin $200-$350 Single $160-$200 (Full breakfast)
Children under 12 $45
Self-contained & garden suite double $280-$350
Visa MC accepted
2 King 4 Queen 3 Twin 2 Single (7 bdrm)
4 in guestlodge, 1 in garden suite, 2 in cottage
Bathrooms: 5 Ensuite 2 Private

Welcome to historic Russell, the Heart of the Bay of Islands and the first settled area of NZ. Take a step back into a bygone era and spend some time with us in our delightful, nostalgic, immaculately restored Victorian villa (Circa 1894). Enjoy your own large guest lounge; tea/coffee and biscuits always available, with open fire in the cooler months, and wrap-around verandahs for you to relax and take in the warm sea breezes. Each of our 4 queen rooms have traditional wallpapers and paintwork, with hand-made patchwork quilts and fresh flowers to create a lovingly detailed, traditional romantic interior. Breakfast is served in our farmhouse kitchen around the large kauri dining table or alfresco on the verandah if you wish. It is an all home-made affair; from the freshly baked fruit and nut bread, to the yummy daily special and the jam conserves. Our self-contained cottage is set in park-like grounds for your privacy and enjoyment: with 2 double bedrooms, it is ideal for a family or 2 couples travelling together. It has a large lounge overlooking the reserve and out into the bay, a sunroom and fully self-contained kitchen. Wonderful for people looking for that special place for peace and time-out. Maximum 4 persons. Breakfast is available if required. Complimentary afternoon tea on arrival. Laundry service available. We look forward to meeting you soon. Our homes are SMOKE-FREE. We are closed June and July.

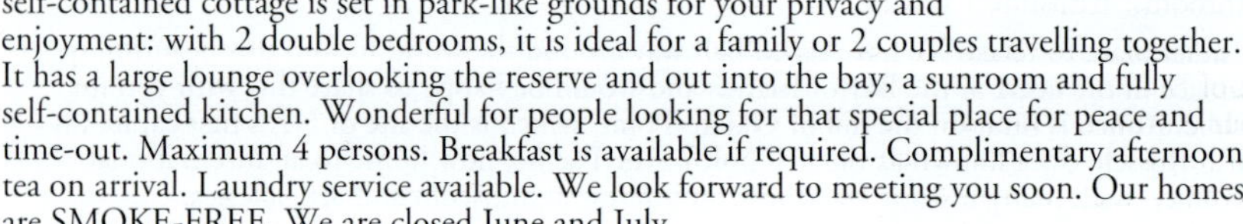

EXPERIENCE OUR HISTORIC B&B. ENJOY A WORLD OF DIFFERENCE.

Bay of Islands - Russell *1 km E of Russell*

B&B Approved

Lesley's *B&B*

Lesley Coleman
1 Pomare Road,
Russell, Northland
Tel (09) 403 7099
or 021 108 0369
three.gs@xtra.co.nz
www.Lesleys.co.nz

Double/Twin $140-$160
Single $110-$135
(Special breakfast)
Children $30
Dinner by arrangement
2 nights minimum
Visa MC accepted
Children welcome
1 Queen 2 Single (2 bdrm)
Main bedroom plus loft room for children
Bathrooms: 1 Private
Clawfoot bath, shower and toilet

Walk beside palms to our secluded home inspired by living in Greece. See Matauwhi Bay and boats from the deck. Enjoy breakfast (with organic emphasis) and eggs from our hens in the cosy guest conservatory. Our guest room has its own entrance and tea/coffee making facilities. Lesley's original artwork on the walls and the private bathroom features a clawfoot bath. Guestbook comments: " We came exhausted and left refreshed!" "Awesome waffles." Billy the terrior lives here too. Ten minutes walk to Russell central. Welcome

Bay of Islands - Russell *0.5 km N of Russell*

B&B Approved

La Veduta *B&B Homestay*

Danielle & Dino Fossi
11 Gould Street,
Russell,
Bay of Islands
Tel (09) 403 8299
Fax (09) 403 8299
laveduta@xtra.co.nz
www.laveduta.co.nz

Double/Twin $180
Single $150-$180
(Full breakfast)
King-size rooms $200-$220
Visa MC accepted
1 King/Twin 1 King 1 Queen
2 Double (5 bdrm)
Bathrooms: 3 Ensuite 2 Private

La Veduta. Enjoy our mix of traditional European culture in the midst of the beautiful Bay of Islands. Historic heartland of New Zealand. La Veduta is the perfect pied a terre for your Northland holiday. We offer our guests a warm welcome and personalised service. All our bedrooms are individually styled, offering full sea view. A delicious cooked breakfast is served on the balcony. We can arrange tours and activities. Restaurants, beach, ferries handy. French and Italian spoken. Complimentary afternoon tea.

Bay of Islands - Russell *0.4 km N of Russell Central*

A Place in the Sun *B&B Separate Suite Apartment with Kitchen*

Pip & Oliver Campbell
57 Upper Wellington Street,
Russell 0202, Bay of Islands

Tel (09) 403 7615
Fax (09) 403 7610
BayView_Russell@paradise.net.nz
www.aplaceinthesun.co.nz

Double/Twin $135-$185
Single $125-$165
(Breakfast by arrangement)
Children by arrangement
Group of 4 $260-$295
(two en-suites plus studio)
Visa MC accepted
Pet free home
2 Queen 1 Double (3 bdrm)
2 queen bedrooms, a double sofa-bed in Bay View studio
Bathrooms: 2 Ensuite

Our special place, 'Romantic Russell', this retired Kiwi sailing couple's perfect anchorage. Two queen bedroom en-suite apartments, Fern or BayView, (separate entrances) ideally combined for two couples. B&B or self-catering options. Ranchsliders open to patio and garden(no stairs).T.Vs Barbecues. Great views overlooking Russell village and the Bay.Sunny, peaceful setting bordering bush reserve (kiwi habitat). Uncrowded beaches, heritage trails, brilliant night sky, cleaner air!. Ideal for relaxing holidays, honeymoons. All cruises depart Russell. Explore or simply unwind. A different world. It's Paradise.

Bay of Islands - Russell *0.2 km N of Russell Central*

Villa Russell *Luxury B&B*

Sue & Steve Western
2 Little Queen Street,
Russell,
Bay of Islands

Tel (09) 403 8845
or 027 492 8912
Fax (09) 403 8845
info@villarussell.co.nz
www.kingfishercharters.co.nz

Double/Twin $185-$320
(Full breakfast)
Rollaway bed available,
Suitable for children up to 6 years
Visa MC accepted
1 King/Twin 2 Queen (3 bdrm)
Spacious rooms with large ensuites
and awesome views
Bathrooms: 3 Ensuite

Enjoy a welcoming visit to Villa Russell, 2 minutes from the beach and Russell's restaurants. Relax with magnificent views of the bay and wharf from the deck of our beautifully restored 1910 Villa, or from one of two spacious suites in the new guest cottage. A short walk takes you to a surf beach or up the historic Flagstaff Hill. Off-street parking provided. Charters on our 11.6 metre yacht Kingfisher may also be arranged to sail the Bay of Islands. Friendly family dog.

Bay of Islands - Russell - Te Wahapu *7 km S of Russell*

B&B Approved

A Tranquil Place *B&B*

Susanne and Uwe
14 Major Bridge Drive,
off Te Wahapu Road,
Russell, 0242

Tel (09) 403 7588
or 021 403 976
Fax (09) 403 7588
TranquilPlace@xtra.co.nz
www.atranquilplace.co.nz

Double/Twin $160-$195
Single $130-$160
(Special breakfast)
Dinner by arrangement
Visa MC accepted
1 Queen (1 bdrm)
Guestroom with separate entrance
Bathrooms: 1 Ensuite

Our cosy home is nestled in native bush on Te Wahapu peninsula opposite historic Russell.You can access the secluded beach via a footpath next to the house and may use our rowing dinghy. Otherwise just relax on our spacious deck, go for a walk, enjoy romantic Russell or join a coach or boat trip to explore the further environment. We speak German and we love sailing, golfing & travelling, have been living in Asia for more than 10 years.

Bay of Islands - Russell - Okiato *9 km SW of Russell*

B&B Approved

Pipiroa Bay Homestay and Garden *B&B Apartment with Kitchen*

Paula & Gary Franklin
348 Aucks Road, Russell, 0272

Tel (09) 403 8856
or 027 295 3640
Fax (09) 403 8856
gpfranklin@xtra.co.nz
www.bay-of-islands.co.nz/accomm/
pipiroa.html

Double/Twin $120-$150
Single $80-$120 (Full breakfast)
Children $20 for each child
Dinner $40 pp includes wine
Waterbased activities from $20 pp
Visa MC accepted
Pet free home
Children and pets welcome
3 Queen 2 Single (4 bdrm)
Bathrooms: 2 Ensuite 1 Guest share

Nestled in the hillside, overlooking historically significant Pipiroa Bay, at Okiato Point, handy to Russell, Opua and Paihia, our warm north facing purpose built homestay bed and breakfast will delight you. As kiwis, with years of sailing experience in the Bay of Islands, we will ensure you enjoy the best the Bay can offer. Choose from our self contained apartment and bed and breakfast suite and savour our delicious breakfast using fresh produce from the garden.Other meals by arrangement.

Bay of Islands - Russell *0.4 km N of Russell village centre*

Russell Bay Lodge *Luxury B&B*
Aom & Dave Metcalfe
71 Wellington Street,
Russell, 0202

Tel (09) 403 7376
or 027 417 3310
Fax (09) 403 7376
info@russellbay.co.nz
www.russellbay.co.nz

Double/Twin $150-$295
(Continental breakfast provisions)
Visa MC accepted
Pet free home
Not suitable for children
3 King (3 bdrm)
Bathrooms: 3 Ensuite

Romantic Russell, luxury accommodation, fabulous bay views. Contemporary Russell Bay Lodge has an idyllic location overlooking Russell and it's beautiful harbour. Just a short walk to waterfront cafes, shops and al fresco dining.The purpose designed accommodation offers king suites, two with mini kitchen, lounge area with TV/DVD/CD/Wifi, own entrance and own patio area.We provide a sumptuous breakfast basket each day.Select from a wide range of local activities, then later relax on the balcony soaking up possibly the best sea views in Russell!

~

Bay of Islands - Russell *0.1 km E of Information Centre*

B&B Approved

The White House *Luxury B&B Guest House*
Emma & Steve Jury
7 Church Street,
Russell, 0202

Tel (09) 403 7676
or 021 241 1010
info@thewhitehouserussell.com
www.thewhitehouserussell.com

Double/Twin $195-$275
Single $175.50-$247.50
(Full breakfast)
We do not cater for children under 12
Visa MC Eftpos accepted
3 Super King Ensuites (3 bdrm)
Bathrooms: 3 Ensuite

Come and have a truly unique stay with us in one of NZs oldest houses (circa 1840) ideally situated in the heart of Russell. A beautifully restored villa with plenty of character. She features 3 well appointed rooms with super-king size beds and fresh new ensuites along with guest lounge and full kitchen. Indulge in absolute luxury, with a dip in the spa pool, read a book on the shaded sundeck or wander to the waterfront. 12 midday check-out, free WiFi & SKY TV.

Bay of Islands - Pakaraka *15 km NW of Pahia/ Kerikeri/Kaikohe*

Jarvis Family Farmstay & Equestrian Centre

B&B Farmstay, also s/c Treetops Cottage

Frederika & Douglas Jarvis
State Highway 1, Pakaraka,
RD2 Ohaeawai, Bay of Islands

Tel (09) 405 9606 or 021 259 1120
baystay@igrin.co.nz www.nzbaystay.com

Double/Twin $120-$130 Single $75
(Continental breakfast)
Children half price up to 9 yrs
Dinner $30 by arrangement
Longer stay - discount
Visa MC accepted Pets welcome
2 Queen 2 Double 1 Twin (4 bdrm) Four poster suite
Bathrooms: 1 Ensuite 3 Private spa bathroom

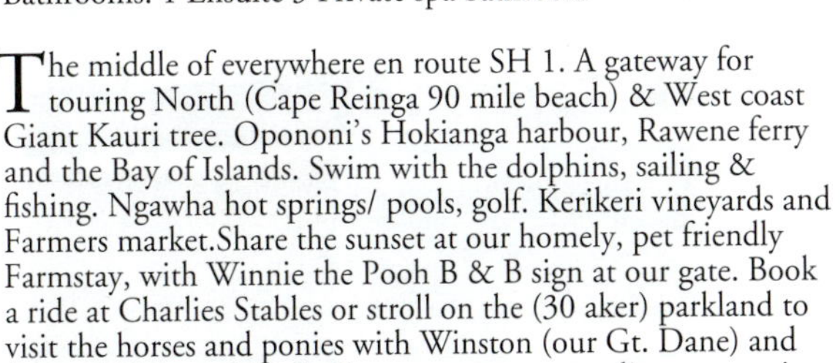

The middle of everywhere en route SH 1. A gateway for touring North (Cape Reinga 90 mile beach) & West coast Giant Kauri tree. Opononi's Hokianga harbour, Rawene ferry and the Bay of Islands. Swim with the dolphins, sailing & fishing. Ngawha hot springs/ pools, golf. Kerikeri vineyards and Farmers market.Share the sunset at our homely, pet friendly Farmstay, with Winnie the Pooh B & B sign at our gate. Book a ride at Charlies Stables or stroll on the (30 aker) parkland to visit the horses and ponies with Winston (our Gt. Dane) and foxy pal Piglet, while the Patron can prepare a dinner party in his kitchen. Breakfast includes home made conserves, an orchard bowl of fruitfullness, (parsley scrambled eggs a 'specialty').Al fresco dining on the deck with local wine and a crackling log chiminea. Queensize honeymoon 4 poster bed suite and Scottish room overlook our fabulous subtropical palm and water garden is a bird lovers 'Bay of Islands' haven.Also in the garden "Treetops Cottage" a s/c studio for a quiet retreat (minimum stay 2 nights) . Dinner available on request.Free wireless broadband availableclick on www.nzbaystay.com for Northland weather reports and local links info

Opononi *6 km W of Opononi*

Koutu Lodge *B&B Homestay*
Tony and Sylvia Stockman
607 Koutu Loop Road,
Opononi,
RD 3,
Kaikohe
Tel (09) 405 8882
Fax (09) 405 8893
koutulodgebnb@xtra.co.nz
www.wairereboulders.co.nz/koutulodge

Double/Twin $90-$110
Single $70
(Full breakfast)
Visa MC accepted
1 King 1 Queen 1 Double (3 bdrm)
Our No1 room has extensive views down the harbour
Bathrooms: 2 Ensuite 1 Private

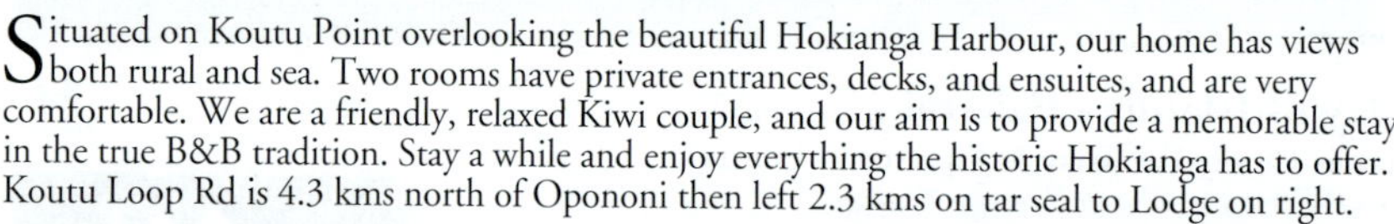

Situated on Koutu Point overlooking the beautiful Hokianga Harbour, our home has views both rural and sea. Two rooms have private entrances, decks, and ensuites, and are very comfortable. We are a friendly, relaxed Kiwi couple, and our aim is to provide a memorable stay in the true B&B tradition. Stay a while and enjoy everything the historic Hokianga has to offer. Koutu Loop Rd is 4.3 kms north of Opononi then left 2.3 kms on tar seal to Lodge on right.

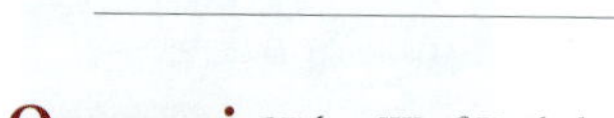

Opononi *57 km W of Kaikohe*

Opononi Dolphin Lodge *B&B Separate Suite*
Sue & John Reynard
Corner of SH12 & Fairlie Crescent,
Opononi
Tel (09) 405 8451
or 021 064 4050
Fax (09) 405 8451
opononidolphinlodge@xtra.co.nz

Double/Twin $85-$120
Single $65-$95
(Continental breakfast)
1x Self Contained unit - Sleeps 6
Visa MC accepted
1 Queen 1 Double 1 Twin
1 Single (3 bdrm)
Bathrooms: 2 Ensuite 1 Private
1 Guest share

Situated on the corner of Fairlie Crescent and SH12, opposite a beach reserve on the edge of the pristine Hokianga Harbour. Our sunsets are breathtaking. 20 minutes from "Tane Mahuta" the largest kauri tree in the world. Step outside for picture postcard views of beautiful blue beconing waters and huge sand dunes. Visit the boulders, sand board, walking tracks, boating, great fishing, local crafts. Come, enjoy the friendly hospitality. The West Coast Diamond in the North awaits you.

Omapere *55 km W of Kaikohe*

Harbourside Bed & Breakfast *B&B*

B&B Approved

Joy & Garth Coulter
State Highway 12,
1 Pioneer Walk,
Omapere

Tel (09) 405 8246
harboursidebnb@xtra.co.nz

Double/Twin $95-$105
Single $70-$80
(Continental breakfast)
Visa MC accepted
1 Queen 2 Single (2 bdrm)
Single beds are king singles
Bathrooms: 2 Ensuite

Our beachfront home on corner State Highway 12 and Pioneer Walk overlooking the Hokianga Harbour is within walking distance of restaurants and bars. Both rooms have ensuites, tea making facilities, refrigerators and TV with separate entrances onto private decks to relax and enjoy superb views. We're close to the Waipoua Forest, West Coast beaches, sand hills and historic Rawene. We have an interest in farming, forestry and education. Stay and share our home and cat. Also available self catering flat.

~

Omapere *60 km W of Kaikohe*

Hokianga Haven Omapere Beachfront *B&B Separate Suite*

B&B Approved

Heather Randerson
226 State Highway 12,
Omapere,
Hokianga

Tel (09) 405 8285
or 021 393 973
Fax (09) 405 8285
tikanga2000@xtra.co.nz
www.hokiangahaven.co.nz

Double/Twin $150-$180
Single$120-$150
(Continental breakfast)
TWO NIGHT MINIMUM stay
October to March
1 Super King
Bathrooms: 1 Private

Snuggled into this peaceful private, beachfront location, our comfortable home embraces the continuously inspiring seascape of the dramatic harbour entrance and magnificent dune. Simply relaxing in this harbourside haven is reviltalizing. Local artists, forest walks, horse riding, harbour cruising, fishing, river and coastal swimming are some of the natural delights to be enjoyed in this historic area. Enjoy light filled, spacious self contained facility with direct beach access. Our dog Niwa is a willing walking companion. Range of healing therapies available.

Dargaville *1.5 km S of Dargaville*

B&B Approved

Kauri House Lodge *Luxury B&B*

Doug Blaxall
PO Box 382, Bowen Street, Dargaville
Tel (09) 439 8082 or 027 454 7769
Fax (09) 439 8082
kaurihouselodge@orcon.net.nz
http://kaurihouselodge.co.nz

Double/Twin $225-$300
Single $200 (Full breakfast)
Visa MC accepted
1 King/Twin 2 King (3 bdrm)
Bathrooms: 3 Ensuite

Kauri House Lodge sits high above Dargaville amongst mature trees. The 1880s villa retains all it's unique charm, style and grace with original kauri panelling and period antiques in all rooms.

Start your day woken by native birds, walk through extensive landscaped grounds or read in our library. In summer enjoy a dip in the large swimming pool. In winter our billiard room log fire is a cosy spot to relax for the evening. Join Doug to explore beautiful mature native bush on the nearby farm overlooking the Wairoa River and Kaipara Harbour. The area offers many activities including deserted white sand beaches, fresh water lakes, river tours, horse treks, bush walks and restaurants.

THE MOST COMMON COMMENT IN OUR VISITOR BOOK: "SAVE THE BEST TO LAST".

I have been hosting Bed & Breakfast for over 30 years, "Perfect Accommodation, good host, these things make holidays worthwhile" - Frank & Annie, Holland "Fantastic house and timber furniture, best we've seen" - Gary & Trish, Australia

Dargaville *2 km E of Dargaville*

Awakino Point Boutique Motel *Separate Suite Apartment with Kitchen*

June & Mick
State Highway 14, Dargaville,
PO Box 168 Dargaville

Tel (09) 439 7870
or 027 451 9474
or 027 479 2126
awakinopoint@xtra.co.nz
www.awakinopoint.co.nz

Double/Twin $115-$135
(Special breakfast)
Each extra person $25
Visa MC Amex accepted
3 Queen 4 Twin (5 bdrm)
1 or 2 b/rm units
Bathrooms: 3 Ensuite

Unique property set on its own acreage surrounded by attractive gardens.Just 2 mins drive from Dargaville on SH14 (The Whangarei Road) The best features of a NZ motel and a b&b have been amalgamated to give our guests the best of both worlds. You will enjoy your own 1 or 2 b/rm self-contained suite with own entrance and private bathroom.An attractive breakfast trolley delivered each morning.Guest laundry & BBQ available. Smoke-free Indoors.

Matakohe *9 km S of Matakohe*

Petite Provence *B&B Homestay*

Linda & Guy Bucchi
703C Tinopai Road,
RD 1
Matakohe

Tel (09) 431 7552
Fax (09) 431 7552
petite-provence@clear.net.nz
www.petiteprovence.co.nz

Double/Twin $145
Single $100
(Continental breakfast)
Dinner $40 by arrangement
Visa MC accepted
2 King/Twin 1 King
2 Queen (3 bdrm)
Bathrooms: 2 Ensuite 1 Private

Ten minutes from Matakohe Kauri museum,eco friendly Petite Provence is set on 7 hectares of rolling farmland. All rooms (insect screens) open onto a covered deck with panoramic and distant water views. Relaxing and peaceful atmosphere. Delicious evening meals, mediterranean, vegetarian, local cuisine. Guy is French, Linda a New Zealander. Our home in France was also a Bed & Breakfast. Loopy is our outside dog.Directions: From Matakohe museum drive 2 kms towards Tinopai, turn left into Tinopai road, drive 7kms. Roadside sign on left.

Paparoa *1 km E of Paparoa*

The Old Post Office Guesthouse *B&B Guest House*

Janice Booth
Corner of State Highway 12
& Oakleigh Road, Paparoa
PO Box 79, Paparoa

Tel (09) 431 6444
paparoa.jan@xtra.co.nz

Double/Twin $100-$110
Single $55-$55
(Continental breakfast)
Dinner $30 - 3 courses
2 bedroom suite from $200 (sleeps 5)
Visa MC accepted
Pet free home Children welcome
2 Queen 1 Double 2 Twin 4 Single
(6 bdrm)
Single, twin, double, queen, 2 bdrm
(1 queen, 3 single)
Bathrooms: 1 Ensuite 4 Private

From the moment you step inside you will succumb to the character and charm of this lovely old historic building (circa 1903), with delightful cottage garden and rural backdrop. Enjoy our true Kiwi hospitality, cuisine and homely atmosphere with separate guests lounges and free tea/coffee. Dinner by prior arrangement. Local restaurants W/Th/F/Sat/Sun only. Spend a day at the world famous Matakohe Kauri Museum only 8km away or if, like us, you enjoy the outdoors, visit Pahi Beach or our local bush reserve.

Please let us know
how you enjoyed your B&B experience.
Ask your host for a comment form
or leave a comment on www.bnb.co.nz.

Whangarei *17 km E of Whangarei*

Parua House *B&B Homestay Farmstay*
Pat & Peter Heaslip
1113 Whangarei Heads Road,
Parua Bay, RD 4, Whangarei 0174
Tel (09) 436 5855 or 021 0250 4389
paruahomestay@clear.net.nz
www.paruahomestay.homestead.com

Double/Twin $150-$175
Single $90-$110 (Full breakfast)
Children half price Dinner $35
Visa MC accepted Children welcome
2 Queen 1 Twin (3 bdrm)
Bathrooms: 2 Ensuite 1 Private

Parua House is a classical colonial house, built in 1883, comfortably restored and occupying an elevated site with panoramic views of Parua Bay and the Whangarei Harbour.

The property covers 29 hectares of farmland including 2 protected reserves, which are rich in native trees (including kauri) and birds.Guests are welcome to explore the farm and bush, milk the jersey cow, explore the olive grove and sub-tropical orchard, or just relax on the veranda soaking up the panoramic view. We are an environmentally friendly homestay. A safe swimming beach adjoins the farm, with a short walk to the fishing jetty; 2 marinas and an excellent golf course are just 2 minutes away.

Our wide interests include photography, patchwork quilting and horticulture. (Cats and an outside corgi) The house is attractively appointed with antique furniture and a rare collection of spinning wheels. Awake to home-baked bread and freshly squeezed orange juice. Dine in elegant surroundings with generous helpings of home produce with our own eggs, home grown vegetables, olives and sub-tropical fruit (home-made ice cream a speciality). Pre-meal drinks and wine are provided to add to the bonhomie of an evening around a large French oak refectory table. As featured on TV's "Ansett NZ Time of Your Life" and "Corban's Taste NZ".

Whangarei *12 km SW of Whangarei*

Owaitokamotu *B&B Homestay*

Minnie & George Whitehead
727 Otaika Valley Road,
Otaika,
Whangarei

Tel (09) 434 7554
Fax (09) 434 7554
minniegeorge@xtra.co.nz

Double/Twin $85-$100
Single $65
(Full breakfast)
Dinner $25 by arrangement
Children and pets welcome
2 King/Twin 2 Queen (3 bdrm)
Bathrooms: 2 Guest share

Come, enjoy the tranquility of Owaitokamotu, place of water. Magnificent rocks of all shapes and sizes, pristine bush, rambling walks, set in 10 acres, easy contour. Created gardens, featuring ponds, bridges, archways, windmill, 1850s style shanty and more. Home wheelchair friendly. All bedrooms private access from exterior. TV, tea/coffee facilities. Join us for 3 course evening meal, $25 by arrangement. Restaurants nearby. Interests: travel, wood carving, our garden. Smoke-free indoors. Laundry facilities available. Warm welcome awaits you.

Whangarei *25 km SE of Whangarei*

Vealbrook B&B - Spirit of Hospitality Award for Excellence in Home Hosting Finalist

Homestay Apartment with Kitchen

Bob & Pre Sturge
2013 McLeod Bay,
Whangarei Heads, RD 4,
Whangarei Heads Road, Whangarei

Tel (09) 434 0098
Fax (09) 434 0098
pretoria@clear.net.nz
www.vealbrook.co.nz

Double/Twin $100
Single $85 (Full breakfast)
Children $15 Dinner $25
Self-contained unit $130
Children welcome
1 King 1 Queen 1 Double
1 Twin 3 Single (3 bdrm)
Bathrooms: 1 Ensuite 1 Guest share 1 Family share
1 bath & two showers & toilets

Stunning harbour views. Coastal scenic walks. Mountains to climb. 20 metres to the beach. Safe swimming, snorkelling, kayaking, good fishing at jetty. Local dairy nearby. Pine Golf Course 15 minutes away. Surfing ocean beach. Pleasant drive round beautiful ocean bays. The house is arranged with antique furniture. Antique lace garments on display. For breakfast enjoy Bob's home-made marmalades jellies. Freshly picked fruit and fruit juice. Vegetables, subtropical fruits. Dinner supplied on request. Pre-meal drinks. Enjoy warmth and friendliness of your hosts.

Whangarei - Onerahi *9 km SE of Whangarei*

B&B Approved

Channel Vista *B&B Apartment with Kitchen Cottage with Kitchen*

Braia & Paul Larsen
254 Beach Road,
Onerahi,
Whangarei

Tel (09) 436 5529
or 021 124 2800
Fax (09) 436 5529
channelvista@igrin.co.nz
www.bnbwhangarei.co.nz

Double/Twin $170
Single $120
(Full breakfast)
Visa MC accepted
Children welcome
2 Queen (2 bdrm)
Bathrooms: 2 Ensuite

Channel Vista is situated on the shores of Whangarei Harbour. We have 2 self-contained units each with their own private decks where you can relax and watch boats go by. Laundry, fax and email facilities available. Local shopping centre only 3 minutes away, 5 minute walk along waterfront to top restaurant. Sports facilities eg, golf, diving, game fishing, bowls etc nearby. We are 1 hour from the Bay of Islands, so it is a good place to base yourself for your Northland holiday.

Whangarei - Taiharuru *25 km E of Whangarei*

B&B Approved

Tidesong *B&B Homestay Apartment with Kitchen*

Ros & Hugh Cole-Baker
Beasley Road,
Taiharuru Estuary,
Whangarei

Tel (09) 436 1959
or 027 636 5888
stay@tidesong.co.nz
www.tidesong.co.nz

Double/Twin $110-$140
Single $85-$90
(Full breakfast)
Dinner $30-$35
Visa MC accepted
Children welcome
3 Queen 1 Single (3 bdrm)
Comfortable, warm and private, separate building from hosts
Bathrooms: 2 Ensuite

From Whangarei drive east for 25 minutes to Taiharuru Estuary. Comfortable secluded accommodation in a separate upstairs flat. Full breakfast with extra home-cooked meals available. Safe kayaking and other boating from our jetty. Large garden with bush tracks and outdoor games. Close to fishing, shellfish, varied birdlife,and great walks on surf beaches and spectacular ridges. Relax afterwards in the gas-fired outdoor garden bath.Try tasting pizzas,and bread baked outside in our new wood-fired oven. Warm,friendly hospitality. Members of Northland Sustainable Business network.

Whangarei *7 km N of Whangarei City*

Lotus Lodge *B&B Farmstay Self Contained Studio (double)*

B&B Approved

Keith & Jill Clarke
58 Great North Road,
Springs Flat,
Kamo,
Whangarei

Tel (09) 435 2294
Fax (09) 435 2294
lotuslodge@clear.net.nz

Double/Twin $100-$140
Single $65-$80
(Continental breakfast)
Dinner By arrangement
2 Double 1 Twin (3 bdrm)
Studio - 1 Double
Bathrooms: 1 Guest share

We invite you to share in our 200 acres of paradise. 2 minutes from Kamo, 5 minutes to golf course. Experience moving cattle/sheep with farm dog Del, view native bush, find amazing limestone rocks,laze in the quietness of the garden, or read in the lounge. Make this your stop for seeing the north - beaches, fishing, diving, kauri forests, shopping, all in a days outing. Our interests: gardening, classic cars, travel, art and people.

Whangarei - Parua Bay *18 km E of Whangarei*

Eden House *B&B Homestay*

Richard & Carole Harris
510 Owhiwa Road, Parua Bay,
RD 1, Onerahi, Whangarei

Tel (09) 436 1938 or 027 366 4272
or 021 112 5532 eden@igrin.co.nz
www.edenhomestay.co.nz

Double/Twin $115-$140
Single $90 (Full breakfast)
Children $60
No charge for a baby sharing the room
Dinner pp, $40 /30 /25 (3/2/1 course)
Wine and drinks list available
Complimentary beverages
Visa MC accepted
Children and pets welcome
1 King/Twin 2 Queen (3 bdrm)
Large, Unique character, personal deck and super views.
Bathrooms: 1 Ensuite 1 Private 1 Family share Luxury en suite or private bathroom.

Relax in a spacious luxury bedroom with your own deck overlooking stunning views to the distant Pacific Ocean. Have the culinary adventure of a delicious Bhutanese meal prepared from the traditional recipes of that tiny Himalayan Kingdom. Nightime tranquillity and abundant bird song. Amenities include, petanque, swimming pool, two lounges, TV/DVD/library, laundry and email. 11 acres of private native forest, creek and peaceful glade. Nearby scenic beaches, walks, activities. Only twenty minutes to charming Whangarei. Pets and children welcome by arrangement.

Whangarei-Kamo *4 km N of Kamo*

B&B Approved

Little Bush *Homestay self contained unit*

Jean & Robert Pedersen
250 Pipiwai Road,
Kamo,
Whangarei, 0121

Tel (09)435 5330
or 021 0272 1759
Fax (09)435 5330
rjpedersen@xtra.co.nz

Double/Twin $110-$130
Single $90-$110
(Full breakfast)
Pet free home
Not suitable for children
2 Queen (2 bdrm)
Bathrooms: 1 Ensuite 1 Private
Private with spa bath

We welcome you to the beauty and tranquillity of "Little Bush".Native trees and birds and an awesome view of Northland Golf Course and beyond will be yours to enjoy as you relax by the pool. 30mins to Tutukaka and other east coast beaches.45mins to Bay Of Islands.Close to Whangarei Falls and many walkways and other attractions.Laundry facilities available Our self-contained unit has full kitchen facilities including dish washer and fridge/freezer. Breakfast provisions supplied if preferred

~

Whangarei *5 km N of Whangarei*

B&B Approved

Brantome Villa Fine Country Boutique Bed & Breakfast

Luxury B&B Homestay Boutique

Valerie & Roger Bloomfield
454 Crane Road, RD 1, Whangarei

Tel (09) 435 2088 or 021 512 006
Fax (09) 435 2089
relax@brantomevilla.co.nz
www.brantomevilla.co.nz

Double/Twin $210-$395
Single $190-$350 (Full breakfast)
Dinner by arrangement $50pp
- main & dessert
Visa MC accepted
Pet free home
Not suitable for children
1 King 1 Queen (2 bdrm)
California King room & Queen room both with ensuites
Bathrooms: 2 Ensuite

Welcome to our special place 'Brantome Villa' our sunny colonial-style home which is now an upmarket boutique B&B. California King & Queen beds, both rooms have ensuites & private entrance (no stairs) A/C, luxury beds & linen etc. Awake to bird song & trees wispering in this beautiful country setting. 2 hours north of Auckland or 10 mins north of Whangarei, perfect base for seeing Northland. Cat in garden. SH1, turn left at Apotu Rd left again Crane Rd, 2k on left.

Ruakaka - Bream Bay *30 km S of Whangarei*

Island View Lodge *Luxury B&B Farmstay Separate Suite Apartment with Kitchen*

B&B Approved

Joyce & Vince Roberts
34 Doctors Hill Road, Ruakaka,
Postal: 34 Doctors Hill Road RD 2 Waipu 0582
Tel (09) 432 7842
or 027 441 9585
or 021 419 515
Fax (09) 432 7847
robertsb.b@xtra.co.nz
www.breambayfarmstay.co.nz

Double/Twin $100-$150
Single $80-$100
(Full breakfast)
Children $30
Dinner $30
Visa MC accepted
Children and pets welcome
2 Queen 2 Double (3 bdrm)
4 in main suite (dble bed setee) in lounge
Bathrooms: 3 Ensuite 3 Private

"Come stressed, leave refreshed"Spectacular is the only words to describe the sea views from this 2 year old home built especially for the discerning travelers. The main suite has its own kitchen & laundry with large lounge area.
We have air con/heat pumps plus under floor heating for your comfort. Have a swim in the heated lap pool or relax in the spa after having a game of pool in the games room. Beautiful beaches, golf course, racetrack where

Vince trains our racehorses and good restaurants are a short drive from our home. Meals include our home grown lamb.As ex dairy farmers with grown up family of four, we have enjoyed hosting B&B for 17 years, other interests include travel, golf & gardening.We look forward to meeting you and helping make your holiday enjoyable.
Indoor heated lap pool and spa, Pool table.

Waipu Cove *10 km S of Waipu*

labonte@xtra.co.nz *Homestay Farmstay Apartment with Kitchen*

B&B Approved

Andre & Robin La Bonte
PO Box 60,
Waipu,
Northland

Tel (09) 432 0645
Fax (09) 432 0645
labonte@xtra.co.nz

Double/Twin $120
Single $75
(Continental breakfast)
Dinner $25 by arrangement
Visa MC accepted
1 King 1 Queen 2 Double 2 Single
(3 bdrm)
Bathrooms: 2 Private

Sleep to the sound of the ocean in a separate studio apartment or in guest bedrooms on our 36 acre seaside property. Explore our limestone rock formations or just sit and relax under the mature trees that grace our shoreline. The beach at Waipu Cove is a 10 minute walk along the sea. We are a licensed fish farm, graze cattle, have flea-free cats and an outside dog. We are ocean and coastal engineers who enjoy hosting guests from around the world. American spoken.

~

Waipu Cove *8 km SE of Waipu*

Flower Haven *B&B Self-contained Downstairs Flat*

Shirley & Brian Flower
53 St Anne Road,
Waipu Cove,
RD 2,
Waipu 0582

Tel (09) 432 0421
bnb@flowerhaven.com
www.flowerhaven.com

Double/Twin$120-$140
(Continental breakfast)
Pet free home
Not suitable for children
2 Double (2 bdrm)
Bathrooms: 1 Private

Flower Haven is elevated with awesome coastal views, being developed as a garden retreat. The accommodation has separate access. Kitchen includes stove, microwave, fridge/freezer, washing machine, TV, radio. Linen, duvets, blankets and bath towels provided. Reduced tariff if continental breakfast not required. Our interests are gardening, genealogy and meeting people. Near bird sanctuary, museums, golf, horse treks, fishing, caving, walking tracks, oil refinery. 5 minutes walk to restaurant, shop, surf beach, rocks. Whangarei 35 minutes, Auckland 1 1/2 hours. Visit our website for more details.

Waipu Cove *9 km SE of Waipu*

Melody Lodge *B&B Homestay*
Melody Gard
996 Cove Road,
Waipu,
Northland 0582

Tel (09) 432 0939
melody@melodylodge.co.nz
www.melodylodge.co.nz

B&B Approved

Double/Twin $90-$120
Single $70-$100
(Continental breakfast)
Not suitable for children
1 King/Twin 1 Queen 2 Single (3 bdrm)
Bathrooms: 1 Ensuite 1 Guest share

Offering panoramic sea views from all rooms, Melody Lodge overlooks the whole of Bream Bay. We extend a warm welcome to our BnB with it's quiet ambience, peaceful garden and spectacular location. Enjoy refreshments on the patio watching weather moods over Bream Head and experience the ethereal magic of our natural forest track. Attached Gallery features works of six local artists plus exclusive souvenirs, cards etc. Resident artist and cat. Beach 1km. Magnificent sandy beaches, great walks, golf, birdllife, restaurants, glowworm caves, museums.

All our B&Bs are non-smoking unless stated otherwise in the text.

Auckland
Waipu
Waipu Cove
Langs Beach
Paparoa
Kaiwaka
Mangawhai
1
Te Hana
Wellsford
Warkworth
1
Puhoi
Waiwera
Orewa
Great Barrier Island
See Auckland City next page
Hobsonville
Kumeu
Waitakere
Devonport
Auckland central
Bethells Beach
Mangere
Papakura
Drury
Ramarama
Miranda
2
1
0 Kilometres 20
0 Miles 12

Auckland City
Silverdale
Whangaparaoa
Okura
Coatesville
Riverhead
Hobsonville
Waiheke Island
Rangitoto Island
Devonport
Auckland Central
Herne Bay
Ponsonby
Grey Lynn
Mission Bay
St Heliers
Orakei
Ranui
Mt Eden
Remuera
Ellerslie
Howick
Titirangi
Mangere Bridge
Mangere
Manukau City
Manurewa
Auckland International Airport
Kilometres
0
5
Miles
0
3
1
28
18
16

Mangawhai Heads *.5 km SE of Mangawhai Heads*

Mangawhai Lodge - a room with a view Boutique B&B Inn    

B&B Separate Suite s/c apartment

Jeannette Forde
4 Heather Street,
Mangawhai Heads 0505

Tel (09) 431 5311
info@seaviewlodge.co.nz
www.seaviewlodge.co.nz

Double/Twin $165-$230
Single $150-$185 (Special breakfast)
Children suit children 10 & over
Mid winter xmas dinner for groups
Visa MC Eftpos accepted
Pet free home
3 King/Twin 2 Queen
8 Single (5 bdrm)
Stylish rooms, all with bathrooms open to verandahs
Bathrooms: 3 Ensuite 2 Private 3 ensuite, 1 s/cont apartment, 1 guest suite

Midway between Auckland airport & the Bay of Islands Mangawhai Lodge offers the perfect beach destination for couples, groups, golfers & singles. Three stylish guest rooms, 1 luxury suite and 1 s/c apartment open to verandahs, seating and views of sea or garden. Two guests lounges offer a stylish, relaxing atmosphere with spectacular sea, and beach views. Championship Golf course adjacent, Off street parking. Enjoy beaches,walkways,bird sanctuary. Walk to cafes and shops. A sumptuous cooked/continental breakfast served. Complimentary internet access. For winter specials visit www.seaviewlodge.co.nz

The difference between a B&B and a hotel is that you don't hug the hotel staff when you leave.

Wellsford - Te Hana *6 km N of Wellsford*

The Retreat Historic Farmhouse *Farmstay*
Colleen & Tony Moore
Te Hana, RD 5, Wellsford 0975
Tel (09) 423 8547
enquiry@sheepfarmstay.com
www.sheepfarmstay.com

Double/Twin $120
Single $80 (Full breakfast)
Dinner $30pp by arrangement
Visa MC Diners accepted
2 Queen 1 Double 1 Single (3 bdrm)
2 in B&B 1 in cottage
Bathrooms: 1 Ensuite 1 Private

Tony and Colleen welcome you to The Retreat, a spacious 1860s farmhouse built for a family with 12 children. Set well back from the road, the house is surrounded by an extensive landscaped garden, including a productive vegetable garden and orchard. Fresh produce from the garden is a feature in our home cooking.

Colleen is a spinner and weaver and our flock of sheep provides the raw material for the woollen goods that are hand-made and for sale from the studio. If you haven't got close up to a sheep this is your chance, as we always have friendly sheep to hand feed. We have hosted guests at The Retreat since 1988 and appreciate what you require.

We know New Zealand well, our families have lived in NZ for several generations and we have visited most places in our beautiful country, so if you have any questions on what to see or do, we are well equipped to provide the answers.

Also available is a self-contained cottage, close to the house, with the option of having meals with us, or self-catering.

The Retreat is very easy to find. Travelling North on SH1, we are 6km north of Wellsford, look for the Weaving Studio sign on your left. You will pass through Te Hana before arriving at The Retreat. Kaiwaka is 13km north of The Retreat.

Warkworth - Sandspit *7 km E of Warkworth*

Belvedere Homestay *Homestay*

M & R Everett
38 Kanuka Road,
RD 2
Sandspit,
Warkworth

Tel (09) 425 7201 or Mobile 027 284 4771
or Mobile 027 343 0905
Fax (09) 425 7201
belvederehomestay@xtra.co.nz
www.belvederehomestay.co.nz

Double/Twin $150-$165 Single $110
(Special breakfast)
Dinner $50 pp
Visa MC accepted
Not suitable for children
2 Queen 1 Twin (3 bdrm)
Bathrooms: 1 Ensuite 2 Private

Sandspit the perfect stop to and from The Bay of Islands. Belvedere has 360 degree views, sea to countryside; it's awesome.

Relaxing decks, barbecue, garden, orchards, native birds and bush, peace and tranquillity with good parking. Air-conditioned, spa, games room, comfortable beds are all here for your comfort.

Many attractions are within 7km and Margaret's flair with cooking is a great way to relax after an adventurous day with pre-drinks, 2 course meal and wine. Have a warm and relaxing stay with Margaret & Ron

SANDSPIT - "THE PERFECT STOP TO AND FROM THE BAY OF ISLANDS"

Warkworth *13 km E of Warkworth*

Maltby Homestay *B&B Self-contained unit*

Barbara & John Maltby
Omaha Orchards,
282 Point Wells Road,
RD 6,
Warkworth

Tel (09) 422 7415
Fax (09) 422 7419
jmaltby@clear.net.nz

Double/Twin $75-$95
Single $65-$75
(Full breakfast provisions)
Children & Extra guest $12
Dinner $20-$25 by arrangement
Check for seasonal specials
1 Queen 1 Double (1 bdrm)
Bathrooms: 1 Ensuite

Our home and self-contained unit is nestled beside the Whangateau Harbour. Relax in the extensive gardens and swim in the beautifully appointed pool.Only 5 minutes by car to the popular 'Boutique' village of Matakana with its movie theatres,shops, eateries etc. Nearby is Omaha Beach, golf,tennis, vineyards, restaurants, art and craft studios, pottery works, and Kawau Island. This is some of the prettiest coastline in New Zealand. John and Barbara look forward to sharing their little slice of paradise with you.

~

Warkworth *4.5 km W of Warkworth*

Willow Lodge *B&B Homestay*

B&B Approved

Colin Hilditch & Vicki Webster
541 Woodcocks Road,
RD 1,
Warkworth 0981

Tel (09) 425 7676
or 021 104 1807
or 021 064 5567
Fax (09) 425 7676
willow_lodge@xtra.co.nz

Double/Twin $110-$130
Single $80-$100
(Full breakfast)
Children $30
Dinner by arrangement
1 Queen 1 Double 2 Twin (4 bdrm)
2 in-house, 2 in semi-detached unit
Bathrooms: 1 Ensuite 2 Private

You've just found what you were looking for - peace and old world charm, 5 minutes drive from picturesque Warkworth (45 minutes from Auckland). Willow Lodge is nestled amid 2 acres of landscaped gardens. We offer in-house or semi-detached accommodation. Enjoy guest TV lounge, tea/coffee, BBQ all of which opens onto a private courtyard. Colin, Vicki and their dog Boss look forward to warmly welcoming you to their home. Much to explore, plenty to enjoy and treasured memories to be created.

Warkworth - Sandspit *10 km E of Warkworth*

B&B Approved

Kotare Lodge *Luxury B&B Apartment with Kitchen*

Judy & Graeme Maker
5 Kotare Place,
RD 2, Sandspit Heights,
Warkworth 0982

Tel (09) 425 7331
or 021 279 8116
Fax (09) 425 0311
makers@ihug.co.nz
www.sandspitkotarelodge.co.nz

Double/Twin $160-$195
Single $150 (Continental breakfast)
2 Guest lounges
Visa MC accepted
Children welcome
1 Queen 1 Twin 1 Single (3 bdrm)
Sofa queen bed
Bathrooms: 2 Private

Kotare Lodge has arguably the best views at Sandspit from Kawau Bay, Hauraki Gulf, Great Barrier, Little Barrier, the rural areas of Matakana and the inner harbour of Sandspit. Relax in your luxury self-contained, air-conditioned apartment including swimming pool, Sky TV and spacious viewing decks. Enjoy bush walks to beaches, visit the many vineyards, galleries, cafes, restaurants, golf courses, Kawau Island ferry, all within a few minutes drive. Spend time cruising Kawau Bay and islands aboard our 54' Riviera launch (extra cost). The perfect stay.

Warkworth *70 km N of Auckland*

B&B Approved

Warkworth Country House *B&B*

Perry & Jan Bathgate
18 Wilson Road,
RD 1,
Warkworth, 0981

Tel 09 422 2485
or 027 600 1510
Fax 09 422 2485
info@warkworthcountryhouse.co.nz
www.warkworthcountryhouse.co.nz

Double/Twin $120-$145
Single $95-$110
(Full breakfast)
Visa MC accepted
1 Queen 1 Twin (2 bdrm)
Bathrooms: 2 Ensuite

Warkworth Country House is 45 minutes north of Harbour bridge and situated in 2 acres of gardens and bush, surrounded by farmland. Each unit has ensuite with private entrance and patio, TV, tea/coffee, heater, electric blankets, radio and toiletries. Enjoy a full or continental breakfast in our dining room then visit one of the local places of interest. Warkworth township with its shops and restaurants is only 3 minutes drive away. We welcome holders of New Zealand Seniors Gold Card - discount applies. We love meeting new people and discussing various travel experiences. We will be happy to assist you in planning your travels around New Zealand over a glass of wine, tea or coffee in the comfort of our home.

Warkworth *1.5 km SE of Warkworth, 10 mins from Matakana*

RibbonWood B&B Apartment *B&B Apartment with Kitchen*

Berris & Alan Spicer
7 Thompson Road,
Warkworth, 0981

Tel (09) 422 2685 or 027 241 9986
Fax (09) 422 2684
berris@ribbonwoodwarkworth.co.nz
www.ribbonwoodwarkworth.co.nz

Double/Twin $110-$150
(Special breakfast)
Varied dinner menu avail. from $18 pp
Extra person $20+
Discount for self cater & longer stays
Visa MC accepted
Pet free home Children welcome
1 Queen 2 Single (2 bdrm)
Queen lounge sofabed
Bathrooms: 1 Private
Luxury Bathroom with separate bath & shower, heated floor

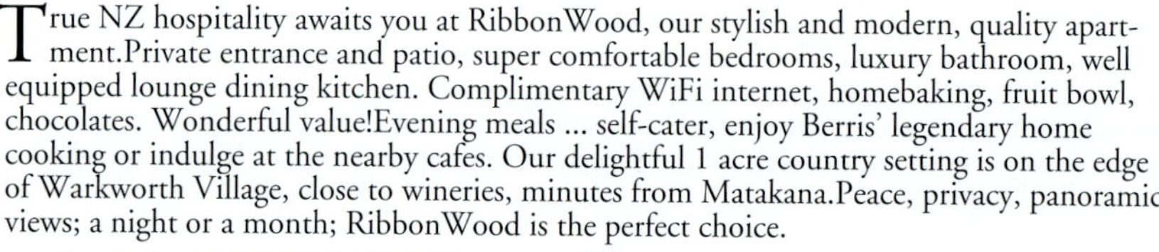
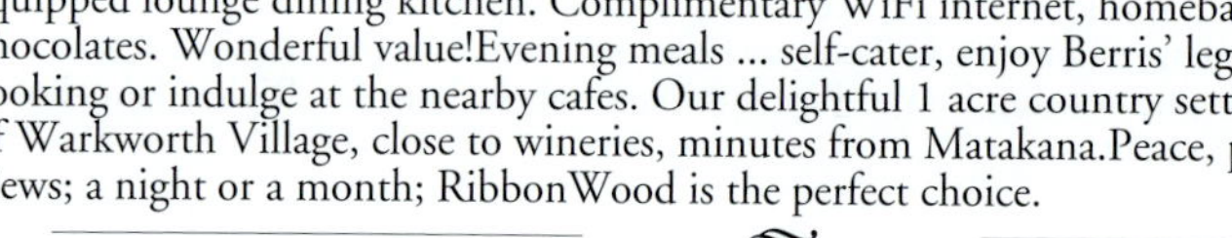

True NZ hospitality awaits you at RibbonWood, our stylish and modern, quality apartment.Private entrance and patio, super comfortable bedrooms, luxury bathroom, well equipped lounge dining kitchen. Complimentary WiFi internet, homebaking, fruit bowl, chocolates. Wonderful value!Evening meals ... self-cater, enjoy Berris' legendary home cooking or indulge at the nearby cafes. Our delightful 1 acre country setting is on the edge of Warkworth Village, close to wineries, minutes from Matakana.Peace, privacy, panoramic views; a night or a month; RibbonWood is the perfect choice.

Warkworth - Snells Beach *7 km E of Warkworth*

Heaven's Haven *B&B*

Beulah Heaven
23 Ariki Drive,
Snells Beach,
Warkworth 0920

Tel 09 425 6545
or 021 289 5523
by.heaven@xtra.co.nz

Double/Twin $125
Single $75-$100
(Full breakfast)
Dinner $50 by arrangement
Visa MC accepted
Not suitable for children
1 Double 2 Twin (2 bdrm)
Bathrooms: 1 Ensuite 1 Guest share

Share this slice of Heaven. Relax and enjoy the stunning sunrises and breath-taking crimson sunsets from this absolute beachfront property. You're on the beach already! Relax with a complimentary bottle of wine on arrival. Enjoy a delicious breakfast with seasonal produce from the pristine Matakana Valley. Relax and soak up the views with Sophie(our genteel dog) or visit the boutique vineyards, cafes, art galleries or many walkways that dot this sparkling area. Dinner by arrangement at $50 per head.

Warkworth - Sandspit *7 km SE of Warkworth*

B&B Approved

EbbTide Homestay *Luxury B&B Homestay*

Shona & Julian Huxtable
36 Kanuka Road,
Sandspit, RD2
Warkworth 0982

Tel 09 425 8681
or 021 238 3850
or 021 144 2038
ebbtidebb@xtra.co.nz

Double/Twin $140-$170
Single $120 (Special breakfast)
Dinner $45 (by prior arrangement)
Not suitable for children
1 King/Twin 1 King
1 Queen (2 bdrm)
1 King or King/Twin and
1 Queen, both en-suite
Bathrooms: 2 Ensuite

Overlooking the stunning Sandspit Harbour EbbTide commands magnificent views enhanced by the call of Skylarks and Tui. Situated within easy reach of Matakana, Warkworth and Kawau. This is an ideal resting place for travellers requiring comfort, tranquility and of course a great breakfast. The tastefully decorated bedrooms have their own en-suite, television, tea/coffee facilities and heating/air conditioning. Relax in the gardens with our pet Collies,a glass of wine and the expectation of a sumptuous dinner cooked by Shona with the use of home-grown produce.

~

Puhoi *9 km N of Orewa*

B&B Approved

Westwell Ho *B&B*

Fae & David England
34 Saleyards Road,
Puhoi, 0951

Tel (09) 422 0064
or 027 280 5795
Fax (09) 422 0064
dhengland@xtra.co.nz

Double/Twin $115
Single $95
(Full breakfast)
Children $35
Visa MC Amex accepted
Children welcome
1 Queen 1 Double 1 Single (2 bdrm)
Bathrooms: 1 Ensuite 1 Private

We welcome you to our sunny colonial-style home in the lovely Puhoi Valley. We are only 2 minutes by car west of Main North Highway up a small road behind the old pub in this historic Puhoi Village. The homestead has wide verandahs around 3 sides where you can relax as you view the gardens and beautiful trees. Nearby are the fantastic Waiwera Thermal Pools, or you could hire a canoe and paddle down the Puhoi River to Wenderholm Beach and Park. Sky TV available.

Puhoi *9 km N of Orewa*

Puhoi Tudor Cottage *B&B or Accommodation Only*

Tina Chamberlin
80 Puhoi Road,
Puhoi,
Auckland 0951

Tel (09) 422 0130
or 0275 39 26 43
Fax (09) 422 0132
orewa@paradise.net.nz

Double/Twin $80-$150
Single $70-$90
(Full breakfast)
Children $35 pp
Dinner $25 pp
Visa MC accepted
Children welcome
1 Queen 1 Double 1 Single (3 bdrm)
Bathrooms: 1 Guest share

We welcome you to our English Tudor cottage situated in the heart of Puhoi's Historic Village and set on an acre of lovely gardens and peaceful surroundings. Located opposite Puhoi Museum, the quaint village church and next to the Puhoi River Canoes. Come enjoy our pet sheep, elderly dog Meg, and doves residing with us. Waiwera Hot pools and Wenderholm Regional Park are minutes away. We look forward to making your stay memorable, with comfortable rooms and good hearty meals. Private guest entrance.

Waiwera *6 km N of Orewa*

Estuary Cottage *B&B*

Jenny & Bob Kelly
15 Weranui Road,
(PO Box 92),
Waiwera, 0950

Tel (09) 426 2621
or 021 426 262
021 02470170
Fax (09) 426 2614
rj.kelly@ihug.co.nz

Double/Twin $110-$130
Single $80-$100
(Full breakfast)
Visa MC accepted
1 Queen 1 Single (1 bdrm)
Large triple, with ensuite
Bathrooms: 1 Ensuite

A comfortable, centrally located B&B in the village of Waiwera - the beautiful Hibiscus Coast thermal area, with a safe scenic ocean beach, native bush covered hills, and world famous hot pools.Estuary Cottage - 'Owaimaru', is located on the tidal waters' edge, and offers quality accommodation with a stunning bedroom view, satellite television, tea & coffee making facilities, refrigerator, hot Spa pool, and a private en-suite. Our guests receive a generous discount to the nearby thermal pools.

Orewa *35 km N of Auckland Central*

Villa Orewa *Luxury B&B Homestay*

Sandra & Ian Burrow
264 Hibiscus Coast Highway,
Orewa,
Auckland

Tel (09) 426 3073
or 021 626 760 (Ian)
or 021 556 960 (Sandra)
Fax (09) 426 3053
rooms@villaorewa.co.nz
www.villaorewa.co.nz

Double/Twin $175-$250
(Full breakfast)
Visa MC accepted
1 King/Twin 2 Queen (3 bdrm)
Greek-style rooms with
white vaulted roofs
Bathrooms: 3 Ensuite

Welcome to our beautifully appointed Mediterranean style home, with white-washed walls and blue vaulted roofs. A taste of the Greek Isles on beautiful Orewa Beach. Stay in 1 of our self-contained rooms, each with private balcony, and enjoy the panoramic beach and sea views, or socialise with us in our spacious living areas. Orewa offers a great range of activities and amenities; with cafes, restaurants, and shopping all within a short level walk. We are sure your stay will be enjoyable and memorable.

~

Orewa - Red Beach *5 km S of Orewa*

Hibiscus House *B&B*

Judy & Brian Marsden
13A Marellen Drive, Red Beach,
Whangaparaoa - Hibiscus Coast,
New Zealand 0932

Tel (09) 427 6303
or 0274 492 025 or 0274 472 056
Fax (09) 427 6303
jb.marsden@clear.net.nz

Double/Twin $110 Single $85
(Continental breakfast)
Only children 12 years or over
Dinner $30 by prior arrangement
Pet free home
2 Queen 2 Twin (3 bdrm)
Tastefully furnished
Have courtyard or balcony
Bathrooms: 2 Ensuite 1 Private modern tile and glass with exellent showers

We offer quality bed & breakfast, opposite a beach for the relaxing break you deserve, on route to Northland. Judy and Brian give friendly, personal hospitality in a very convenient location. Handy to shops, markets, cinema, beaches, golf courses and a leisure centre complex with heated swimming pool. Easy walks to surf, tennis and squash clubs. RSA 5 minutes away. Gulf Harbour Marina for ferries, fishing and sailing. Restaurants/bars/cafes for all tastes and occasions 5-15 minutes away. Sorry no pets. Children over 12 welcome. We have an outdoor spa pool available all year round.

Orewa *35 km N of Auckland*

Art & The Sea B&B *Apartment with Kitchen*

B&B Approved

Vicki & John Lambert
12 Chelverton Terrace,
Red Beach,
Whangaparaoa,
Auckland 0932

Tel (09) 426 1060
or 021 426 107
vickilambert@actrix.co.nz
www.homeexchange.com ID#62402

Double/Twin $160
Single $140
(Full breakfast provisions)
Pet free home
Not suitable for children
1 Queen (1 bdrm)
Large bedroom with queen bed
Bathrooms: 1 Private Shower

Enjoy beautiful sea views and peace and quiet in this top-class cul-de-sac, where only a reserve separates you from beautiful Red Beach. Spread yourselves out in over 80sq.m. of exclusive use living area, with art, sky TV, stereo, books and games, well-equipped kitchen, washing machine, and patio with barbeque, table & chairs and sun-lounger. All this plus shops, golf courses, restaurants and tourist attractions while only 30mins north of Auckland city. To view living areas, visit www.homeexchange.com ID#62402.Breakfast provisions included.

~

Whangaparaoa *4 km E of Orewa*

Duncansby by the Sea *B&B*

B&B Approved

Kathy & Ken Grieve
72 Duncansby Road,
Whale Cove,
Stanmore Bay,
Whangaparaoa

Tel (09) 424 0025
or 027 200 9688
or 0274 4222 78
Fax (09 424 0025
duncansby@xtra.co.nz
www.duncansbybnb.co.nz

Double/Twin $125
Single $95
(Full breakfast)
Visa MC accepted
2 Queen (2 bdrm)
Bathrooms: 1 Ensuite 1 Private

Duncansby, our new home, offers relaxing panoramic sea views of the Hibiscus Coast. Located at Whale Cove between Red Beach and Stanmore Bay, our modern sunny well appointed rooms have own entrances, TV, decks, white linen, tea/coffee facilities. Paradise for golfers with 3 local courses including International Gulf Harbour Course with its boating marina. Bird watchers visit Tiritiri Island Bird Sanctuary, walk Shakespeare Park. Enjoy petanque, 9 superb beaches, excellent local restaurants and cafes. Only 35 minutes north of Auckland City, we welcome you.

Auckland

Whangaparaoa *8 km E of Orewa*

Verdelais *Luxury B&B Homestay Boutique Wedding Venue*
Glenys and David Ferguson
36 Tindalls Bay Road, Tindalls Bay, Whangaparaoa
Tel (09) 424 7031 or 0210 414 322
Fax 09 424 7031 glenys@verdelais.co.nz
www.verdelais.co.nz

Double/Twin $180-$205 Single $180 (Full breakfast)
Visa MC accepted
1 King/Twin 2 Queen (3 bdrm)
2 Queen, 1 King/TwinBathrooms: 2 Ensuite 1 Private

Verdelais is a luxury beachfront Bed and Breakfast and Boutique Wedding venue. It offers beauty, peace and comfort with genuine hospitality.

It is ideal for a weekend rest, a small wedding, local event, mini conference or a break in your journey.We have three rooms:- the Verdelais Suite is a garden suite with king size beds or twin beds, full bathroom with spa bath, private entrance and patio. The Coral and Aquarius Rooms have queen size beds, ensuites and spectacular views of the bay. All rooms have TV/DVDs, tea and coffee making facilities, home made cookies and reverse-cycle air-con.Sky and internet facilities are available in the comfort of our two lounge areas. We have ample and secure off-street parking.

Breakfast is a signature meal with seasonal vegetables and fruit home grown and freshly picked. Fresh eggs are laid daily by our four chooks.Enjoy a drink before dinner from our well stocked bar. Dinner is served by request at our dining table or on the veranda taking in the view of the bay. Alternatively there are a variety of international restaurants at nearby Manly Village.

Take a walk through our garden and down to the beach for a swim, there are three other safe beaches within easy walking distance. If you are lucky you may see dolphins swimming in the bay.Verdelais is ideally situated near Gulf Harbour International Golf Course and Marina, Waiwera Thermal Pools, Ferry to city and islands and the wineries. There are so many other attractions in the locality too numerous to list.Timmy our tabby and Monty our golden lab are happy and friendly members of our family.We look forward to your stay with us.

Whangaparaoa *5 km E of Orewa*

Peone Place *B&B Homestay Apartment with Kitchen*
Elizabeth Horne
35 Surf Road,
Whangaparaoa, 0932
Tel (09) 424 1455
info@peone.co.nz
www.peone.co.nz

Double/Twin $130-$160
Single $30
(Continental breakfast)
Children negotiable
Dinner by arrangement
Visa MC Eftpos accepted
2 King/Twin 1 Queen
3 Single (4 bdrm)
Bathrooms: 1 Private 1 Guest share

Welcome to our large, comfortable home. Enjoy genuine, warm hospitality, wide sea views, or relax in our peaceful private garden with resident tuis.We have two double bedrooms & a self-contained apartment.(Sleeps 5) Enquire about extended stay/group rates.Attractions: beaches, thermal pools, golf courses, walks & quality restaurants. Peone Place is an ideal base for trips to boutique wineries, colourful markets, distinctive galleries & potteries, or nearby beautiful islands including Tiritiri Matangi Bird sanctuary. Guest ferry discounts available, "Tiri" lunches & maps. Be at ease at Peones!

~

Silverdale - Waitoki *14.5 km SW of Silverdale*

Plover Lodge *B&B*
Michael & Pauline Tuckett
149 Ireland Road,
Waitoki,
RD 1,
Kaukapakapa 0871
Tel (09) 420 5282
ploverlodge@slingshot.co.nz
www.vianet.travel/visit/24426

Double/Twin $140
Single $100
(Full breakfast)
Visa MC accepted
Pet free home
Not suitable for children
1 Double (1 bdrm)
Bathrooms: 1 Ensuite

Magnificent sunsets can be seen from your own air-conditioned lounge overlooking a lush valley, only 12 minutes from Silverdale,??s motorway exit and 35 minutes from Auckland Harbour Bridge. Come and relax on your own patio on this 7 acre property, meet the animals, or go for a stroll to Riverhead Forest and enjoy the spectacular views. Enjoy a delicious wholesome breakfast made with fresh home baked bread served in the separate dining room. Michael, Pauline and their 2 cats welcome you to their home.

Auckland

Kumeu *26 km NW of Auckland*

Calico Lodge *B&B Countrystay B & B*

Kay & Kerry Hamilton
250 Matua Road, RD 1, Kumeu

Tel (09) 412 8167 or 0800 501 850 or 027 286 6064
bed@calicolodge.co.nz www.calicolodge.co.nz

Double/Twin $150-$195
Single $130-$160 (Full breakfast)
Visa MC accepted Pets welcome
1 King 2 Queen 2 Twin (4 bdrm)
Warm, decorated with quilts and artwork
Bathrooms: 2 Ensuite 2 Private Bathroom amenities, heated, hairdryer, double spa bath.

Kerry and Kay, Zippy our little dog, 3 cats and tame sheep welcome you to Calico Lodge.Amidst the wineries, wedding venues, and cafes of Kumeu and Waimauku, near Muriwai west coast beach our modern home on 4 acres has beautiful trees and gardens.

Under an hour from Auckland Airport, Calico Lodge is an ideal base to start or end your New Zealand holiday.

Stay in the country and explore Auckland City sights only 26 kms away or Waitakere Rain forest 12 kmsGolf courses, 6 nearby are scenic and challenging.Quilting, patchwork and teddy bears (many for sale) adorn the bedrooms and lounge in a separate guest wing with private entrance.

Two minutes SH16, peace and stunning bush views complete the picture. We love to share our little piece of paradise.

Calico Lodge has free wireless broadband and a computer is available to check your email.Calico Lodge is endeavouring to be as eco friendly as possible.100% New Zealand owned and operated.

Kumeu *29 km NW of Auckland*

Mockingbird Hill *B&B Homestay Cottage with Kitchen countrystay*

Bob & Sue Leech
25 School Road,
Waimauku, 0881

Tel (09) 411 9696
or 027 203 6897
info@mockingbirdhill.co.nz
www.mockingbirdhill.co.nz

Double/Twin $134-$170
Single $107-$116
(Full breakfast)
Children welcome
Dinner by arrangement
Equestrian Facilities
Pets welcome
3 Queen 1 Double 1 Single (3 bdrm)
2 bedrooms B&B, 1 bedroom cottage
Bathrooms: 1 Private 1 Guest share

Bob and Sue warmly invite you to share their Lifestyle and Homestay, nestled in its own valley on the fringe of Waimauku village. The homestead surrounded by rambling relaxing gardens is also home to "Shorty", our westie, cats "Romney" and "Mouse", native and exotic birds and a small flock of Wiltshire sheep and cattle. Close to wineries, restaurants, cafes, function centres, 6 golf courses, beaches and forests. Equestrian facilities are available to accommodate your horses. Pets welcome by arrangement.

Hobsonville *20 km NW of Auckland*

Eastview *B&B Homestay Separate Suite*

Joane & Don Clarke
2 Parkside Road,
Hobsonville, Auckland

Tel (09) 4169254
or 027 437 3400
enquiries@eastview.co.nz
www.eastview.co.nz

Double/Twin $120-$135
Single $85-$100 (Full breakfast)
Children $30 (cot available)
Dinner by arrangement
Extra adult discount in the Marina Suite
Visa MC accepted
Children welcome
2 Queen 2 Single (3 bdrm)
Marina Suite has 2 bedrooms,
Rosies Retreat has a queen-bed
Bathrooms: 2 Private
1 for Marina Suite, 1 for Rosies Retreat

Situated at the western end of Auckland's beautiful harbour. Eastview is easy to find from the airport or travel routes north and south. Well located for exploring Auckland. Panoramic water/city views. Near to Kumeu wine country (popular for weddings), superb beaches, rainforest clad hills, gannet colony. We offer many personal homely touches. 2 sunny accommodation areas. A 2 bedroomed suite, and a queen bedroom with private bathroom. A great place to relax after your trip or a day's sightseeing. Friendly cat.

Hobsonville *20 km NW of Auckland City*

Hobsonville House *B&B*

B&B Approved

Anne and Greg Watt
373 Hobsonville Road, Hobsonville, 1008

Tel (09) 416 9293 or 021 957 935
Fax (09) 416 9292
annewatt@ihug.co.nz
www.hobsonvillehouse.co.nz

Double/Twin $120-$145 Single $85
(Full breakfast)
Children welcome by arrangement;
sharing with parents $30
Dinner with the family by arrangement: $25pp
Large room accommodates 3, with kitchenette
Visa MC accepted Children welcome
1 King/Twin 1 King (2 bdrm)
Comfortable Kind Beds Set in a modern renovated environment
Bathrooms: 2 Ensuite Ensuite bathrooms attached to both bed rooms.

Welcome to our comfortable newly renovated house on the outskirts of Auckland City. We are 3rd generation New Zealanders, and proud to offer you a wonderful experience in our family home; we have three young adult children and no pets. Our passions are wine, food, coffee and travel. If you are on business or traveling you can find us at the end of the North Western Motorway, The surrounding district offers travelers many unspoilt beaches, vineyards, gorgeous countryside plus the harbour to explore We have a lounge area for you relax and enjoy after a days outing or for a quiet drink before dinner. Here you can meet and chat with fellow guests, play cards or chess or read from the library.

~

Bethells Beach *15 km W of Swanson*

Bethells Beach Cottages - Natural Luxury for Humans Being

B&B Approved

Luxury Cottage with Kitchen Fully self contained Apartment and 2 cottage - 120 seater celebration pavilion

Trude & John Bethell-Paice
PO Box 95057,
Swanson, Auckland

Tel (09) 810 9581
Fax (09) 810 8677
info@bethellsbeach.com
www.bethellsbeach.com

Double/Twin $285, $335, $395
(Special breakfast)
Children under 12 half price
Dinner 2 course $45pp 3 course $55pp
Breakfast $35pp
Visa MC accepted
Children welcome
3 Queen 2 Double 3 Single (4 bdrm)
Bathrooms: 3 Private

Love dances in the beauty of NatureWhen you stay at Bethells Beach Cottages you become one with the elements. The sights and sounds of nature will awaken your passionate spirit and time will cease to exist. Whether walking the beach, relaxing in your cottage, or sitting in the Scandinavian hot tub watching the sun set you will know that love is everywhere but here it flows a little more easily.Welcome to our website.

Waitakere Ranges - Swanson *4 km W of Swanson*

Panorama Heights *B&B*
Allison & Paul Ingram
42 Kitewaho Road,
Swanson,
Waitakere City,
Auckland

Tel (09) 832 4777
or 0800 692624
Outside Auckland Booking
nzbnb4u@clear.net.nz
www.panoramaheights.co.nz

Double/Twin $160
Single $135
(Full breakfast)
Dinner by request
Visa MC accepted
2 Queen 1 Twin (3 bdrm)
Bathrooms: 3 Ensuite 1 Private

Paul & Allison invite you to vist and share our extremely special location high in the Waitakere Ranges with tranquility,privacy and magnificent panoramic views across Native Rainforest to Auckland City and Rangitoto Island beyond. Explore 250km walking/hiking trails in surrounding Regional Park, West Coast beaches(Piha,Karekare,Bethells, Muriwai) Wineries,2 Scenic Golf courses. Train to City is nearby. Excellent quality accommodation is here for you to Enjoy. Your hosts who reside nextdoor encourage relaxation while we spoil you. Please Phone/Email for Bookings/Directions.

Waitakere Ranges *15 km NW of Henderson*

Wairere Lodge *B&B Homestay*
Bob and Heather Harmes
351 Wairere Road,
Waitakere,
Auckland, 0782

Tel 09 8109 467
info@wairerelodge.co.nz
www.wairerelodge.co.nz

Double/Twin $130-$150
Single $95-$105
(Full breakfast)
Dinner 3 courses $40,
2 courses $30,
1 course $20
Wine and beer available to purchase
Visa MC accepted
2 Queen (2 bdrm)
Double - robes and slippers available
Bathrooms: 1 Guest share

Heading north on northwestern motorway, take Lincoln Road turn off; second set of lights turn right into Universal Drive, 2 km to roundabout, straight through on to Swanson Road; 4 km; turn right into Waitakere Road; 3 km, over the railway overbridge, turn left into Bethells Road; 1/2 km right into Wairere Road.

Ranui *15 km W of Auckland*

The Garrett *B&B Homestay*
Alma & Rod Mackay
295 Swanson Road,
Waitakere City,
Auckland 0612

Tel (09) 833 6018
Fax (09) 833 6018
rodalmamacka@paradise.net.nz

Double/Twin $90
Single $60
(Continental breakfast)
2 King/Twin 1 King
2 Single
(2 bdrm)
Bathrooms: 1 Ensuite

Just 15 minutes from Auckland City, 5 minutes from Henderson. The Garrett offers villa style accommodation with ensuite. Twin beds or king-size available. Accommodation for extra guests with folding beds on request; suitable for business people. High ceilings, period furniture and decor create a charming atmosphere in this delightful homestay, just minutes from Waitakere City. Attractions include wine trails, Art Out West - including Lopdell House Gallery, Waitakere Ranges, bush walks, Aratiki Centre, and golf courses. Westcity Shopping Centre, Lynn Mall and St Lukes.

Ranui *15 km W of Auckland*

The Brushmakers Cottage *B&B Apartment with Kitchen*
Jeanette & Roger Brown
20 Clearview Heights, Ranui,
Waitakere City, Auckland 0612

Tel (09) 833 8476
or 021 725 627
Fax 09 833 8476
r.g.brown@xtra.co.nz

Double/Twin $95-$150
Single $80-$110
(Continental breakfast)
Dinner by arrangement
Extra guests $25
Not suitable for children
3 Queen 1 Twin (4 bdrm)
Two bedrooms in apartment -
Two bedrooms in B&B
Bathrooms: 1 Ensuite 2 Private 1 Family share

Choose between luxury self-contained apartment, featuring full kitchen, dishwasher, dining/lounge, TV/DVD, laundry, or traditional B&B. Backing onto a vineyard this peaceful location has views of both the Waitakere ranges and central Auckland. 10 minutes walk from train and bus stations and only 20 minutes drive from downtown Auckland. Close to both east and west coast beaches, gannet colony, golf courses, winery, cafes, restaurants and shopping malls. A great base for exploring Auckland.Wireless internet connection.Ask about long stay discounts.

Okura *20 km N of Auckland Central*

Okura B&B *B&B Separate Suite*

Judie & Ian Greig
20 Valerie Crescent,
Okura,
North Shore City,
Auckland

Tel (09) 473 0792
Fax (09) 473 1072
ibgreig@paradise.net.nz

Double/Twin $110
Single $85
(Full breakfast)
Visa MC accepted
1 Queen 1 Single (2 bdrm)
Both in separate suite
Bathrooms: 1 Private
Own shower

Situated on Auckland's North Shore, Okura is a small settlement bounded by farmland and the Okura River, an estuary edged with native forest. If you like peace, quiet, with only bird song nearby, estuary and forest views, then this is for you. Accommodation includes your own, not shared, TV lounge, tea-making facilities, fridge, shower and toilet. Nearby is a wide variety of cafes, shops, beaches, walks, North Shore Stadium, Massey University and golf courses. Okura - one of Auckland's best kept secrets.

Okura - North Shore *20 km NE of Auckland Central*

Okura River Cottage *B&B Cottage with Kitchen*

Elizabeth & David Keay
12 Deborah Place,
Okura,
North Shore City

Tel (09) 473 6298
or 027 542 6699
okuracottage@xtra.co.nz
www.okuracottage.co.nz

Double/Twin $120-$195
(Special breakfast)
Visa MC accepted
1 Queen 1 Double (2 bdrm)
Queen in cottage,
double in main house
Bathrooms: 1 Ensuite 1 Private

Okura River Cottage is nestled alongside Auckland's prettiest river. The view from the cottage is stunning. Imagine waking up to sun streaming on calm waters and bush clad hills. Bird life is amazing. Swimming beaches minutes away with bush walks at your doorstep. Self contained top quality detached cottage. Scrumptious kiwi home baking awaits your arrival. Ideally situated for a first or last stop from the airport. We and our two Scottish Terriers extend a warm welcome to you at this beautiful tranquil place.

Coatesville - Albany *7 km N of Albany*

Camperdown *B&B Farmstay*

Chris & David Hempleman
455 Coatesville/Riverhead Highway,
RD 3, Albany,
Auckland

Tel (09) 415 9009
Fax (09) 415 9023
chris@camperdown.co.nz
www.camperdown.co.nz

Double/Twin $140
Single $100
(Full breakfast)
Children $50
Dinner $40
Children welcome
1 King/Twin 1 King 2 Queen
2 Single (5 bdrm)
Bathrooms: 2 Private 1 Guest share

We are only 20 minutes from Auckland City, relax in secluded tranquillity. Our home opens into beautiful gardens, native bush and stream offering the best of hospitality in a friendly relaxed atmosphere. On the farm we have sheep, cattle and pet lambs Our spacious guest areas consist of the entire upstairs. Guests may use our games room, play tennis on our superb court, row a boat on the lake, or just stroll by the stream. Camperdown is easy travelling to the main tourist route north.

Coatesville/Riverhead *30 km N of Auckland City*

Coatesville Lavender Hill *Luxury B&B Farmstay Bedroom/Ensuite/Dining/Lounge*

Tricia Henderson
11A Beacon Road,
Coatesville, Auckland 0793

Tel (09) 412 5275
or (09) 412 5270 or 021 728 051
Fax 09 412 5275 ring first
tricia@lavenderhill.co.nz
http://lavenderhill.co.nz

Double/Twin $150-$200
Single $100 (Full breakfast)
Dinner by arrangement to suit
BBQ facilities available
Visa MC Amex Eftpos accepted
Not suitable for children
4 King/Twin (4 bdrm)
Four Superking w/Ensuite
Bathrooms: 4 Ensuite
Showers + mobility facilities

Luxury B&B farmstay accommodation in Coatesville/Riverhead; near Albany, Kumeu, Westgate. Superior Sealy beds, three rooms with ensuite, one room with separate mobility bathroom and ramp to outside. Set amongst the lavender beds, olive groves and lemon orchards. Views to City, harbour and Riverhead Forest. Wireless broadband available. Please provide credit card details when confirming your booking. Full cooked breakfast available @ $15pp.

Devonport *4 km N of Auckland Central*

B&B Approved

Karin's Garden Villa *B&B Cottage with Kitchen Apartment*

Karin Loesch & Family
14 Sinclair Street, Devonport, Auckland 0624

Tel (09) 445 8689
Fax (09) 445 8689
stay@karinsvilla.com
www.karinsvilla.com

Double/Twin $155-$185
Single $95-$150 Continental breakfast)
Children $25 Self-contained cottage $195
Visa MC accepted
1 King/Twin 2 Double 3 Single (4 bdrm)
Bathrooms: 1 Ensuite 1 Private 1 Guest share

Tucked away at the end of a quiet cul-de-sac, Karin's Garden Villa - a Devonport dream - offers real home comfort with its light cosy rooms, easy relaxed atmosphere and the warmest of welcome from Karin and her family.

A beautifully restored spacious Victorian villa surrounded by large lawns and old fruit trees. Karin's Garden Villa has also been featured on NZ and Australian television advertising for its relaxed, peaceful setting. Just 5 minutes stroll from tree-lined Cheltenham Beach, sailing, golf, tennis, shops and restaurants and only a short drive or pleasant 10 minute walk past extinct volcanoes to the picturesque Devonport centre with its many attractions.

Your comfortable room offers separate private access through french doors, opening onto wide verandahs and cottage garden. And for those visitors wanting ultimate comfort and privacy, there is even a self-contained studio cottage with balcony and full kitchen facilities to rent. For longer stays enquire about our new open-plan private Garden Apartment (sleeps 2-4) in the heart of Devonport. Sit down to a nutritious breakfast in the sunny dining room with its large bay windows overlooking everflowering purple lavender and native gardens.

Feel free to use the kitchen, laundry and wireless broadband. Karin comes from Germany and she and her family have lived in Indonesia for a number of years. We have seen a lot of the world and enjoy meeting other travellers. Always happy to help you arrange island cruises, rental cars, bikes and tours.Come as guests - leave as friends.

Devonport *1.5 km N of Devonport*

Ducks Crossing Cottage *B&B Homestay*

Gwenda & Peter Mark-Woods
58 Seabreeze Road,
Devonport,
Auckland

Tel (09) 445 8102
Fax (09) 445 8102
duckxing@xtra.co.nz

Double/Twin $100-$130
Single $70-$85
(Special breakfast)
Children $30
Pet free home
Children welcome
1 King/Twin 1 Queen
1 Single (3 bdrm)
Bathrooms: 1 Ensuite 2 Private

Welcome to our charming modern home in a garden setting. Peaceful, spacious, sunny bedrooms with television and clock radios. Tea, coffee and home-cooking available. We overlook Waitemata Golf Course and are 5 minutes from Narrow Neck Beach. Devonport Village, with cafes, restaurants and antique shops is 2 minutes by car or 15 minutes walk. Hosts are well travelled,informative and enjoy hospitality. Directions:airport door to door shuttle, or drive Route 26, Seabreeze Road, first house on left. Good off-street parking, courtesy ferry pick up on request.

Devonport *01 km E of Devonport*

Rainbow Villa *B&B*

Judy McGrath
17 Rattray Street,
Devonport,
Auckland

Tel (09) 445 3597
Fax (09) 445 4597
rainbowvilla@xtra.co.nz
www.rainbowvilla.co.nz

Double/Twin $150-$160
Single $100-$150
(Full breakfast)
Visa MC accepted
Pet free home
Not suitable for children
1 King 1 Queen 1 Twin 2 Single (3 bdrm)
3 elegant bedrooms
Bathrooms: 3 Ensuite

Welcome to our Victorian villa (1885) nestled in a quiet cul-de-sac on the lower slopes of Mt Victoria. 3 elegant spacious rooms with ensuites, Sky TV. Spa pool in the garden. We serve a delicious full breakfast, coffee and tea available at all times. Situated just 100 metres from historic Devonport Village, 5 minute walk to ferry, only 10 minute 'cruise' to downtown Auckland. Directions: Rattray Street is first on left past Picture theatre. Shuttles available at airport. Not suitable for children or pets.

Devonport *0.25 km E of Devonport Township*

The Jasmine Cottage *B&B Cottage with kitchenette*

B&B Approved

Joan & John Lewis
20 Buchanan Street,
Devonport,
Auckland

Tel (09) 445 8825
Fax (09) 445 8605
joanjohnlewis@xtra.co.nz
www.photoalbum.co.nz/jasmine/

Double/Twin $120
(Full breakfast)
1 Queen (1 bdrm)
Bathrooms: 1 Ensuite

Welcome to our cosy smoke-free quiet and private guest cottage. We are right in the heart of historic Devonport Village with all its attractions, cafes, beaches, golf course, scenic walks. The ferry to Auckland City and the Hauraki Gulf is 3 minutes walk away. A breakfast basket is delivered to your door and provides fruit juice, cereals, home made muesli and yoghurt, a platter of seasonal fruits, breads, jams, spreads, free-range eggs, breakfast teas and freshly brewed coffee. TV, fax.

Devonport *0.5 km N of Devonport*

Mahoe *B&B Apartment with Kitchen*

B&B Approved

Judith & David Bern
15B King Edward Parade,
Devonport, 0624

Tel (09) 445 1515
or 027 291 3727
Fax (09) 445 1515
info@mahoe.co.nz
www.mahoe.co.nz

Double/Twin $170-$200
(Breakfast by arrangement)
Children By arrangement
Visa MC accepted
2 Queen 1 Double (3 bdrm)
1 Queen/1Double B&B,
1 Queen Apartment
Bathrooms: 1 Ensuite 1 Private

Mahoe is an old school house transported from Huntly in 1985. Situated on the Devonport waterfront up a driveway in a peaceful setting. The upstairs B&B has queen room with deck and double room with lounge. The bathroom is separate. Our B&B is suitable for one couple or 3 or 4 people who are family or friends. We can accommodate 3 couples by including the apartment, which has a separate entrance and is fully equipped.

Devonport *0.3 km N of Information Office*

SEASAW *Luxury B&B Stand Alone Lucxury Cottage*

B&B Approved

Kerry and Ramazan Semiz& family
1 Hastings Parade,
Devonport,
Auckland

Tel (09) 445 96 99
or 021 86 87 97
Fax (09) 445 9760
info@seasawbnb.com
www.seasawbnb.com

Double/Twin $120-$150
(Continental breakfast)
Children welcome
Baby cot in separate room
1 Queen 1 Single (1 bdrm)
1 Cot, 1 Stretcher, spacaes friendly
Bathrooms: 1 Ensuite with luxury bath

Welcome to SEASAW Bed & Breakfast. A private,stand alone sunny cottage situated in the heart of historic Devonport Village. Only ten minute ferry cruise to downtown Aucland city. Breakfast is delivered to your door which includes fresh juice, tropical and seasonal fruits served with our homemade muesli and yogurts, a selection of assorted breads, free range eggs with breakfast teas and freshly brewed coffee. You may enjoy your breakfast in the privacy of your room or served on the sunny deck.

~

Auckland - Herne Bay *2.5 km W of Auckland central*

Moana Vista *Luxury B&B Homestay Guest House*

Qualmark ★★★★ plus guest & hosted · @home New Zealand · B&B Approved

Tim Kennedy & Matthew Moran
60 Hamilton Road,
Herne Bay,
Auckland

Tel (09) 376 5028
or 0800 213 761
Fax (09) 376 5025
info@moanavista.co.nz
www.moanavista.co.nz

Double/Twin $240-$350
Single $180-$240
(Full breakfast)
Visa MC Amex Eftpos accepted
Pet free home
Children welcome
2 Queen 1 Twin (3 bdrm)
Bathrooms: 2 Ensuite 1 Private

Just minutes stroll from the Waitmata Harbour, nestled in the exclusive enclave of Herne Bay. This charming, renovated 2 storey villa is owned and operated by your friendly hosts, Tim and Matthew. 2 of the upper rooms have lovely harbour views. All rooms have LCD TVs with sky digital, DVD players and complimentary wireless internet access. In the evening you can wander up the road to visit any one of the award winning Ponsonby restaurants.

Auckland - Ponsonby *1 km NW of Auckland Central*

The Great Ponsonby Arthotel *B&B Hotel*
Sally James & Gerard Hill
30 Ponsonby Terrace, Ponsonby, Auckland 1011

Tel (09) 376 5989 or 0800 766 792
Fax (09) 376 5527
info@greatpons.co.nz www.greatpons.co.nz

Double/Twin $180-$400
Single $180-$350 (Special breakfast)
Visa MC Diners Amex Eftpos accepted
Children and pets welcome
6 King/Twin 5 Queen (11 bdrm)
Bathrooms: 11 Ensuite

Relax in a quiet, heritage, 1890's villa in the middle of cosmopolitan Auckland, just 2 minutes stroll to Ponsonby's vibrant cafes, restaurants, and galleries. Fifteen minutes by eco bus, five minutes by taxi to the waterfront or a 30 minute amble through Ponsonby's interesting streets. Close to Eden Park, the Zoo and all main attractions.

Wake up to an award winning breakfast in the lively dining room or al fresco on the balcony. Socialise and read in the large comfortable lounge, on your balcony, or relax with a glass of wine in the wisteria covered courtyard.Each of our eleven individually designed guestrooms has original Pacific and New Zealand artworks that reflect the brightness of this part of the world.In the main house are villa rooms with queen beds. The courtyard and palm garden studios are roomier and have self catering facilities as well. An upstairs penthouse suite has expansive views from the deck out to the mountains.All rooms are non smoking, have opening windows, ipod docks and access to free wifi. A laptop and extensive guest library of New Zealand books, films and music is also available.

Your hosts are knowledgeable about the area and are more than happy to help you with travel plans over a complimentary aperitif.We are committed to sustainability and we have two bikes for your enjoyment.

Auckland - Ponsonby *1.5 km W of Auckland Central*

B&B Approved

Colonial Cottage *B&B Homestay*

Grae Glieu
35 Clarence Street,
Ponsonby,
Auckland 1034

Tel (09) 360 2820
Fax (09) 360 3436
bnb@colonial-cottage.com

Double/Twin $100-$120
Single $80-$100
(Special breakfast)
Dinner $25 by arrangement
Pet free home
1 King 1 Queen 1 Single
(3 bdrm)
Bathrooms: 1 Guest share

Delightful olde-world charm with modern amenities to assure your comfort - accent on quality. Hospitable and relaxing. Quiet with green outlook. Close to Herne Bay and Ponsonby Road cafes and quality restaurants. Airport shuttle service door-to-door. Handy to public transport, city attractions and motorways. Smoke-free indoors. Alternative health therapies and massage available. Special dietary requirements catered for. Organic emphasis. Single party bookings available.

Auckland CBD *0.5 km E of Auckland CBD*

B&B Approved

Braemar on Parliament Street *B&B*

Susan Sweetman
7 Parliament Street,
Auckland City Central, 1010

Tel (09) 377 5463
or 021 640 688
Fax (09) 377 3056
braemar@aucklandbedandbreakfast.com
www.aucklandbedandbreakfast.com

Double/Twin $225-$350
(Full breakfast)
Visa MC Diners Amex Eftpos accepted
Children and pets welcome
3 Queen 1 Double (4 bdrm)
Bathrooms: 1 Ensuite 1 Private
1 Guest share 1 Family share

A lovingly restored late Victorian townhouse in the Auckland CBD, Braemar provides comfortable, elegant accommodation to the discerning traveller. All upstairs bedrooms have posturepedic beds. All bathrooms have large claw foot baths. Complimentary toiletries, tea & coffee. Children welcome. Pets by prior arrangement.Toy poodles and cat live on site. Wireless broadband.

Auckland - Remuera *3 km E of Auckland Central*

Omahu Lodge *Luxury B&B*

Robyn & Ken Booth
33 Omahu Road, Remuera, Auckland 1050
Tel (09) 524 5648 or 021 954 333
or 027 475 4466 Fax (09) 524 5108
info@omahulodge.co.nz www.omahulodge.co.nz

Double/Twin $195-$295 Single $160-$200 (Full breakfast)
Walking distance to great restaurants -
Visa MC accepted
Pet free home Not suitable for children
1 King/Twin 1 King 2 Queen 1 Twin 1 Single (4 bdrm)
All ensuited with views and complimentary refreshments
Bathrooms: 4 Ensuite 1 Private
Plus luxurious separate bath suite

Omahu Lodge offers luxury Bed and Breakfast accommodation with total privacy in a peaceful residential setting. The Lodge is very spacious with beautifully appointed bedrooms all with ensuites, fine bed linen, heated towels, bathrobes, slippers, hair dryers, ironing and tea/coffee facilities. Rooms have views of Cornwall Park, Mt Hobson, Mt St John, the eastern suburbs or the pool and spa complex from the Poolside Suite. Relax with a complimentary drink and snacks in the large lounge amongst the antiques, in the separate entertainment room with a large plasma television, DVD and CD player or enjoy the solar heated pool, sauna or spa. Omahu Lodge is a boutique resort. The city centre and Auckland's renowned harbour are just 10 minutes away by car. Remuera, Parnell, Newmarket's exclusive shopping, restaurants, Epsom Showgrounds and public transport are easy walking distance. Walks in Cornwall Park, Mt Hobson and Mt St John add to the peaceful ambience of the suburban setting. A sumptuous breakfast is served in the conservatory overlooking the pool, on the patio beside the pool or room service is available. Check www.tripadvisor.com for Auckland B&B rating and guest comments.

Auckland - Remuera *1.5 km E of Newmarket*

Green Oasis *B&B Homestay Apartment with Kitchen*

James & Joy Foote
25A Portland Road,
Remuera,
Auckland 1050

Tel (09) 520 1921
Fax (09) 522 9004
footes1@xtra.co.nz
www.babs.co.nz/greenoasis

Double/Twin $120
Single $80
(Full breakfast)
Children $65
laundry/ironing-small charge b/a
Visa MC accepted
Children welcome
1 Queen 1 Single (2 bdrm)
Bathrooms: 1 Private

Green Oasis, a secluded, tranquil location in a much loved garden of native trees and ferns, 10 minutes to city centre. Close to the museum, antique & specialty shops, restaurants & cafes. An informal home of natural timbers, sunny decks where you will find us relaxed, welcoming and sensitive to your needs. Your accommodation, entered from a private garden, is self-contained with kitchen/dining room, tea/coffee making facilities, washing machine, TV. Special breakfast of seasonal and home-made taste sensations!

Auckland - Mt Eden *2 km S of Auckland Central*

Bavaria B&B Hotel *B&B*

Ulrike & Rudolf
83 Valley Road,
Mt Eden,
Auckland 1024

Tel (09) 638 9641
Fax (09) 638 9665
bavaria@xtra.co.nz
www.bavariabandbhotel.co.nz

Double/Twin $145-$155
Single $105-$115 (Full breakfast)
Children over 2 years $25
Extra adult $ 50
Please inquire about our reduced rates from May-September
Visa MC Amex Eftpos accepted
Children welcome
1 King/Twin 4 Queen 2 Double 2 Twin 2 Single (11 bdrm)
Bathrooms: 11 Ensuite

Charming small hotel in quiet, historic, residential surroundings. Close to city with excellent connections to town. Mt. Eden summit with panoramic views easily accessible, immaculate quality rooms with ensuites, phones; wireless internet access available, free use of guest computer in lounge, healthy breakfast buffet-style, complimentary tea/coffee/biscuits, sunny lounge and peaceful garden, good shopping, fine restaurants & cafes nearby, off-street parking, friendly and welcoming atmosphere. Ask us for advice on rental cars, tours etc.

Auckland - Ellerslie *5 km SE of Auckland*

Ellerslie Bed & Breakfast Inn *Luxury B&B*

AnnaBella & Brian Gillies
6 Walpole Street,
Ellerslie,
Auckland

Tel (09) 589 1997
or 021 582 522
or 0800 589 199
Fax (09) 589 1994
info@ellersliebbi.co.nz
www.ellersliebbi.co.nz

Double/Twin $150-$180
Single $120-$150
(Full breakfast)
Visa MC accepted
Not suitable for children
2 Queen 1 Twin 2 Single (3 bdrm)
Bathrooms: 3 Ensuite

Some Guest Book comments - Welcome to EBBI which offers Wonderful Warm Hospitality - Great Facilities, Delicious full Breakfasts! & Situated midway between Airport and Auckland city. We are a quick walk - 8 minutes to train - bus- restaurants-shops! We have a Burmese cat "Purkins". We offer a truly fantastic start or finish to your NZ holiday! Plus - Free off street parking - Free Wireless (within reason) - Free computer to check emails. What more could you want? Phone AnnaBella now to reserve your room.

Auckland - Orakei/Okahu Bay *4.8 km E of Auckland Central*

Nautical Nook/Free Sailing *B&B Homestay*

Trish & Keith Janes
23B Watene Crescent,
Orakei,
Auckland

Tel (09) 521 2544
or 0800 360 544
or 027 439 7116
nauticalnook@bigfoot.com
www.nauticalnook.com

Double/Twin $130-$151
Single $97
(Full breakfast)
Visa MC accepted
Children welcome
2 King/Twin (2 bdrm)
Bathrooms: 2 Ensuite

Friendly, relaxed beachside hospitality overlooking park/harbour, 4.8km from downtown. 100 metres from Okahu Bay. Gourmet breakfast. Stroll along picturesque promenade to Kelly Tarlton's Underwater World, Mission Bay beach and cafes. Bus at door to downtown, ferry terminal, museums. Unwind for 2-3 day stopover. Complimentary sailing on the harbour on our 34' yacht. We have a wealth of local knowledge and international travel experience and can assist with sightseeing, travel planning. Welcome! Pay cash and deduct 7.5% off listed rates. Excellent website! Free Wireless Internet.

Auckland - Mission Bay *6 km E of Auckland Central*

B&B Approved

Cockell Homestay *Homestay*

Jean & Bryan Cockell
41 Nihill Cresent,
Mission Bay,
Auckland

Tel (09) 528 3809
cockells@xtra.co.nz

Double/Twin $105
Single $85
(Full breakfast)
Dinner $30 by arrangement
Visa MC accepted
Pet free home
Not suitable for children
1 Double (1 bdrm)
Bathrooms: 1 Private

We warmly welcome you to our comfortable split level home. The upper level is for your exclusive use including a private lounge. 5 minutes walk to Mission Bay beach, cafes and restaurants and 10 minutes scenic car or bus ride to down town Auckland and ferry terminal for harbour and islands in the Gulf. We are retired and look forward to sharing our special part of Auckland with you.Please phonefor directions or airport shuttle bus to our door.Please no smoking.

~

Auckland - St Heliers *10 km E of Auckland*

B&B Approved

McPherson B&B *B&B*

Jill & Ron McPherson
102 Maskell Street,
St Heliers,
Auckland

Tel (09) 575 9738
Fax (09) 575 0051
ronjillmcpherson@xtra.co.nz

Double/Twin $130
Single $90
(Continental breakfast)
1 Queen 1 Twin (2 bdrm)
Bathrooms: 1 Private

Welcome to our modern home with off-street parking in a smoke-free environment. 1 group of guests is accommodated at a time. Having travelled extensively ourselves we are fully aware of tourists' needs. 8 minutes walk to St Heliers Bay beach, shops, restaurants, cafes, banks and post office. Picturesque 12 minutes drive along the Auckland waterfront past Kelly Tarlton's Antarctic and Underwater Encounter to downtown Auckland. Interests including all sports, gardening and Jill is a keen cross-stitch embroiderer. Not suitable for children/pets.

Auckland - St Heliers *12 km E of Auckland Central*

The Munro's *B&B Homestay*
Margaret and Don Munro
12 Emerson Street,
St Heliers,
Auckland 1071

Tel (09) 528 0459
Fax (09) 528 0459
dmlmunro@xtra.co.nz

Double/Twin $100-$120
Single $80-$90
(Full breakfast)
Dinner by arrangement
Special dietary needs please inform at time of booking
Pet free home
Not suitable for children
2 King/Twin 1 King (1 bdrm)
Bathrooms: 1 Ensuite

Our spacious guest room has a king/twin comfortable beds, ensuite, tea/coffee etc; private entry and off-street parking.Wireless internet access for use with your own laptop. Located only 2km from St Heliers Bay, beach shops restaurants. 10km scenic waterfront drive to CBD & Harbour. Tamaki Campus of Auckland University is 1.5km. Airport a 45min drive or a taxi/shuttle bus will bring you to our door. Convenient for travel to city by bus or train, or accessing North/South motorways.

~

Auckland - St Heliers *12 km E of Auckland*

Seaside B & B *B&B Twin, Double or single bookings*
Alan & Diane Hay
3/40 Vale Road,
St Heliers, 1071

Tel (09) 575 4954
or 021 025 72440
alan.diane@ihug.co.nz
www.seasidebb.net

Double/Twin $90-$120
Single $70-$80
(Continental breakfast)
Children $20 under 12
See our website for family deals
Cash payment only
Children welcome
1 Double 2 Twin (2 bdrm)
1 Twin, 1 Double
Bathrooms: 1 Private 1 Family share

A pleasant quiet home in a top suburb. 300 metres to a safe swimming beach, childrens playground on the shore, and shopping/dining area.Good bus connections to city from 40 metres away.Hosts are experienced travellers who know what older travellers value, and as grandparents understand travelling with children.Bedroom and bathroom facilities are clean and pleasant and maintained to a high standard. Breakfast can be served on a garden patio or inside as desired. Arrival information and help is available.

Auckland - Howick *2 km N of Howick*

B&B Approved

French Lavender *B&B*

Michael & Barbara Davis
40 McCahill Views,
Howick,
Auckland

Tel (09) 535 4910
enquiries@frenchlavender.co.nz
www.frenchlavender.co.nz

Double/Twin $100
Single $80
(Continental breakfast)
Family Rates Available
Visa MC accepted
Children welcome
1 Queen 2 Single (2 bdrm)
Bathrooms: 1 Guest share

Set in a quiet cul-de-sac, French Lavender is a modern two storey home with the guest rooms on the upper level, sharing a private balcony overlooking the garden and 180-degree views. The guest lounge provides a separate spot for relaxation, peace and quiet. Your hosts have travelled extensively, enjoy meeting people, visiting local restaurants as well as gardening and an occasional round of golf. Stroll in the garden; watch the birds and fish or make friends with our two cats.

~

Auckland - Titirangi *15 km W of Auckland Central*

B&B Approved

Kaurigrove *B&B*

Gaby & Peter Wunderlich
120 Konini Road,
Titirangi,
Waitakere 0642,
Auckland

Tel (09) 817 5608
or 027 275 0574
kaurigrove@yahoo.co.nz

Double/Twin $100-$110
Single $60-$65
(Continental breakfast)
Visa MC accepted
Children welcome
1 Queen 1 Single (2 bdrm)
Bathrooms: 1 Private

Welcome to our home! Kaurigrove offers a tranquil location amidst kauri trees in a park-like setting yet close to shops, cafes and restaurants. Situated at Titirangi, we are near Auckland's historic west coast with its magnificent beaches and vast native bush with a wonder-world of walking tracks. Gaby and Peter, your hosts of German background, are keen travellers themselves and are happy to introduce you to the highlights of Auckland and its surrounding areas. Non-smoking inside residence.

Auckland Airport - Mangere Bridge *14 km S of Auckland Central*

Mangere Bridge Homestay *Homestay*

Carol & Brian
1 Boyd Ave,
Mangere Bridge,
Auckland

Tel (09) 636 6346
Fax (09) 636 6345
mangerebridgehomestay@xtra.co.nz

Double/Twin $100-$125
Single $80-$100
(Full breakfast)
Children $20, 12 & under
Dinner $30 by prior arrangement
2 King/Twin 1 Double (3 bdrm)
Bathrooms: 3 Ensuite

We invite you to share our home, which is within ten minutes of Auckland Airport, an ideal location for your arrival or departure of New Zealand. We enjoy meeting people and look forward to making your stay an enjoyable one. We welcome you to join us for dinner by prior arrangement. Courtesy car to or from airport, bus and rail. Off street parking available. Handy to public transport. Short stroll to the waterfront. Please no smoking indoors. Our cat requests no pets. Inspection welcome.

Airport - Mangere *4 km N of Airport*

Airport Bed & Breakfast *B&B Guest House*

Laurel Blakey
1 Westney Road,
Corner of Kirkbride Road,
Mangere

Tel 0800 247 262
or (09) 275 0533
airportbnb@xtra.co.nz
www.airportbnb.co.nz

Double/Twin $90-$120
Single $75-$105
(Continental breakfast)
Visa MC Diners Amex
Eftpos accepted
Children welcome
1 King 3 Queen 5 Double
1 Twin 7 Single (10 bdrm)
Bathrooms: 4 Ensuite 3 Guest share

Just 5 minutes drive from Auckland Airport a friendly welcome and great value accommodation awaits. 10 smart rooms, 4 ensuites, central heating, large lounge/dining room with TV/Sky, air conditioning, Internet access, WiFi. 2 minutes walk to city bus stop - see Auckland by bus and ferry on the $11.00 day pass. Restaurants/takeaways nearby. Car, cycle and luggage storage. Rental cars and NZ wide sightseeing tours booked. Courtesy airport transfer 6.30am -8.45pm. Buffet breakfast, complimentary tea/coffee.

Auckland - Manukau *6.5 km NE of Manukau*

B&B Approved

Calico Cottage *B&B*

Patty & Murray Glenie
7 Inchinnam Road,
Flat Bush,
Auckland
Tel (09) 274 8527
Fax (09) 274 8528
MG-PT@xtra.co.nz

Double/Twin $110
Single $85
(Full breakfast)
Children $15
Visa MC accepted
Children and pets welcome
1 Queen 1 Single (2 bdrm)
Bathrooms: 1 Ensuite

Welcome to Calico Cottage. We are on 2 acres with garden, paddocks, sheep, chickens - free range eggs, and 1 dogwho lives outdoors. Peaceful and yet only 10 minutes from both Manukau City Centre and Botany Town Centre and 20 minutes from Auckland Airport. Transport to and from airport arranged if required. We have a double bedroom with new ensuite and a TV room adjoining for your own use. We look forward to your visit.

Auckland - Manurewa *2 km S of Manukau City*

B&B Approved

Hillpark Homestay *B&B Homestay*

Katrine & Graham Paton
16 Collie Street,
Manurewa,
Auckland 2102
Tel (09) 267 6847
or 021 207 2559
Fax (09) 267 8718
stay@hillpark.co.nz
www.hillpark.co.nz

Double/Twin $100
Single $60 (Full breakfast)
Children $20
Dinner $20 by arrangement
Visa MC accepted
Children welcome
1 Queen 4 Single (3 bdrm)
Bathrooms: 1 Ensuite 1 Guest share

Welcome to our sunny, spacious home and meet our friendly tonkinese cat. We are 15 minutes from Auckland Airport, 20 minutes from Auckland City centre, on the route south and the Pacific Coast Highway. Nearby are restaurants, Auckland Regional Botanic Gardens, TelstraClear Pacific Events Centre, Tipapa Events Centre, Manukau City Shopping Centre, Manukau Superclinic and Surgery Centre. Our interests include teaching, classical music, painting, gardening, photography, Christian activities, reading and travel. We are a smoke-free home. Directions: please phone or visit our website.

Papakura *1.5 km W of Papakura*

Campbell Clan House *B&B*

Colin & Anna Mieke Campbell
57 Rushgreen Avenue,
Pahurehure,
Papakura

Tel (09) 298 8231
or 027 496 7754
Fax (09) 298 7792
colam@pl.net
www.campbellclan.co.nz

Double/Twin $130
Single $80 (Special breakfast)
Children negotiable
Dinner $30-$50 prior booking only
Discount for 3+ nights
Visa MC accepted
Pet free home
2 Queen 2 Single (3 bdrm)
Bathrooms: 2 Ensuite 1 Private

We offer you above average facilities in a peaceful attractive location. Buses,trains,shops and restaurants are a short walk away. We are 2 minutes from the motorway and Karaka Bloodstock, 15 minutes from airport and enroute to Firth of Thames and the Coromandel. Our separate upstairs guest accommodation includes 3 double bedrooms, large comfortable lounge with tea/coffee, tourist information, TV and private balcony overlooking estuary. We offer internet and laundry facilities and discount for 3 or more nights.

Take time to enjoy your journey and the company of your hosts.

Drury *3 km E of Drury*

B&B Approved

The Drury Homestead *B&B*

Carolyn & Ron Booker
349 Drury Hills Road, Drury, South Auckland
Tel (09) 294 9030 or 021 157 6531
or 021 158 5061 Fax (09) 294 9035
druryhome@paradise.net.nz

Double/Twin $140 Single $90 (Full breakfast)
Children negotiable
3 Queen 1 Twin (4 bdrm)
Bathrooms: 3 Ensuite 1 Private

The Drury Homestead is a wonderful old colonial house, built in the 1860s and lovingly restored by your hosts Carolyn and Ron.With 4 beautifully decorated rooms to choose from where would you like to sleep? Upstairs looking out over the creek and bush is The River Room with queen-size bed and en suite. Dunedin has magnificent views across the countryside, a queen bed and en suite.Cape Reinga has twin king-single beds and it's own bathroom with shower, toilet, vanity and claw-foot bath and oh what views from the bath!Downstairs is The Lily Room, a self-contained studio with kitchen facilities , a queen size bed and en suite and own entrance and verandah. Ideal for a longer stay. We also have a cot and pull-out beds available for children.

We offer a discount for those staying 3 nights or more.We are situated on a rural block, minutes from the motorway, 35 minutes from Auckland CBD and 20 minutes from the airport. Set amidst paddocks with surrounding bush and a stream, the only noise you will hear are the birds and the sound of the tumbling stream.We love our lifestyle here and would like to make your stay in New Zealand a truely memorable one.

The guest lounge is the perfect retreat or somewhere you can get to know Ron! Carolyn's breakfasts are famed for their fresh home-made ingredients and have received high praise. We value your time with us and look forward to welcoming you to our Homestead.Local restaurants are nearby in Drury.Family cat and dog.

Ramarama *7 km S of Drury*

B&B Approved

Thistledown Lodge *B&B Homestay*

Sue & Archie McPherson
42 Coulston Road,
Ramarama,
Pukekohe RD2

Tel (09) 238 1912
or 027 473 6313
inquiries@thistledownlodge.co.nz
www.thistledownlodge.co.nz

Double/Twin $140
Single $90
(Special breakfast)
Children negotiable
Dinner by arrangement
Visa MC accepted
1 King 2 Queen (3 bdrm)
Bathrooms: 3 Private

This peaceful country setting will be the perfect start or end to your holiday. Discover the secret of Archie's breakfasts which delight and surprise guests. The English-style country house has an idyllic setting down a leafy lane. Relax in quiet and spacious second floor bedrooms or unwind in the spa (jacuzzi) . Guest lounge/games room available. Easy to find from Ramarama motorway exit, secure off-street parking and just 25 minutes from Auckland Airport.

The best part about a homestay is that you share the family's living area.

Waikato,
King Country
Kopu
2
Mangatarata
Te Kauwhata
Huntly
27
1
Hamilton
Raglan
23
Tamahere
Cambridge
Ohaupo
1
Tirau
Te Awamutu
31
3
Otorohanga
Waitomo
0
Kilometres
20
0
Miles
12
Te Kuiti
Piopio
3
30

Mangatarata *13 km W of Ngatea*

Clark's Country Touch *Farmstay*

Betty & Murray Clark
249A Highway 27,
Mangatarata,
RD 6,
Thames 3576

Tel (07) 867 3070
or 021 808 992
Fax (07) 867 3070
bmclark@xtra.co.nz

Double/Twin $110
Single $80
(Continental breakfast)
Children discount
Dinner by arrangement
Visa MC accepted
Children welcome
1 King/Twin 1 Queen (2 bdrm)
Bathrooms: 1 Private Shower

We welcome you to our new home which is warm, spacious and designed for your comfort in a quiet location with panoramic rural views. Our guest rooms are private, with bathroom between, and a sliding cavity door gives the option of creating an ensuite to the queen-sized bedroom. We are close to the Hauraki Golf Course and Bowling club, Seabird coast, Miranda Hot Pools, Ngatea Gemstone Facotry, Water Gardens and Thames Coromandel Coast, and one hour south-east of Auckland Airport. Warm country hospitality awaits you.

Te Kauwhata *7 km E of Te Kauwhata*

Herons Ridge *Farmstay Separate Suite*

David Sharland
1131 Lake Waikare Scenic Drive,
RD 1,
Te Kauwhata

Tel (07) 826 4646
Fax (07) 826 4171
davidteytey@xtra.co.nz
www.huntly.net.nz/herons.html

Double/Twin $140-$180
Single $70-$90
(Full breakfast)
Dinner by arrangement
Self-contained studio $140
Not suitable for children
Pets welcome
1 Queen (1 bdrm)
En suite with private lounge and kitchen
Bathrooms: 1 Ensuite

Welcome to your home in the Waikato. Our quality Garden Studio overlooking the pool and garden is the perfect setting for your stay. The farm, set amongst ponds and pinewoods, enhance our rural location close to Lake Waikare. Meet our cats Shabby and Chilly, and our two farm dogs. Meals are served inhouse by arrangement. Country walks, golf and hot springs - the choice is yours. From SH1 go through Te Kauwhata village, 6kms East along Waerenga Road, 1km on right - Welcome.

Glen Murray - Te Kauwhata *22 km W of Te Kauwhata*

B&B Approved

Awaroa Vineyard Cottage *Luxury Cottage with Kitchen*

Jan and Brian White
121 Insoll Road, Glen Murray,
RD 2 Huntly 3772
Tel (09) 233 3289
or 021 773 327
Fax (09) 233 3290
awaroavineyard@xtra.co.nz
www.awaroa-vineyard-cottage.co.nz

Double/Twin $135-$150
Single $135
(Full breakfast provisions)
Children $20 pp up to age 10 yrs
Dinner by arrangement
Extra adults $30pp
Visa MC Diners Amex accepted
Children welcome
1 King/Twin 1 Queen (2 bdrm)
Luxury linen, electric blankets & bedside lamps
Bathrooms: 1 Private - Separate toilet, bathroom with shower

Escape the city and retreat to our self-contained two-bedroom vineyard cottage at peaceful Glen Murray. Enjoy spectacular views across the vineyard and rolling countryside. One hour from Auckland, Hamilton, Cambridge, Thames, Raglan & Port Waikato. 15 minutes from SH1 at Rangiriri and Te Kauwhata. Full breakfast provisions supplied including fresh farm eggs. Jan, Brian and Tigger (our small dog) will give you a warm welcome and leave you to relax in private surroundings.

Huntly *4 km NW of Huntly*

B&B Approved

Parnassus Farm & Garden *B&B Farmstay Cottage with Kitchen*

Sharon & David Payne
Te Ohaki Road,
RD 1, Huntly
Tel (07) 828 8781
or 021 458 525
Fax (07) 828 8781
parnassus@xtra.co.nz
www.parnassus.co.nz

Double/Twin $120-$140
Single $70-$100
(Full breakfast)
Children according to age
Dinner by arrangement
Visa MC Eftpos accepted
Children welcome
2 King/Twin 2 Double 2 Single (3 bdrm)
Warm private rooms with quality mattresses & bed linens
Bathrooms: 3 Private 1 Guest share

For over 10 years Parnassus has been providing accommodation for both international and local travellers. Dinner, Bed and Breakfast is our speciality featuring farm & kitchen garden produce.The Farmhouse has two well-appointed rooms with private bathrooms and offers full breakfast. The Dairyman's and Gardener's cottages allow for self-contained stays with breakfast supplies provided. Families are welcome and enjoy our wide range of animals and birds. Parnassus is an hour from Auckland and central to many tourist destinations, bush, wetland walks, golfing & wine-tasting opportunities.

Raglan *20 km S of Raglan*

Matawha *Farmstay*

Jenny & Peter Thomson
61 Matawha Road,
RD 2,
Raglan

Tel (07) 825 6709
Fax (07) 825 6715
jennyt@wave.co.nz

Double/Twin $120
Single $60
(Full breakfast)
Dinner $20
Cash or cheque only please
Not suitable for children
1 King 1 Double 4 Single (3 bdrm)
Bathrooms: 1 Private 1 Guest share
1 Family share

We live on the west coast and our family has farmed this land for 100 years. Come and enjoy our private beach, expansive garden, home-grown vegetables, spa, 2 cats and the peace of no other buildings or people for miles. Take bush or mountain walks, a scenic drive, go surfing or fishing, or maybe find the hot-water beach! Auckland 2.5 hours, Hamilton 1 hour, Raglan 30 minutes.

Hamilton *3 km N of Hamilton*

Kantara *Homestay*

Mrs Esther Kelly
7 Delamare Road,
Bryant Park,
Hamilton

Tel (07) 849 2070
or 027 263 9442
esther@slingshot.co.nz

Double/Twin $110-$135
Single $80
(Full breakfast)
Dinner $25
Pet free home
Not suitable for children
1 Double 1 Twin (2 bdrm)
Bathrooms: 1 Ensuite 1 Private

I have travelled extensively throughout New Zealand and overseas and welcome tourists to my comfortable home. I live close to the Waikato River with its tranquil river walks and St Andrews Golf Course. My interests are travel, golf, Mah Jong. Tea/coffee making facilities are available. I look forward to offering you friendly hospitality. Directions: from Auckland - leave main Highway north of Hamilton at round intersection into Bryant Road (large Blue sign-St Andrews. Turn left into Sandwich Road and second street on right.

Hamilton *1.5 km E of Hamilton Central*

B&B Approved

Matthews B&B *B&B Homestay*

Maureen & Graeme Matthews
24 Pearson Avenue,
Claudelands,
Hamilton

Tel (07) 855 4269
or 027 474 7758
Fax (07) 855 4269
mgm@xtra.co.nz
www.matthewsbnb.co.nz

Double/Twin $100-$140
Single $55-$75
(Full breakfast)
Children half price
Dinner $25
Pet free home
1 Double 1 Twin (2 bdrm)
Bathrooms: 1 Guest share 1 Family share

Welcome to our home 2 seconds off the city bypass on Routes 7 & 9 at Five Crossroads. We are adjacent to the Waikato Events Centre, Ruakura Research Station, handy to the university and only 3 minutes from central city. Our home is a lived-in comfortable home, warm in winter and cool in summer, with a pool available. We enjoy spending time with visitors from NZ and overseas. We have travelled extensively and enjoy helping to plan your holiday. Dinner by arrangement.

Hamilton *3 km N of Hamilton Central*

B&B Approved

Ebbett Homestay *B&B Homestay*

Glenys & John Ebbett
162 Beerescourt Road,
Hamilton

Tel (07) 849 2005
johnebbett@xtra.co.nz

Double/Twin $120
Single $85
(Full breakfast)
Dinner $30
Pet free home
Not suitable for children
2 Single (1 bdrm)
2 single beds in 1 bedroom
Bathrooms: 1 Private

Only minutes from town centre, our 18 year old home has a spectacular view of the Waikato River (New Zealand's longest) and easy access to Hamilton's popular river walk. We enjoy sharing travel anecdotes, but also respect our guests' wish for privacy. Your room has its own tea/coffee facility and private bathroom. Only 85 minutes from Auckland International Airport, we appeal to tourists arriving or departing New Zealand. Our interests include people, music, sport, travel, gardening and community. 16 years of happy hosting.

Hamilton - Ohaupo *4 km SW of Hamilton*

Green Gables of Rukuhia *B&B*

Earl & Judi McWhirter
35 Rukuhia Road,
RD 2,
Ohaupo

Tel (07) 843 8511
or 021 583 462
Fax (07) 843 8514
judi.earl@clear.net.nz

Double/Twin $100-$130
Single $55-$70
(Continental breakfast)
Dinner by arrangement
Visa MC accepted
Children welcome
2 Double 1 Twin (3 bdrm)
Bathrooms: 1 Guest share

Warm, comfortable smoke-free family home in a quiet rural setting, close to Hamilton, Airport and field days (Mystery Creek). Free pick up/delivery airport, bus, train terminal all part of the friendly service. 5km to Vilagrad Winery; 2 minutes walk to Gostiona Restaurant. 2 storeyed house with guest bedrooms and lounge downstairs; dining and hosts upstairs. Continental breakfast with fresh home-baked bread. Judi lectures statistics, University of Waikato. Earl is a school teacher. Non-smokers preferred.

Hamilton *28 km S of Hamilton*

Country Quarters Homestay *B&B Homestay*

Ngaere & Jack Waite
11 Corcoran Road,
Te Pahu,
Hamilton

Tel (07) 825 9727
graeme.waite@xtra.co.nz

Double/Twin $80-$100
Single $40-$50
(Full breakfast)
Children $10
Dinner $25
Children and pets welcome
1 Queen 1 Twin 3 Single (5 bdrm)
Bathrooms: 2 Guest share
Bathroom & Shower room

We welcome you to the peace and tranquillity of country life. Our place is central from Te Awamutu and Hamilton, located in the little farming community of Te Pahu, right under Mount Pirongia. We are in the middle of a block of chestnut trees and are quite secluded. Our home is very large and roomy and we have special facilities for the elderly person. Comfort and nice meals is what we offer you.

Hamilton - Tamahere *10 km S of Hamilton*

Lenvor B&B *B&B Homestay*

Lenora & Trevor Shelley
540E Oaklea Lane,
RD 3,
Tamahere,
Hamilton

Tel (07) 856 2027
Fax (07) 856 4173
lenvor@clear.net.nz

Double/Twin $110-$130
Single $70-$80
(Full breakfast)
Children $10-$25
Dinner by arrangement
Children welcome
3 Queen 3 Single (4 bdrm)
Bathrooms: 1 Ensuite
2 Guest share 1 Family share

Lenora and Trevor warmly invite you to relax and to share the comfort of our home Lenvor, which is set in a rural area, down a country lane. Our 2 storeyed home has guest rooms and small lounge upstairs; dining, lounge and hosts downstairs. 10 minutes to Hamilton or Cambridge, 5 minutes to Mystery Creek or airport. Lenora's interests are floral art and cake icing. Trevor enjoys vintage cars. Centrally situated for day trips to Coromandel, Tauranga, Rotorua, Taupo and Waitomo Caves.

Hamilton - Ohaupo *15 km S of Hamilton*

Ridge House *B&B Homestay*

Margaret Birtles & Matthew Harris
15 Great South Road,
Ohaupo 3803

Tel (07) 823 6555
or 021 260 6504
Fax (07) 823 6550
m.a.birtles@xtra.co.nz

Double/Twin $90-$120
Single $70
(Continental breakfast)
Children $15
Dinner $20 by arrangement
Visa MC accepted
Children and pets welcome
2 Queen 1 Single (2 bdrm)
Ensuite, and double bedroom
Bathrooms: 1 Ensuite 1 Guest share

We welcome you to come and visit our home with its wonderful lake and pastoral views. We are just 6 minutes to Hamilton Airport and can arrange pick up from there and car storage ($10). This is an ideal base for trips to Hamilton, Te Awamutu, Waitomo Caves, Cambridge, Rotorua and Tauranga. Mystery Creek (home of the Field Days) and popular golf courses are close by. Games room, and garden to relax in.

Hamilton *12 km SW of Hamilton*

Uliveto Countrystay *Homestay Countrystay B&B*

Peter & Daphne Searle
164 Finlayson Road, RD 10,
Ngahinapouri, Hamilton

Tel (07) 825 2116
or 027 200 5320
or 027 755 8289
uliveto@xtra.co.nz
www.uliveto.co.nz

Double/Twin $140
Single $110-$140
(Full breakfast)
Dinner by arrangement
Visa MC accepted
Not suitable for children
2 Queen (2 bdrm)
Choose from either The Lavender or The Olive Room
Bathrooms: 2 Ensuite Private ensuite

Come and enjoy the peace and tranquility of the beautiful countryside with us and our chocolate labrador, Bella. Wander in our olive grove and gardens or relax on your private deck. Hamilton City,the airport and National Fieldays are 20 minutes away.Nearby attractions include - Waitomo Caves,lavender farm, golf course,horse treks/tramping tracks on Mt Pirongia, Bridal Veil Falls, Raglan beaches and cafes. To complete your day, share dinner and wine with us or relax in the guest lounge or our therapeutic spa.

Hamilton CBD *0.2 km N of Hamilton CBD*

Home Hospitality *B&B Homestay*

Diana & Fred Houtman
7A Hamilton Parade, Hamilton

Tel 07 838 1538
or 021 170 3210 text only
frediana@ihug.co.nz
www.accommodationinnewzealand.co.nz//homehospitality

Double/Twin $120
Single $70
(Full breakfast)
Not suitable for children
Dinner $30 - advance notice required
Separate rate for special events
Please enquire.
Pet free home
1 Queen 2 Single (2 bdrm)
1 Queen ; 1 Twin/King
Bathrooms: 1 Guest share

Comfortable self-contained accommodation in a quiet riverside cul-de-sac in the centre of Hamilton. Private sitting room for guests, with tea/coffee making facilities. Leave your car in our secure off-road parking area & walk to restaurants, shops, theatres, sports venues, conference centres - no parking hassles. A handy point from which to explore a large area of central NZ. Hosts are well travelled & enjoy meeting new people. Dutch spoken. Credit cards NOT accepted.

Hamilton - Whatawhata *10 km W of Hamilton*

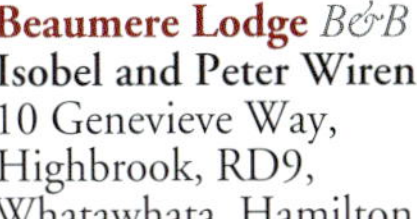

Beaumere Lodge *B&B*

Isobel and Peter Wiren
10 Genevieve Way,
Highbrook, RD9,
Whatawhata, Hamilton

Tel (07) 829 8652
or 027 232 9149
Fax (07) 829 8652
beaumere@wave.co.nz

Double/Twin $100-$130
Single $60-$80
(Full breakfast)
Children by negotiation
Dinner & light meals b/a
No Eftpos/CC available
Children and pets welcome
1 Queen 1 Twin (2 bdrm)
Bathrooms: 1 Private
Sep Spa-Bath/Sep toilet

Wonderful country setting, magic views and sunsets over the Hakaramatas. Romantic fairy-lit gardens. Guest wing, own patio, spa. One-group bookings. Close Golf, Zoo, Tree Arboratum, Bridal Veil Falls, Raglan seaside resort 25 mins. Glowworm Caves 1 hour. En route Auckland-Waitomo-Taupo. Semi-retirees with a friendly cat, enjoy golf, bowls gardening, travel, and Isobel sings in a choir. Peter has lived in Japan and Korea so we are always delighted to help with language and travel plans. You are assured of a memorable stay.

~

Hamilton - Te Pahu *20 km W of Hamilton*

Harmony Hours Retreat and B&B *B&B Retreat*

Chrystene Hansen and Bill Bailey
1385 Te Pahu Road,
RD 5, Hamilton, 3285

Tel 0 7 825 9877
or 021 128 6083
relax@harmonyhours.co.nz
www.harmonyhours.co.nz

Double/Twin $120-$150
Single $100-$100
(Special breakfast)
Children up to 12years $50
Dinner by arrangement $25 pp
24 hour stay, all meals,
healing therapies available
Visa MC accepted
1 Queen 1 Single (1 bdrm)
One spacious upstairs room, TV, stereo balcony, spa pool
Bathrooms: 1 Ensuite

Relax in this beautiful, spacious, upstairs room with lovely views of rural waikato including Mount Pirongia. Soak in the spa pool on your very own balcony under a night sky. Bill and Chrystene offer a relaxing experience and are negotiable with meal times. Meals are homegrown, sprayfree or organic. Enjoy our 2 acre block, which also has gardens an orchard and sheep. Muffy is our resident cat. Enquire with Chrystene for a massage/healing. 20 minutes to Hamilton, 30 to Raglan, 90 to Auckland Airport

Hamilton-Matangi *10 km SE of Hamilton*

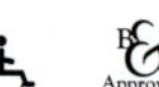

Kowhai Lodge *B&B Homestay*

Sheila and John
81 Butcher Road,
RD4
Hamilton, 3284

Tel (07) 8296 014
kowhai.lodge@yahoo.co.nz

Double/Twin $120
Single up to $95
(Full breakfast)
Dinner by arrangment
Pet free home
2 Queen 1 Twin (3 bdrm)
Bathrooms: 3 Ensuite

Sheila and John would like to welcome you to Kowhai Lodge, a new pet free home built in Matangi. Located 90 minutes from Auckland Airport and just 15 minutes from Hamilton city centre. A few minutes drive from State highway 1 & 1B, Matangi is centrally situated for Hamilton airport, Mystery Creek Event Centre and day trips to Rotorua, Tauranga or Waitomo Caves. Matangi is ideal for couples looking for the tranquility of the countryside in comfortable surroundings; rooms have tea/coffee making facilities and ensuites.

Cambridge *5 km SW of Cambridge*

Birches *Cottage with Kitchen Farmhouse Bed & Breakfast or Self Contained Cottage*

B&B Approved

Sheri Mitchell & Hugh Jellie
263 Maungatautari Road, Cambrige
PO Box 194, Cambridge

Tel (07) 827 6556
or 021 882 216
Fax (07) 827 3552
birchesbandb@xtra.co.nz
www.birches.co.nz

Double/Twin $130-$140
Single $80
(Special breakfast)
Children by arrangement
Dinner by arrangement
Visa MC accepted
1 Queen 1 Double 1 Single (2 bdrm)
Bathrooms: 1 Ensuite 1 Private

Our character farmhouse offers open fires, tennis, swimming pool and hottub in country garden amongst renown horse studs. Proximity to Lake Karapiro makes Birches an ideal base for lake users. Hugh, a veterinarian, and I are widely travelled. Olivia, 17 leaves St Peter's Cambridge end 2009. We have farm pets and a cat. Cherry Tree Cottage is ideal for couples wanting privacy. The twin room in farmhouse has private bathroom with spa bath. We serve delicious farmhouse breakfasts alfresco or in dining room.

Cambridge *2 km S of Cambridge*

Glenelg *B&B Homestay*

B&B Approved

Shirley & Ken Geary
6 Curnow Place,
Cambridge

Tel (07) 823 0084
glenelgbnb@ihug.co.nz
www.cambridge.co.nz

Double/Twin $110
Single $85
(Full breakfast)
Children $25
Dinner $25 by arrangement
Children and pets welcome
3 Queen 1 Twin (4 bdrm)
Bathrooms: 3 Ensuite 1 Private

Glenelg welcomes you to your home away from home. We offer spacious, quality accommodation, that is warm, quiet and private, overlooking Waikato farmland. There is plenty of off-street parking. Beds have electric blankets and woolrests. There are 200 rose bushes in the garden. Five minutes to Lake Karapiro. Mystery Creek, where NZ National Field Days and many other functions are held, is only 15 minutes away. Laundry facilities available. Homemade Kiwi dinners are available by arrangement.

Tirau *10 km S of Matamata*

B&B Approved

Oraka Deer Park *Luxury B&B Homestay Farmstay Separate Suite Cottage with Kitchen*

Linda & Ian Scott
71 Bayly Road,
RD1,
Tirau 3484

Tel (07) 883 1382
or 027 245 2888
or 027 473 2657
Fax (07) 883 1384
oraka@xtra.co.nz
www.oraka-deer.co.nz

Double/Twin $100-$250
Single $90-$200
(Breakfast by arrangement)
Dinner by arrangement
Visa MC accepted
Children and pets welcome
2 King 1 Double 1 Single (3 bdrm)
Cottage: superking, double & single, sofa bed in lounge
Bathrooms: 2 Ensuite Showers

Scott Family, Ian & Linda and twins Lani & Travis, Labrador Tilly and two burmese. This is a working deer farm, restaurant and tourist business. Lovely garden with mature trees & flower borders, swimming pool & spa, tennis & petanque. Private & peaceful green Waikato countryside.

Te Awamutu *2 km S of Te Awamutu*

Leger Farm *B&B Farmstay*
Beverley & Peter Bryant
114 St Leger Road,
Te Awamutu
Tel (07) 871 6676
Fax (07) 871 6679

Double/Twin $125-$140
Single $85-$100
(Full breakfast)
Dinner $35
1 Queen 1 Double 1 Twin
3 Single (4 bdrm)
Bathrooms: 1 Ensuite 1 Private
1 Guest share 1 Bath

Leger Farm is a private residence with country living at its finest. The discerning leisure traveller seeking quality accommodation, in peaceful, relaxing surroundings, will find warm hospitality and every comfort here. Spacious bedrooms share stunning views of surrounding countryside. Each bedroom has its own balcony with garden vistas. We farm cattle and sheep, and are centrally based for visiting Waitomo Caves and black water rafting, Rotorua with its thermal activity and NZ's dramatic West Coast and ironstone sands. Golf course nearby for relaxation. Smoke-free home.

Otorohanga - Waitomo District *10 km S of Otorohanga*

Redwood Lodge *Luxury B&B Homestay*
Julie & Donovan Neuhoff
222 Puketawai Road,
RD 6, Otorohanga
Tel (07) 873 6685
or 027 569 6567
welcome@redwood-lodge.co.nz
www.redwood-lodge.co.nz

Double/Twin $140-$170
Single $110-$130
(Full breakfast)
Children B/A
Dinner Available on request
One, two or three courses
Visa MC Eftpos accepted
1 King/Twin 3 Queen 2 Single (4 bdrm)
Individually decorated and furnished
Bathrooms: 4 Ensuite

Only 10 minutes from Waitomo Caves, Redwood Lodge offers travellers affordable luxury in a tranquil setting. Julie & Donovan welcome you to their well-appointed and comfortable home offering 4 good-sized heated/air conditioned en-suite rooms, each provided with tea/coffee making facilities. Enjoy our 8 acres of parklike grounds, our guest lounge and games room with TV and pool table. A hot spa, sauna and in-ground swimming pool are all available to our guests.

Waitomo Caves *9.7 km W of Waitomo Village*

Te Tiro *B&B Farmstay Cottage with Kitchen*

B&B Approved

Rachel & Angus Stubbs
970 Caves Te Anga Road,
RD 8 Te Kuiti,

Tel (07) 878 6328
Fax (07) 878 6328
tetiro@waitomocavesnz.com
www.waitomocavesnz.com

Double/Twin $110 Single $70
(Continental breakfast provisions)
Children $15 pp
Dinner by prior arrangment
Familys of 5 welcome,
we add extra mattress to loft
Visa MC accepted
Children and pets welcome
2 Queen 4 Single (2 bdrm)
Cottages one room, queen down,
two single mattresses in loft
Bathrooms: 2 Private Two bathrooms with shower, toilet and washbasin.

Te Tiro (The View) welcomes you. Enjoy fantastic panoramic views of the central North Island and mountains. At night enjoy glowworms nestled in lush NZ bush only metres from your cottage. Situated on an established sheep farm with 350 acres of reserve bush. Our self-contained pioneer style cottages can accommodate up to 5 people in a cosy open plan room. Hosts Rachel and Angus have 30 years of tourism experience between them and would be happy to advise you on the wonders of Waitomo.

Waitomo Caves *16 km S of Otorohanga*

Waitomo Caves Guest Lodge *B&B Studio units each with own entrance*

B&B Approved

Janet & Colin Beeston
7 Te Anga Road,
Waitomo Caves Village

Tel (07) 878 7641
or 0800 465 762
Fax (07) 878 7466
waitomocavesguestlodge@xtra.co.nz
www.waitomocavesguestlodge.co.nz

Double/Twin $100-$110
Single $75 (Continental breakfast)
Children $10-5yrs, $15 5-10yrs,
$20 10-15yrs Extra adult $25
Visa MC Eftpos accepted
Children welcome
7 Queen 9 Single (8 bdrm)
A variety of double, twin & family rooms
Bathrooms: 7 Ensuite 1 Private
There is a bath in the private bathroom

We are right in Waitomo Caves village, adjacent to a shop and 2 cafes, and an easy walking distance to the Museum/i-SITE, Glowworm Caves, adventure caving offices and other eating places. Our quality ensuite studio units are in a beautiful peaceful garden setting, with lovely views over the surrounding countryside. You can expect a warm welcome from Colin, Janet and Gypsy the family dog. We can give you knowledgeable advice, make bookings for local activities and help you with your itinerary.

Te Kuiti - Waitomo District *2 km N of Te Kuiti*

Simply the Best B&B *B&B Farmstay*

Margaret & Graeme Churstain
129 Gadsby Road,
RD 5,
Te Kuiti

Tel (07) 878 8191
or 027 666 9343
Fax (07) 878 5949
enquiry@simplythebestbnb.co.nz
www.simplythebestbnb.co.nz

Double/Twin $90
Single $50
(Continental breakfast)
Children negotiable
Pets - cats on property
2 Queen 1 Twin (3 bdrm)
spacious and comfortable
Bathrooms: 1 Ensuite 1 Private 1 Guest share

Just 2.5hours from Auckland Airport our peaceful farmlet, signposted off SH3, northern end of Te Kuiti, we welcome you to 'Simply the Best' way to break a journey or to begin or end your New Zealand adventure. Happy to share our knowledge of the local area, Waitomo Caves, Blackwater rafting 10minutes away. Our comfortable 1 level home is unique for easy access from all rooms to decks overlooking stunning rural views. We offer secure parking, restaurants nearby, and 'above all' a place to remember.

Te Kuiti - Waitomo District *21 km W of Te Kuiti*

Tapanui Cottage *B&B Cottage with Kitchen*

Craig and Sarah Fagan
1714 Oparure Road,
RD 5,
Te Kuiti

Tel (07) 877 8498
or 027 251 1340
Fax (07) 877 8432
info@tapanuicottage.co.nz
www.tapanuicottage.co.nz

Double/Twin $150-$200
Single $70-$90
(Continental breakfast)
Visa MC accepted
Children welcome
1 King/Twin 1 Queen 2 Single (4 bdrm)
Bathrooms: 1 Private

The elegant self-contained cottage is a serene and secluded country retreat located near the renowned Waitomo Glow-Worm Caves. Tapanui Cottage offers accommodation totally unlike any run-of-the-mill hotel or motel accommodation in New Zealand.Situated on a 2,500 acre working sheep and cattle farm Tapanui Cottage is surrounded with sheep, cattle, deer and goats roaming the hillsides. Experience New Zealand farming hospitality while recharging from Waitomo activities. We welcome guest after 2pm

Waikato

Pio Pio - Waitomo District *19 km S of Te Kuiti*

B&B Approved

Carmel Farm *B&B Homestay Farmstay*
Barbara & Leo Anselmi
1832 SH3, PO Box 93, Pio Pio
Tel (07) 877 8130
or 0800 877 813
Fax (07) 877 8130
Carmelfarms@xtra.co.nz

Double/Twin $120 Single $80
(Continental breakfast)
Dinner $25pp
Children and pets welcome
2 King/Twin 4 Single (4 bdrm)
Bathrooms: 1 Ensuite 1 Guest share

Barbara and Leo Anselmi operate a 2000 acre sheep, beef and dairy farm. You will be welcomed into an established homestead set in a picturesque limestone valley.

You will be treated to delicious home-cooked meals and the warmth of our friendship.

Whether mustering mobs of cattle and sheep, viewing the milking of 550 Friesian cows, driving around the rolling hills on the 4 wheeled farm-bike, basking in the sun by the pool or enjoying the gardens, you will feel relaxed and rejuvenated. Whether you seek excitement or tranquility, Carmel Farm is the perfect retreat.

We are ideally located for you to explore many other attractions. We are adjacent to a beautiful 18 hole golf course which welcomes visitors. The property is a short distance from black water rafting and canoeing activities, The Lost World Cavern, and the famous Waitomo Caves. Nearby are bush walks, waterfalls, and the home of the rare kokako bird. The Mangaotaki stream is a mecca for the trout enthusiast. We can help to arrange activities for people of all ages and interests; from garden visits to horse riding. (P.S. In the TV lounge there is Sky for those all-important rugby matches.) Please let us know your preference.

We are 140km from Rotorua/Taupo. Directions: Travel 19km south of Te Kuiti on SH3 towards Piopio. Carmel Farm is on the right. We can arrange to pick up from Otorohanga, Te Kuiti or Waitomo, if required.

Coromandel Peninsula
Waiheke Island
Beachlands
Whitford
Clevedon
Papakura
Kaiaua
rury
Bombay
Mercer
Kuaotunu
Opito Bay
Coromandel
Whitianga
Hahei
Cooks Beach
Hot Water Beach
Tairua
Te Puru
Thames
25
Whangamata
2
Paeroa
Karangahake
Waihi
Waihi Beach
0
Kilometres
20
0
Miles
12

Paeroa - Karangahake *7 km S of PAEROA*

Karangahake Gold 'n Views B&B *Guest Suite. Modern self contained cottage and the Ohinemuri Historic cottagee*

Pamela and Nigel Blaikie
21 John Cotter Road,
Karangahake - RD 4, Paeroa 3674
Tel 0800 023 259 or 021 902 780
Fax (07) 862 6905
goldnviews@orcon.net.nz
www.goldnviewsbnb.co.nz

Double/Twin $100-$180 (Full breakfast)
Children under 12 years $30
Dinner $30 by arrangement
Cottage breakfast provisions available
Visa MC accepted
Children and pets welcome
1 Queen 1 Double (2 bdrm)
B&B:1plus double sofabed . Cottage:1 plus double sofabed
Bathrooms: 1 Ensuite B&B ensuite shower. Cottage - shower.

CURRENT SPECIALS! see www.goldnviewsbnb.co.nz Nestled beneath Mt. Karangahake among the stunning scenic views of the Karangahake Gorge, Pam and Nigel welcome you to this peaceful location. Only minutes from the Ohinemuri winery,a cafe, trout fishing, and the famous Windows walkway. Our homestay offers the Guest Suite with Queen bed,`ensuite and own lounge with TV and coffee making facilities. Our modern Cedar wood self contained cottage offers one bedroom, and one double sofabed. Our Ohinemuri historic cottage offers two bedrooms plus sofabed and river views.

Thames *8 km SE of Thames*

Wharfedale Country House *Homestay Farmstay Apartment with Kitchen*

Rosemary Burks
RD 1, Kopu,
Thames
Tel (07) 868 8929
Fax (07) 868 8926
wharfedale@xtra.co.nz

Double/Twin $150
Single $100
(Full breakfast)
Visa MC accepted
Not suitable for children
1 Double 2 Single (2 bdrm)
Bathrooms: 2 Private

For 17 years our guests have enjoyed the beauty of Wharfedale which has featured in Air NZ's "Airwaves" and Japan's "My Country" magazines. We invite you to share our idyllic lifestyle set in 9 acres of park-like paddocks and gardens, surrounded by native bush. Delight in private river swimming, abundant bird life. We enjoy wholefood and organically grown produce. There are cooking facilities in the studio apartment. Cool shade in summer and cozy log fires and electric blankets in winter. Golf club nearby.

Thames *6.4 km E of Thames*

B&B Approved

Mountain Top B&B *Homestay*

Elizabeth McCracken & Allan Berry
452 Kauaeranga Valley Road,
RD 2, Thames

Tel (07) 868 9662
Fax (07) 868 9662
mountain.top@slingshot.co.nz

Double/Twin $115-$120
Single $80
(Full breakfast)
Children half price
Dinner $30-$35
Visa MC Diners Amex accepted
Children and pets welcome
1 Queen 2 Twin (2 bdrm)
Bathrooms: 1 Guest share

Allan and I grow mandarins, native trees and raise coloured sheep on a small organic farm. Our private, peaceful, guest wing with lounge, TV and extensive library has bedrooms and decks with superb views overlooking river, forest swimming pools and mountains. Nearby Forest Park has wonderful walking tracks. We have a productive, rambly garden, Jack Russell Roly, cat Priscilla. No cell phone coverage - best to phone mornings or evenings. We love entertaining and cooking for people, mostly from farm produce. Let's look after you.

~

Thames *8 km E of Thames*

B&B Approved

Huia Lodge *B&B*

Celia & Murray Newby
589 Kauaeranga Valley Road,
Thames,

Tel (07) 868 6557
Fax (07) 868 6557
celian@wave.co.nz
www.thames-info.co.nz/HuiaLodge

Double/Twin $110
Single $75
(Full breakfast)
Extra person $40
Visa MC accepted
2 Queen 2 Single (2 bdrm)
spacious suites ,Queen and single beds, ensuiteBathrooms: 2 Ensuite

Each unit has an ensuite and tea/coffee facilities. Relax and enjoy the tranquility of the valley, hike in the nearby Forest Park or circle the Peninsula to view the famous Coromandel scenery. We enjoy meeting travellers, love the rural lifestyle, grow fruit/vegetables, and enjoy the peace with our pet dog on our 3 acre paradise. Turn at BP corner (south end of township)into Banks Street then follow Parawai Road into the valley. We're 8km from BP. Just 1 1/2 hours from Auckland.

Thames *2.5 km SE of Post Office*

The Heights *Luxury B&B*
Vicky & Phil English
300 Grafton Road, Thames, 3500
Tel (07) 868 9925 or 0800 68 9925 (NZ)
0808 337 7020 (UK) 1800 557 671 (AUS)
info@theheights.co.nz
www.theheights.co.nz

Double/Twin $195-$225
Single $185-$210
(Full breakfast)
Dinner $50-$60 per person by pre-arrangement
Ariel premium non-alcoholic wines $25
Visa MC Diners Amex accepted
Not suitable for children
2 King (2 bdrm)
2 King bedrooms, one can be reconfigured as 2 singles
Bathrooms: 2 Ensuite

tourism INDUSTRY MEMBER · Qualmark ★★★★ · @ home · B&B Approved

Photos can't do justice to the breathtaking panoramic views of sea, mountains and countryside at The Heights.

Relax in luxury with your own private deck or patio, king bed, ensuite, tea making, fridge, SKY TV, DVD, Internet, and all the special touches for a memorable stay. Hosts Vicky and Phil love sharing with you all the best spots to visit, and our friendly cats add to the welcome.

The 100 km of views from the deck from Te Moana are worth the short climb of stairs, while garden-view Te Koru features its own fireplace.

Only 1.5 hours from Auckland International Airport, take time to pamper yourself at The Heights. Qualmark Enviro Silver award winner.

Thames *3 km S of Thames*

Totara Valley Barns *B&B Apartment with Kitchen*
Shona & Bruz MacGregor
65 Totara Valley Road,
RD 1, Thames

Tel (07) 868 9730
or 027 310 3644
info@totarabarns.co.nz
www.totarabarns.co.nz

Double/Twin $135-$155
Single $135
(Continental breakfast)
Dinner $35 Delicious Kiwi meals
or order a BBQ Box cook yourself
Visa MC accepted
Not suitable for children
2 Queen (2 bdrm)
Comfortable queen beds
with own ensuite
Bathrooms: 2 Ensuite

Unique, quality separate accommodation in a beautifull rural garden setting. 90 minutes south of Auckland Airport, Totara Barns is perfect as a relaxing getaway or as a base to explore the Coromandels exciting attractions. Separate guest accommodation with ensuites and spacious guest lounge. Enjoy the quiet surroundings, safe off-road parking, a generous continental breakfast and beautiful garden to unwind in at days end. Evening meal available using home-grown produce. Your local hosts, Shona and Bruz, assure you of true Kiwi hospitality.

Thames *5 km S of Thames*

Thorold Country House *Luxury Homestay Cottage with Kitchen*
Wendy & Gary
36 Ngati Maru Highway,
Kopu, Thames, 3578

Tel (07) 868 8480 or 021 253 6746
thorold@xtra.co.nz
www.thoroldcountryhouse.co.nz

Double/Twin $195-$250
Single $150 (Full breakfast)
Dinner available by prior
arrangement, special diets catered for
Garden cottage $250 double,
Extra person $50, max 4
Visa MC accepted
Children welcome
2 Queen 2 Twin (4 bdrm)
Queen & Twin in Homestay
and Garden Cottage
Bathrooms: 2 Private
Private bathroom in both Homestay and Garden Cottage

Relax in our private, peaceful, quality country home situated on 6 acres just 70 minutes from Auckland Airport. The ideal base to explore the beautiful Coromandel Peninsula. Views extend over the Coromandel Hills and Firth of Thames. Luxury guest rooms open onto wide verandas with private seating areas overlooking park like grounds. The Garden Cottage is a spacious home from home with large lounge, dining room, kitchen, bathroom, BBQ. Tennis court, secluded swimming pool set in subtropical gardens, WiFi, open log fire for cooler evenings.

Thames *1 km N of Information Centre*

B&B Approved

Ocean View on Thames *B&B Homestay Apartment with Kitchen*

Julie & Steve McLellan
509 Upper Albert Street,
Thames, 3500

Tel (07) 868 3588
sjmclellan@xtra.co.nz
http://retreat4u.co.nz

Double/Twin $140-$160
Single $125 (Full breakfast)
Extra persons in apartment $30 each
Visa MC Eftpos accepted
Pet free home
Children welcome
3 Queen 1 Twin (4 bdrm)
Homestay 2 Queen.
Apartment 1 Queen, 1 Twin
Bathrooms: 2 Private
Private in home, 1 bathroom in apartment

Peace, tranquility, wonderful views and a very warm welcome await you at Ocean View, with its beautifully landscaped gardens and array of native birds. Thames is a great base from which to explore the stunning and varied scenery of the Coromandel Peninsula, or just enjoy a quiet relaxing break. Ten-minute walk to town centre, restaurants and the coast. Facilities include: off-road parking, laundry service, free WiFi, barbecue, outdoor spa pool with sea view, in-room fridge, tea/coffee, safe, hairdryer, TV, clock radio.

Thames - Totara *5 km SE of THAMES*

Cotswold Cottage *Luxury B&B Cottage with Kitchen*
Luxury Boutique Country House

Graham & Jacqueline Hamlett
46 Maramarahi Road,
Totara, Thames

Tel (07) 868 6306
or mobile 021 1133 463
Fax (07) 868 6202
cotswoldcot@gmail.com
www.cotswoldcottage.co.nz

Double/Twin $110-$195
Single $110-$145
(Full breakfast)
Delicious evening meals $35-$45
Visa MC accepted Pet free home
Not suitable for children under 10
1 King/Twin 5 Queen 1 Single 6 bdrm)
5 Queen Double 1 Twin King single
Bathrooms: 5 Ensuite 1 Private
Neatherwood suite private double spar bath, sitting area

Relax and unwind in our lovingly restored 1920's villa just one hour from Auckland 3 minutes from historic Thames. This is a wonderful base for travellers touring the Coromandel and surrounding areas. With breath taking sea,river and mountain views.Wi fi internet, laundry service, an outside hot spa pool and private off street car parking. Holiday, honeymoon and speciality packages, plus sightseeing and adventure days out can be arranged. Generous gourmet breakfasts inc evening meals available.

Thames Coast - Te Puru *12 km N of Thames*

Te Puru Coast Bed & Breakfast *B&B Homestay*

Bill & Paula Olsen
2A Tatahi Street, Te Puru,
Thames Coast, Thames

Tel (07) 868 2866
or 027 656 6058
Fax (07) 868 2866
tepurucoastbnb@xtra.co.nz
www.tepurucoastbnb.co.nz

Double$120-$140
Single $100-$100
(Full breakfast)
Twin $120
Children $25 under 12 years of age
Dinner $35pp,
Includes New Zealand wine or beer
Pet free home
1 Queen 1 Twin 2 Single (2 bdrm)
Large Queen bedroom, Twin/Single
Bathrooms: 1 Ensuite 1 Private

Welcome to the beautiful Thames Coast. Our modern comfortable home is 80 metres off the main coast road. Guest lounge has TV,books and tea & coffee facilities. You may choose a continental or cooked breakfast and evening meals are on request ($35.00pp) with complimentary New Zealand wine or beer. Our large deck is yours to enjoy or take a 2 minute walk to the beach. A warm welcome greets you on arrival with tea or coffee and homemade cookies.

Coromandel *10 km S of Coromandel*

AJ's Homestay *B&B Homestay*

Annette & Ray Hintz
24 Kowhai Drive,
Te Kouma, RD, Coromandel

Tel (07) 866 7057
or 027 458 1624
Fax (07) 866 7057
rm.aj.hintz@actrix.co.nz

Double/Twin $110-$135
Single $85-$95
(Special breakfast)
Dinner $40--$45
Visa MC accepted
Children welcome
1 King/Twin 2 Queen 1 Single (3 bdrm)
3 bedrooms
Bathrooms: 1 Ensuite 1 Family share

AJ's Homestay with panoramic sea views overlooking the Coromandel Harbour, spectacular sunsets. A 5 minute walk to a safe swimming beach.Our games room has a billiard and table tennis table.Wireless internet available. Dinner by arrangement. Directions: Thames coast main road (SH25) approximately 50 minutes. At the bottom of the last hill overlooking the Coromandel Harbour. Turn sharp left, at the Te Kouma Road sign. Travel past the boat ramp, next turn left. Kowhai Drive, we are number 24.

Coromandel *3 km S of Coromandel*

Jacaranda Lodge *B&B*

B&B Approved

Robin Münch
3195 Tiki Road,
Coromandel, RD 1

Tel (07) 866 8002
or 021 252 6892
Fax (07) 866 8002
info@jacarandalodge.co.nz
www.jacarandalodge.co.nz

Double/Twin $120-$165
Single $70-$130
(Special breakfast)
Visa MC accepted
Pet free home
Not suitable for children
4 Queen 1 Twin 1 Single (6 bdrm)
Bathrooms: 2 Ensuite 1 Private 1
Guest share Spotlessly clean

Robin invites you to share her spacious home set on 6 acres of tranquil country paradise. Located 3km south of Coromandel Town, Jacaranda Lodge provides the perfect escape: relax in one of the guest lounges; stroll around the delightful gardens; experience Coromandel's walks, unique attractions and spectacular coastline. Delicious continental breakfasts include fresh organic produce from Jacaranda's orchard. Large, comfortable bedrooms. Wireless internet connection. Fully equipped guest kitchen (additional charge may apply). Special dietary needs can be catered for, including kosher. Sleep, eat, enjoy.

Coromandel - Te Kouma *8 km S of Coromandel*

Te Kouma B&B *B&B Separate Suite Apartment with Kitchen*

Kurt & Jo Muller
50 Puriri Road,
Te Kouma,
Coromandel

Tel (07) 866 7971
or 021 263 5533
Fax (07) 866 7971
ko_jm_muller@xtra.co.nz

Double/Twin $120-$140
Single $95-$100
(Continental breakfast)
Children welcome
Dinner lots of options in Coromandel
Pet free home
2 Queen 2 Twin (3 bdrm)
Queens have ensuites. Twins share bathroom
Bathrooms: 2 Ensuite 1 Family share

Our well appointed home has the best views in the area. Kurt speaks German and makes delicious wholemeal breads, served for your breakfast with home preserved fruits and jams. Jo collects pacific seashells and old china. We live in a very tranquil place, abounding with bellbirds, tuis and pigeons, over looking Coromandel Harbour. Fishing trips can be arranged, Coromandel town 10 minutes North. Thames 45 minutes South.

Coromandel Town *0.5 km S of Coromandel Town*

The Green House *Luxury B&B*

Malcolm & Denise Stone
505 Tiki Road,
Coromandel Town

Tel (07) 866 7303
or 027 232 6396
or 027 464 0050
Fax (07) 866 7303
m.d.stone@slingshot.co.nz
www.greenhousebandb.co.nz

Double/Twin $145-$165
Single $120-$125
(Continental breakfast)
Visa MC accepted
Not suitable for children
1 King 1 Queen (2 bdrm)
Guest rooms are upstairs
Bathrooms: 2 Ensuite
New ensuite bathrooms

This relaxed home has extremely comfortable facilities, stunning views over hills and sea, and is minutes walk to the excellent restaurants of Coromandel Town. Upstairs, the dedicated guest lounge has a lovely airy feeling with vaulted ceiling and the folowing facilities: complimentary tea/coffee, fridge, TV, computer, videos, book swap etc. The bedrooms, one with private deck, the other sea views, are separated by the guest lounge. Both rooms have excellent ensuite facilities. Generous hospitality is offered by Malcolm & Denise to make your stay memorable.

Coromandel *0.5 km E of Coromandel*

Breakaway B&B *B&B Separate Suite Tea/coffee, TV, microwave, fridge*

Michael & Ross
39 Whangapoua Road,
Coromandel

Tel (07) 866 8310
or 027 363 9960
Fax (07) 866 8310
info@breakaway-bb.co.nz
www.breakaway-bb.co.nz

Double/Twin $165-$165
Single $165-$165
(Continental breakfast)
$25 for each extra person
Visa MC accepted
Not suitable for children
Pets welcome
2 Queen 2 Twin (4 bdrm)
All units are seperate from the home and private.
Bathrooms: 4 Ensuite 4 Private Unit 2 ,twin,large shower room ideal 4 wheel chair use

Allow time in your travels to stop with us. Michael & Ross invite you to a quiet and relaxing stay in their rural country setting in park-like grounds. Just a 1 minute drive or a 10 minute level walk to Coromandel town which offers an excellent variety of restaurants and cafes. Also a good selection of quality craft shops. A continental breakfast is served in the conservatory overlooking the garden with views of the Coromandel Harbour. The fishing is great !!!Pets are welcome by arrangement.

Kuaotunu *17 km N of Whitianga*

Kaeppeli's *B&B Farmstay*
Jill Kaeppeli
40 Gray Ave, Kuaotunu, 3592
Whitianga

Tel (07) 866 2445
or 027 656 3442
Fax (07) 866 2445
paradise@kaeppelis.co.nz
www.kaeppelis.co.nz

Double/Twin $130-$190
Single $95-$140 (Full breakfast)
Children negotiable
Dinner $40 by arrangement,
Swiss Chef
Visa MC Eftpos accepted
Children and pets welcome
1 King 2 Single
Bright sunny cosy rooms with glorious views
Bathrooms: 2 Ensuite Bath & Shower with ocean views

"Back to Paradise" A unique peaceful, secluded, haven with stunning sea, bush and rural views above the Pacific Ocean. Relax, unwind, enjoy the natural beauty that surrounds you. Comfortable sunny rooms with private decks and entrances. Swiss Chef prepares dinner by arrangement using fresh local mostly organic produce. Panoramic gazebo dining room. Clean, safe, white, sandy unspoilt beaches, kayaking, tennis, bush walks, horsetrekking, fishing, golf, arts and crafts. Ideal for exploring Coromandel. Swiss/ German spoken. Children welcome. Pets to pamper. Our view? Simply the best.

Kuaotunu *16 km N of Whitianga*

@ The Peacheys *B&B Homestay Homestay*
Yvonne & Dale Peachey
15 Kawhero Drive,
Kuaotunu RD 2,
Whitianga

Tel (07) 866 5290
Fax (07) 866 4592
DYPeachey@xtra.co.nz
www.thepeacheys.co.nz

Double/Twin $140
Single $110
(Special breakfast)
Dinner $35 pp Reservations please
Visa MC accepted
Not suitable for children
1 King 1 Queen 3 Single (2 bdrm)
Spacious rooms with comfortable beds
Bathrooms: 2 Ensuite

We welcome you to our piece of paradise on the Coromandel Peninsular.Seven safe beaches all close by, & ours is 100 metres from your spacious & well appointed room. Short & picturesque drives to Whitianga & Coromandel & local attractions, cafes & resturuants. You are welcome to dine with us,Monday,Tuesday & Wednesday evenings. Reservations essential please. Laundry & Bicycles available. We have a very shy cat, Chelsea. We will enjoy meeting you & welcome you to our home.

Kuaotunu *17 km N of Whitianga*

Drift In B&B *B&B Homestay*

Yvonne & Peppe Thompson
16 Grays Avenue,
Kuaotunu, RD 2, Whitianga

Tel (07) 866 4321
or 027 245 3632
Fax (07) 866 4321
driftin@paradise.net.nz
www.coromandelfun.co.nz/driftin

Double/Twin $135
Single $75 (Full breakfast)
Children negotiable
Dinner main and dessert $30
Visa MC accepted
1 Queen 2 Single (2 bdrm)
Reading lights, tea and coffee tray in room, comfortable beds
Bathrooms: 1 Guest share
With bath and shower

Welcome is assured. This tranquil comfortable modern cedar home is designed to take full advantage of the sun and breathtaking island views by day and moonlit night. An unique beach theme pervades house and garden, small dog in residence. Just a minute stroll to white sand beaches for safe swimming and fossicking. Breakfast is a memorable occasion with sight and sounds of birds and sea complementing an excellent range of home cooking. Drift in, relax and enjoy this unique and special part of New Zealand.

~

Opito Bay *27 km NE of Whitianga*

@home NEW ZEALAND B&B Approved

At Opito *B&B*

Max & Bev
13 Stewart Place,
Opito Bay, RD 2
Whitianga

Tel (07) 866 0317
or 027 418 5588
max-bev@xtra.co.nz

Double/Twin $120-$150
Single $110 (Full breakfast)
Children $20
Dinner $30 by arrangement
Visa MC accepted
Pet free home
Children welcome
1 Queen (1 bdrm)
Plus sofa bed in guest room
Bathrooms: 1 Private
Shower over 'shub' (mini-bath)

A warm kiwi welcome awaits you with complimentary tea & coffee and home baking on the deck. Our clean comfortable B&B offers you your own entrance,queen room, bathroom, guest area with sofa-bed, fridge, toaster, electric jug etc. Enjoy soaking in our spa after a swim or walk along Opito's beautiful, safe, white sandy beach, just 2 minutes stroll away. Restaurants at Whitianga or Matarangi or join us for a home cooked dinner or you may choose to self-cater on the BBQ. Laundry facilities available.

Whitianga *1 km S of Whitianga*

B&B Approved

Cosy Cat Cottage *B&B Cottage with Kitchen*

Gordon Pearce
41 South Highway (town end),
Whitianga
Tel (07) 866 4488
cosycat@xtra.co.nz
www.cosycat.co.nz

Double/Twin $95-$125
Single $80-$90
(Full breakfast)
Cottage $90-$180
Visa MC accepted
Children welcome
2 Queen 1 Double 1 Single (3 bdrm)
2 queen rooms and 1 single room with cat decor
Bathrooms: 2 Ensuite 1 Private

Welcome to our picturesque 2 storied cottage filled with feline memorabilia! Relax with complimentary tea or coffee served on the veranda or in the guest lounge. Enjoy a good nights rest in comfortable beds and choose a variety of treats from our breakfast blackboard menu. You will probably like to meet Honey the cat or perhaps visit the cat hotel in the garden. A separate cottage is available with queen beds, bathrooms and kitchen. Friendly helpful service is assured - hope to see you soon!

Whitianga - Cooks Beach *17 km N of Tairua*

@home New Zealand · B&B Approved

Mercury Orchard *B&B Cottage with Kitchen*

Heather and Barry Scott
141 Purangi Road,
Cooks Beach, Whitianga
Tel (07) 866 3119
Fax (07) 866 3115
relax@mercuryorchard.co.nz
www.mercuryorchard.co.nz

Double/Twin $165-$180
Single $120-$140
(Full breakfast)
Children $20
Fig Tree Cottage $180
Paua Bach $180
Visa MC accepted
Children welcome
1 King 1 Queen 2 Single (3 bdrm)
Bathrooms: 2 Ensuite

Paua Bach and Fig Tree Cottage are nestled amongst 5 acres of peaceful country gardens and orchard. Self- contained country style luxury with french doors opening onto your private deck. Crisp cotton bed linen, bathrobes, fresh fruit, flowers and candles. Special to the Bach, an old fashioned outdoor bath. Enjoy a Mercury Orchard full breakfast while listening to the birdsong. Barbeque your evening meal Kiwi style. Hot Water Beach,Cooks Beach and Cathedral Cove are 7-8 minutes drive. We share our home with two small dogs.

Whitianga *4 km N of Whitianga*

At Parkland Place *Luxury B&B*
Maria & Guy Clark
14 Parkland Place,
Brophys Beach, Whitianga

Tel (07) 866 4987
or 021 404 923
Fax (07) 866 4946
parklandplace@wave.co.nz
www.atparklandplace.co.nz

Double/Twin $165-$200
(Full breakfast)
Children negotiable
Dinner by arrangement
Visa MC Eftpos accepted
Pet free home
Children welcome
1 King/Twin 4 King 2 Single (5 bdrm)
Bathrooms: 5 Ensuite

Enjoy European hospitality in Whitianga's most luxurious hotel style B&B. Maria, a ship's chef from Poland and New Zealand husband Guy, a master mariner, will make your stay a memorable experience. Large luxuriously appointed rooms. Magnificent breakfasts. Superb candle-lit dinners or BBQ by arrangement. Sunny picturesque outdoor area with spa pool. Large guest lounge with TV, library, music and refreshments. Situated near the beach and next to reserves and farmland ensures absolute peace and quiet. Privacy and discretion assured. You will not regret coming.

Whitianga - Coroglen *14 km S of Whitianga*

Coroglen Lodge *B&B Farmstay Separate Suite*
Wendy & Nigel Davidson
2221 State Highway 25,
RD 1,
Whitianga 3591

Tel (07) 866 3225
Fax (07) 866 3235
info@coroglenlodge.co.nz
www.coroglenlodge.co.nz

Double/Twin up to $100
Single $60-$80
(Continental breakfast)
Visa MC accepted
Children welcome
2 Queen 2 Single (3 bdrm)
Bathrooms: 2 Guest share

Coroglen Lodge is situated on 17 acres of farmland with cattle, sheep and alpacas. Nestled in the hills with views of the Coromandel Ranges, this is rural tranquillity. Halfway between Whitianga township and Hot Water Beach there is easy access to both areas and all attractions. Guest area is separate, relaxed, and spacious with a large sunny lounge area for your comfort. Wendy spins and knits with wool from her sheep and alpacas, and Nigel has a collection of vintage tractors.

Whitianga *6 km N of Whitianga*

On The Beach *B&B*

B&B Approved

Gordon and Diana Barnaby
66 State Highway 25,
Simpson's Beach,
RD2
Whitianga, 3592

Tel 07 866 2433
or 027 245 7496
info@onthebeachwhitianga.co.nz
www.onthebeachwhitianga.co.nz

Double/Twin $120-$180
(Continental breakfast)
Children Up to 12 yrs free
Dinner By request
Visa MC Amex accepted
Children welcome
2 King 1 Queen 1 Single (3 bdrm)
Fully equipped
Bathrooms: 3 Ensuite

Diana and Gordon look forward to exceeding your expectations when you choose to stay with them. They have travelled extensively and are aware of what their guests would expect when they are away from home. They look forward to making you welcome and to fulfil you needs.

Hahei *38 km S of Whitianga*

The Church *Separate Suite Cottage No Kitchen Cottage with Kitchen*

B&B Approved

Richard Agnew & Karen Blair
87 Beach Road, Hahei,
RD 1, Whitianga

Tel (07) 866 3533 or 0274 596 877
Fax (07) 866 3055
info@thechurchhahei.co.nz
www.thechurchhahei.co.nz

Double/Twin $105-$180
Single $105-$180
(Breakfast by arrangement)
Children $10-$15 Extra Adult $20
Dinner Menu a la carte
Visa MC Eftpos accepted
Children welcome
11 Queen 1 Double 11 Twin
13 Single (11 bdrm)
A selection of bedroom types
Bathrooms: 11 Ensuite

The Church is Hahei's unique accommodation and dining experience. The Church building provides a character dining room/licensed restaurant for delicious evening meals. 11 cosy wooden cottages scattered through delightful bush and gardens offer a range of accommodation and tariffs, ensuites,microwave,toaster, fridge, tea and coffee facilities. Some cottages fully self-contained with woodstoves for winter.Breakfast tray by arrangement. Small conference facilities. Enjoy the nearby wonders of Cathedral Cove, Hot Water Beach, and the Coromandel Peninsula. Seasonal rates.Winter specials. Smoking outside.

Hot Water Beach *28 km N of Tairua*

Auntie Dawns Place *Apartment with Kitchen*

Dawn & Joe Nelmes
15 Radar Road,
Hot Water Beach,
Whitianga RD 1

Tel (07) 866 3707
or 021 215 6300
dawn@auntiedawn.co.nz
www.auntiedawn.co.nz

Double/Twin $100-$135
Single $30-$60
(Continental breakfast)
Visa MC accepted
2 Queen 1 Double 1 Single (2 bdrm)
1 Queen in each apartment
Bathrooms: 2 Private

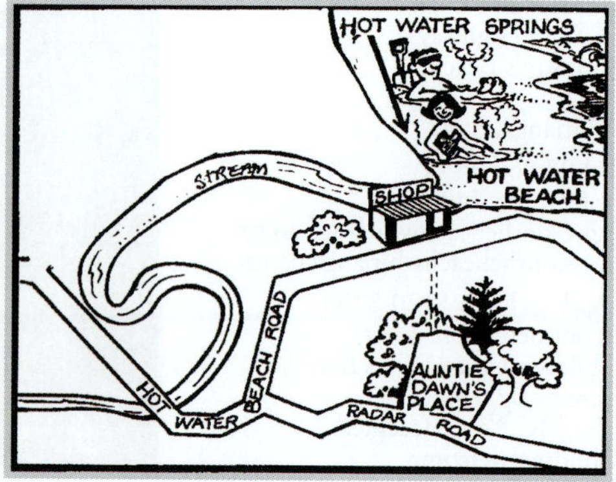

Hot Water Beach is a surfbeach. At low tide hotwater bubbles up in the sand and you dig yourself a "hotpool".Our house is surrounded by huge Pohutukawa trees, 3 minutes walk from hotsprings. We have 6 hens and Joe makes home-brew beer. Each apartment is comfortably furnished with a queen bedroom & spare bed in the living room. Tea, coffee, bread, butter, jam, milk, cereals provided, guests prepare breakfast at preferred time. Directions: turn right into Radar Road before cafe.

~

Tairua *45 km E of Thames*

Approved

Harbour View Lodge *Luxury B&B*

Eve and Alan Roper
179 Main Road,
Tairua

Tel (07) 864 7040
or 027 479 7851
Fax (07) 864 7042
info@harbourviewlodge.co.nz
www.harbourviewlodge.co.nz

Double/Twin $190-$220
Single $160-$190
(Full breakfast)
Visa MC accepted
Not suitable for children
1 King/Twin 2 Queen (3 bdrm)
Bathrooms: 3 Ensuite

Peace & tranquility is yours when you stay in one of our luxury rooms with ensuite. Enjoy the swimming pool and garden,or try out our kayaks. Start your day with a sumptuous breakfast while enjoying the breathtaking views of Tairua Harbour & Paku Mountain. A short stroll will take you to cafes, restaurants, shops and safe beaches. We can also help you plan your daily activities. We have friendly pets for you to enjoy.

Whangamata *.2 km N of town centre*

Sandy Rose Bed & Breakfast *B&B*

Shirley & Murray Calman
122 Hetherington Road,
(Corner Hetherington
& Rutherford Roads),
Whangamata

Tel (07) 865 6911
sandyrose@whangamata.co.nz
http://sandyrose.whangamata.co.nz

Double/Twin $140
Single $100
(Special breakfast)
Visa MC accepted
Pet free home
Not suitable for children
2 King/Twin 1 Queen
1 Double (3 bdrm)
Bathrooms: 3 Ensuite

A charming B&B in the Coromandel Peninsula's popular holiday destination, we have 3 tastefully decorated guest bedrooms, all with ensuite bathrooms, comfortable beds and in-room TVs. Complimentary tea & coffee is available in the guest lounge. We are ideally located, close to Whangamata's shops, cafes and restaurants, and an easy stroll to the surf beach, harbour and wharf. Enjoy our extensive special breakfast and use our home as a base to relax and enjoy the natural attractions that Whangamata and area has to offer.

Whangamata *2 km S of Town Centre*

Kotuku *B&B Homestay*

Linda & Peter Bigge
422 Otahu Road,
Whangamata

Tel (07) 865 6128
or 027 358 1227
Fax (07) 865 6128
bookings@kotukuhomestay.co.nz
www.kotukuhomestay.co.nz

Double/Twin $100-$120
Single $80-$100
(Full breakfast)
Visa MC accepted
3 Queen (3 bdrm)
Bathrooms: 3 Ensuite

We offer comfortable homestay accommodation in a purpose built home. Rosie, our friendly dog and Elizabeth, the cat, will give you a warm welcome too! Relax in the spacious lounge or private patio, take an outdoor spa. Kotuku is situated at the quieter end of Whangamata, just a short stroll to the lovely Otahu Estuary Reserve; ideal for walking, swimming and kayaking. Golf courses(two), shops,cafes a short drive and the surf beach an easy ten minute walk. Do use our bikes and kayaks.

Waihi *1 km S of Waihi*

West Wind Gardens *B&B Homestay*

Josie & Merv Scott
58 Adams Street,
Waihi

Tel (07) 863 7208
westwindgarden@xtra.co.nz
www.athomenz.org.nz

Double/Twin $90
Single $50
(Continental breakfast)
Children $20
Dinner $20
Visa MC accepted
Children welcome
1 Double 2 Single (2 bdrm)
Bathrooms: 1 Guest share

We offer a friendly restful smoke-free stay in our modern home and garden. Waihi is the gate way to both the Coromandel and the Bay of Plenty with its beautiful beaches. Waihi is a historic town with a vintage railway and a working gold mine discovered 1878 closed 1952. Reopened in 1989 as a open-cast mine.Beach 10 minutes away, beautiful walks, golf courses, trout fishing. Enjoy a home cooked meal or sample our restaurants. Our interests are gardening, dancing and travel.

Waihi *2 km W of Waihi*

Ashtree House *B&B rural b@bplus private unit*

Anne & Bill Ashdown
20 Riflerange Road,
Waihi

Tel (07) 863 6448
or 027 492 8915
Fax (07) 863 6443
ash.tree@clear.net.nz
http://ash.tree@clear.net.nz

Double/Twin $100
Single $60 (Full breakfast)
Children under 10 $10
Dinner $20pp booking required
Garden Unit $40pp
Children welcome
1 Queen 1 Double 2 Single (3 bdrm)
Queen, double unit with single beds
Bathrooms: 2 Private 1 Guest share
1 in house bathroom

Modern brick home set on the side of a hill with extensive views and access to trout river. Private guest wing comprising 2 double bedrooms, large private bathroom with shower and bath. Guest lounge with TV, stereo and large selection of New Zealand books. Laundry and separate toilet. 8 acres, large attractive garden and pond area. 1 house dog. Situated 2 minutes to centre of Waihi, complete privacy and quiet guaranteed. Self-contained unit with wheelchair facilities. 5 minutes to beautiful Karangahake Gorge.

Waihi *0.5 km W of Waihi*

Chez Nous *B&B Homestay*

B&B Approved

Sara Parish
41 Seddon Avenue,
Waihi

Tel (07) 863 7538
or 027 644 5562
sarap@slingshot.co.nz

Double/Twin $65
Single $45
(Continental breakfast)
Children $20
Dinner $20pp by arrangement
Visa MC accepted
Children welcome
1 Queen 1 Twin (2 bdrm)
Bathrooms: 1 Guest share

Enjoy a relaxed and friendly atmosphere in a spacious, modern home in an attractive garden setting. Shops and restaurants are within easy walking distance. Discover past and present gold mining activities (tours available), sandy surf beaches, bush walks, 18 hole golf course, art, craft and wine trails. Waihi is an ideal stopover for the traveller who wants to explore the Coromandel Peninsula, Bay of Plenty and Waikato.

Waihi *1 km NE of Waihi*

Dragonfly Garden Bed and Breakfast *B&B*

B&B Approved

Bert and Kathy
11 Parry Palm Ave,
Waihi, 2981

Tel (07) 863 9034
or 027 236 1997
wattsdue@paradise.net.nz
www.dragonflygardenbnb.co.nz

Double/Twin $130-$150
Single $90 (
Full breakfast)
Dinner BBQ, outside garden oven
Not suitable for children
Pets welcome
1 Queen 1 Twin (2 bdrm)
Bathrooms: 2 Ensuite

Enjoy these charming and comfortable detached bedrooms with ensuites which are ideally situated amoungst 1 1/2 acres of mature trees and gardens with fishponds.We offer laundry facilities, outdoor garden oven, fireplace and BBQ area. Situated 1 minute from Waihi Centre, 8 minutes from Karangahake george and 15 minutes from the beach. This area offers something for everyone. Your friendly hosts Bert and Kathy and Roco (the Tibetan Terrier) look forward to looking after you.

Waihi Beach *11 km E of Waihi*

Waterfront Homestay *Apartment with Kitchen*

Kay & John Morgan
17 The Esplanade
(off Hinemoa Street),
Waihi Beach

Tel (07) 863 4342
or 021 170 5058
Fax (07) 863 4342
k.morgan@xtra.co.nz

Double/Twin $120-$150
(Breakfast by arrangement)
Self catering breakfast option
Visa MC accepted
Pet free home
Children welcome
1 Queen 3 Single (2 bdrm)
Bathrooms: 1 Private

Waterfront Homestay. Fully self-contained, 2 double bedrooms. Situated on beach at north end.Suitable for 2 couples or small family group. Unit is lower floor of family home. Walk from front door directly onto an uncrowded sandy beach. Safe ocean swimming, surfcasting, surfing and coastal walks. Restaurants within walking distance or use facilities provided with accommodation. Waterfront Homestay is situated close to popular scenic coastal walks to Orokawa and Homunga Bays. Tariff $120 - 150 per couple, bed and breakfast. Hosts John & Kay Morgan.

~

Waihi Beach *11 km E of Waihi*

Seagulls Bed & Breakfast *B&B*

Marie & Steve Quinlan
8 West Street
(off Pacific Road),
Waihi Beach

Tel (07) 863 4633
or 021 0290 9880
Fax (07) 863 4634
seagullsquinlan@clear.net.nz

Double/Twin $120-$150
Single $100-$110
(Full breakfast)
Children welcome
2 Queen 1 Single (2 bdrm)
Queen size
with extensive sea and beach views
Bathrooms: 1 Guest share
Large modern with bath and shower

Relax and unwind at beautiful Waihi Beach - gateway to Coromandel Peninsular, historic Karangahake Gorge, Orokawa/Homunga walkways and Bay of Plenty. Enjoy spectacular panoramic views of main beach (3minutes walk) and Mayor Island. Watch the sunrise, listen to tuis sing in bush on boundary. Modern spacious luxury home with your own TV lounge, tea/coffee facilities, bedrooms all with sea views. Excellent outdoor area, cafes/restaurants RSA closeby, swimming, surfing, fishing, beach and bush walks. Breakfasts include fresh seasonal fruits, homemade preserves, organic produce.

Waihi Beach *12 km N of Katikati*

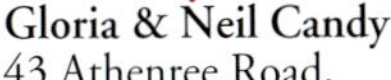

The Candy's B&B *B&B Cottage with Kitchen*

Gloria & Neil Candy
43 Athenree Road,
Athenree,
Waihi Beach

Tel (07) 863 1159
Fax (07) 863 1196
neilcandy@ihug.co.nz

Double/Twin $130-$135
Single $80-$100
(Continental breakfast)
Dinner $32pp
2 King 2 Twin (3 bdrm)
1 Bedroom Cottage self contained ,
2 at main house
Bathrooms: 1 Ensuite 1 Private
1 Guest share
Bath available at the B&B

Take time out: relax. Our modern home is on three acres, with beautiful harbour views: each room has a private patio. Walk to Athenree Hotpools, drive 3 minutes to Waihi Surf Beach, 10 minutes south to Katikati, 2 Local Golf Courses, Morton Estate Winery, . 10 minutes north to Waihi Goldmine, walks and excellent restaurants. Neil loves fishing, and Gloria loves crafts. Meals on request. This is paradise and our city pets agree. New 1 bedroom cottage self contained no meals supplied

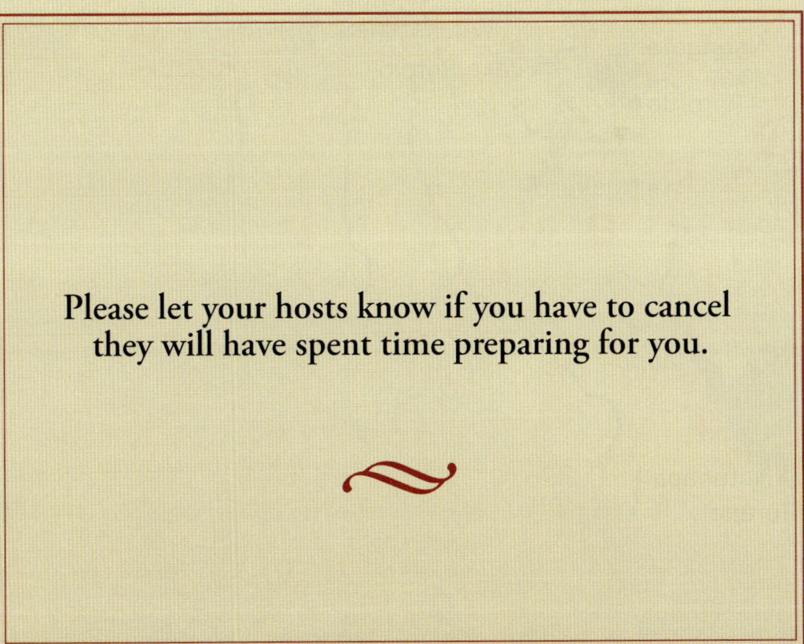

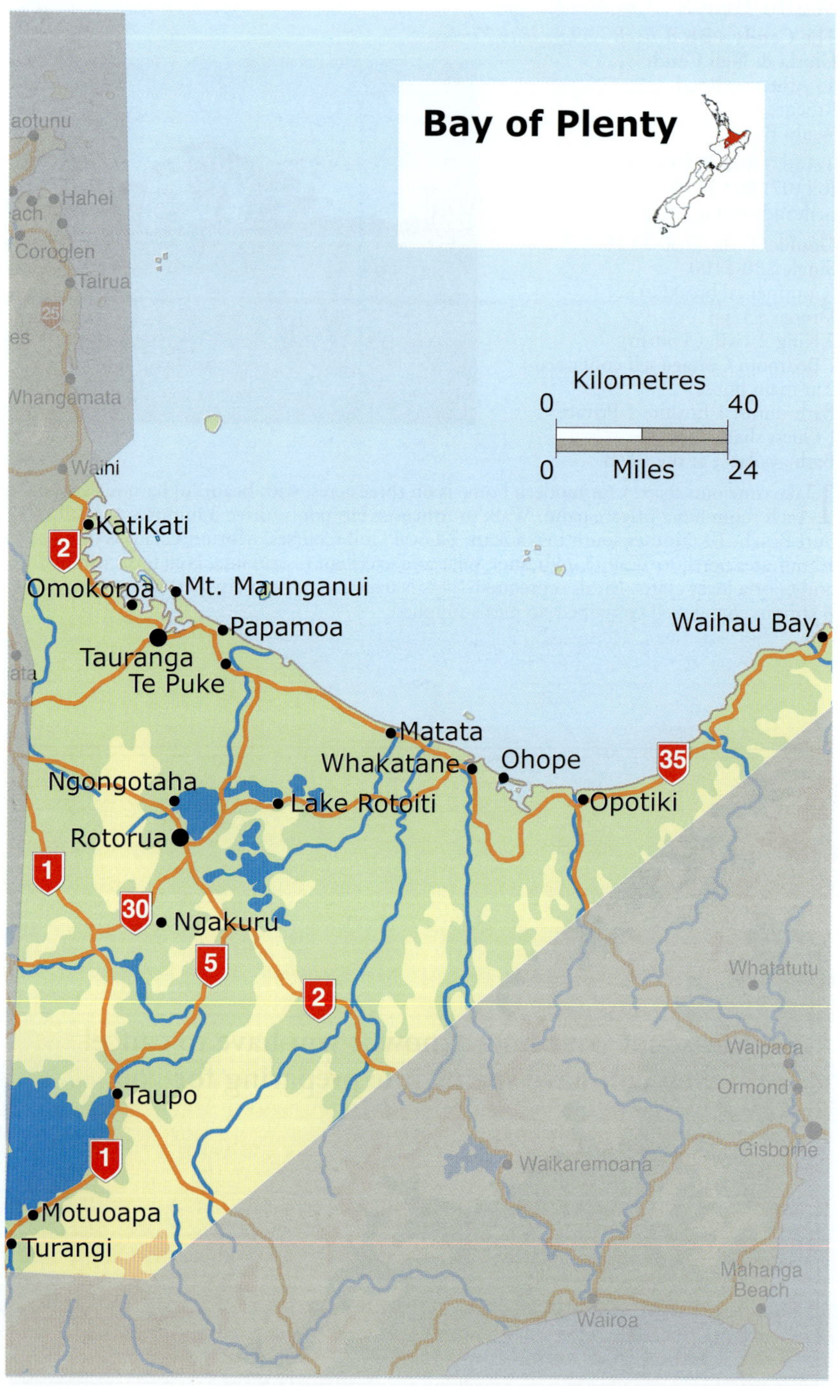
Bay of Plenty
Kilometres
0
40
0
Miles
24
Katikati
Omokoroa
Mt. Maunganui
Papamoa
Tauranga
Te Puke
Matata
Whakatane
Ohope
Opotiki
Waihau Bay
Ngongotaha
Lake Rotoiti
Rotorua
Ngakuru
Taupo
Motuoapa
Turangi
Hahei
Coroglen
Tairua
Whangamata
Waihi
Whatatutu
Waipaoa
Ormond
Gisborne
Waikaremoana
Mahanga Beach
Wairoa
2
25
1
30
5
2
1
35

Katikati *3 km N of Katikati*

Aberfeldy *B&B Farmstay*

B&B Approved

Mary Anne & Rod Calver
164 Lindemann Road,
RD 1, Katikati

Tel (07) 549 0363
or 0800 309 064
027 590 9710
Fax (07) 549 0363
aberfeldy@xtra.co.nz
www.aberfeldy.co.nz

Double/Twin $120
Single $75 (Full breakfast)
Children $40
Dinner by arrangement
Visa MC accepted
Children and pets welcome
1 Queen 1 Twin 1 Single (2 bdrm)
Bathrooms: 1 Private
We take one party only at a time

Home in extensive gardens with private sunny accommodation. The lounge opens onto a patio, and has fridge,microwave, TV, tea and coffee making facilities. 1 party at a time . We farm sheep and cattle. Rod's associated with Kiwifruit and is a Rotarian. Panoramic views of bush-clad hills, farmland and harbour. Activities include farm walks, meeting tame animals especially Piglet & Lucy the Kune Kune pigs. Golf course, horse riding, and beaches nearby. Our Australian terrier Monty and Pearl our farm dog will welcome you .

Katikati *8 km N of Katikati*

Cotswold Lodge Countrystay *B&B*

Qualmark ★★★★ guest & hosted · @home New Zealand · B&B Approved

Alison & Des Belsham
183 Ongare Point Road,
RD 1,
Katikati

Tel (07) 549 2110
Fax (07) 549 2109
relax@cotswold.co.nz
www.cotswold.co.nz

Double/Twin $150-$170
Single $110
(Special breakfast)
Dinner by prior arrangement
Visa MC accepted
2 Queen 1 Twin (3 bdrm)
Quality Furnished bedrooms
with ensuite bathroom
Bathrooms: 3 Ensuite

We offer warm hospitality and a little luxury, in our rural home, set amidst orchards, with views to Kaimai Ranges, and situated 8 mins north of Katikati and 15 mins from Waihi Beach.Welcoming afternoon tea on arrival. Yummy breakfast.Quality accommodation with ensuite bathrooms.Guest capacity 4. Relax in the undercover hot-tub or play petanque in the garden. We have a friendly Labrador. We will look forward to meeting you.

Katikati *9 km N of Katikati*

B&B @ Panorama Country Lodge *Luxury B&B*

Barbara & Phil McKernon
901 Pacific Coast Highway (SH2),
RD 1, Katikati

Tel (07) 549 1882
or 0211 655 875
Fax (07) 549 1882
mckernon@xtra.co.nz
www.panoramalodge.co.nz

Double/Twin $170-$200
Single $130-$150
(Special breakfast)
Visa MC accepted
1 King 1 Queen 1 Twin (2 bdrm)
Bathrooms: 1 Ensuite 1 Private

Perfectly situated between beautiful Waihi Beach and Katikati. Nestling in the foothills of the Kaimai Ranges, magnificent ocean views from every room! Relax in spacious and peaceful guest suites, quality furnishings, french doors to swimming pool and terrace, TV, CD, DVD, slippers & robes, coffee & tea, delicious breakfasts, served: in-suite, terrace or dining room. Explore the grounds, orchards, paddocks and meet 'our boys' the alpacas, not forgetting our very friendly dog, Kaimai. Nearby: cafes, wineries, beaches, golf, bushwalks... 'We love it here...so will you!'

Katikati *5 km SE of Katikati*

Tranquility Lodge *B&B Homestay*

Gayle & Capt Reynold Alvins
325 Rea Road,
RD 2,
Katikati, 3178

Tel 07 549 3581
or 027 452 2960
Fax 07 549 3582
info@tranquilitylodge.co.nz
www.tranquilitylodge.co.nz

Double/Twin $165
Single $130
(Special breakfast)
Children by arrangement
Visa MC accepted
Children and pets welcome
2 King (2 bdrm)
Luxury King bedrooms
Bathrooms: 2 Ensuite

Nestled in a peaceful valley, warm kiwi hospitality and superior accommodation await you. Have a seat on your own private deck, view our farmyard pets & Maremma dogs. Relax to the tune of birdsong & stream while viewing the Kaimai Ranges, or play Petanque. Each King suite is sumptuously furnished, with finen linens, bathrobes, slippers, toiletries & hairdryers. So get away from the crowds & discover Katikati. You will find golf, DaySpa, Winery, beaches, bushwalks & much more all within easy reach of our home.

Katikati *9 km SW of Katikati*

Burr-wood Countrystay *B&B Homestay*

B&B Approved

Maureen and Alan Cook
449 Lund Road
RD 2, Katikati, 3178
Tel (07) 549 2060
Fax (07)549 2061
nzjewellery@clear.net.nz

Double/Twin $120-$130
Single $90-$100
(Full breakfast)
Not suitable for small children
Dinner $30 per head -
2 courses plus wine
Visa MC accepted
Pet free home
1 Queen 2 Single (2 bdrm)
one queen and one twin
Bathrooms: 1 Private
We take one party only at a time

Burr-wood is set in a 2 1/2 acre garden and surrounded by native bush. An elevated situation, we overlook a panorama of land,sea, harbour and islands. Enjoy breakfast which includes homemade bread and jams; complimentary pre-dinner drinks, Dinner is available by arrangement. We are 5mins from SH2 and within easy reach of Bay of Plenty attractions We make unique N.Z.Native Timber jewellery. Only one party at a time.home baking,tea/coffee on arrival. Bathrobes,tea/coffee in rooms. Laundry.Internet for emails.

Omokoroa *13 km N of Tauranga*

Serendipity *B&B Homestay B & B and Homestay*

B&B Approved

Sarath and Linda Vidanage
77 Harbour View Road,
Omokoroa,
Tauranga
Tel (07) 548 2044
or 021 999 815(cell)
sarathv@yahoo.com
www.serendipitybnb.com

Double/Twin $125-$135
Single $85
(Full breakfast)
Children $30
Dinner $40 Visa
MC accepted
Children welcome
4 Double (3 bdrm)
Bathrooms: 2 Private
2 bathrooms available

Welcome to our home and garden nestled above spectacular Omokoroa Beach. The beach is a short walk down the steps. Leisurely walking treks take you through the groves and gardens of the peninsula. A beautiful golf course and local hot pools are minutes away. We are a well-traveled couple who have found our paradise. We love to cook and offer a varied cuisine from traditional to exotic. The best of Tauranga and The Bay of Plenty. Free tel. to U.S /Canada,U.K high speed internet

Omokoroa *17 km N of Tauranga*

Seascape *B&B*

Sue & Geoff Gripton
5 Waterview Terrace,
Omokoroa

Tel (07) 548 1027
or 021 171 1936
grippos@xtra.co.nz
www.seascapenz.com

Double/Twin $120-$130
Single $90
(Full breakfast)
Visa MC accepted
1 Double 2 Single (2 bdrm)
Bathrooms: 1 Ensuite

Come share our stunning views of Tauranga Harbour and Kaimais. On our doorstep are beaches, walkways, golf, hot pools, boat ramps etc. Just halfway between Tauranga and Katikati, we offer a double room with ensuite and TV, twin room with shared bathroom, both with tea/coffee. Enjoy a cooked or continental breakfast with homemade bread and jams while gazing at view. Only 3 1/2 kilometres from SH2, left at third roundabout, 1st right, 1st left into Waterview Terrace. Geoff, Sue and our cat will welcome you.

Omokoroa - Tauranga *15 km N of Tauranga*

Wildhaven Farm *Luxury B&B*

Robert & Bryony Cross
Wildhaven Farm, 257
Whakamarama Road,
RD 6, Tauranga

Tel (07) 552 5484
or 021 618 201
Fax (07) 552 5484
roberthhcross@eol.co.nz
www.wildhaven.co.nz

Double/Twin $150
Single $150 (Full breakfast)
Children $20 per child per night
3 course dinner $35 pp b/a
Payment by cash/cheque/internet
Children welcome
1 Double (1 bdrm)
Luxury bedroom with en-suite facilities
Bathrooms: 1 Ensuite Large shower room with heated towel rail and hair dryer

We warmly welcome guests to our little slice of paradise. Our 77 acre working farm has uninterrupted coastal views of Mount Maunganui, north to the Alderman Islands, which you can enjoy from the extensive landscaped gardens and heated swimming pool. We have one large air-conditioned double bedroom, a fold down sofa bed and a cot provides sleeping accommodation for children. Your hosts are, Robert & Bryony and their two children Emma (11) and Freddie (9) and their friendly dog, Hugo.

Tauranga *2 km N of Tauranga Central*

Harbinger House *B&B Homestay*

B&B Approved

Helen & Doug Fisher
209 Fraser Street,
Tauranga

Tel (07) 578 8801
or 027 236 8660
or 0274 583 049
Fax (07) 579 4101
d-h.fisher@xtra.co.nz
www.harbinger.co.nz

Double/Twin $90-$110
Single $75-$95
(Continental breakfast)
Children half price
Dinner $35
Visa MC accepted
2 Queen 2 Single (3 bdrm)
Bathrooms: 1 Guest share

Harbinger House provides affordable luxury in the heart of Tauranga, being close to hospital, conference facilities, downtown and a new shopping mall 100 metres away. Our upstairs has been renovated with your comfort in mind, using quality furnishings, linen, bathrobes, fresh flowers, tea and coffee. Laundry facilities are available. The queen rooms have separate vanities and private balconies. Breakfast is continental using fresh local ingredients where possible. Complimentary pick up from public transport depots and off-street parking is provided.

Tauranga *8 km NW of Tauranga*

Oakridge Views *B&B*

B&B Approved

Diane & Trevor Hinton
557 Cambridge Road,
Tauriko,
Tauranga

Tel (07) 543 0292
or 027 285 2189
Fax (07) 543 0294
oakridge.views@xtra.co.nz
www.oakridgeviews.co.nz

Double/Twin $110-$135
Single $75-$95
(Continental breakfast)
$10 extra for cooked breakfast
Children under 12 $30
Children and pets welcome
1 Queen 1 Twin (2 bdrm)
1 queen, 1 twin king singles
Bathrooms: 1 Ensuite 1 Guest share

Welcome to Oakridge Views, where your comfort is our concern. Enjoy our panoramic views of gardens and rolling hills. Relax in our comfortable 1 level home away from home with an acre of gardens. Handy to some of the top restaurants in the bay. Only 10 minutes to downtown Tauranga and over the harbour bridge to Mt Maunganui. Attractions include garden walks, tramping, parks, wineries, beaches, golf courses. Spa pool available.

Tauranga - Matua *3 km N of Tauranga*

Aramoana *B&B*
Doreen Anderson
9 Seaway Terrace,
Matua,
Tauranga

Tel (07) 576 3058
or 027 320 0203
Fax (07) 576 3758
andersondem@xtra.co.nz
www.aramoanabnb.co.nz

Double/Twin $120
Single $80
(Full breakfast)
Children $35
Eftpos accepted
Pet free home Children welcome
1 Queen 1 Twin (2 bdrm)
Relax in comfort and warmth
Bathrooms: 1 Guest share

Relax in comfort by the sea with fabulous views of the harbour and Mt Maunganui. Watch the ships coming and going to the port. Enjoy the lights at night and the moonlight sparkling on the water. Walk along the beach to parks. Dine or shop in nearby Cherrywood village or drive to golf, the nearest course only 4 minutes away. Use Aramoana as your base to explore the bay. Your host has extensive knowledge of the area and will make you very welcome.

~

Tauranga - Oropi *3 km SE of Greerton*

Oropi B and B *B&B Cottage No Kitchen Seperate Suite, No Kitchen*
Linda and Mike Neill
203 Oropi Road,
Tauranga, 3173

Tel (07) 543 1995
or 027 20 750 42
lindahwills@kinect.co.nz

Double/Twin $100-$130
Single $90-$100
(Continental breakfast)
Children welcome
Dinner $40 per guest
Extra guests are $20 per person
Visa MC accepted
Children and pets welcome
1 Queen 1 Double 2 Single (2 bdrm)
Two bedrooms with fold out double sofa-bed in lounge
Bathrooms: 1 Ensuite 1 Private

We are a family of four with a private building for guests in which there are two bedrooms, lounge and ensuite.Guests can use their own barbeque or our pitanque court.Our property has ample parking for boat, caravan or cars off the road.We overlook a public 9-hole golf course on on side of our property and on the other a white-baiting stream!The Tauranga racecourse is 5mins drive from us.We will endvour to make your stay with us as comfortable as possible.

Tauranga - Plummers Pt. *15 km N of Tauranga*

B&B Approved

Te Puna Estuary B&B *B&B Self contained*

Kirsty & Graham Walker
99 Jess Road,
Te Puna,
Tauranga 3172

Tel (07) 548 2939
or (021) 527 352
tepunaestuarybnb@vodafone.co.nz

Double/Twin $100-$120
(Continental breakfast provisions)
Not suitable for children
Pets welcome
1 Queen (1 bdrm)
Bathrooms: 1 Ensuite

Lovely quiet, self contained with kitchen, TV and stereo. Located on tidal estuary. Close to restaurants and wedding venue. Perfect for a romantic idyll or weekend retreat. Extensive gardens including ponds. Feed ducks and chooks and enjoy our fresh fruit and produce. Take the harbourside walk to the Point. Sea fishing by arrangement (Weather and captain dependent!) Mineral pools nearby at Omokoroa. Close to Bethlehem shopping centre and Te Puna Quarry Park. Directions: Plummers Point Rd is opposite the Caltex petrol station at Whakamarama on SH2.

Mt Maunganui *4 km N of Mt Maunganui*

B&B Approved

Homestay on the Beach *Luxury Homestay Apartment with Kitchen*

Bernie & Lolly Cotter
85C Oceanbeach Road,
Mt Maunganui

Tel (07) 575 4879
Fax (07) 575 4828
bernie.cotter@xtra.co.nz

Double/Twin $130-$140
Single $100
(Continental breakfast)
Children negotiable
Suite Double $160,
Extra guests $30pp
Children welcome
2 Queen 1 Single (2 bdrm)
Bathrooms: 1 Ensuite 1 Private

Welcome to our magnificent home by the sea. Choose from our self-contained suite, sleeping 2 couples and 1 single (suitable for children) with private deck. 1 min to beach for those casual walks. Upstairs is our Queen ensuite with TV. Your continental breakfast includes eggs any style. International golf course 500 metres. The famous "Mount Walk" up or around with 360 degree views is breathtaking. 4kms to shops, hot salt water pools, and restaurants for your enjoyment.

Mt Maunganui *9 km S of Mt Maunganui*

Pembroke House *B&B*

Cathy & Graham Burgess
12 Santa Fe Key,
Royal Palm Beach,
Papamoa/ Mt Maunganui
Tel (07) 572 1000
PembrokeHouse@xtra.co.nz
www.pembrokehouse.co.nz

Double/Twin $100-$110
Single $80
(Full breakfast)
Children $35
Visa MC accepted
2 Queen 1 Twin (3 bdrm)
All bedrooms have own ensuite or private bathroom
Bathrooms: 2 Ensuite 1 Private

A modern home. Cross the road to the Ocean Beach, where you can enjoy swimming, surfing and beach walks. Enjoy stunning sea views while dining at breakfast. Near Fashion Island and Palm Beach Shopping Plaza, restaurants and golf courses. Stay with us and visit nearby attractions at Mount Maunganui, Tauranga, Rotorua and Whakatane. Separate guest lounge with TV and tea making facilities. Cathy, a schoolteacher, and Graham, semi-retired - your hosts. We are widely travelled and enjoy meeting people. Unsuitable for pre-schoolers.

Mt Maunganui - Papamoa *9 km SE of Mount Maunganui*

B&B Approved

Hesford House *B&B Homestay*

Sally & Derek Hesford
45 Gravatt Road,
Royal Palm Beach,
Papamoa 3118/Mt Maunganui
Tel (07) 572 2825
or 021 257 7384
derek.sally@clear.net.nz
www.hesfordhouse.co.nz

Double/Twin $90-$140
Single $70-$90 (Full breakfast)
Children Negotiable
Visa MC accepted
Pet free home
2 Queen 1 Twin (3 bdrm)
Light and airey, cool in summer, warm in winter
Bathrooms: 1 Ensuite 1 Guest share

Enjoy wonderful kiwi B&B hospitality. A short stroll to the fabulous Papamoa Beach for excellent swimming and surfing or enjoy fine dining at the Bluebiyou Restaurant (function/wedding venue). Explore local shops, supermarket, cafes, restaurants and internet cafe opposite. Close to Blokarts, golf, fishing, walks etc. View our beautiful garden while sampling our delicious breakfast. Your spacious room includes TV, tea/coffee and small fridge. Enjoy day trips to Rotorua (50 mins drive) Whakatane (White Island) and the Coromandel (1hr). Courtesy pickup from public transport.

Mt Maunganui *3.5 km SE of Mt. Maunganui Centre*

Beachside *B&B B&B with free wireless internet*

Lorraine & Jim Robertson
21B Oceanbeach Road,
Mt Maunganui
Tel (07) 574 0960
or 021 238 0598
info@beachsidebnb.co.nz
www.beachsidebnb.co.nz

Double/Twin $100-$140
Single $80-$100
(Full breakfast)
Visa MC accepted
1 King/Twin 2 Queen (3 bdrm)
Bathrooms: 2 Ensuite 1 Private

We are 30 seconds to NZ's most popular beach, but still close to the action and golf courses but far enough away to be quiet. **Free wireless internet**, off-street parking, courtesy transport to/from local airport/buses. Enjoy stunning sea views from our guest lounge while indulging in a generous cooked breakfast plus seasonal fresh fruit salad, home-baked bread & real expresso coffee. We are widely travelled, enjoy meeting and helping our guests. Use our B&B as a base to explore White Island, Rotorua & Coromandel Peninsula.

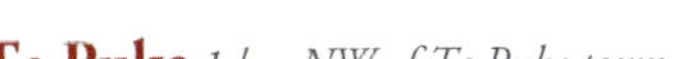

Te Puke *1 km NW of Te Puke town*

Princess Street Apartment. *B&B Apartment with Kitchen*

The Wilson Family
7 Princess Street,
Te Puke, 3119
Tel (07) 573 9345
Fax (07) 573 9354
ruth_wilson@xtra.co.nz

Double/Twin $90
Single $70
(Continental breakfast provisions)
Children $15 per child
Children welcome
1 King/Twin 2 Twin (2 bdrm)
2 double bedrooms.
Bathrooms: 1 Ensuite 1 Private

Fully self contained apartment situated in a quiet cul-de-sac in central Te Puke within walking distance to the township. Enjoy the many restaurants, cafes and shops. The modern apartment, with a full kitchen, laundry facilities, Sky T.V. overlooks a solar heated swimming pool and a tranquil garden setting for your enjoyment.View the many amenities Te Puke has to offer - Kiwifruit Capital of the World, lovely beaches, numerous excellent golf courses nearby, and a 30-40 minute drive from Tauranga, Mount Maunganui, Whakatane and Rotorua.

Te Puke *3.5 km S of Te Puke*

Aotea Villa *B&B Self Contained Bungalow*

Peter & Nanette Miller
246 Te Matai Road,
Te Puke 3188,

Tel (07) 573 9433
Fax (07) 573 9433
Millerph@xtra.co.nz
www.aoteavilla.co.nz

Double/Twin $120
Single $90
(Breakfast by arrangement)
Children $30 < 13yrs
Visa MC accepted
Children and pets welcome
2 Queen 1 Single (2 bdrm)
Villa, 1 double ,
Bungalow 1 double, 1 single
Bathrooms: 1 Ensuite 1 Guest share
Villa guest share, bungalow ensuite

Welcome to our relaxing and comfortable 1910 villa situated in the heart of the Bay of Plenty in pictuesque kiwifruit and avocado countryside. We are minutes from Te Puke, 45 minutes from Whakatane and Rotorua and 20 minutes from Tauranga and Mount Maunganui. Relax on our wisteria covered verandahs and view our beautiful sunsets. Laundry and internet facilities. Guest lounge and games room. Stunning local restaurants, excellent golf course, bush walks and trout fishing close by. Visit our website for more information.

Matata *34 km W of Whakatane*

Pohutukawa Beach B&B & Cottage *B&B Farmstay Cottage with Kitchen*

Christine & Jorg Prinz
693 State Highway 2,
RD 4,
Whakatane

Tel (07) 322 2182
Fax (07) 322 2186
joe@prinztours.co.nz
www.beachbnb.co.nz

Double/Twin $100-$140
Single $100
(Continental breakfast)
Self-contained cottage (sleeps 6)
$160-$180
Visa MC accepted
Children welcome
3 Queen 1 Double 1 Twin (4 bdrm)
Bathrooms: 2 Ensuite 1 Private

Enjoy the fantastic views over the Pacific Ocean in this beautiful rural and cosy setting. We run an organic cattle farm and orchard. We are involved in health care and wellness and provide on site family and medical counseling for those guests in respite. Two ensuite rooms. Self-contained or fully serviced guest house for six people. Relax at the pool, sauna or garden, cuddle the dogs and cat or 'have a chat' to the friendly farm animals. English and German spoken. You are welcome!

Matata - Pikowai *30 km NW of Whakatane*

Fothergills on Mimiha *B&B Farmstay Cottage with Kitchen*
S/C Suite with kitchen
Separate fully equipped Cottage

Bev & Hilton Fothergill
84 Mimiha Road, Pikowai,
Matata, Whakatane

Tel (07) 322 2224 or 0274 60 5958
021 1315 171 Fax (07) 322 2224
bev@fothergills.co.nz
www.fothergills.co.nz

Double/Twin $150-$160
Single $110-$130 (Special breakfast)
Children $20 under 13
$30 teens & extra adults
Dinner $50 each, by arrangement
Cottage 2-nights minimum, $320
$750 p.w. double Visa MC accepted
Children and pets welcome
2 King/Twin 2 Queen 1 Twin (4 bdrm) Two bedrooms in B&B suite + 2 bedrooms in cottage
Bathrooms: 1 Ensuite 2 Private - 1 bathroom in each venue

Just off SH2 and the beach, you'll find our stylish, comfortable, peaceful B & B suite and cottage, and us, your friendly, helpful, hospitable hosts. Breakfasts, served in house or garden, are garden-fresh, home-made and delicious. Mimiha Cottage, is fully equipped; a home-away-from-home. Stroll in our idyllic garden, play petanque, walk along the unspoilt beach, up the country road or climb the wonderful hills, with our two fox terriers for company. After a busy day, soak in the outdoor spa. Come and enjoy this slice of heaven!

If you would like dinner most hosts require 24 hours' notice.

Whakatane *7 km W of Whakatane*

Whakatane Homestay- Leaburn Farm *Farmstay Homestay on a dairy farm*

Kathleen & Jim Law
237 Thornton Road, RD 4, Whakatane 3194
Tel (07) 308 7487
or 021 212 1196
Fax (07) 308 7437
kath.law@xtra.co.nz
www.whakatanehomestay.co.nz

Double/Twin $100 Single $65 (Full breakfast)
Dinner $25-$35 negotiable
Visa MC accepted
Pet free home Pets welcome
1 Queen 2 Single (2 bdrm)
Large rooms-Single bedroom has handbasin only.
Bathrooms: 1 Guest share

Looking for peace and quiet, or do you want to explore this sunshine coast? If stimulating conversation or a browse in an extensive library is something you enjoy, you are welcome here.

Other guests comments over the 26 years we have been home-hosting, include: *"Fantastic value for money with a very interesting friendly couple"* Alan & Janet..U.K. *"Our first experience of B & B has left a wonderful impression."* David & Terri.NZ . *"Wish we could be friends for life"*.Jim and Pat U.S.A.

As young oldies, we enjoy company, farming tales, travel, business interests, and your choice of topic.

We are handy to the golf course, 7km to thriving Whakatane Township. Special interests of genealogy, Lions Club,and bowls . We have a cafe/restaurant,and gift shop on the property.

Our queen-bedded guest room is adjacent to a spa bathroom, separate shower and toilet, and is shared only with other guests if the twin bedroom is occupied. Be as busy as you like or enjoy restful country atmosphere. Pamper yourselves at our place.

Whakatane *10 km S of Whakatane*

Baker's *B&B Homestay Cottage with Kitchen*

B&B Approved

Lynne & Bruce Baker
40 Butler Road, RD 2, Whakatane

Tel (07) 307 0368
or 027 284 6996
Fax (07) 307 0368
bakers@world-net.co.nz
www.bakershomestay.co.nz

Double/Twin $120-$140
Single $90-$110
(Continental breakfast)
Children $20
Dinner $50 by arrangement
(wine included)
Self-contained private cottage available
Visa MC accepted
Children and pets welcome
1 King/Twin 2 Queen 2 Single (4 bdrm)
Garden Room queen, lovely garden aspect
Bathrooms: 2 Ensuite 1 Private Fully tiled private ensuites

Friendly welcome to our lovely country home nestled amongst mature gardens croquet lawn and Avocado orchard. Enjoy our Swimming or spa pool Choose between our delightful fully self-contained 2 bedroom cottage or be pampered with bed & our special breakfast in our warm spacious home. Sky TV in our comfortable guest lounge Lynne & Bruce are keen outdoor hosts enjoying fishing,surfing, gardening and travel White Island tours, dolphin watching, fishing and diving activities can be arranged for your memorable

Whakatane *1.5 km SE of Whakatane Central*

Crestwood Homestay *B&B Separate Suite*

B&B Approved

Janet & Peter McKechnie
2 Crestwood Rise,
Whakatane, Bay of Plenty

Tel (07) 308 7554
or 0800 111 449
or 027 624 624 8
Fax (07) 308 7551
pandjmckechnie@xtra.co.nz
www.crestwood-homestay.co.nz

Double/Twin $140
Single $120 (Continental breakfast)
Dinner $45pp by arrangement
Visa MC accepted
1 Queen 2 Single (2 bdrm)
Sitting room and bedroom
lead onto balcony
Bathrooms: 1 Private - Separate toilet
One party booking only

Hill top seclusion with spectacular sea views. Three minutes drive to town and jetty for White Island/dolphin watching tours. Trout fishing paradise with scenic bush and rivers nearby.Private upstairs suite with living area, sunny balcony, tea-making facilities, fridge, television, phone, wireless internet.Rooms are warm, comfortable and spacious.Suite is yours alone with separate entry and safe off road parking.Ideal for group of four travelling together. Complimentary bottle of wine for three or more nightsInterests are coastguard activities, flyfishing, bush walks and rugby.

Ohope Beach *8 km N of Whakatane*

The Rafters *Apartment with Kitchen*

Pat Rafter
261A Pohutukawa Avenue,
Ohope Beach
Tel (07) 312 4856
Fax (07) 312 4856
The_Rafters_Ohope@xtra.co.nz
www.wave.co.nz/pages/macaulay/The_Rafters.htm

Double/Twin $80
Single $75
(Accommodation only)
Children $10
Extra adult $20, limit 1
Children and pets welcome
1 King 1 Single (2 bdrm)
Bathrooms: 1 Ensuite

Breakfast is not supplied, Unit is self-contained. Minimum 2 night stay. Maximum 3 guests.

Sea views: White, Whale islands, East Coast. Safe swimming. Many interesting walks. Golf, tennis, bowls, all within minutes. Licensed Chartered Club Restaurant opposite. Trips to volcanic White Island, fishing, jet boating, diving, swimming with dolphins arranged. Full cooking facilities; private entrance, sunken garden, BBQ. Complimentary: tea, coffee, biscuits, fruit, newspaper, personal laundry service.

Pat's interests are: philosophy, theology, history, English literature, the making of grape wines and all spirits, golf, bowls, music and tramping. I have a friendly weimaraner dog.

Courtesy car available. House trained animals welcomed. 4 restaurants and oyster farm within 5 minutes drive. I look forward to your company and assure you unique hospitality.

Directions: on reaching Ohope Beach turn right, proceed 2km to 261A (beach-side) name "Rafters" on a brick letterbox with illuminated B&B sign.

Ohope Beach *6 km E of Whakatane*

Shiloah *B&B Homestay Cottage with Kitchen*

Pat & Brian Tolley
27 Westend,
Ohope Beach

Tel (07) 312 4401
Fax (07) 312 4401

Double/Twin $90-$100
Single $50-$60
(Full breakfast)
Children half price
Dinner $18-25 by arrangement
Self-contained unit available
1 Queen 1 Twin 4 Single (2 bdrm)
Bathrooms: 2 Private 1 Guest share
(2 Private in house, 1 Guest share in cottage - Showers only)

Homestay: paradise on the beach - view White Island and enjoy our hospitality. Facilities available for disabled guests - 5% discount. Well travelled. Also available is a self-catered unit, separate from our B&B, with 1 twin bedroom, set of bunks and bed settee if required, complete with shower and kitchenette. Tariff; $60 own bedding, extra if supplied. Access to beach across road. Fishing, swimming, surfing, and bush walks.

~

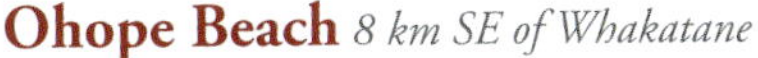

Ohope Beach *8 km SE of Whakatane*

Oceanspray Homestay *Homestay Apartment with Kitchen Cottage with Kitchen*

Frances & John Galbraith
283A Pohutukawa Avenue,
Ohope, Bay of Plenty

Tel (07) 312 4112 or 027 286 6824
Fax (07) 312 4192
frances@oceanspray.co.nz
www.oceanspray.co.nz

Double/Twin $150-$170
Single $80-$100
(Full breakfast provisions)
Children negotiable
Visa MC accepted
Children welcome
3 Queen 2 Twin (5 bdrm)
3 Bedrooms in apartment,
2 bedrooms in cottage
Bathrooms: 1 Ensuite 2 Private
Apartment - ensuite & bathroom, Cottage - own bathroom

Welcome to our beachfront home. Wonderful sea views from our upstairs decks. Our modern downstairs 3 bedroom apartment is self-contained with own kitchen, lounge, two bathrooms (one ensuite). Adjacent to our house is a 2 bedroom, modern, self-contained cottage. Families welcome. Home comforts - Sky TV, books,/DVDs/toys for children. Continental breakfast provisions are supplied into your unit. John's pursuits are kayaking and longline fishing. Frances enjoys entertaining and providing excellent cuisine. Our very sociable cats, Barnaby & Cleo, will also greet you with a warm welcome.

Ohope *10 km SE of Whakatane*

Moanarua Beach Cottage *Cottage with Kitchen*

Miria & Taroi Black
2 Hoterini Street,
Ohope

Tel (07) 312 5924
or 021 255 6192
info@moanarua.co.nz
www.moanarua.co.nz

Double/Twin $1,115-$150
Single $100-$130
(Continental breakfast)
Children 1 baby or small child
Dinner by arrangement
Pets welcome
1 King (1 bdrm)
Bathrooms: 1 Ensuite

Naumai, haere mai Miria and Taroi welcome you to a unique cultural experience in a romantic hideaway, a restful retreat nestled between the ocean and the harbour in sunny Ohope. Feel free to use BBQ, luxury spa and expansive decks with views of ocean and harbour. Chat with us about local history and Maori art works that adorn our home, cottage and garden. Kick back, relax in your private fully self-contained cottage or enjoy many local activities. Boat tours and kayaks available for hire.

Ohope Beach *7.5 km E of Whakatane*

Seaview Bed and Breakfast *B&B Homestay*

Lynnette and Ross Nicholson
33 Waterford Avenue,
Waterford Estate,
Ohope

Tel 07 312 6005
or 021 207 3838
Fax (07) 312 6005
r.lnicholson@xtra.co.nz
www.seaviewbb.co.nz

Double/Twin $110-$140
Single $90-$120
(Special breakfast)
Children welcome by negotiation
Dinner $35pp by arrangement
Visa MC accepted
1 Queen 1 Double 1 Twin (3 bdrm)
Bathrooms: 1 Guest share

Relax and enjoy the quiet gated location of Seaview with the lovely Ohope Beach just metres away. Lovely views from our upstairs deck.br/>Guests have their own lounge downstairs - TV/Video, Tea/Coffee facilities, BBQ, Microwave. Special picnic hampers can be ordered in advance. Home baking and preserves. Laundry available.Golf Club, Restaurants, Playground all close by. Lynnette and Ross, who are former farmers, have many interests including Sea/Lake Fishing, Reading, Sports, Cooking.Together with 'Two Bob", a spoilt cat, we will ensure you enjoy your stay at Ohope

Opotiki *18 km E of Opotiki*

Coral's B&B *B&B Farmstay Cottage with Kitchen*

Coral Parkinson
Morice's Bay,
Highway 35,
RD 1,
Opotiki

Tel (07) 315 8052
or 021 299 9757
coralsb.b@wxc.net.nz

Double/Twin $95-$130
Single $70-$90
(Continental breakfast)
Children $15
Breakfast $10pp by arrangement
Children and pets welcome
2 Queen 2 Single (3 bdrm)
Bathrooms: 1 Private

We provide self-contained accommodation located on our hobby farm. As well as pets and farm animals we collect varied memorabilia. Enjoy the beach and bird life; swim at nearby sandy surf beach. Fish, ramble over the rocks, explore caves. Our 2 storied cottage features lead-light windows, native timbers, large decks look out across the bay and native bush. 3 golf courses within an hours drive; covered parking, home-made bread and preserves. We have a clasic English Daimler car Visit our local Marae.

Opotiki - Waihau Bay *112 km N of Opotiki*

Waihau Bay Homestay *B&B Homestay Apartment with Kitchen*

Noelene & Merv Topia
10942 State highway 35
Waihau Bay, RD 3,
Opotiki

Tel (07) 325 3674
or 0800 240 170
n.topia@clear.net.nz
www.waihaubayhomestay.co.nz

Double/Twin $85-$120
Single $55-$75
(Continental breakfast)
Children half price
Dinner $35
Visa MC Eftpos accepted
Children and pets welcome
2 King 1 Queen 2 Twin 2 Single (4 bdrm)
Bathrooms: 3 Ensuite 1 Private
All bathrooms are suitable for disabled

Surrounded by unspoiled beauty come and enjoy magnificent views, stunning sunsets, swim, go diving, kayaking (we have kayaks) or just walk along the sandy beach. You are most welcome to join Merv when he checks his craypots and his catches are our cuisine specialty. Fishing trips, horse treks and guided cultural walks are also available. We have 2 self-contained units with disabled facilities, and a double room with ensuite. Our cat Tosca and our small dog Kaykay enjoy making new friends.

Rotorua *4 km SW of Rotorua*

Hunts Farm *Farmstay*
Maureen & John Hunt,
363 Pukehangi Road, Rotorua (Home 1: Top Photo)
Tel (07) 348 1352 or 027 486 3477
Sonya Hunt & Dave Cronshaw
359 Pukehangi Road, Rotorua
Tel 07 348 2874 or 027 486 3477
sonyahunt@xtra.co.nz

B&B Approved

Double/Twin $125 Single $80 (Full breakfast)
Children $30 Children welcome
Home 1: 1 King/Twin 1 Queen 2 Single (2 bdrm)
Home 2: 1 Queen 1 Double 2 Single (2 bdrm)
Bathrooms: 3 Ensuite

Come and relax in our neighbouring new homes as we help you plan your itinerary and book your local tours. Explore our 150 acre scenic farm running beef and deer. Views of farm, lake, forest and city are uninterrupted panoramic and magical. Guest areas have private entrances, lounges with tea/coffee facilities and fridges.

Home 1 (363) Maureen and John Hunt: Single story ranch style home, private guest wing with TV. Rosie our chief farm helper who lives in her kennel in the garden at 363 replaces our grown family. Two triple rooms each with ensuite and private terrace. 1 Queen with Single and ensuite, 1 King Twin with single and ensuite.

Home 2 (359) Sonya Hunt and Dave Cronshaw: Upstairs private guest wing available to one group at a time only. Well suited for family groups. Enjoy our 12 m swimming pool and spacious lawns and gardens. At 359 the family includes 2 children and cat. 1 Queen 1 double 2 single with ensuite. Complementary high speed wireless internet available.

Rotorua *2 km N of Rotorua centre*

B&B Approved

Rotorua Lakeside Homestay *Homestay*

Ursula & Lindsay Prince
3 Raukura Place,
Rotorua

Tel (07) 347 0140
or 0800 223 624
Fax (07) 347 0107
the-princes@xtra.co.nz

Double/Twin $110-$120
Single $90-$100
(Special breakfast)
1 King/Twin 1 Queen (2 bdrm)
Bathrooms: 1 Ensuite 1 Private

We invite you to share our spacious, modern home in its tranquil lake setting. Hosts since 1988, our interests include world affairs and environmental issues. We enjoy outdoor activities - feel free to use our Canadian canoe. Now retired, we have lived overseas and still travel extensively. At breakfast (home-made goodies) we'll help you plan activities and arrange bookings. Minimum stay 2 nights.Directions: From Lake Road turn into Bennetts Road, then first left into Koutu Road, then first right into Karenga Street. Turn RIGHT into Haumona Street, a left turn at the end brings you down Raukura Place to our door.$5.00 discount off per night for three or more nights.

Bay of Plenty

Rotorua - Ngakuru *32 km S of Rotorua*

B&B Approved

Te Ana Farmstay *Farmstay Cottage No Kitchen*

The Oberer Residence: Heather Oberer
Poutakataka Road,
Ngakuru, RD 1, Rotorua

Tel (07) 333 2720
or 021 828 151
Fax (07) 333 2720
teanafarmstay@xtra.co.nz
www.teanafarmstay.co.nz

Double/Twin $110-$150
Single $90 (Special breakfast)
Children negotiable
Dinner by prior arrangement
Children welcome
2 Queen 4 Single (4 bdrm)
2 homestead rooms, garden views;
2 roomed cottage
Bathrooms: 2 Ensuite 1 Family share

Te Ana, The Oberer family sanctuary since 1936, offers peace and tranquility in a spacious rural garden setting affording magnificent views of lake, volcanically-formed hills and lush farmland. Enjoy a leisurely stroll before joining host for a very generous country breakfast. Ideal base from which to explore the Rotorua and Taupo attractions, Waiotapu and Waimungu Thermal Reserves, Waikite Thermal mineral swimming pool and Tamaki Tours Hangi. Families welcomed by Jack, our loyal Jack Russell. Farm tour and fishing rod available.

Rotorua *4 km S of Rotorua*

Serendipity Homestay *B&B Homestay*
Kate & Brian Gore
3 Kerswell Terrace,
Tihi-o-Tonga, Rotorua
Tel (07) 347 9385
or 027 609 3268
b.gore@clear.net.nz
www.serendipityhomestay.co.nz

Double/Twin $140-$150
Single $85 (Full breakfast)
Children under 12 $35
Dinner $35 by arrangement
Visa MC accepted
Pet free home
Children welcome
1 Queen 2 Single (2 bdrm)
Electric blankets and wool underlay ensure your comfort
Bathrooms: 1 Private - Spa bath plus shower

Marvel at unsurpassed views of geysers, city, lakes and beyond. Relax in all day sun, on the deck, in the conservatory or in the privacy of our garden. Indulge in comfort, home-cooked cuisine and the friendly folk who have been enjoying hosting for many years. Our interests are, golf, tramping, travel, the environment, antiques and sharing our extensive local and national knowledge with you. Let us advise you on the 'must see' list while in Rotorua and other highlights of our beautiful country. Welcome!

Rotorua *14 km NE of Rotorua*

Brunswick *B&B*
Joy & Lin Cathcart
99 Brunswick Drive,
RD 4,
Rotorua 3074
Tel (07) 350 1472
or mob 021 256 5355
Fax (07) 350 1472
joylin@clear.net.nz

Double/Twin $125
Single $85
(Full breakfast)
Visa MC accepted
Pet free home
Not suitable for children
1 King (1 bdrm)
Bathrooms: 1 Private
The bathroom is adjacent to the bedroom

With peaceful surroundings and beautiful views over Lake Rotorua "Brunswick" is 15mins from Rotorua City centre and 5mins from Rotorua Airport. Having retired from dairy farming Lin now enjoys his golf: Joy plays bridge and gardening is a shared hobby.Our guest room has TV, hot drink facilities,refrigerator and balcony.The bathroom has both bath and separate shower.We are smoke free. Joy's home baking and a warm welcome await you!

Rotorua - Central *0.1 km S of Rotorua Central*

Tresco Classical Oasis B&B *Luxury B&B*

Cottage with 1 bedroom, double bed, and kitchen

Trinka & Trevor
3 Toko Street, Rotorua

Tel (07) 348 9611 or Reservations 0800 873 726
or 021 355 777 Fax (07) 348 9611
trescorotorua@xtra.co.nz www.trescorotorua.co.nz

Double/Twin $180 Single $120 (Full breakfast)
Call for special offers Visa MC Eftpos accepted
Pet & smoke free home
3 Queen 1 Twin 1 Single 1 Queen+ 1 Single (triple)
(5 bdrm)
Bathrooms: 3 Ensuite 1 Private 2 Guest share

Classic Tresco… offers the discerning traveler the opportunity to experience true 100% New Zealand Hospitality.

Just a two minute walk from the city, Tresco is the Classic Private Hotel Bed and Breakfast where the most important thing is the comfort and wellbeing of our guests.

Even when the clean crisp nip of winter cools our Rotorua, guests are snuggly warmed by the comprehensive Geothermal heating throughout Classic Tresco. Piping hot waters from deep in the earth are given up to keep our guests in luxurious comfort.

Tresco has its own Geothermal pool, Roman Bath style, for guests to enjoy. The Geothermal pool is complimented by our sauna.

After a day of marveling at what our spectacular Rotorua has to offer, you can relax and let the mineral waters wash away the worries of the world. The pool is maintained at a constant 40 degrees.

Tresco lets you rediscover the complete joy of the traditional Bed and Breakfast where the levels of service exceed your wishes.

Warm nights and a hearty breakfast prepares you for your days of discovery

100% pureTresco

Rotorua *5 km SE of Rotorua*

Walker Homestay & B&B *B&B Homestay Self contained Cottage*

Colleen & Isaac Walker
13 Glenfield Road,
Owhata, Rotorua

Tel (07) 345 3882
or 021 050 9633
colleen.walker@clear.net.nz

Double/Twin $98-$130
Single $70-$110
(Continental breakfast)
Children half price
Dinner $25-$40 by arrangement
Extra guest $20
Visa MC accepted
Children welcome
1 Queen 1 Double 1 Twin (3 bdrm)
2 in cottage, 1 in house
Bathrooms: 1 Ensuite 1 Private
Cottage has own bathroom, Room in house - ensuite

2 bedroom cottage in own garden area has lounge, kitchen, bathroom,and laundry. Guest room in house has ensuite; tea/coffee facilities; microwave; separate entrance; access to hosts living area. Complete privacy or become one of the family. Colleen is a business administration tutor and Isaac (Ike), a NZ Maori, is a coach driver with a background of farming and paper industry, keen fisherman and golfer. Both are Lions. 2 friendly dachshunds will welcome you. 24 hours notice for Dinner. Off-road parking.

~

Rotorua *3 km W of Rotorua*

West Brook *B&B Homestay*

Judy Bain
378 Malfroy Road,
Rotorua

Tel (07) 347 8073
Fax (07) 347 8073

Double/Twin $100
Single $50
(Continental breakfast)
Children under 12 half price
Dinner $25
Visa MC accepted
Children welcome
4 Single (2 bdrm)
Bathrooms: 1 Family share

Judy, a Rotorua Host Lion Member with years of hospitality involvement lives 3km from city on western outskirts. Interests include meeting with the people, the farming scene, International and local current affairs. Assistance with sight seeing planning and transport to and from tourist centre available. Both well appointed comfy guest rooms are equipped with electric blankets. The friendly front door welcome and chatter over the meal table add up to my motto: home away from home.

Rotorua - Ngongotaha *17 km N of Rotorua*

Clover Downs Estate *Luxury B&B Homestay Farmstay*

Lyn & Lloyd Ferris
175 Jackson Road, RD 2, Ngongotaha, Rotorua
Tel (07) 332 2366 or 021 712 866 Fax (07) 332 2367
Reservations@cloverdowns.co.nz
www.accommodationinrotorua.co.nz

Bay of Plenty

Double/Twin $250-$350 Single $235-$335
(Special breakfast) Children negotiable
Visa MC Diners Amex accepted Children welcome
2 King/Twin 1 King (3 bdrm)
Super-king size rooms, with ensuite bathrooms
Bathrooms: 3 Ensuite Governor's Suite has bath and shower

Welcome to Clover Downs Estate, a luxury bed & breakfast retreat in stunning rural surroundings near Rotorua. Enjoy the comfort of superior accommodation while experiencing New Zealand farm life. Clover Downs is a unique place to stay. Stituated just 15 minutes north of Rotorua city centre in the secluded country setting of Ngongotaha it is a B & B farmstay like no other.

Large comfortable king-size suites comprising of ensuite bathroom, tea & coffee facilities, refrigerator, TV, stereo, wireless internet and individual outdoor decks to provide you with a place to rest and relax in peace and tranquility
Take our complimentary farm tour 9am each morning and feed ostriches by hand see trained sheep dogs rounding up sheep, pat a deer and get within a few feet of our magnificent elk stag. In the evenings, enjoy a glass of wine on your own private verandah overlooking the lush pasture.

Your hosts, Lyn & Lloyd will ensure that your retreat is comfortable and memorable. We can also help arrange other activities so that you can experience all that Rotorua has to offer - geothermal wonderlands with geysers and bubbling mud pools and the rich Maori culture, excellent fishing, sightseeing and other exciting pursuits.
For dining out, the city has an impressive array of cafes and restaurants which offer cuisine from all over the world to tempt the palate or maybe indulge in a traditional hangi feast.
We strive to exceed our guest's expectations through an ineffable blend of warmth, generosity and detail.

Directions: Take State Highway 5 to roundabout. Travel thru Ngongotaha village on Hamurana Road, go over railway line the take 3rd left into Central Road. Turn 1st right into Jackson Road, Clover Downs Estate is number 175 on left hand side.

Rotorua *4 km E of Rotorua*

Aroden B&B Homestay *B&B Homestay*
Leonie & Paul Kibblewhite
2 Hilton Road,
Lynmore,
Rotorua

Tel (07) 345 6303
or 027 696 4211
Fax (07) 345 6353
aroden@xtra.co.nz

Double/Twin $130-$145
Single $90-$110
(Full breakfast)
Children negotiable
Visa MC accepted
2 Queen (2 bdrm)
Bathrooms: 1 Ensuite 1 Private

A great central location: city 5 minutes, Whakarewarewa Forest adjacent (glow-worms at night!), lakes and thermal nearby. Enjoy Aroden's style, peace and character: 2 lounge areas, well-appointed rooms, comfortable beds and fine linen, modern bathrooms (excellent showers), central heating/open fire, patio, spa and luxuriant garden with native tree collection. Leonie, background in teaching, and Paul, scientist, are fifth generation Kiwi with real knowledge of this remarkable area. And meet Taupo, Paul's delightful guide dog. Breakfast is special - this couple enjoys food! Leonie parle francais.

~

Rotorua *10 km N of Rotorua*

Ngongotaha Lakeside Lodge *B&B Homestay*
Lyndsay & Graham Butcher
41 Operiana Street,
Ngongotaha,
Rotorua

Tel (07) 357 4020
or 0800 144 020
or 027 385 2807
Fax (07) 357 4020
lake.edge@xtra.co.nz
www.lakesidelodge.co.nz

Double/Twin $170-$230
Single $150-$200
(Full breakfast)
Children over 10 welcome
Visa MC accepted
Children welcome
1 King 1 Queen 3 Single (3 bdrm)
3 ensuite bedrooms
Bathrooms: 3 Ensuite

Arrive, settle in and make yourselves at home in our Award Winning Lakeside Bed & Breakfast. Enjoy stunning panoramic views, well appointed rooms with all the comforts of home, fly fishing, bird watching, great food and warm, friendly, relaxed, hospitality. Quiet, peaceful, close to major tourist attractions, and away from the sulphur fumes. Come, stay awhile, relax and enjoy. We promise you a great stay!

Rotorua *10 km SE of Rotorua centre*

B&B Approved

Lake Okareka B&B *B&B Homestay*

Patricia & Ken Scott
10 Okareka Loop Road,
R.D 5,
Rotorua

Tel (07) 362 8245
or 0800 652 735
patricia.scott@xtra.co.nz
www.lakeokarekabnb.co.nz

Double/Twin $150
Single $120
(Special breakfast)
Visa MC accepted
2 Queen (2 bdrm)
Bathrooms: 2 Ensuite

A very warm welcome awaits you at tranquil Lake Okareka, one of the most beautiful Lakes in the area. Our modern home captures magnificent Lake views and beyond to Mt Tarawera. Stroll along the waters edge, enjoy the native bush, ferns and birdlife. Use our local knowledge on all nearby hot pools, fishing, scenic, thermal, adventure and cultural activities. Excellent swimming, complimentary kayaks available. Our environment is quiet and peaceful yet only ten minutes from Rotorua. The perfect retreat with space, privacy and home comforts.

Rotorua *1 km N of rotorua*

Robertson House *B&B*

John Ballard
70 Pererika Street,
Rotorua

Tel (07) 343 7559
Fax (07) 343 7559
info@robertsonhouse.co.nz

Double/Twin $140-$190
Single $110-$155
(Continental breakfast)
Extra person $50
Pets welcome
1 King/Twin 2 Queen
2 Double 2 Single (5 bdrm)
Bathrooms: 5 Ensuite

Our historic home, only 2 minutes drive from city centre, was built by one of Rotoruas forefathers, in 1905. Under the auspices of the Historic Places Trust it has been carefully renovated, retaining its colonial charm. Relax in its warm comfortable atmosphere, or take time out on the verandah and enjoy our old English cottage garden resplendent with colour and fragrance, citrus trees and grape vines. Our friendly hosts are happy to assist with information and bookings for Rotorua's Maori cultural and sightseeing attractions.

Rotorua *2 km N of Rotorua centre*

Rotorua's Legend on the Lake Homestay *B&B Homestay Apartment with Kitchen*

Murray & Heather Watson
33 Haumoana Street, Koutu, Rotorua
Tel (07) 347 1123 or 027 492 7122
Fax (07) 347 1313
muzzandheb@kol.co.nz
www.troutnz.co.nz

Double/Twin $150
Single $150 (Full breakfast)
Children $20
Dinner $45 per person by arrangement
Additional Adults $30/night per person
Visa MC accepted
Pet free home
2 Queen 1 Double 1 Single (3 bdrm)
Bathrooms: 1 Ensuite 1 Private

On arrival you will be greeted with our magnificent, quiet and secluded lakes-edge view and a genuine Kiwi welcome. Please join us beside the lake for refreshments as we would love to help you plan your stay by sharing our local knowledge of the area and its many attractions.

Hearing the tranquil lapping of the lake you will find it hard to believe you are only 3 minutes drive from the city centre. You will find your self-contained apartment to have all the comforts of home (washing machine, TV, DVD, video, stereo, oven, microwave and dishwasher). Separate bedroom (queen) and living area/kitchen with ensuite access from both rooms.Free email access.

Our smoke-free apartment ensures a freshness you will enjoy. Breakfast includes fruit, yoghurt, cereal, juice and tea/coffee followed by a cooked breakfast - all this and you can choose the time you would like to have it served. Breakfast is a great time to get to know us and for us to help you make best use of your time in this volcanic thermal paradise.

We are more than happy to assist with local bookings and recommend you sample some of the strong local Maori culture. Murray operates a trout fishing charter business on Lake Rotorua from our Lakeside jetty.Special rates apply.We have both travelled extensively, internationally and throughout New Zealand and enjoy meeting people from all over the world. We have been running homestays for the last 15 years and really know how to make your time here enjoyable and comfortable.

Feel free to sit on the lawn and watch the spectacular sunsets we are lucky enough to enjoy almost every night.We hope you will arrive as our guests and leave as our friends."Humble luxury here"

Rotorua - Lake Rotoiti *20 km NE of Rotorua*

Lakestay Rotoiti *B&B*

Graeme & Raewyn Natusch
173 Tumoana Road,
Lake Rotoiti,
RD 4,
Rotorua

Tel (07) 345 4089
or 027 418 8404
Fax (07) 345 4089
lakestayrotoiti@xtra.co.nz

Double/Twin $120-$150
(Full breakfast)
Dinner $35
Self-contained studio $120-$150
Off season rates May-Oct
Visa MC accepted
2 Queen (2 bdrm)
Bathrooms: 2 Ensuite

Lakestay Rotoiti, a very special destination for the discerning couple or individual travellers both summer and winter with friendly informative hosts and siamese cat. One of just 3 lakefront properties in a beautiful secluded sandy bay surrounded by native bush, forest and stunning lake views from all living and guest bedrooms. Excellent swimming, trout fishing, walking tracks and natural rejuvinating hot baths nearby. Guests enjoy complimentary use of kyaks, dingy, windsurfer and bicycles. Wonderful evening dinner by arrangement. Directions are essential. A truely unique experience.

Rotorua *5 km SW of Post Office*

Arias Farmlet in Town *B&B Farmstay Separate Suite Cottage with Kitchen*

Kerris & Chris
396 Clayton Road, Rotorua

Tel 021 753 691
or (07) 348 0790
Fax (07) 348 0863
ariasfarm@xtra.co.nz
www.ariasfarm.com

Double/Twin $99-$135
Single $80-$100 (Full breakfast)
Children 0-3yrs Cot $25,
5-12 yrs $40
Dinner Mains $15pp,
3-Crse(Soup, Mains, Dessert) $30pp
Laundry full load + dry $10
Visa MC accepted
Pet free home Children welcome
1 King 3 Queen 1 Twin 2 Single (4 bdrm)
King, Queen, & Family Rooms
Bathrooms: 1 Ensuite 1 Private 1 Guest share Ensuite or private

Cute farm animals to pet yet so close to town right in suburbs! Brand new modern lodge on 3 acres with lots of space for families or couples wanting peace. King & Queen beds, ensuite & private bathrooms. Air con & central heating. Unlimited tea/coffee. Laundry, internet, off-street parking. Full breakfast w/fresh eggs, luxury spa after a busy day. Join our fun-loving family with 2 kids, or enjoy your own privacy. Special winter rates, incl semi self-contained 2 bedroom Cabin.

Rotorua *6 km NW of City*

Affordable Westminster Lodge and Cottage *B&B Farmstay Cottage with Kitchen Fully self contained units*

Gillian and Barry Gillette
58A Mountain Road, Rotorua, 3201

Tel (07) 348 4273 or 0800 937 864
Fax (07) 348 4205
westminster@slingshot.co.nz
www.westminsterlodge.co.nz

Double/Twin $110-$150 Single $80-$110 (Special breakfast)
Children $20 per child under 14
Fully cooked breakfast for extra $12.00 per person
Visa MC Eftpos accepted   Children welcome
5 Queen 1 Double 6 Twin 2 Single (8 bdrm)
2 bedrooms in cottage 6 in lodge
Bathrooms: 3 Ensuite 3 Private 1 Guest share
Family rooms have bath and shower

Affordable Westminster Lodge and Cottage are English Tudor style homes nestled on the slopes of Mt Ngongotaha overlooking the city of Rotorua. So country, yet only 6 minutes to the city centre. Panoramic views in the day and fairy land at night.We offer superior Bed and Breakfast accommodation in fully self contained units or lodge rooms at affordable prices or you can choose the self catering cottage Children are welcome in our large family rooms.The Lodge is Qualmark 3Star Plus and the Cottage a 4Star

All rooms have tea and coffee making facilities fridge and microwaveUnits have a fully equiped kitchenette for self catering option.Enjoy our delicious special breakfast with fresh fruit salad yoghurt and cereal, hot apple muffins (baked daily) and a freshly laid egg or a scrumptious fully cooked breakfast at a small extra cost.

Experience all the comforts of home in a warm and friendly atmosphere, ensuring your stay in our family home will always be remembered. Breathe in the fresh mountain air and relax in our spa pool that overlooks the city at the end of your busy day.We are a family of eight with five adopted children one still living at home.We have miniature cows friendly sheep, rabbits chickens, and Mrs Pig. Our house pets are a cockatoo Paulie, and Holly and Benji our little dogs. All the animals are friendly and can be hand fed.

Rotorua - The Redwoods *4 km E of Rotorua*

B&B @ The Redwoods *Luxury B&B Homestay*

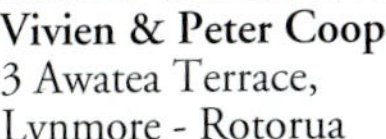

Vivien & Peter Cooper
3 Awatea Terrace,
Lynmore - Rotorua
Tel (07) 345 4499 or 027 270 3594
Fax (07) 345 4499
bnb@theredwoods.co.nz
www.theredwoods.co.nz

Double/Twin $130-$160
Single $130-$160 (Full breakfast)
Single bed available
for child to share room
Dinner $45 Host experience in
hospitality industry and silver service
Visa MC accepted
Pet free home Children welcome
2 Queen 1 Single (2 bdrm)
New Luxurious Ensuite Bedrooms
Bathrooms: 2 Ensuite Excellent shower

Secluded yet central! Two new luxurious ensuite guestrooms with private entrance, guest-only lounge, dining and outdoor living. Decor is simple yet stylish, lounge opens onto courtyard and garden. We live upstairs in a split level home in quiet cul-de-sac; enjoy our company or the privacy of your own space. We combine interaction with discretion. Redwood Forest on your doorstep, city and lakes 5 minutes away with Rotorua's many attractions very accessible. Safe off-street parking. All our guests have enjoyed our personal service and quality recommendations.

If you need any information ask your hosts, they are your own personal travel agent and guide.

Rotorua - Ngongotaha *12 km N of Rotorua*

Panorama Country Homestay *Luxury B&B Homestay Farmstay*

David Perry & Christine King
144 Fryer Road, Hamurana, RD 2, Rotorua
Tel (07) 332 2618 or 021 610 949 Fax (07) 332 2618
panoramahomestay@xtra.co.nz
http://panoramahomestay.co.nz

Double/Twin $190-$290 Single $135-$155 (Special breakfast)
Dinner by arrangement Discount for over 2 nights stay
Visa MC accepted
1 King 1 Queen (2 bdrm)
1 Superking/twin
Bathrooms: 1 Ensuite 1 Private
Queen room with private bathroom has large plunge bath

Aptly named Panorama is your ideal base to stay near Rotorua's many attractions. Take in the magnificent views overlooking Lake Rotorua and legendary Mokoia Island, Mt Tarawera and surrounding country side.

Feel the peace and tranquility as you relax under the stars in the outdoor heated massage spa pool, then curl up in front of the log fire in winter to stay cosy and warm. You may prefer to enjoy an energetic game of tennis on the championship sized court or take in many of the fantastic walks then come home and stretch out on the extra large beds in Panorama's peaceful surrounds for a perfect nights sleep.

The three spacious, luxury bedrooms have private bathrooms/ensuites containing, toiletries, heated towel rails, hairdryers, shaving points and heaters. The large comfortable inner spring beds are warmed with electric blankets, woollen underlays and feather quilts in winter. In the living area, the formal lounge has a native timber, cathedral ceiling, and an open fire where you can relax with a book and listen to soft music.

The large house is centrally heated, screened and wheelchair accessible. Only 15min from Rotorua, Panorama is situated on the northern side of the lake away from the sulphur smells. There is ample room for safe off street parking and helicopter access. Pet lambs and sheep can be fed by hand. Dave and Chris welcome you to spend a few days at Panorama where hospitality is ensured in their country home. They have lived in Rotorua for many years and have a wealth of knowledge to assist you in enjoying your stay and the local attractions. They would be happy to help you with any bookings you may require.

Rotorua - Rerewhakaaitu *45 km SE of Rotorua*

Ashpit Place *B&B Homestay Farmstay*

Alison & Scott Marshall
815 Ashpit Road,
Rerewhakaaitu,
Rotorua 3073

Tel (07) 366 6709
or 021 117 0317
Fax (07) 366 6710
samarshall@clear.net.nz
www.ashpitplace.co.nz

Double/Twin $190
(Continental breakfast)
Visa MC accepted
1 King/Twin 1 Queen (2 bdrm)
Bathrooms: 2 Ensuite
Spa bath in one suite

Relax and enjoy the panoramic views of Lake Rerewhakaaitu and Mt Tarawera with farming and forestry vistas from the lounge and dining areas. We have some of the best sunsets in the world. The property is in a quiet rural area which is at lakes edge where you can walk at your leisure. We are in between the thermal areas Waiotapu and Waimangu, central to Rotorua and Taupo and on the way to Whirinaki National Park.

Bay of Plenty

Rotorua - Hamurana *20 km N of Rotorua*

Lakeview Heights *B&B Farmstay*

Liz & John Dentice
269 Te Waerenga Road,
Rotorua, 3072

Tel (07) 332 3570
or 021 0224 2513
Fax (07) 332 3570
john-lizdentice@xtra.co.nz
www.lakeviewheightsnz.co.nz

Double/Twin $120-$180
Single $80-$120 (Full breakfast)
Children welcome
Dinner by arrangement
Visa MC accepted
Children and pets welcome
2 Queen 2 Twin 2 Single (3 bdrm)
Family room with queen & 2 singles,
2 queen rooms
Bathrooms: 1 Ensuite 1 Private 1 Guest share

Our country home has three guest rooms with superb views across the lake to the city and the volcanic Mount Tarawera in the distance. We are bordered by a Scenic Reserve with native trees,ferns Tuis and Bell birds. John & Liz are well travelled with farming backgrounds and would be delighted to give you a tour of Arab horses, sheep and calves. Fluff the house cat and two Cavalier King Charles Spaniels will make you welcome. Trout fishing, golf course and Rotorua's arttractions all nearby.

Taupo *3 km E of Central Taupo*

Hill Top Park Homestay *B&B Homestay*

Colleen & Bob Yeoman
61 Puriri Street,
Taupo 3330

Tel (07) 377 0283
Fax (07) 377 4683

Double/Twin $140
Single $80
(Full breakfast)
Children $40
Dinner $40 by arrangement
Children welcome
1 Queen 1 Twin (2 bdrm)
Bathrooms: 1 Ensuite 1 Guest share
We take only one party at a time

Bob and I have enjoyed hosting for many years, our lovely new home in Hill Top Park with beautiful mountains views makes our guests' stay in Taupo very special. All attractions are nearby, golf courses, thermal pools, Huka Falls and fishing. We are retired sheep and cattle farmers, who enjoy travelling and meeting other travellers. Bob excels at golf and is in charge of cooked breakfasts. Home-made jams and marmalade are my specialty. Please phone for directions. Good off street parking

Taupo - Acacia Bay *6 km W of Taupo*

Leece's Homestay *Homestay*

Marlene Leece
98 Wakeman Road,
Acacia Bay,
Taupo 3330

Tel (07) 378 6099
or 021 0243 9190
Fax (07) 378 6092

Double/Twin $110 Single $80
(Continental breakfast)
1 King 1 Queen 2 Single (2 bdrm)
Bathrooms: 1 Ensuite 1 Guest share

Your host Marlene & Jaspa (my Birman cat) extend a warm welcome to our large wood interior home with woodfire for winter and north facing sunny deck from guest bedroom. Also magnificent view of Lake Taupo from lounge and front deck. There are bush walks and steps down to lake to swim in summer with an extended new piece of road. Easy walking and different view. Awaiting your arrival with anticipation of making friends. Please phone for directions.

Taupo *1 km S of Taupo*

Pataka House *B&B Homestay Separate Suite*

Raewyn & Neil Alexander
8 Pataka Road, Taupo

Tel (07) 378 5481
Fax (07) 378 5461
pataka-homestay@xtra.co.nz
www.patakahouse.co.nz

Double/Twin $130
Single $90
(Full breakfast)
Children $30 upto 13 years
Separate suite $140
Visa MC accepted
Children welcome
2 Queen 4 Single (4 bdrm)
Extra comfortable beds in all rooms
Bathrooms: 1 Ensuite 1 Private 1
Guest share all renovated bathrooms

Pataka House is highly recommended for its hospitality. We assure guests that their stay lives up to New Zealand's reputation as being a home away from home. We are easily located just 1 turn off the lake front and up a tree-lined driveway. Our garden room is privately situated, has an appealing decor and extremely popular to young and old alike. Stay for 1 night or stay for more as Lake Taupo will truly be the highlight of your holiday. Mika, a burmese, loves visitors.

Taupo *1 km N of Taupo Central*

Lakeland Homestay *Homestay*

Lesley & Chris
11 Williams Street,
Taupo

Tel (07) 378 1952
or 0274 877 971
Fax (07) 378 1912
lakeland.bb@xtra.co.nz

Double/Twin $130-$140
Single $70
(Continental breakfast)
Visa MC accepted
1 Queen 2 Twin (2 bdrm)
Bathrooms: 1 Ensuite 1 Family share

Nestled in a restful tree-lined street, a mere 6 minutes stroll from the lake's edge and shopping centre Lakeland Homestay is a cheerful and cosy home that enjoys views of the lake and mountains. Keen gardeners, anglers and golfers Chris and Lesley work and play in an adventure oasis. By the way we have two cats, Caddy and Monica.Laundry facilities are available and a courtesy car is available for coach travellers, there is off-street parking. Please phone for directions.

Taupo *14 km NW of Taupo*

Minarapa *B&B Country Stay*

Barbara & Dermot Grainger
620 Oruanui Road,
RD 1,
Taupo

Tel (07) 378 1931
info@minarapa.co.nz
www.minarapa.co.nz

Double/Twin $140-$170
Single $110-$130
(Full breakfast)
Children price on application
Dinner by arrangement
Visa MC accepted
1 King/Twin 2 Queen 2 Twin (4 bdrm)
Spacious well-appointed rooms
with tea/coffee facilties
Bathrooms: 2 Ensuite 1 Private
Large rooms with heated towel rails and heater

Wend your way along a wonderful tree-lined drive into rural tranquillity. Minarapa, our extensive country retreat, 12 minutes from Taupo, 45 minutes to Rotorua, is within easy reach of Orakei Korako, Huka Falls and other tourist attractions. Wander here among colourful tree-sheltered gardens, play tennis, billiards, or ball with Toby the dog, visit friendly farm animals or relax in our guest lounge. Retire to spacious, comfortably appointed guest rooms, two with balcony and TV. All offer individual character and tea/coffee facilities.

Taupo *15 km N of Taupo*

Brackenhurst *B&B Homestay Farmstay Separate Suite Cottage with Kitchen*

Barbara & Ray Graham
801 Oruanui Road,
RD 1, Taupo

Tel (07) 377 6451
or 0274 456 217 mob
Fax (07) 377 6451
rgbg@xtra.co.nz

Double/Twin $110-$150
Single $65-$65
(Full breakfast)
Children $35
Dinner $45
Visa MC accepted
Pet free home
Children and pets welcome
2 Queen 1 Double 4 Single (4 bdrm)
Bathrooms: 2 Ensuite 2 Private

Brackenhurst is a modern Lockwood home on 14 acres of peaceful countryside with fantails, tuis and bellbirds in the large garden. highland cattle and sheep. A warm welcome with peace and tranquility. . We are half a kilometre from SH1 and close to Huka Falls, geothermal activities, golf courses a days outing to Rotorua, Waitomo Caves or Napier. Private guests wing in the house or separate annex offer away from home comforts. Breakfast to suit, continental style or full English. Dinner available by arrangement.

Taupo *15 km N of Taupo*

Maimoa House *B&B Homestay Farmstay Separate Suite Apartment with Kitchen*
Self contained apartment very popular

Margaret & Godfrey Ellis
41 Oak Drive, off Palmer Mill Road,
Taupo

Tel (07) 376 9000
or 021 233 4640
mewestview@xtra.co.nz
www.maimoahomestay.co.nz

Double/Twin $110-$150
Single $80
(Special breakfast)
Children $30
Dinner $35 by arrangement
10% discount for 3 nights or more
Visa MC accepted
Children and pets welcome
2 Queen 1 Double 1 Twin 1 Single (3 bdrm)
Our rooms are airy & spacious with great views
Bathrooms: 1 Ensuite 1 Guest share Large Spa bath, seperate shower, toilet

Hello and welcome to our peaceful home with spectacular views over the mountains to the lake.Our spacious new apartment is very popular, including our special breakfast. Join us for a 3 course dinner We are very happy to arrange on-going recommended B&Bs, local trips & excursions. We have a friendly lab dog,a Balinese cat and a few cows.We are close enough to Rotorua & Napier for days out. Our interests include church activities, travelling and chatting over a glass of wine.

Taupo *1 km N of Taupo*

Fourwinds Bed & Breakfast *B&B Homestay*

Catherine Culling
57 Woodward Street,
Taupo, 3330

Tel (07) 376 5350
Fax (07) 376 5360
bnb@fourwindsbedandbreakfast.co.nz
www.fourwindsbedandbreakfast.co.nz

Double/Twin $120-$140
Single $100-$120
(Full breakfast)
Visa MC accepted
Not suitable for children
1 Double 2 Single (2 bdrm)
Bathrooms: 1 Private
Toilet is separate from bathroom

A warm welcome and a refreshing cup of tea awaits your arrival at Fourwinds. Close to all Taupo attractions and town, with panoramic views of the Lake, Kaimanawa Ranges and mountains. The generous breakfast is served in dining room overlooking the wonderful view. Taupo is an excellent base for day trips to Rotorua, Waitomo, Hawkes Bay and Tongariro National Park. Catherine and Ambee (Cat) enjoy meeting guests from all corners of the world and look forward to you staying with us.

Taupo *2 km S of Taupo*

Above The Lake - Taupo *B&B*

Angela & Bruce Christoffersen
46 Rokino Road,
Taupo, 3330
Tel (07) 378 8738
or 027 272 9857
windsor-charters@xtra.co.nz
www.taupostay.com

Double/Twin $160-$190
Single $150-$180
(Full breakfast)
Visa MC accepted
1 King 2 Queen (3 bdrm)
Bathrooms: 1 Ensuite 1 Private
1 Guest share

On arrival, relax and enjoy magical lake, mountain and Taupo town views. Your supremely comfortable accommodation is centrally located in the heart of Taupo. Easy to find, and just a short stroll to the lake and Taupo√??s own, hot water beach. Walking distance to award winning restaurants. Join your hosts, Bruce, Angela & golden retriever named Koda for coffee or a glass of wine. Make use of our extensive local knowledge to plan your Taupo experience.

Taupo - Acacia Bay *5 km W of Taupo*

Te Moenga Lodge *B&B Separate Suite*

Brent & Jacque McClellan
60 Te Moenga Park,
Reeves Road,
Taupo, 3330
Tel (07) 378 0437 or 027 452 1459
Fax (07) 378 0438
info@temoenga.com
www.temoenga.com

Double/Twin $150-$295
Single $130-$220
(Continental breakfast)
Children 2yrs+ $50 per head
Local restaurant at end of road
Visa MC Amex Eftpos accepted
Children welcome
3 King/Twin 1 Queen (4 bdrm)
2 x private chalets 2 x studio
roomsBathrooms: 4 Ensuite Chalets have double spa bath

Climb the tree-lined road to the homestead on the hill. Close the door on the everyday and relax so far above the lake it seems you're looking down from the sky.Choose a studio room with ensuite, television, tea/coffee making facilites or a private chalet with king/twin beds, separate lounge, television, spa bath, tea/coffee making facilities. Own the breath-taking view from your chalet for the length of your stay. Brent, Jacque, 3 children and pet boxer dog welcome you to experience Te Moenga Lodge.

Taupo - Acacia Bay *5 km W of Taupo*

The Loft *B&B*

B&B Approved

Jane Redfern and John de Latour
3 Wakeman Road,
Acacia Bay, Taupo
Tel (07) 377 1040
or 027 485 1347
Fax (07) 377 1049
book@theloftnz.com
www.theloftnz.com

Double/Twin $145-$185
Single $100-$120 (Full breakfast)
Children $50-$75
Dinner $30-$45 per person
Washing/internet available - POA
Visa MC accepted
Pet free home Children welcome
3 Queen 3 Single (3 bdrm)
Well apppinted rooms with view of native bush
Bathrooms: 3 Ensuite

Situated five minutes from Taupo township and a few minutes walk to the lake and a very good restaurent. The Loft is set in a cottage garden adajacent to a native bush reserve. Hosts Jane & John look forward to your visit.Enjoy a scrumptious breakfast of fresh fruit salad, orange juise, fresly baked crossants , wonderful poached or scrambled eggs with bacon mushrooms and our own delicious tomatoes when in season. Tea and coffee making facilities on landing upstairs.

Taupo *1.5 km N of Taupo*

Rive Gauche *Luxury B&B Separate studio unit*

Lynne Fauchelle
128 Ferndale Way, RD 1, Taupo 3377
Tel (07) 377 6167
or 021 050 6735
or 0274 894 250
lynnejim4@clear.net.nz
www.rivegauchetaupo.co.nz

Double/Twin $175-$225
Single $150-$175 (Full breakfast)
Children negociable.
Rollaway bed available
Restaurant 4 minutes walk away
Lynne parle français
Visa MC accepted
Pet free home
2 King 1 Queen 1 Single (3 bdrm)
2 rooms have Sky TV, Wifi access available
Bathrooms: 3 Ensuite, Fully tiled with heater, heated towel rail and extractor

Set on a 1 hectare site on the left bank of the Waikato River just 2 minutes from Taupo town centre, Rive Gauche was purpose-built in 2007 to offer quality lodge-style B&B accommodation. We have 3 options: a separate studio with lovely river views, a queen room and a king plus king single. Our B&B rooms have access to a kitchenette with fridge. Facilities include air conditioning, Sky TV and Wifi. We love to travel and can advise you on your itinerary. Fluent French spoken.

Taupo *13 km N of Taupo*

Bellbird Ridge Alpaca Farm *B&B Farmstay Cottage with Kitchen*
Rex and Donna Ferrall
68 Tangye Road, RD 1, Taupo

Tel (07) 377 1996 or 027 552 2055
or 021 522055
Fax (07) 377 1992
info@bellbirdridge.co.nz
www.bellbirdridge.co.nz

Double/Twin $180-$180
Single $150-$150
(Full breakfast provisions)
Children $50 under 12
Dinner 1 course $30, 2 courses $40
or 3 courses $50
BYO beverages or purchase from hosts
Visa MC Eftpos accepted
Children and pets welcome
1 King/Twin 2 Queen 1 Single (4 bdrm)
Bathrooms: 1 Ensuite 1 Private

Take a break and unwind in our charming and secluded self-contained one bedroom cottage, enjoy our beautiful garden and friendly alpacas, located only 10 mins from Taupo. The cottage has a separate queen bedroom, kitchen/dining/lounge area & deck with BBQ. Generous breakfast provisions are provided. Also available in a separate guest wing in the homestead, where you would be our only guests, are a super king, 1 queen, 1 queen & a single bedrooms with your own bathroom.

~

Taupo - Countryside *35 km NW of Taupo*

South Claragh & Bird Cottage *Luxury B&B Homestay Cottage with Kitchen*
Lynn Betts & Mike A'Court
South Claragh,
3245 Poihipi Road, Taupo

Tel (07) 372 8848
or 021 125 3263
Fax (07) 372 8047
info@countryaccommodation.co.nz
www.countryaccommodation.co.nz

Double/Twin $130-$150
Single $80-$100 (Special breakfast)
Children $25 (cottage) $45 (B&B)
Dinner restaurants close by
Bird Cottage $130 double
Visa MC accepted
Children welcome
2 Queen 1 Double 2 Single (4 bdrm)
1 in cottage, 3 in B&B
Bathrooms: 2 Ensuite 1 Family share

Taupo's best kept secret.Turn into our leafy driveway and relax in 3 acres of rambling gardens and stay in our centrally heated farmhouse. Both deluxe ensuites have tv/dvd's refridgerators and coffee making facilities.Each room also has it's own access and private balcony.While here stroll arround and say hello to our highland cattle.If you would prefer more privacy stay in Bird Cottage a charming fully self contained cottage situated in it's own wood.Also includes heated outdoor spa (fee applies)bbq and washing machine.

Taupo *2.5 km S of Taupo*

B&B @ Number Ten *B&B*

B&B Approved

Ann & John Page
10 Coprosma Crescent,
Taupo, 3330

Tel (07) 378 6823
or 021 237 2405
Fax (07) 378 6823
ajpage@nettel.net.nz
www.bnb-at-number-ten.co.nz

Double/Twin $150-$175
(Full breakfast)
Not suitable for children
Visa MC accepted
2 Queen (2bdrom)
Bathrooms: 2 Ensuite

We look forward to welcoming you to our new home, built in a quiet area of Taupo. Close to the Waipahihi Botanical Gardens and thermally heated pools. Our sunny guest rooms open onto individual couryards with peaceful glimpses of the lake. Bedrooms are well appointed with comfortable beds, electric blankets, televisions, tea and coffee making facilities, heatpump/airconditioning units, heated towel rails, underfloor heating and hair dryers. The view from our upstairs dining room will encourage you to get out and about and explore the beauty of Taupo.

Turangi *1 km S of Turangi Information Centre*

Brown Trout House *B&B Homestay*

B&B Approved

Bruce & Nita Wilde
11 Kokopu Street,
Turangi, 3334

Tel (07) 386 0308
or 027 253 3415
Fax (07) 386 0308
kohinoor@xtra.co.nz
www.browntrouthouse.co.nz

Double/Twin $120-$150
Single $80-$90
(Full breakfast)
Children negotiable
Lunches and dinner
by prior arrangement
Visa MC accepted
1 King/Twin 1 Queen 2 Single (3 bdrm)
Bathrooms: 1 Private 1 Family share

Welcome to Brown Trout house overlooking the Tongariro River in Turangi, halfway between Auckland and Wellington. Your bedroom opens on to the spacious deck. Have refreshments or step out our gate on to the Tongariro River Walkway or in to world famous fishing pools. Bruce is a keen fisherman willing to share his knowledge. Shuttle pickup for the Tongariro Crossing arranged. Choose walks, golf, skiing or a hot swim 5 mins drive away. Friendly experienced hosts willing to give genuine kiwi hospitality.

Turangi *15 km W of Turangi*

B&B Approved

Omori Lake House *Luxury Lodge*

Niel & Raewyn Groombridge
31 Omori Road,
Omori

Tel (07) 386 0420
or 021 667 092
stay@omorilakehouse.co.nz
www.omorilakehouse.co.nz

Double/Twin $160
Single $160
(Special breakfast)
Dinner by arrangement
Visa MC accepted
Pet free home
Not suitable for children
2 King (2 bdrm)
Bathrooms: 2 Ensuite

Our new boutique accommodation high above Omori has stunning views across to Taupo. There are two en-suite guest rooms with king beds, tea/coffee facilities and private deck. Raewyn loves to cook and eating well is part of the experience. Enjoy barbeques or meals with kiwi classics Omori on the menu.We are close to a variety of activities including fly-fishing,The Tongariro Alpine crossing, bush walks, thermal pools and ski slopes.

~

Turangi - Motuoapa *10 km N of Turangi*

B&B Approved

Meredith House *B&B Self-contained*

Frances & Ian Meredith
45 Kahotea Drive,
Motuoapa, R.D.2,
Turangi 3382

Tel (07) 386 5266
or 0274 406 135
Fax (07) 386 5270
meredith.house@xtra.co.nz

Double/Twin $120-$150
Single $85
(Breakfast by arrangement)
Self-contained $130-160
Visa MC accepted
Children welcome
1 Queen 3 Single (2 bdrm)
Bed settee & single in lounge if needed
Bathrooms: 2 Ensuite

Stop and enjoy this outdoor Paradise. Just off SH1 (B&B Sign). Overlooking Lake Taupo, our 2 storey home offers ground-floor self-contained accommodation with own entrance. Full breakfast on request. Fully equipped kitchen, dining room, lounge. 2 cosy bedrooms (each with TV). Vehicle/boat off-street parking. Minutes to marina and world-renowned lake/river fishing. Beautiful bush walks. 45 minutes to ski fields and Tongariro National Park. Our association with Tongariro/Taupo area spans over 30 years, through work and outdoor pursuits. Welcome to our retreat.

Turangi *54 km S of Taupo*

B&B Approved

Founders@Turangi *B&B Homestay*

Peter & Chris Stewart
253 Taupahi Road,
Turangi
Tel (07) 386 8539
Fax (07) 386 8534
chris@founders.co.nz
www.founders.co.nz

Double/Twin $180
Single $120
(Special breakfast)
Visa MC Eftpos accepted
Pet free home
Not suitable for children
2 King/Twin 1 King
3 Queen (4 bdrm)
Bathrooms: 4 Ensuite

Welcome to Turangi and our New Zealand colonial-style home. Relax and enjoy the unique beauty of the Trout Fishing Capital of the World. Many outdoor activities are available at this place for all seasons, with the Tongariro River, mountains of Tongariro National Park and magnificent Lake Taupo on our doorstep. Enjoy breakfast in our sunny dining room or pre-dinner drinks by the fire apres ski in the winter!We are happy to cook early breakfasts for Tongariro Alpine Crossing adventurers!

~

Turangi *16 km NW of Turangi*

B&B Approved

Wills' Place *B&B*

Jill & Brian Wills
145 Omori Road, Omori
Tel (07) 386 7339
or 027 228 8960
Fax (07) 386 7339
b.g@willsplace.co.nz
www.willsplace.co.nz

Double/Twin $135-$150
Single $100-$120
(Full breakfast)
Children negotiable
Dinner by arrangement
Visa MC accepted
Pet free home
Children welcome
2 Queen 2 Single (2 bdrm)
Private suite with 2 bedrooms
Bathrooms: 1 Private Bath with shower over

A lakeside home and superior guest suite with wonderful views. Fishing, boating, swimming, walks. Off the beaten track, yet only 10-15 minutes to shops, restaurants, thermal pools, Tongariro River, rafting, etc. 40 minutes to World Heritage Tongariro National Park. Private suite with two bedrooms, full size bathroom with bath and shower, living area, tea-making facilities, fridge, microwave, television, laundry, email access. Private patio overlooking the lake. Suite yours alone with separate entry and safe parking. Discount for three or more nights.

Turangi *2 km N of Turangi*

At the Tongariro Riverside B & B *B&B Homestay*

Leslie & Maryke Wilson
72 Herekiekie Street,
Turangi, 3334
Tel (07) 386 7447
or 021 161 6215
info@bytheriver.co.nz
www.bytheriver.co.nz

Double/Twin $125
Single $100
(Special breakfast)
Dinner $40 pp with wine, b/a
1 King/Twin (1 bdrm)
Overlooks the world famous
Tongariro River
Bathrooms: 1 Ensuite

Location! Location! Location! Right alongside the world famous Tongariro river. Trout fishing - just metres from your king/twin ensuite bedroom (latest tiled walk-in shower). Wonderful sunsets in a peaceful and tranquil setting. Situated halfway between Auckland and Wellington with secure on- site parking. Leave your car with us for the Tongariro Alpine Crossing - (Shuttles arranged). Skifields just 40 minutes away. Free WIFI, Air-Conditioning, Flat screen TV, Tea/Coffee making facilities and fridge. Generous continental breakfast (fresh fruit and cheese etc). Restaurants just a stroll away.

Turangi *0.5 km E of Turangi*

Ika Lodge *B&B Apartment with Kitchen Cottage with Kitchen*

Margaret & Kenneth Toon
155 Taupahi Road,
Turangi, 3334
Tel (07) 386 5538
or 027 292 5023
ikalodge@ika.co.nz
www.ika.co.nz

Double/Twin $140-$165
Single $120
(Full breakfast)
Dinner on request
Visa MC Diners Eftpos accepted
Children welcome
5 Queen 1 Double 1 Twin
1 Single (7 bdrm)
2 B&B Suites, 2 bedroom Apartment,
3 bedroom Bungalow
Bathrooms: 2 Ensuite 2 Guest share
2 ensuites, apartment 1 shared, bungalow 1 shared

Ika Lodge offers superior bed and breakfast homestay suites, 2 bedroom apartment and 3 bedroom bungalow on the banks of the Tongariro River and minutes from some of the worlds best trout fishing. A perfect base for the Tongariro National Park ski fields and the famous Tongariro Crossing trek all in a tranquil garden setting.

Gisborne
Waihau Bay
Te Kaha
Maraenui
35
Tolaga Bay
2
Waipaoa
Gisborne
2
0 Kilometres 20
0 Miles 12

Tolaga Bay *3 km N of Tolaga Bay*

Papatahi *Homestay Separate Suite*

Nicki & Bruce Jefferd
427 Waiapu Road,
Tolaga Bay
Tel (06) 862 6623
or 021 283 7178
Fax (06) 862 6623
nickibrucej@xtra.co.nz

Double/Twin $120
Single $70
(Full breakfast)
Children half price
Dinner $35pp
Children welcome
1 Queen 1 Double 2 Single (3 bdrm)
Bathrooms: 1 Ensuite 1 Guest share

Papatahi Homestay... easy to find being just 3km north of the Tolaga Bay township, on the Pacific Coast Highway. We have a comfortable, modern, sunny home set in a wonderful garden. Papatahi offers separate accommodation with ensuite. A golf course, fishing charters, the Tolaga Bay Cashmere Co. and several magnificent beaches are all just minutes away. Daily farm activities are often of interest to our guests. Friendly farm pets add to the experience! Great country meals and good wine are a speciality. Inspection will impress!

Waipaoa *20 km N of Gisborne*

B&B Approved

The Willows *Farmstay*

Rosemary & Graham Johnson
Waipaoa,
RD 1,
Gisborne
Tel (06) 862 5605
or 027 483 7365
waipaoa@bordernet.co.nz

Double/Twin $90
Single $50
(Full breakfast)
Children 10% discount
Dinner $30 by arrangement
2 Queen 2 Single (3 bdrm)
Bathrooms: 1 Private 1 Guest share

Our home is situated on a hill amid a park-like garden with some wonderful trees planted by our forefathers. We enjoy the amenities available in the city and also the country life on our 440 acre property involving cattle, sheep, grapes and cropping. We now offer a double bedroom with a private bathroom. The bedroom has its own access so you can enjoy privacy if you so desire. We are situated 20km north of Gisborne on SH2 through the scenic Waioeka Gorge.

Gisborne *0.5 km N of Gisborne Central*

Sea View *B&B Homestay*
Raewyn & Gary Robinson
68 Salisbury Road,
Gisborne

Tel (06) 867 3879
or 021 031 1514
raewyn@regaleggs.co.nz

Double/Twin $100-$120
Single $90
(Continental breakfast)
Children welcome
1 Queen 1 Double 1 Twin
1 Single (3 bdrm)
Bathrooms: 2 Private

Absolute luxury and comfort. Beachfront bed & breakfast. Seaview is situated on the foreshore of Waikanae beach with unsurpassed panoramic views of Young Nicks Head and Poverty Bay. Just 50 metres from front door to golden sand, and warm blue waters. Only 2 minutes drive to the city (easy walking distance) and visitor information centre.Enjoy safe swimming and great surfing. 5 minutes to international golf course and Olympic pool complex. We offer 2 double bedrooms and twin room. 2 private bathrooms. Internet facilities available.

Gisborne *5 km NE of Gisborne*

Beach Stay *B&B*
Peter & Dorothy Rouse
111 Wairere Road,
Wainui Beach,
Gisborne

Tel (06) 868 8111
Fax (06) 868 8162
pete.dot@xtra.co.nz

Double/Twin $90-$110
Single $60
(Full breakfast)
Children $10
Dinner $25 pp
Pets welcome
1 Queen 2 Single (2 bdrm)
Bathrooms: 1 Ensuite 1 Private

We welcome you to our home which is situated right on the beach front at Wainui. The steps from the lawn lead down to the beach, which is renowned for its lovely clean sand, surf, pleasant walking and good swimming. Gisborne can also offer a host of entertainment, including golf on 1 of the finest golf courses, charter fishing trips, wine trails, Eastwood Hill Arboretum etc, or you may wish to relax on the beach for the day.

Gisborne *2.0 km NE of Gisborne*

Thistles *Homestay*
Barrie & Lesley Munday
137 Riverside Road,
Gisborne

Tel (06) 868 8900
or 021 127 9841
or 021 035 0587
thistles137@gmail.com

Double/Twin $120
Single $90
(Full breakfast)
Pet free home
Children welcome by arrangement
1 Queen 1 Double (2 bdrm)
Bathrooms: 1 Private

Thistles quiet location offers comfortable modern homestyle hospitality. An ideal base for exploring the Historic East Coast, the first landing sites of Captain Cook and the Chardonnay Capital of New Zealand.Tours of local vineyards and wineries can be arranged. Unwind in the spa bath before savouring the delights of the many restaurants in Gisborne. French,German and Scottish dialect spoken! Secure parking available.

Gisborne *14 km S of Gisborne*

B&B
Approved

Fairlight *B&B*
Kay and Don Orchiston
52 Saddler Road,
RD 2,
Gisborne 4072

Tel (06) 862 8499
or 027 440 9556
orchiston@clear.net.nz

Double/Twin $120
Single $80
(Full breakfast)
Children by arrangement
Dinner by arrangement
Children and pets welcome
1 King 1 Queen 1 Double
3 Single (4 bdrm)
Bathrooms: 1 Private
1 shower as well

Our home is situated on a hill with expansive views of the sea, city and rural wine region. We are 14 kms south of the city. Gisborne has beautiful beaches, scenic walks, restaurants and excellent sport facilities.We have 2 friendly sheep dogs and 2 elusive bengal cats.Visitors welcome to experience handling sheep and cattle. Trout fishing and deep sea fishing by prior arrangement.

Taranaki, Wanganui, Ruapehu, Rangitikei
Te Awamutu
Otorohanga
Waitomo
Te Kuiti
Piopio
Taumarunui
Piriaka
Owhango
New Plymouth
Egmont National Park
Stratford
Ohakune
Raetihi
Taihape
Waitotara
Wanganui
Marton
Fielding
Colyton
Newbury
Woodville
Oroua Downs
Palmerston North
Tokomaru
Foxton
Pahiat
Eketahuna
Levin
Otaki
Te Horo
0 Kilometres 40
0 Miles 24

New Plymouth - Brixton *12 km N of New Plymouth*

Loggers Retreat *B&B Cottage with Kitchen*

John & Brenda Reumers
42 Richmond Road,
Waitara, 4373

Tel (06) 754 3131
or (06) 754 7668
Fax (06) 7547668
loggersretreat@xtra.co.nz
www.windwand.co.nz/loggersretreat.htm

Double/Twin $130
Single $80
(Full breakfast provisions)
Pet free home
Not suitable for children
1 Double (1 bdrm)
Loft sleeping quarters
Bathrooms: 1 Private
Private outside bath

A rustic character-filled private board and battened 2 storyed cottage. Private outside bath area.Situated on 6 acres of beautiful rural land, which hosts a hand-built double storyed log home and native gardens. Pond area,bridge and belted gallowways grazing surrounding paddocks. Only 12kms north of New Plymouth on SH3,five minutes from local airport, all under the watchful gaze of Mt Taranaki.

~

New Plymouth *3 km S of New Plymouth*

Oak Valley Manor *B&B Farmstay*

Pat & Paul Ekdahl
248 Junction Road,
RD 1,
New Plymouth

Tel (06) 758 1501
or 027 442 0325
Fax (06) 758 1052
paul@oakvalley.co.nz
www.oakvalley.co.nz

Double/Twin $150
Single $125
(Continental breakfast)
Children $1 per year up to 15 years
Visa MC accepted
Children and pets welcome
2 Queen 1 Single (2 bdrm)
Bathrooms: 2 Ensuite

Your hosts, Pat and Paul, 2 friendly people with experience in the hospitality industry, invite you to a unique bed & breakfast in their beautiful home with views of Mt Taranaki from all rooms. These beautiful views make an everlasting impression. Guests can choose their own privacy or socialise with us. We have a variety of animals, donkey, ducks, geese and an ex guide dog. Golf course 5 minute drive. Multiple night rates available.

New Plymouth *25 km N of New Plymouth*

Cottage by the Sea *Cottage with Kitchen Garden studios with kitchens*

B&B Approved

Nancy & Hugh Mills
66 Lower Turangi Road,
RD 43, Waitara

Tel (06) 754 4548 or (06) 754 7915
cottagebythesea@clear.net.nz
www.cottagebythesea.co.nz

Double/Twin $155-$195
Single $145-$185
(Breakfast by arrangement)
Restaurant and takeaway nearby
Extras $25 each/per night
Visa MC accepted
Not suitable for children
1 King/Twin 3 Queen
2 Double (4 bdrm)
Cottages sleep 2-4; studios sleep 2
Bathrooms: 4 Ensuite
1 ensuite per accommodation

Find yourself, lose yourself - the choice is yours. Peacefulness and privacy are our specialty - a perfect place to unwind. Enjoy the everchanging seaviews, discover our tranquil sunken garden, wander down 100 handcrafted steps to the secluded blacksand beach. Two 1-bedroom cottages and two, open-plan studios, nestled in their own gardens with kitchens and ensuites. Minutes from cafes, coastal walks, gardens. Minutes from cafes, coastal walks, gardens and Mt Taranaki. Two small poodles may greet you. See our website for more photos and details.

New Plymouth *3 km W of CBD*

Vineyard Holiday Studio *B&B Separate Suite*

B&B Approved

Shirley & Trevor Knuckey
12 Scott Street,
Moturoa,
New Plymouth

Tel (06) 751 2992
or 027 310 3669
Fax (06) 751 2995
shirley12vineyard@xtra.co.nz

Double/Twin $90
Single $60
(Full breakfast)
Children $20
2 adults, 2 children $125
Visa MC accepted
Children welcome
1 King/Twin 1 Double
2 Single (1 bdrm)
Bathrooms: 1 Ensuite

Situated in New Plymouth's harbour-view Moturoa suburb. Enter through hobby vines to the spacious upstairs open-plan penthouse; 360 views of harbour, mountains, city; coast north and south. Shoreline pleasures nearby including eateries. Guests may be self-contained. Lock-up garage, separate entrance, mini-kitchen. Private balcony, dining-table, full AV options,wireless Internet. Extra bed(s) by arrangement. Ideally situated for exploring Taranaki's attractions, or the perfect R&R retreat. There is a pet cat.

New Plymouth *8 km N of New Plymouth*

Rockvale Homestay *B&B Homestay*

Jeannette & Neil Cowley
97 Manutahi Road,
RD 2, New Plymouth

Tel (06) 755 0750
or 027 682 1236
Fax (06) 755 0750
rockvale@farmside.co.nz
www.rockvalehomestay.co.nz

Double/Twin $120
Single $90
(Full breakfast)
Children $35 under 12 yrs
Dinner $30 by arrangement
Visa MC accepted
Children welcome
1 Queen 2 Single (2 bdrm)
1 Queen, 1 Twin
Bathrooms: 1 Private

Welcome to our large, country home, surrounded by deer farm, with Mt Egmont as a backdrop. Guests' double room and lounge open onto balcony, with rural views. Relax in spa on deck. Your comfort is our concern. We host 1 guest party at a time. Join us for dinner, in our spacious living area or the deck in summer. We are close to airport, city, beaches, parks and mountain. Six golf courses are within easy drive. We welcome you to our home. Families welcome.

New Plymouth *0.5 km W of New Plymouth*

Airlie House *B&B Apartment with Kitchen*

Gabrielle Masters
161 Powderham Street,
New Pymouth

Tel (06) 757 8866
or 021 472 072
Fax (06) 757 8866
email@airliehouse.co.nz
www.airliehouse.co.nz

Double/Twin up to $155
Single up to $120
(Full breakfast)
Children negotiable
Studio $155 double
Visa MC Eftpos accepted
Children welcome
1 King/Twin 2 Queen
2 Single (3 bdrm)
Bathrooms: 1 Ensuite 2 Private 1 claw bath

Airlie House is a 110 year old character home nestled among mature trees and garden. This beautiful home provides 2 guest bedrooms with ensuites or private bathrooms, plus a studio apartment with its own kitchen and private bathroom. Located in central New Plymouth Airlie House is an easy 5 minute walk from shops, restaurants, the sea front, parks and many other local attractions. All rooms have many amenities available for your comfort, including Sky Digital TV, broadband and wireless internet access.

New Plymouth *5 km W of New Plymouth centre*

B&B Approved

Whaler's Rest *B&B*

Maureen & Denis Whiting
86A Barrett Road,
New Plymouth 4310
Tel (06) 751 4272
or 027 328 0268
whalersrest@clear.net.nz
www.whalersrest.co.nz

Double/Twin $100
Single $80
(Full breakfast)
Children $20
Children and pets welcome
1 Double 1 Twin (2 bdrm)
Bathrooms: 1 Ensuite 1 Private

Large double bedroom with ensuite, and your own deck for drinks, plus twin room with private bathroom. Breakfast, continental or cooked. We are on the gateway to Surf Highway, 10 minutes to Oakura beach and 5 minutes to New Plymouth City featuring the Wind Wand, coastal walkway, Puke Ariki Museum and Pukekura Park. Your hosts Maureen and Denis who love their tennis and garden welcome you. We have a very sociable labrador Stella, and 2 cats, Tuffy and Biscuit. Please phone for bookings and directions.

New Plymouth *0.01 km N of New Plymouth City*

B&B Approved

Timata Ora *Luxury B&B Luxury B&B 5 min walk from CBD*

Carol & Rodney Hall
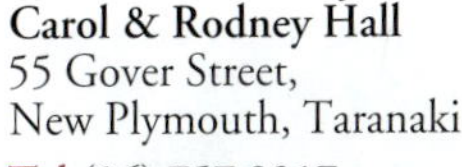
55 Gover Street,
New Plymouth, Taranaki
Tel (06) 757 9917
or 0274 523 885
Fax (06) 759 1654
carol_rodney@iconz.co.nz
www.timataora.com

Double/Twin $125-$135
Single $115-$135 (Full breakfast)
Family suite $220 when both bedrooms used
Visa MC Eftpos accepted
4 Queen 1 Twin (5 bdrm)
All large with own bathrooms, TV, coffee, tea & extras
Bathrooms: 4 Ensuite
All suites each have own bathroom

We warmly welcome guests to our fully refurbished central city home. A 1920's heritage home, Timata Ora offers 4 luxurious queen suites (1 with 4 Poster) each with own bathroom, TV, fridge, hair drier, iron/ironing board, heated towel rails, complimentary beverages and in room treats. The family suite has an additional twin bedroom along with the queen bedroom. Gregarious cat Murphy (the Butler) shares Timata Ora. Breakfast in your suite, dining room, in the conservatory or on the terrace.

New Plymouth *2 km NE of Post Office*

The Grange *B&B*
Rachael Nielsen and Alan Clarke
44B Victoria Road,
Brooklands,
New Plymouth
Tel (06) 759 8004
or 027 434 5680
grangebandb@xtra.co.nz

Double/Twin $120-$140
Single $80-$90
(Full breakfast)
Visa MC Diners Amex accepted
Pets welcome
1 King/Twin 2 Queen (3 bdrm)
1 Queen room has patio,
over looking bush
Bathrooms: 3 Ensuite

Come and stay in our modern award-winning home built with the privacy and comfort of our guests in mind. With unique bush views and a house designed to take full advantage of the sun, our guests can enjoy relaxing in the lounge or the extensive tiled courtyards and listen to the sounds of the native birds. The Grange is centrally heated, security controlled and located adjacent to the renowned Pukekura Park and Bowl of Brooklands. The city is 10 minutes walk.

~

New Plymouth - Bell Block *7 km N of New Plymouth*

K & J's Bed and Breakfast *B&B*
Keith and Joy Hosking
94 Parklands Avenue,
New Plymouth, 4312
Tel (06) 755 4199
or 027 294 9682
Fax (06) 755 4199
kjhosking@xtra.co.nz

Double/Twin up to $110
Single up to $80
(Continental breakfast)
Not suitable for children
2 Queen (2 bdrm)
1 down stairs and 1 upstairs
Bathrooms: 1 Ensuite 1 Private

Lovely sea and mountain views very close to airport. 10 minutes to central New Plymouth. Restaurant, Bank and shopping facilities in walking distance.Able to walk to the beach. Situated in quiet street. 2007 winner of 'Supreme House of the Year' award. Broadband and Wireless available

Stratford *0.5 km N of Stratford*

B&B Approved

Stratford Lodge (Stallards) B&B *B&B Homestay Farmstay Guest House*

Billieanne & Corb Stallard
3514 State Highway 3,
Stratford Northern Boundary

Tel (06) 765 8324
Fax (06) 765 8325
stallardbb@infogen.net.nz
www.stratfordlodge.co.nz

Double/Twin $90
Single $55 (Full breakfast)
Children $20
Double is 2 people
Family room sleeps 4 $98
Visa MC accepted
Pet free home Children welcome
2 Double 2 Twin 2 Single (4 bdrm)
Antique romantic
Bathrooms: 4 Ensuite 1 Guest share

Graceful"Upstairs Downstairs" comfort. A down to earth gardeners rest Aga cooked or continental breakfast included. Free self-catering kitchen, tea, coffee, biscuits. Homely or private. Own key. Optional separate lounge. Restaurants, taverns, shops nearby. Rooms are antique, romantic with TV, heaters, electric blankets, serviced daily. Gardens, BBQ, row boat, bush bath, river walks. 15 minutes to Mt Egmont ski fields, tramping. Centrally located easy distance to New Plymouth, museums, famous gardens, tourist attractions. Interests include gemstones travel, art. Welcome. AA accredited.

Egmont National Park *9 km W of Stratford*

B&B Approved

Anderson's Alpine Lodge *Homestay Farmstay*

Berta Anderson
922 Pembroke Road,
R.D. 21, Stratford 4391,
Taranaki

Tel (06) 765 6620
or 0274 412 372
andersonsalpinelodge@xtra.co.nz
www.andersonsalpinelodge.co.nz

Double/Twin $160-$190
Single $160
(Full breakfast)
Dinner by prior arrangement
Visa MC accepted
Children and pets welcome
1 King/Twin 1 Double 1 Twin (3 bdrm)
Secluded , romantic rooms with
Swiss alpine ambiance
Bathrooms: 3 Ensuite

Swiss style lodge rests in 5 acres of native bush capturing majestic views of Mount Egmont/Taranaki. Landscaping includes New Zealand natives, lakes, waterwheel and bushwalks. Three charming rooms with ensuite, one with spa bath. Egmont National Park opposite front gate. 5km to spectacular walking tracks, summit climb (guides available) and skiing. Helicopter rides by request.Trout streams, gardens and museums nearby. 9km to Stratford. Swiss Berta Anderson has lived on the mountain since 1976.

Waitotara - Wanganui *29 km W of Wanganui*

Ashley Park *Farmstay Cottage with Kitchen*

Wendy Pearce
State Highway 3,
Box 36,
Waitotara,
Wanganui

Tel (06) 346 5917
Fax (06) 346 5861
ashley_park@xtra.co.nz
www.ashleypark.co.nz

Double/Twin $100-$140
Single $100
(Full breakfast)
Dinner $30
Visa MC Diners Eftpos accepted
1 Queen 4 Single (3 bdrm)
Bathrooms: 1 Ensuite 1 Guest share

We have a 500 acre sheep and cattle farm and live in a comfortable home, set in an attractive garden with a swimming pool and tennis court. Also in the garden is an antique shop selling Devonshire teas. 100 metres from the house is a 4 acre park and lake, aviaries and a collection of hand fed pet farm animals. We welcome guests to have dinner with us. Self-contained accommodation is available in the park.

~

Wanganui *2 km NW of Wanganui City centre*

Kembali *B&B Homestay*

Marylyn & Wes Palmer
26 Taranaki Street,
St Johns Hill, Wanganui

Tel (06) 347 1727
or 027 741 7517
or 027 244 4347
wespalmer@xtra.co.nz

Double/Twin $110-$125
Single $80-$95
(Full breakfast)
Small charge for laundry facilities
Visa MC accepted
Pet free home
Not suitable for children
1 Queen 1 Twin (2 bdrm)
Firm beds, attractive decor, centrally heated
Bathrooms: 1 Private

Kembali is a modern, centrally heated, sunny home in a quiet street overlooking trees and wetlands. Upstairs guest bedrooms, bathroom and lounge (with TV, fridge, tea/coffee) are for 1 party/groups exclusive use. Retired, no pets, children married, we offer a restful stay. We enjoy meeting people, gardening, travel, reading and have Christian interests. Off-street parking and laundry available. 5 minutes drive to city, heritage buildings, restored paddle steamer, restaurants, museum, art gallery and walks. We look forward to welcoming you.

Wanganui *.5 km N of Wanganui centre*

Braemar House *B&B Guest House*

B&B Approved

Clive Rivers
2 Plymouth Street, Wanganui
Tel 06 348 2301
Fax (06) 348 2301
contact@braemarhouse.co.nz
www.braemarhouse.co.nz

Double/Twin $80-$110
Single $75-$85
(Full breakfast)
Children $10
Dinner $25 by arrangement
Visa MC Eftpos accepted
Not suitable for children
4 Queen 1 Double 3 Twin (8 bdrm)
Individually period designed
Bathrooms: 4 Guest share
Deluxe sized bath Powerful Showers

Welcome to 'Olde Worlde Charm'. This restored historic Homestead, nestled alongside the Wanganui River, has a homely ambience making your stay restful and enjoyable. The graceful entrance leads to eight centrally heated, period-designed bedrooms,drawing room and dining room. Laundry, wireless internet, fully equipped kitchen available. Off-street parking set in beautiful gardens.Close to the city and tourist attractions, The paddle steamer Waimarie passes daily in front of the Homestead. We look forward to you visiting Braemar House.

~

Wanganui *20 km NW of Marton*

Te-Aunui Farmstay *B&B Farmstay Cottage with Kitchen*

B&B Approved

Mike & Marg Webster
RD 11,
Wanganui
Tel (06) 327 3821
TE-AUNUI@xtra.co.nz
www.te-aunuifarmstay.co.nz

Double/Twin up to $130
Single $75
(Special breakfast)
Children $25
Dinner $40 by arrangement
Children and pets welcome
1 King 1 Queen 2 Single (3 bdrm)
Bathrooms: 1 Private

Te-Aunui is a 300 acre sheep and beef farm. We offer a fully self-contained 3 bedroomed homestead fr guests to explore the farm from or join Marg and I as we work our way through the farm year, shearing, rearing calves, lambing etc. Farm tours and home cooking a speciality. Te-Aunuiis an ideal base to tour the Rangitikei from with one of Marg's picnic hampers. TV, phone and internet access but no cell phone coverage in the valley.

Taumarunui *5 km NE of Taumarunui*

Matawa Country Home *Farmstay*

Shirley & Allan Jones
213 Taringamotu/Ngapuke Road,
Taumarunui

Tel (07) 896 7722
Fax (07) 895 6927
costleyj@farmside.co.nz

Double/Twin $100-$120
Single $70-$80
(Full breakfast)
Children half price
Dinner by arrangement
Visa MC accepted
Children welcome
1 King 1 Twin (2 bdrm)
Bathrooms: 1 Guest share

Our spacious home is situated 5km from the centre of Taumarunui surrounded by a peaceful one acre garden with a native bush backdrop filled with NZ native birds. The bedrooms open on to a large verandah. Laundry available. A stream runs along one boundary of the 80 acre property suitable for walks and summertime swimming. A golf course is located within 2 km, along with guided mountain walks, canoeing, hot pools, scenic flights, skiing, trout fishing and white-water rafting are all within an hours drive.

Taumarunui - Owhango *15 km S of Taumarunui*

Fernleaf *B&B Farmstay Cottage No Kitchen*

Carolyn & Melvin Forlong
58 Tunanui Road,
RD 1,
Owhango

Tel (07) 895 4847
or 0800 FERNLEAF
or 0210 275 3847
or 0210 275 3848
Fax (07) 895 4837
fernleaf.farm@xtra.co.nz

Double/Twin $100-$150
Single $85-$100
(Full breakfast)
Dinner $30
Visa MC Diners Amex accepted
Children welcome
2 Queen 1 Double 1 Twin (4 bdrm)
Bathrooms: 2 Ensuite 1 Guest share

Relax in the tranquil Tunanui Valley just 500 metres from SH4. Close for convenience, far enough away for peace and quiet. We are the third generation to farm Fernleaf and our Romney sheep flock has been recorded every year for ninety years . The views from various vantage point on the farm are awesome, taking in the mountains: Ruapehu, Ngaruahoe, Tongariro and Taranaki. Enjoy our generous country hospitality, wonderful breakfast, a beautiful dalmatian Sally, and friendly cats. Other meals by arrangement. "River Fishing" nearby.

Raetihi *0.5 km N of Raetihi*

B&B Approved

Log Lodge *Luxury B&B*

Jan & Bob Lamb
5 Ranfurly Terrace,
Raetihi
Tel (06) 385 4135
Fax (06) 385 4835
Lamb.Log-Lodge@Xtra.co.nz

Double/Twin $115
Single $60
(Full breakfast)
Children under 14 $40
Spa $5 per person
Visa MC accepted
1 Queen 1 Double 4 Single
Open plan
Bathrooms: 2 Private
We only accept one booking at a time

A unique opportunity to stay in a modern authentic log home sited high on 7 acres on the edge of town. Completely private accommodation, with own bathroom. All sleeping on mezzanine, your own lounge with wood fire, snooker table, TV/video, stereo and dining area, opening onto large verandah, with swimming pool and spa available. Panoramic views of Mts Ruapehu, Ngauruhoe and Tongariro. Tongariro National Park and Turoa Skifield are a half hour scenic drive.

~

Ohakune *6 km W of Ohakune*

B&B Approved

Mitredale *Homestay Farmstay*

Audrey & Diane Pritt
Smiths Road,
RD, Ohakune
Tel (06) 385 8016
or 027 453 1916
Fax (06) 385 8016
mitredale@ihug.co.nz

Double/Twin $110
Single $60
(Continental breakfast)
Dinner $35pp by arrangement
Visa MC accepted
Pets welcome
1 Double 2 Single (2 bdrm)
Comfortable, cosy electric blankets on all beds
Bathrooms: 1 Family share

We farm sheep, bull beef and run a boarding kennel in a beautiful peaceful valley with magnificent views of Mt Ruapehu. Tongariro National Park for skiing, walking, photography. Excellent 18 hole golf course, great fishing locally. We are members of Ducks Unlimited (a conservation group)and our local wine club. We have 2 labradors. We offer dinner traditional farmhouse (Diane, a cook book author), or breakfast with excellent home-made jams. Take Raetihi Road, at Hotel/BP Service Station corner. 4km to Smiths Road. Last house 2km.

Ohakune *0.9 km SE of Junction*

Dakune Lodge *B&B Ski Lodge*

Nicolas & Tasha Cowell
42 Park Avenue,
Ohakune, 4625

Tel (06) 385 8448
Fax (06) 385 8448
info@dakunelodge.co.nz
www.dakunelodge.co.nz

Double/Twin $110-$160
Single $110
(Continental breakfast)
Summer Rate $30 per person
Visa MC Amex Eftpos accepted
2 Queen 5 Double 11 Single (9 bdrm)
Bathrooms: 3 Guest share

A beautiful wooden Lodge with mountain views in a quiet location, yet near the Junction. Warm comfortable accommodation for singles, couples, families or groups with shared bathrooms. Facilities include sauna, spa,games and drying rooms, in-house massage clinic. Socialise by the log fire in our large friendly lounge. Meals by request. Open all year round - wonderful memories are made here!

~

Taihape *6 km S of Taihape*

Grandvue *Homestay*

John & Dianne McKinnon
110 Wairanu Road,
RD 4, Taihape 4794

Tel (06) 388 1308
or 027 244 1309
Fax (06) 388 1308
grandvue@xtra.co.nz

Double/Twin $95
Single $65
(Special breakfast)
Children 12 and under $25
Dinner by arrangement
Visa MC accepted
Children and pets welcome
1 Queen 2 Twin (2 bdrm)
Portacot available
Bathrooms: 1 Guest share
Tiled shower/Spa bath

Relax in comfort in our cosy modern home situated in the heart of the Rangitikei on 90 acres of farmland. Only 6 minutes south of Taihape,2 minutes off State Highway 1.Our home situated in spacious grounds boasts magnificent views of mountains and ranges. One hour to Mt Ruapehu, two hours to Taupo and three to Wellington with many local activity options available. Comfortable beds with electric blankets. Paddock facilities available for travelling animals.

Taihape/Rangitikei *26 km NE of Taihape*

Tarata Fishaway *Luxury B&B Homestay Farmstay*

Stephen & Trudi Mattock
Mokai Road, RD 3, Taihape
Tel (06) 388 0354 or 027 279 7037
027 227 4986 Fax (06) 388 0954
fishaway@xtra.co.nz www.tarata.co.nz

B&B Approved

Double/Twin $120-$220 Single $60-$110
(Continental breakfast provisions)
Children under 12 half price
Dinner $40 pp by arrangement
Visa MC accepted Children and pets welcome
4 King/Twin 5 Queen 1 Double/Twin 3 Single (9 bdrm)
Bathrooms: 4 Ensuite 1 Guest share spa bath

We are very lucky to have a piece of New Zealand's natural beauty. Tarata is nestled in bush in the remote Mokai Valley where the picturesque Rangitikei River meets the rugged Ruahine Ranges. With the wilderness and unique trout fishing right at our doorstep, it is the perfect environment to bring up our 3 children. Stephen offers guided fishing and rafting trips for all ages. Raft through the gentle crystal clear waters of the magnificent Rangitikei River, visit Middle Earth and a secret waterfall, stunning scenery you will never forget.Our spacious home and our large garden allow guests private space to relax and unwind. Whether it is by the pool on a hot summers day with a good book, soaking in the spa pool after a day on the river or enjoying a cosy winters night in front of our open fire with a glass of wine. Come on a farm tour meeting our many friendly farm pets, experience our nightlife on our free spotlight safari and Tarata is only 6km past the new flying fox and bungy jump.Stay in our Homestead or in Tarata's fully self-contained River Retreats where you can enjoy a spa bath with million dollar views of the river and relax on the large decking amidst native birds and trees. Peace, privacy and tranquillity at its best! We will even deliver a candle light dinner to your door. We think Tarata is truly a magic place and we would love sharing it with you.
Directions: Tarata Fishaway is 26 scenic kilometres from Taihape. Turn off SH1, 6km south of Taihape at the Gravity Canyon Bungy and Ohotu signs. Follow the signs (14km) to the bungy bridge. We are 6 km past here on Mokai Road. Features & Attractions: Trout Fishing and Scenic Rafting, Visit LOTR, 6kms Past Bungy, Flying Fox, Mini Golf (with a difference), swimming pool, spa pools, bush walks, spotlight safaris, camp outs, claybird shooting.

Taihape *1 km S of Taihape*

Llanerchymedd *Luxury B&B Apartment with Kitchen*

Alan & Jan Thomas
10 Dixon Way,
Taihape

Tel (06) 388 0283
or (06) 388 0666
or 021 127 6211
Fax (06) 388 0683
alajan@xtra.co.nz

Double/Twin $90
(Continental breakfast provisions)
Children $20 per head
Additional charge $20 per head
Children welcome
1 Queen 1 Double 2 Single (1 bdrm)
Bathrooms: 1 Ensuite

We are a married couple with two children and two cats. LLanerchymedd is a quiet residence, with established gardens. We are two minutes from Taihape and are easily located, 1km south of the town with panoramic views of Mt Ruapehu. A tranquil walk up into the gardens is well rewarded with fantastic views. Take a glass of wine with you and relax in the top gazebo - you will feel on top of the world.

Taihape *32 km E of Taihape*

River Valley Lodge *Adventure Lodge*

Brian & Nicola Megaw
Mangahoata Road,
Pukeokahu, Taihape, 4792

Tel (06) 388 1444 o
r 0800 248 666
Fax (06) 388 1859
thelodge@rivervalley.co.nz
www.rivervalley.co.nz

Double/Twin $169-$169
Single $158-$158
(Full breakfast)
Children please refer to our website
Dinner please refer to our website
Visa MC Amex Eftpos accepted
Children welcome
6 King/Twin 2 King (8 bdrm)
All ensuited rooms with splittable king size beds
Bathrooms: 8 Ensuite
All rooms specified have ensuite showers and toilets

River Valley, is an Adventure Lodge. It is a place that is our home, where we have put down deep roots. It is a place where we feel that the spirit in which we do something, is an essential part of any experience. We actively search for ways in which we can offer you, our guests, experiences that are meaningful and personal. Experiences that are creative, where you feel uplifted, where we can share our stories, and you can share yours.

Marton *45 km N of Palmerston North*

B&B Approved

Rea's Inn *B&B Homestay*

Keith and Lorraine Rea
12 Dunallen Avenue,
Marton 4710

Tel (06) 327 4442
or 027 479 9589
Fax (06) 327 4442
keithandlorraine@xtra.co.nz
www.bnb.co.nz/reasinn.html

Double/Twin $95
Single $55
(Continental breakfast)
Children half price
Dinner $30
Visa MC accepted
Children welcome
1 Queen 1 Twin (2 bdrm)
Bathrooms: 1 Guest share

We have a warm comfortable home offering hospitality, peace and tranquility. Situated in quiet cul-de-sac with a private garden setting. Guests stay in separate wing of home. Close to Nga Tawa and Huntley Schools. Ideal for weekend retreat or stopover. (Only 2 hours from Wellington Ferry). Your comfort and pleasure are important to us. Clients enjoy our homemade hot bread served at breakfast. Our birman cat likes people too, and we all welcome you to come, relax and enjoy the friendly atmosphere at Rea's Inn.

Hawkes Bay
Tiniroto
Mahanga Beach
Mahia Beach
2
5
Eskdale
Bay View
Napier
Taradale
Hastings
Havelock North
50
2
Otane
Waipawa
Waipukurau
2
52
0 Kilometres 40
0 Miles 24

Mahia Peninsula - Mahanga Beach *50 km N of Wairoa*

B&B Approved

Reomoana *B&B Apartment with Kitchen Cottage with Kitchen*

Louise Schick
629 Mahanga Road, RD 8
Mahanga Beach, Mahia,
Hawkes Bay 4198

Tel (06) 837 5898
Fax (06) 837 5990
reomoana@paradise.net.nz
www.reomoana.co.nz

Double/Twin $120-$150
Single $60
(Continental breakfast)
Children $20
Dinner $35
Visa MC accepted
Children and pets welcome
2 Queen 1 Twin 1 Single (4 bdrm)
Bathrooms: 1 Ensuite 1 Private

Reomoana - The voice of the sea. Overlooking the Pacific with breathtaking views this rustic home with handcrafted features combines New Zealand and Hungarian creativity. Situated on a hillside the property is grazed by sheep and cattle, where walks may be enjoyed through QE 2 convenanted native bush. 5mins. walk to 8Kms. of white sandy beach, a recreational paradise for swimming, surfing and fishing. Attractions:- Morere Hot Springs, Marae visits, Golf-course and fishing charters. 6Kms. to Cafe Mahia and Sunset Point Restaurants.

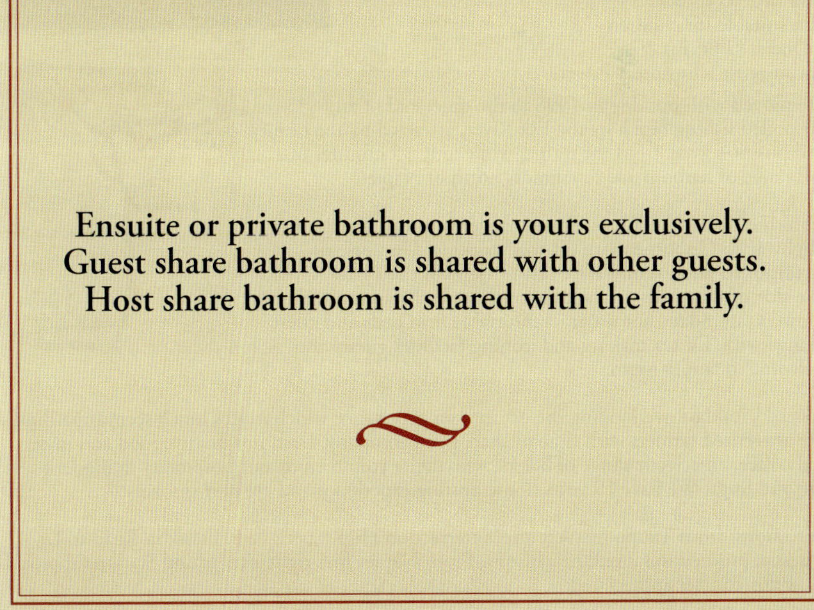

**Ensuite or private bathroom is yours exclusively.
Guest share bathroom is shared with other guests.
Host share bathroom is shared with the family.**

Bay View - Napier *12 km N of Napier*

Kilbirnie *Homestay*
Jill & John Grant
84 Le Quesne Road, Bay View, Napier
Tel (06) 836 6929 or 027 234 7363
jill.johng@xtra.co.nz
www.bnb.co.nz/kilbirnie.html

Double/Twin $90-$110
(Special breakfast)
Dinner $40pp by arrangement
Visa MC accepted
Not suitable for children
2 Queen (2 bdrm)
Bathrooms: 1 Ensuite 1 Private

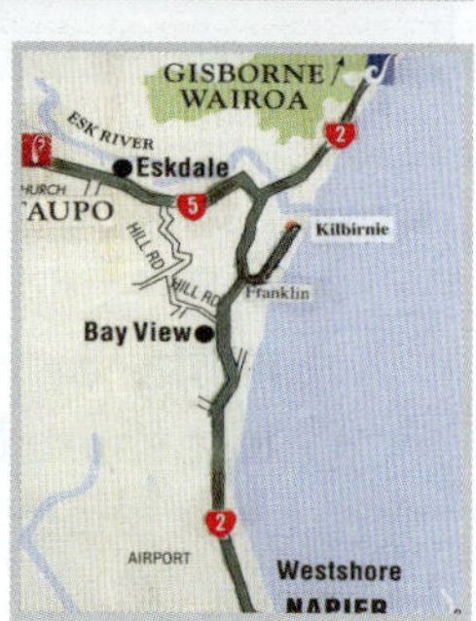

We moved with our dog in 1996 to the quiet end of an unspoiled fishing beach by the Esk River, attracted by the beauty and position away from the traffic, while only 15 minutes of a full range of harbourside restaurants north of Napier.

Kilbirnie is near the Taupo Road intersection with the Pacific Highway to Gisborne, with off-road parking. Upstairs, air-conditioned guest rooms have restful views of the Pacific Ocean one side or vineyards on the other, private bathrooms, excellent showers, abundant hot water, comfortable firm beds and guest lounge with TV tea making and ironing facilities,guests also welcome in family room.

Special breakfast overlooking the ocean is an experience which makes lunch seem superfluous. We are retired farmers with time to share good company, fresh imaginative food and juice, real coffee, an eclectic range of books, who invite you to enjoy our hospitality in modern surroundings. We have 19 years home hosting experience and are non-smokers.

Directions: from Taupo first left after intersection Highways 2 & 5. Franklin Road to Le Quesne, proceed to far end beachfront. From Napier first right after Mobil Station (approx 1 K). Prior contact appreciated.

Bay View - Napier *12 km N of Napier*

The Grange *B&B Farmstay & Self-contained Lodge*

Roslyn & Don Bird
263 Hill Road, Eskdale, Hawkes Bay
PO Box 136 Bay View, Hawkes Bay

Tel (06) 836 6666 or 027 28 15738
Fax (06) 836 6456 thefarmstay@xtra.co.nz www.thefarmstay.com

Farmstay/Double $110-$130 Single $85 (Full breakfast)
The Lodge/Double from $140, Single $100, Extra Persons $30pp,
Optional breakfast $15pp
3 course Dinner with wine $55pp Visa MC accepted Children welcome
1 King/Twin 1 King 2 Double 2 Single
2 in farmstay, 1+ Loft in Lodge (3 bdrm)
Bathrooms: 1 Private, 1 Farmstay Guest share
(Maximum 4 guests share luxury bathroom, separate toilet)

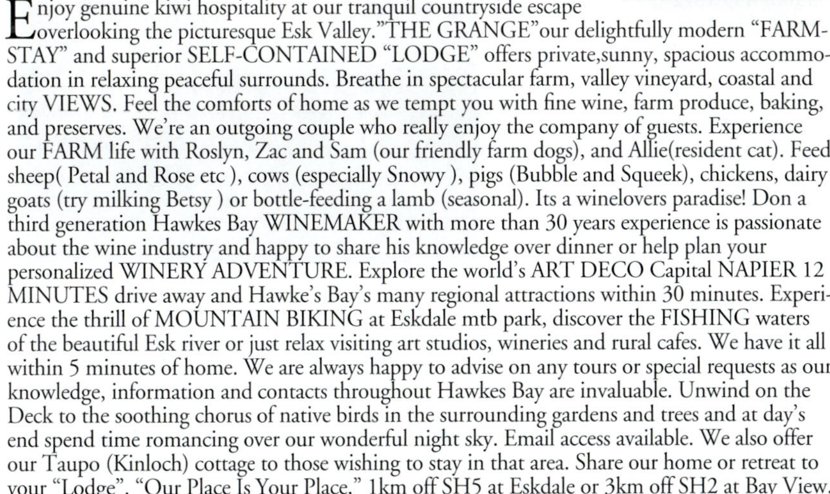

Enjoy genuine kiwi hospitality at our tranquil countryside escape overlooking the picturesque Esk Valley."THE GRANGE"our delightfully modern "FARM-STAY" and superior SELF-CONTAINED "LODGE" offers private,sunny, spacious accommodation in relaxing peaceful surrounds. Breathe in spectacular farm, valley vineyard, coastal and city VIEWS. Feel the comforts of home as we tempt you with fine wine, farm produce, baking, and preserves. We're an outgoing couple who really enjoy the company of guests. Experience our FARM life with Roslyn, Zac and Sam (our friendly farm dogs), and Allie(resident cat). Feed sheep(Petal and Rose etc), cows (especially Snowy), pigs (Bubble and Squeek), chickens, dairy goats (try milking Betsy) or bottle-feeding a lamb (seasonal). Its a winelovers paradise! Don a third generation Hawkes Bay WINEMAKER with more than 30 years experience is passionate about the wine industry and happy to share his knowledge over dinner or help plan your personalized WINERY ADVENTURE. Explore the world's ART DECO Capital NAPIER 12 MINUTES drive away and Hawke's Bay's many regional attractions within 30 minutes. Experience the thrill of MOUNTAIN BIKING at Eskdale mtb park, discover the FISHING waters of the beautiful Esk river or just relax visiting art studios, wineries and rural cafes. We have it all within 5 minutes of home. We are always happy to advise on any tours or special requests as our knowledge, information and contacts throughout Hawkes Bay are invaluable. Unwind on the Deck to the soothing chorus of native birds in the surrounding gardens and trees and at day's end spend time romancing over our wonderful night sky. Email access available. We also offer our Taupo (Kinloch) cottage to those wishing to stay in that area. Share our home or retreat to your "Lodge". "Our Place Is Your Place." 1km off SH5 at Eskdale or 3km off SH2 at Bay View.

Bay View - Napier *10 km N of napier*

B&B Approved

Bay Bach *B&B Homestay*
Jill and Iain Angus
117 Rogers Road,
Napier, 4104

Tel (06) 836 5141
or 021 105 7512
Fax (06) 836 5141
jill-iain@xtra.co.nz
www.baybach.co.nz

Double/Twin $155
Single $125
(Special breakfast)
Children by arrangement
Dinner $50pp by arrangement
Eftpos accepted
Children and pets welcome
1 King/Twin 1 King (2 bdrm)
2 ensuite rooms with patios
Bathrooms: 2 Ensuite

A warm friendly welcome awaits you at Bay Bach. Our architectural award winning uniquely stylish home has been built with your comfort and relaxation as it's primary goal. The beds and linen are of the highest quality and comfort. You have your own patio, entrance and car park with a two minute stroll to the sea. It's a short drive to our beautiful Art Deco city, Napier. Wineries and restaurants abound Hear the sea and look down the grapes to the hills as you breakfast.

~

Napier *1.2 km N of Napier Central*

Hillcrest *B&B Homestay*
Nancy & Noel Lyons
4 George Street,
Hospital Hill,
Napier

Tel (06) 835 1812
lyons@inhb.co.nz
www.hillcrestnapier.co.nz

Double/Twin $110
Single $80
(Continental breakfast)
Visa MC accepted
Pet free home
Not suitable for children
1 Double 2 Single (2 bdrm)
Bathrooms: 1 Guest share

If you require quiet accommodation just minutes from the city centre, our comfortable home provides peace in restful surroundings. Relax on wide decks overlooking our garden, or enjoy the spectacular sea views. Explore nearby historic places and the botanical gardens. Your own lounge with tea/coffee making; laundry and off-street parking available. We have travelled extensively and welcome the opportunity of meeting visitors. Our interests are travel, music, bowls and embroidery. We will happily meet you at the travel depots. Holiday home at Mahia Beach available.

Napier *5 km S of Napier*

Snug Harbour *Homestay*

Ruth & Don McLeod
147 Harold Holt Avenue,
Napier

Tel (06) 843 2521
Fax (06) 843 2520
donmcld@clear.net.nz
www.snugharbour.co.nz

home NEW ZEALAND · B&B Approved

Double/Twin $100-$120
Single $85
(Full breakfast)
Dinner $40 by arrangement
Visa MC accepted
Pet free home
1 Queen 1 Twin (2 bdrm)
Twin room has super single beds
Bathrooms: 1 Ensuite 1 Family share

Ruth & Don welcome you to their comfortable home with its rural outlook and sunny attractive patio. The garden studio with ensuite and tea making facilities has its own entrance. We are situated on the outskirts of Napier City, the art deco city of the World, and in close proximity to wineries and many other tourist attractions. We both have a background in teaching, with interests in travel, gardening and photography.

Napier *1 km N of Napier on hill above city*

The Coachhouse *Cottage with Kitchen*

Jan Chalmers
9 Gladstone Road,
Napier

Tel (06) 835 6126
or 021 251 5847
janchalmers@paradise.net.nz
www.thecoachhouse.co.nz

B&B Approved

Double/Twin $100
Single $80
(Continental breakfast provisions)
Children $25 - babies free
$140 for 3, $160 for 4
Visa MC accepted
Children and pets welcome
1 Queen 2 Single (2 bdrm)
Bathrooms: 1 Private

On the hill over-looking a gorgeous Mediterranean garden and sea views, the historic Coach-house is tastefully renovated and totally self-contained. It contains 2 bedrooms, open plan kitchen, dining, living rooms, bathroom and separate loo. The breakfast supplies include homemade jam and marmalade. TV and radio included and fresh flowers in all rooms. The sunny deck has a table and chairs and gas barbecue. Off-street parking and easy access plus peace and privacy complete the picture.

Napier - Taradale *7.5 km SW of Napier*

'279' Church Road *B&B Homestay*

Sandy Edgington
279 Church Road,
Taradale, Napier

Tel (06) 844 7814
or 021 447 814
sandy.279@homestaynapier.co.nz
www.homestaynapier.co.nz

Double/Twin $120-$150
Single $90-$100
(Full breakfast)
Dinner by arrangement
Smoking area available
Visa MC accepted
Not suitable for children
1 Queen 1 Double 1 Single (2 bdrm)
Spacious
Bathrooms: 1 Guest share
Separate toilet

279, an elegant and spacious home set amongst mature trees and gardens, offers excellent hospitality in a relaxed, friendly atmosphere to domestic and international visitors. Located adjacent to Mission Estate and Church Road Wineries, restaurants and craft galleries, 279 is within a short drive of Art Deco Napier, Hastings, golf courses, and tourist activities. I welcome you to 279 and will help make your visit the highlight of your travels.

Napier - Taradale *10 km W of Napier*

Otatara Heights *B&B Apartment with Kitchen*

Sandra & Roy Holderness
57 Churchill Drive,
Taradale,
Napier

Tel (06) 844 8855
Fax (06) 844 8855
sandroy@clear.net.nz

Double/Twin $100
Single $75
(Continental breakfast)
Extra guest $40
1 Queen 1 Double (1 bdrm)
Bathrooms: 1 Private

Comfortable, quiet apartment in the heart of our foremost wine producing area. Superb day and night views over Napier and local rural scenes. 10 minutes drive to the art deco capital of the world. 2km to Taradale Village. Safe off-street parking. Top quality restaurants and wineries nearby. We are a friendly couple who have enjoyed B&B overseas and like meeting people. Our interests are travel, theatre, good food and wine. Bella, our cat, keeps to herself. Handy to EIT and golf course.

Napier - Marine Parade *0.1 km N of Napier*

Mon Logis *B&B*

Gerard Averous
415 Marine Parade,
PO Box 871,
Napier

Tel (06) 835 2125
or 0274 72 5332
Fax (06) 835 8811
monlogis@xtra.co.nz
www.babs.co.nz/monlogis

Double/Twin $200-$220
Single $160-$180
(Full breakfast)
Visa MC Diners Amex accepted
Not suitable for children
2 King/Twin 2 King (4 bdrm)
Bathrooms: 3 Ensuite 1 Private

A little piece of France nestled in the heart of the beautiful wine-growing region of Hawkes Bay. Built as private hotel in 1915, this grand colonial building is a few minutes walk from the city. Now lovingly renovated Mon Logis will cater to a maximum of 8 guests. Downstairs, an informal guest lounge invites relaxation, television viewing or a quiet time reading. Guests can help themselves to coffee/tea and home-made biscuits at any time.

Napier *1 km N of Napier*

Cobden Garden Homestay *Luxury B&B Homestay*

Rayma and Phillip Jenkins
1 Cobden Crescent,
Bluff Hill,
Napier

Tel (06) 834 2090
or 0800 426 233
or 027 6951240
Fax (06) 834 1977
info@cobden.co.nz
www.cobden.co.nz

Double/Twin up to $220
Single $150-$190
(Full breakfast)
Children negotiable
Visa MC Diners Amex
Eftpos accepted
2 King/Twin 1 King 1 Single (3 bdrm)
Bathrooms: 3 Ensuite

We invite you to share our sunny, colonial villa on Bluff Hill. Enjoy spacious bedrooms furnished for your comfort with; quality bedding, lounge furniture, TV with DVD player, refreshments, robes, hairdryer. Relax in the garden, on the veranda or in a guest lounge. Check emails on the guest computer with wireless access. Join us for complimentary tasting of local wine and hors- d'oeuvres each evening. Choose breakfast from a selection of homemade and local foods. Your stay will be memorable. Three unobtrusive cats in residence.

Napier Hill *1 km N of Napier*

Maison BÈarnaise *B&B Homestay*

Christine Grouden & Graham Storer
25 France Road,
Bluff Hill,
Napier 4110
Tel (06) 835 4693
or 0800 624 766
Fax (06) 835 4694
chrisgraham@xtra.co.nz
www.maisonbearnaise.co.nz

Double/Twin $160-$180
Single $120-$150
(Full breakfast)
Visa MC accepted
Not suitable for children
2 Queen (2 bdrm)
Bathrooms: 2 Ensuite

Christine, Graham & Brewster (shy cat), welcome you to our attractive, peaceful oasis. Walk to city centre, restaurants, Bluff lookout. Off-street parking, wireless email access, laundry service available. Large bedrooms have views, comfortable beds, electric blankets, and DVD-television. Relax with tea / coffee in your room or guest lounge where newspapers, magazines, books are at your disposal. Delicious breakfasts including home grown and local produce served in dining room or colourful courtyard. Friendly adult retreat. Christine, Napier born, happily shares her wealth of local knowledge.

~

Napier *0.5 km N of Napier Central*

Seaview Lodge *B&B Homestay*

Catherine & Evert Van Florenstein
5 Seaview Terrace,
Napier
Tel (06) 835 0202
or 021 180 2101
cvulodge@xtra.co.nz
www.aseaviewlodge.co.nz

Double/Twin $150-$170
Single $120-$130
(Continental breakfast)
Visa MC accepted
1 King/Twin 1 King 1 Single (3 bdrm)
Bathrooms: 1 Ensuite 2 Private

Seaview Lodge is a lovingly renovated, spacious late Victorian home. This inner city, beachside bed and breakfast offers a warm welcome and spectacular views. Enjoy breakfast on the lower verandah while watching the waves break on the shore. In the evening relax in the spacious guest lounge or on the upstairs balcony. Situated across the road from the beach, hot pools and conference complex and a three minute stroll to the city centre makes Seaview Lodge an ideal place to explore Napier from.

Napier - Puketapu *25 km W of Napier*

B&B Approved

Te Puna Farmstay *ECOSTAY*

Sarah & Tony
255 Apley Road,
Puketapu RD 6,
Napier 4021
Tel (06) 844 8753
or 021 165 8306
or 027 366 0126
tonykeele@clear.net.nz
www.farmstaynapier.co.nz

Double/Twin $130
Single $75
(Full breakfast)
Dinner $30 by prior arrangement
Children and pets welcome
1 King/Twin (1 bdrm)
King/twin is superking/twin
Bathrooms: 1 Ensuite

We have completed our lodge and are delighted to offer "low carbon footprint" ECOSTAYS using rainwater and no mains power.You are welcome to our small farm with cattle, sheep, ducks, hens, dogs and indoor cats.Enjoy home-cooked dinner with our own chemical-free meat, seasonal produce and local wines. Just 20 minutes from Napier, our track is best negotiated with 4-wheel drive.

Napier *1 km N of Napier Central*

at home NEW ZEALAND   B&B Approved

Villa Vista B&B *B&B*

Tina Roulston & Tim Barker
22A France Road,
Bluff Hill,
Napier
Tel (06) 835 8770
or 027 435 7179
Fax (06) 835 8770
accommodation@villavista.net
www.villavista.net

Double/Twin $140-$150
Single $110-$125
(Special breakfast)
Children negotiable
Visa MC accepted
Children welcome
3 Queen 1 Single (3 bdrm)
Spacious, comfortable, relaxed, home baking provided.
Bathrooms: 3 Ensuite

A grand Edwardian villa blessed with fantastic views over the sea to Cape kidnappers from every large and private bedroom. Ensuite, air-conditioning, television, tea/coffee making facilities & home baking in each bedroom. Selection of continental and cooked breakfasts are served in the spacious dining room. Amicable children and pets residing. Welcome to Napier.

Napier *3 km S of Napier*

Art Deco Te Awa *B&B*
Kay & Rod Goodspeed
19 Te Awa Avenue,
Napier
Tel (06) 835 1618
or 027 211 0023
Fax (06) 835 3689
kaypat1@xtra.co.nz

Double/Twin $130-$150
(Full breakfast)
Pet free home
1 Queen 1 Double 1 Twin (3 bdrm)
Bathrooms: 2 Ensuite 1 Private

Art Deco Te Awa is spacious, executive quality accommodation. Ideal for visiting NZ's Art Deco City. Breakfast includes locally grown fresh fruit, home made muesli and preserves. Quality beds with fine linen. Guest rooms include one spacious double room with ensuite bathroom,one queen with ensuite bathroom and one twin with private bathroom, all with heated towelrail, hairdryer and complimentary toiletries. Five minutes to city centre. Ten minutes to airport. Walking distance to the beach and 18 hole golf course. Easy access to Hawke's Bay's wineries.

Napier *1 km N of Napier*

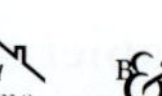

Spence Bed & Breakfast *B&B Homestay*
Kay & Stewart Spence
17 Cobden Road,
Bluff Hill, Napier 4110
Tel (06) 835 9454
or 0800 117 890
Fax (06) 835 9454
ksspence@actrix.gen.nz
www.spencebnb.co.nz

Double/Twin $160-$170
Single $120-$140
(Full breakfast)
Visa MC accepted
Pet free home
Children welcome
1 Queen 1 Single (1 bdrm)
Queen & single beds
Bathrooms: 1 Ensuite

Welcome to our comfortable near new home. Quiet area, 10-15 minutes walk from Art Deco City centre. Guest suite opens outside to patio, and colourful garden. Lounge includes double bed settee,wireless internet access, TV, kitchenette with tea making facilities, fridge and microwave. Bedroom has queen and single beds, ensuite bathroom. We have hosted for over 10 years and enjoy overseas travel. Able to meet public transport. Directions: port end Marine Parade, Coote Road, right into Thompson Road, left into Cobden Road opposite water tower.

Napier *1.5 km N of Post Office*

B&B Approved

A Room with a View *B&B Homestay*

Robert McGregor
9 Milton Terrace,
Napier

Tel (06) 835 7434
or 027 249 2040
Fax (06) 835 1912
roomwithview@xtra.co.nz

Double/Twin $130-$130
Single $100-$100
(Continental breakfast)
Visa MC accepted
1 Queen (1 bdrm)
Spacious bedroom with panoramic view
Bathrooms: 1 Private with bath & shower, directly oppposite bedroom

After 10 years hosting with my late wife, I'm continuing to enjoy companionship, conversation and laughter with guests. Fourth generation property, 130 year old garden, spacious room, panoramic sea view. 15 minute walk to restaurants at historic Port Ahuriri or our world famous Art Deco city centre. Private bathroom. Free laundry facilities, pick-up service, internet. Off-street parking. Smoke-free inside please. I'm interested in travel, gardening, the arts, and especially local history, as until retirement I was Chief Executive of the Art Deco Trust.

Napier - Westshore *3 km N of Post Office*

B&B Approved

Touch th' Tide *B&B Homestay*

Peter and Cheryl Sugden
7 Charles Street,
Westshore,
Napier 4142

Tel Landline (06) 835 7280
or Mobile 027 222 9321
or Mobile 027 478 9093
suggy@xtra.co.nz

Double/Twin $140-$160
Single $95-$95
(Full breakfast)
Children welcome by arrangement
Visa MC accepted
2 Queen 2 Single (2 bdrm)
Each room has a high quality queen and single bed
Bathrooms: 1 Private 1 Guest share

Welcome. Enjoy breakfast on the terrace. Watch the yachts, the distant port, people fishing or meandering along the beach reserve. Swim. Walk to the cafes in Ahuriri's historic village or drive a few minutes to the world renowned Art Deco City. Visit the gannet colony, wineries, play golf or walk the estuary with its water sport facilities. We are a retired, well traveled pharmacist and nurse who have lived locally for many years so can help plan your day. We share our home with you.

Napier *2.5 km W of City*

Logan B & B *B&B Homestay*

Pam & John Thompson
15 Logan Avenue,
Napier, 4110

Tel (06) 843 7558
or 027 660 6982
Fax (06) 843 7569
pam.john@xtra.co.nz

Double/Twin $130-$130
Single $110-$110
(Continental breakfast)
1 Queen (1 bdrm)
Beautifully appointed in Art Deco style
Bathrooms: 1 Private
Spacious with spa bath & shower right next to room

We are Art Deco enthusiasts living in an iconic home situated in Napier's renowned Art Deco suburb. A simple 'walk around the block' from our front door enables you to complete much of the 'Marewa Meander' Art Deco tour. Better still, you are just 5 minutes drive from Napier's inner city which is packed with more Art Deco interest, cafes, and shopping. Winery tours are readily available and we have good local knowledge. Excellent off-street parking and pick-up service by arrangement. 2 friendly cats in residence.

Napier - Greenmeadows *4 km S of Napier*

Greenmeadows on Gloucester Apartment and B&B *B&B Apartment with Kitchen*

Jennifer Leedes
47Gloucester Street, Napier, 4112

Tel (06) 845 4836 or 027 232 4355
Fax (06) 845 4837
leedes@xtra.co.nz
http://greenmeadowsongloucester.co.nz

Double/Twin $95-$125
Single $95-$115
(Continental breakfast)
Children special conditions apply
Dinner not avalaible
Visa MC Eftpos accepted
Pet free home Children welcome
4 Queen 4 Twin 4 Single (4 bdrm)
Queen and long king singles, extra bed if required
Bathrooms: 1 Ensuite in Apartment 1 Guest share in house

Fabulous spacious property built in 2008. Guest are offered B&B in the house or Luxurious Self contained Apartment which sleeps up to 6 persons. Breakfast: outdoors in summer. The garden is newly planted. Jennifer a Wine Tour/Coach Charter Operator for 23 years is a people person and has a wealth of knowledge to share. Close by are Cafes, Restaurants, Golf, Mission and Church Road Wineries. A short drive to Art Deco Napier and tourist attractions. 15 minutes to Hastings. No pets on site. Bike hire available on site.

Napier Hill *0.1 km W of Napier*

B&B Approved

Turret House *B&B Homestay*
Jaime and Deborah Taylor
26 May Ave, 4110
Tel (06) 835 4280
or 027 478 4228
Fax (06) 835 4280
turrethouse@actrix.co.nz

Double/Twin $130-$130
(Continental breakfast)
Visa MC accepted
Children welcome
3 Queen 1 Twin (4 bdrm)
Bathrooms: 2 Guest share
One bathroom with clawfoot bath

Welcome to our 1908 Edwardian Villa built to take advantage of the panoramic views from Cape Kidnappers to the Ruahine Ranges. Enjoy breakfast watching the sunrise over the sea or relax with a glass of wine as the sun sets behind the hills.In a quiet cul de sac with level access and good parking.Facilities include Sky TV and swimming pool.Tea and coffee available all day. Originally from England we have lived in South Africa, moving to New Zealand 15 years ago.We have two friendly Jack Russell dogs.

Hastings City *1 km N of Hastings Central*

B&B Approved

McConchie Homestay *Homestay*
Barbara & Nina McConchie
115A Frederick Street,
Hastings
Tel (06) 878 4576
or 027 478 4576
barbaramcconchie@xtra.co.nz
www.bnb.co.nz

Double/Twin $100
Single $65
(Full breakfast)
Children $25
Dinner $25 by arrangement
Visa MC accepted
1 Queen 2 Single (2 bdrm)
Bedroom with 2 single beds
opens out to a deck.
Bathrooms: 1 Guest share

Enjoy our peaceful garden back section, no traffic noises, yet central to Hastings City. My 2 cats say 'Hi'. Nearby are parks, golf courses, wineries, orchards and the best icecream ever. Short trips take you to spectacular views, Cape Kidnapper's gannet colony, or Napier's art deco, hot pools, or just relaxing and enjoying great hospitality. Directions: from Wellington, arriving Hastings City, turn left into Eastbourne Street, right into Nelson Street, right into Frederick Street, cross Caroline Road. Driveway on right. 115A first house off driveway.

Hastings *14 km NW of Hastings*

Grandvue Country Stay *B&B Homestay*
Dianne & Keith Taylor
Grandvue, 2596 State Highway 50, RD 5 Hastings 4175
Tel (06) 879 6141 or 027 668 0252
Fax 06 879 6988 homestays@xtra.co.nz
www.bnb.co.nz/grandvuehomestay.html

Double/Twin $100-$120 Single $65 (Full breakfast)
Children negotiable Dinner $30 pp Visa MC accepted
Pet free home Children welcome
1 King/Twin 1 Queen (2 bdrm)
Bathrooms: 1 Ensuite 1 Family share

Recently retired and moved from our farm but still the same genuine and caring hospitality. Enjoy with us in a relaxed atmosphere in our extensive private garden the wonderful views over vineyards in the Gimlett Gravels and Ngatarawa area, and to Havelock North hills in the distance. Comfortable beds with firm mattresses make for a good nights sleep (electric blankets for winter warmth). Sit and chat when time allows over a generous breakfast cooked or continental with homemade preserves and goodies - inside or alfresco. Dinner available on request.

Our interests include tramping, bushwalks, gardening, travel and genealogy. Having travelled extensively we do enjoy meeting local and overseas visitors. Let us advise you on all the wonderful things to see and do while in our lovely Hawkes Bay. There are many wineries close by with restaurants, Safari trips to the gannets, Orchard tours, Trout fishing, Golf courses, Panoramic views from Te Mata Peak, Havelock North with boutique shops and cafes and Napier the Art Deco City of the world are just a few.

We can arrange tours for you too, and also advise you on your travel through NZ. After more than 20 years of hosting we have an ever increasing circle of friends with many returning. Please read our guests comments on our B&B Book website. Guests are welcome to use the swimming pool in summer and the tennis court. Dianne is one of a few in NZ who has a certificate in Homestay Management. We look forward to meeting you, and our aim is to make your stay memorable. Arrive as a guest and leave as our friends. Easy access and plenty of parking..

Hastings *3 km S of Hastings*

Raureka *B&B Separate Suite*

B&B Approved

Rosemary & Tim Ormond
26 Wellwood Road,
RD 5,
Hastings

Tel (06) 878 9715
or 021 104 5124
Fax (06) 878 9728
r.t.ormond@xtra.co.nz

Double/Twin $110
Single $90 (Full breakfast)
Visa MC accepted
Pet free home
Not suitable for children
1 Queen (1 bdrm)
Bathrooms: 1 Ensuite
Shower only

Quietness and privacy,in an Orchard setting, are the main ingredients of staying at Raureka. The accommodation is situated separately from the house but close enough for visitors to feel welcome and cared for. Hosts Rosemary and Tim will provide help and advice for planning a successful day around this beautiful region. Fresh flowers, home-baking and complimentary wine are among the many treats ensuring your stay here is a home away from home. Relax by our pool or enjoy the ambience of our property.

Havelock North - Hastings *16 km S of Havelock North*

Wharehau *Homestay Farmstay*

@home New Zealand · B&B Approved

Ros Phillips
1604 Middle Road,
Havelock North, RD 11,
Hastings 4178

Tel (06) 877 4111
or 021 0271 9215
Fax (06) 877 4115
ros.phillips@xtra.co.nz
www.wharehau.co.nz

Double/Twin $120
Single $60 (Full breakfast)
Children half price
Dinner $30
Beach bach$130/$150
Visa MC accepted
Children welcome
2 Queen 2 Twin 1 Single (4 bdrm)
Bathrooms: 1 Guest share 1 Family share

Wharehau is in the beautiful Tuki Tuki valley -a great base for Hawkes Bay experience. Quarter of an hour travel from Hastings or Havelock North in the midst of Wine Country. Close to golf courses, Splash Planet, gannets and art deco. Or enjoy the peace and space on the farm. Weather permitting a farm 4WD tour is available. Walks available locally. Trout fishing (local guide can be hired) in the Tuki Tuki River. Comfortable beach bach at Kairakau Beach is available for rent.

Havelock North *5 km N of Havelock North*

Totara Stables *B&B Homestay*

Sharon A. Bellaart & John W. Hayes
324 Te Mata - Mangateretere Road,
Havelock North,
RD 2,
Hastings

Tel (06) 877 8882
or 027 486 3910
Fax (06) 877 8891
bookings@totarastables.co.nz
www.totarastables.co.nz

Double/Twin $150-$165
Single $120
(Special breakfast)
Visa MC accepted
Not suitable for children
1 King/Twin 1 Queen 1 Twin (3 bdrm)
Bathrooms: 1 Ensuite 1 Private

Offering a unique Bed & Breakfast experience in a lovingly restored 1910 villa. Take a peek into the museum of early pioneer farming displayed in the century old stables or marvel at the simplicity of early stationary motors. Feed the hand reared deer, view the classic 1951 Sunbeam Talbot motor car and 1946 Ford Jailbar pickup. We are located in the heart of the Te Mata wine region only minutes from the pictureque village of Havelock North. Non-smoking and not suitable children under 12 years.

Havelock North *3 km S of Havelock North*

Endsleigh Cottages/Muritai *Luxury Cottage with Kitchen Guest House 3 Self contained cottages and Large Villa*

Denis & Margie Hardy
22 Endsleigh Road,
Havelock North

Tel (06) 877 7588
or 0274 443 800
Fax (06) 876 0275
endsleigh.cottages@xtra.co.nz
www.endsleigh.cottages.co.nz
www.muritai.co.nz

Double/Twin $100-$350
Single $100-$250
(Breakfast provisions first night)
Muritai Villa $1,000pn -
Sleeps 13 comfortably
Visa MC Amex accepted
Pet free home Children welcome
4 Queen (6 bdrm)
Cottages 4 bedrooms Muritai 6 bedrooms
Bathrooms: 3 Ensuite Cottages 3 baths Muritai 5 bathrooms

From Havelock North take Middle Road south for 3km. Cross intersection with Gilpin & Iona Roads, then left into Endsleigh Road. Cottages on right. Muritai - 68 Duart Road Havelock North

Havelock North *2 km NE of Havelock North*

B&B Approved

Options *B&B Homestay*

Rosemary & Graham Duff
92 Simla Ave,
Havelock North, 4130

Tel (06) 877 0257
or 027 653 7270
Fax (06) 877 0257
gr.duff@xtra.co.nz

Double/Twin $130-$150
Single $100-$120
(Full breakfast)
Children negotiable
Dinner by arrangement
Visa MC accepted
Pet free home
1 King 1 Queen 1 Twin
1 Single (3 bdrm)
Bathrooms: 1 Ensuite 1 Private

Options offers: Near Te Mata Peak; Views; 5 minutes to Havelock North village; Wine, gannets and Art Deco all within 30 minutes; Swimming pool and spa; Private sheltered patios; Pet free home; Wireless internet connection; Breakfast inside or outside depending on the weather; Optional evening meal at an additional cost; A home away from home.

Havelock North *0.5 km S of Havelock North*

@home New Zealand

B&B Approved

The Loft Art Studio and Bed & Breakfast *B&B Premium Boutique*

Iris and John
10 Woodford Heights,
Havelock North, 4130

Tel (06) 877 5938
or 021 474 729
or 027 276 1238
Fax (06) 877 5938
theloft@hawkesbayaccommodation.com
www.hawkesbayaccommodation.com

Double/Twin $145-$240
(Special breakfast)
Dinner in romantic setting $50pp b/a
Visa MC accepted
Pet free home
1 King 1 Queen (2 bdrm)
King room with ensuite,
Queen room with ensuite
Bathrooms: 2 Ensuite King room has spa bath & shower; Queen has shower

Come and be pampered in our paradise. We, Iris and John, 4th generation New Zealand-ers will welcome you with complimentary refreshments. Our architectural home has many unique features and superb views of Hawke's Bay. Use the courtyard and /or deck. Delicious breakfasts. Soak luxuriously in the spa bath and view the stars through the glass ceiling. Luxury linen, comfortable beds.John is an artist with a house studio to visit. We are close to our best attractions and can advise you on excursions. Cycles available.

Havelock North *3 km S of Havelock North*

Havelock House *Luxury B&B Apartment*

Diana & Jeff Arnold
77 Endsleigh Road,
Havelock North, 4130

dianaarnold@xtra.co.nz
www.havelockhouse.co.nz

Double/Twin $180-$200
Single $150-$180
(Full breakfast)
Children negotiable
Dinner by arrangement
Local restaurants close by
Visa MC accepted
Pet free home
1 King/Twin 1 King
King double & king twin ensuite
Bathrooms: 2 Ensuite

Relax and unwind in our comfortable Hawkes Bay home - one of the finest architecturally built houses in the Bay with its fabulous swimming pool, tennis court, quiet outside decks and stunning shaded gardens.Diana and Jeff will help you plan your days - close to some of the finest wineries & restaurants in New Zealand - Craggy Range, Black Barn, Clearview..CapeKidnappers, Art Deco Napier, Te Mata Peak and farmers markets.

Havelock North *1 km S of Havelock North Village Centre*

The Whitehouse Homestay B&B *Luxury Homestay B&B*

Doug Henderson and Karin Campbell
14 Woodford Heights,
Havelock North, 4130

Tel (06) 877 0522
or 021 13 48 109
info@thewhitehousebandb.co.nz
www.thewhitehousebandb.co.nz

Double/Twin $145-$195
(Special breakfast)
Children by arrangement
Dinner by arrangement with soft music and candlelights
Hire car - Mazda MX5 Roadster
Visa MC Amex accepted
Pet free home
1 King 1 Queen (2 bdrm)
Woodford Suite King size bed, Iona Suite Queen size bed
Bathrooms: 1 Ensuite 1 Private
Woodford (Private) spa bath, shower. Iona ensuite, shower

Welcome to THE WHITEHOUSE, an adventure with a difference. We offer luxury homestay B&B accomodation in the heart of Havelock North, only minutes from cities, Hastings & Art Deco Capital, Napier. These locations offer boutique shopping and casual or fine dining, also short drive to wonderful wineries that makes this region so very special.We offer two luxury suites, 'Woodford' & 'Iona', refreshments, homebaking on arrival, relax on the decks & soak up the stunning views. Hire Mazda MX5 Roadster enjoy Wineries, Golf, Art Deco, Cape Kidnappers.

Otane *8 km N of Waipawa*

Ludlow Farmstay *Luxury B&B Farmstay Cottage with Kitchen*

Gwen and Neil White
53 Drumpeel Road,
RD 1, Otane/Waipawa

Tel (06) 856 8348
or 027 441 8354
Fax (06) 856 8348
ludlow.white@xtra.co.nz
www. ludlowfarmstay.co.nz

Double/Twin $160
Single $100
(Full breakfast provisions)
Children $20-$30 cot/highchair
Dinner $35 by arrangement
1 King/Twin 1 Queen 1 Double
2 Twin (3 bdrm)
Twin room can be made as a King
Bathrooms: 1 Private Shower only

Ludlow is a Working 555 hectare extensive cropping farm, growing mainly wheat and barley, squash pumpkins, sweetcorn and peas with lamb and beef finishing. Our recently renovated shearers' cottage is situated in private surroundings, 50 metres from main homestead, with full kitchen facilities, laundry, open fire and views over the Drumpeel Valley Farmland, with stock grazing alongside the cottage. Swimming pool and Astrograss tennis court available for guests' use. Farm tour available on request. Expect a warm welcome from the Jack Russell terrier.

Waipawa *40 km S of Hastings*

B&B Approved

Abbotsford Oaks *Luxury B&B*

Nicolette Brasell & Chris Davis
85 Abbotsford Road,
Waipawa,
Central Hawke's Bay

Tel (06) 857 8960
or 027 296 1160
Fax (06) 857 8961
nicolette@abbotsfordoaks.co.nz

Double/Twin $175-$325
Single $140-$280
(Full breakfast)
Dinner by arrangement
Visa MC accepted
Not suitable for children
2 King 2 Queen (4 bdrm)
Bathrooms: 1 Ensuite 3 Private

Abbotsford Oaks was purpose built as a children's home in the 1920s and has been extensively renovated to provide quality boutique bed and breakfast accommodation with that wow factor. It has spacious an elegantly furnished rooms, high quality linens and 3 bedrooms have their own sitting rooms. Set in 3.5 acre of parklike grounds it is the perfect base to explore the many attractions hawke's Bay has to offer or as a corporate retreat. Our cats love it and we think you will too.

Waipawa *1 km NE of Waipawa*

Abbot Heights *Luxury B&B*

Jacqui & Charlie Hutchison
6 Parkland Drive,
Waipawa
Tel 027 433 0146
or (06) 857 8585
Fax (06) 857 8580
chipper.c@xtra.co.nz

Double/Twin $150
Single $100
(Continental breakfast)
Not suitable for children
2 Queen (2 bdrm)
Crisp, modern, clean airy, spacious luxurious rooms
Bathrooms: 1 Ensuite 1 Private
Private bathroom has spa bath

Welcome to Abbot Heights. Your friendly hosts (and cat Myrtle) look forward to your stay at their stunning modern manor set in 12 acres of private park and gardens.Enjoy tea or coffee on arrival or relax in your spacious room. Facilities include a splendid private lounge small library, luxury goose down duvets, plush bathrobes,electric blankets and private entrance.Read a book by the fire in winter or find a shady spot in the garden or courtyard in summer. It's all about your comfort.

Waipukurau *4.5 km S of Waipukurau*

Pukeora Vineyard Cottage *Cottage with Kitchen*

Kate Norman
Pukeora Estate,
208 Pukeora Scenic Road,
RD 1,Waipukurau
(off SH2 south of Waipukurau)
Tel (06) 858 9339
or 021 205 1307
or 021 701 606
Fax (06) 858 6070
cottage@pukeora.com
www.pukeora.com

Double/Twin $125
Single $95
(Continental breakfast)
Children $25
Visa MC Eftpos accepted
2 Queen 2 Twin 1 Single (3 bdrm)
Bathrooms: 1 Private

Enjoy exclusive hire of our charming, hilltop cottage with stunning views over the vineyard, river, plains and beyond. The spacious 1920's cottage, with rimu floors, sunny verandah, open plan lounge/kitchen with log fire, is a private annex to our house. Pukeora Estate, set on 32 Ha, includes a 5 Ha vineyard, boutique winery and functions venue. Your hosts Kate and Max, with daughters Jessica (age 7) and Marika(6), puppy Clara and 3 cats, welcome you. Endless outside space for children. Washing machine. Wine tasting/sales available.

Waipukurau *2 km S of Waipukurau*

Woburn Homestead *Luxury B&B*

Heatha Edwards & Philip Allerby
216 Hatuma Road,
RD 1, Waipukurau

Tel (06) 858 9668
or 0274 529 112
heatha.woburnhomestead@xtra.co.nz
www.woburnhomestead.co.nz

Double/Twin $250-$300
Single up to $150
(Special breakfast)
Dinner available by prior arrangement
Visa MC accepted
Not suitable for children, sorry
2 Queen 2 Twin (3 bdrm)
2 with queen beds and 1 with 2 twin beds
Bathrooms: 3 Ensuite

Welcome to Woburn Homestead, an exquisite 7 bedroom home with 6 bathrooms, built in 1893 and listed with the NZ Historic Places Trust.

Heatha and Philip adore sharing their home, and there are 3 tubby Labradors, who relentlessly patrol the grounds for any stray snacks or crumbs!

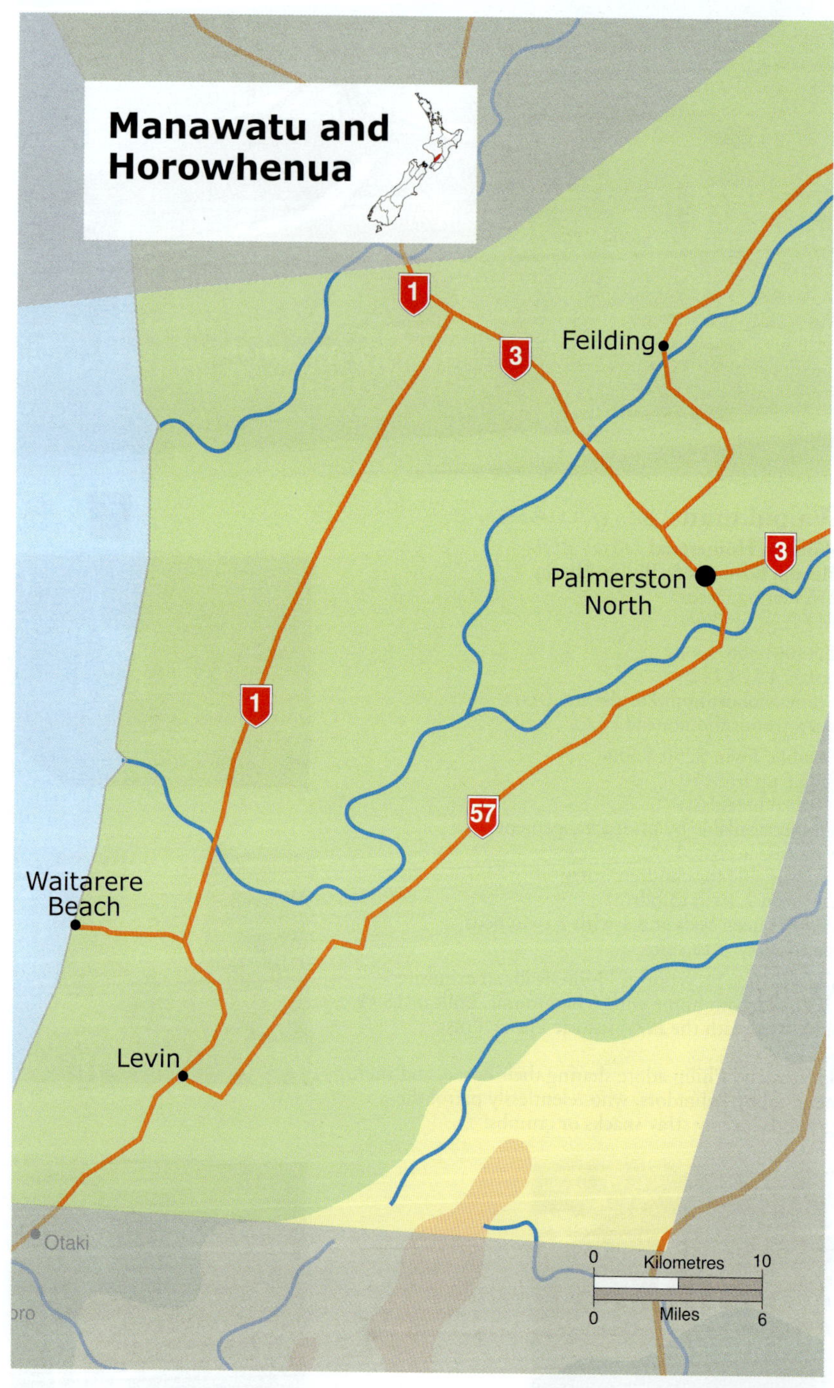
Manawatu and Horowhenua
Feilding
Palmerston North
Waitarere Beach
Levin
Otaki
1
3
57
0 Kilometres 10
0 Miles 6

Feilding *0.25 km N of Feilding Central*

Avoca Homestay *Homestay*

Margaret Hickmott
12 Freyberg Street,
Feilding

Tel (06) 323 4699
margh-avoca@inspire.net.nz

Double/Twin $100
Single $75
(Full breakfast)
Dinner $25 by arrangement
1 Queen 2 Twin (2 bdrm)
Bathrooms: 1 Ensuite 1 Family share

Enjoy a break in friendly Feilding, 14 times winner of New Zealand's Most Beautiful Town Award. You are assured of a warm welcome and an enjoyable stay in a comfortable smoke-free home set in an attractive garden with mature trees and a colourful shrubbery. Off-street parking is provided for your vehicle. The main bedroom has a queen-size bed, ensuite and an outside entrance for your sole use. We are within easy walking distance of the town centre and well situated for the Manfield Park complex.

Feilding *1 km E of Feilding Town Centre*

B&B Approved

Feilding Mahoe B&B *B&B Guest House Self contained B&B*

David & Lesley Klue
171 South Street,
Feilding, 5301

Tel (06) 323 0311
or 027 277 0235
purplepear@xtra.co.nz

Double/Twin $120-$180
Single $70-$100
(Continental breakfast provisions)
Dinner by arrangement
Off street parking,
Full cooking and Laundry Facilities
Eftpos accepted
Children and pets welcome
1 Queen 1 Single (1 bdrm)
Extra beds available
Bathrooms: 1 Ensuite

We enjoy our semi rural lifestyle with our three children, small dog, cat, four sheep and pig nestled amongst old native and fruit trees. Your privacy is assured in the guest house, separate from the main house, with views to gardens and a swimming pool. Situated just 1km from Manfield Park, and the town centre - you can enjoy great shopping and cafes, or alternatively, Palmerston North city is only a 15min drive. Welcome to Mahoe, your stay would be our pleasure.

Feilding *1.5 km W of Feilding*

Minffordd Cottage *Cottage with Kitchen*

Bob and Jenny Phillips
153, Halcombe Road,
RD 5 Feilding, 4775

Tel Mobile 021 331 449
or Land line (06) 323 1182
bjphillips@xtra.co.nz
www.minffordd.co.nz

Double/Twin $130-$150
Single $120
(Continental breakfast provisions)
Children over 6 $10
Alpaca Association of
New Zealand members $110
Visa MC accepted
Pet free home
1 Queen 2 Single (2 bdrm)
Bathrooms: 1 Guest share

Relax in our quiet, rural location, five minutes from Feilding and Manfield Park and 20 minutes from Palmerston North. Feilding has won the Keep New Zealand Beautiful award for 13 years and events include Farmers Market (Friday), tour of the largest lifestock market in the Southern Hemisphere (Fridays), Steam engine trips and Manfeild events. The cottage has gas hob, microwave, laundry, fridge freezer, and barbecue: Sky T.V., broadband and ample parking. Continental breakfast provided. Come and see our alpacas and sleep under an alpaca duvet.

Palmerston North *3 km NW of Palmerston North Centre*

B&B Approved

Bradgate *B&B Homestay*

Frances
3 Celtic Court,
Roslyn,
Palmerston North

Tel (06) 355 5956
or 021 0241 1864
Fax (06) 355 5956
vige@value.net.nz

Double/Twin $90
Single $50
(Full breakfast)
Dinner $30
1 Queen 1 Double 1 Twin (3 bdrm)
Bathrooms: 1 Guest share

Welcome to Bradgate, a four bedroomed brick townhouse located in a quiet cul-de-sac. 34 years ago my husband and I came to New Zealand. We owned a restaurant opposite Virginia Lake Wanganui, after retiring we ran a bed & breakfast overlooking the river. Having shifted to Palmerston North it was time to open up our home again. I have a Labrador named Crunchy. I enjoy playing golf, gardening and meeting people. Close to airport, will pick up if required. Non-smoking house, dinner by arrangement.

Palmerston North *3 km W of Palmerston North*

Andellen *Farmstay Guest House*

Kay and Warren Nitschke
580 Kairanga Bunnythorpe Road, R D 8, Palmerston North
Tel 027 244 1393 or (06) 355 4155
or 021 900 226 Fax (06) 355 4155
kw@inspire.net.nz

Double/Twin $110 Single $70
(Continental breakfast provisions)
Children $20 under 12
Dinner $30pp by arrangement
Visa MC accepted
Children and pets welcome
2 Queen 2 Single (3 bdrm)
Electric blankets on all beds
Bathrooms: 1 Ensuite 1 Private
Gorgeous spa bath in large bathroom

Welcome to ANDELLEN. Enjoy your very own separate modern three bedroom house with both a private and tranquil setting looking out over the farm.

Kay, Warren and Libby (13 years) would love to have you stay. Set on 70 acres with lovely native gardens and plenty of room for children to run around or play on the trampoline or jungle gym.

We offer guests the opportunity to relax in an elegant, tranquil country setting. Accomodation includes private lounge, TV and gorgeous spa bath. Seasonal farm activities available. Children very welcome. City 3km away. We have a small pet dog and cat and generally there are horses, sheep and cattle on the farm. Dinner by arrangement. Plenty of parking for cars, trucks and trailers. The Airport and hospital are only a few minutes away. Cattle or horses are welcome as yarding and paddock facilities are available.

Palmerston North *5.5 km E of City Centre*

Clairemont *B&B*
Joy & Dick Archer
10 James Line,
RD 10,
Palmerston North

Tel (06) 357 5508
or 021 063 6951
clairemont@ihug.co.nz

Double/Twin $80
Single $50
(Continental breakfast)
Not suitable for children
1 Double 1 Twin (2 bdrm)
Bright light rooms, comfortable beds
Bathrooms: 1 Guest share

Welcome to Clairemont. We are a rural spot within the city boundary, plenty of trees and a quite extensive garden. On our 1 1/4 acres we keep a few sheep, silky bantams, and our little dog Toby. We are handy to river walks, golf course, and shops are a few minutes away. We have a cosy, spacious family home we would like to share with you. Our interests are walking, gardening, model engineering and barbershop singing. Good off-street parking. Supper provided.

Palmerston North *13 km E of Palmerston North*

Country Lane Homestay *B&B Homestay*
Fay & Allan Hutchinson
52 Orrs Road,
RD 1 Aokautere,
Palmerston North

Tel (06) 326 8529
or 027 448 5833
Fax (06) 326 9216
countrylane@xtra.co.nz

Double/Twin $100-$140
Single $75-$95
(Full breakfast)
Dinner $25-$30
Not suitable for children
1 King/Twin 1 King 1 Queen
1 Double 1 Single (3 bdrm)
Bathrooms: 1 Ensuite 2 Private
1 Family share

Luxury country living, short distance from Palmerston North, near Manawatu Gorge, below wind farm. 10km from Pacific College and 2km from Equestrian Centre. Excellent stop over en route to/from Wellington or East Coast. Our home is newly decorated, with antiques in a country traditional style surrounded by our garden. Sawmill on the property, coloured sheep, horses and calves. Manawatu River borders our property. It is our pleasure to provide home-cooked meals with some local produce. Directions: please phone. A brochure with map is available.

Palmerston North *5 km SW of Central Palmerston North*

B&B Approved

Udys on Anders *B&B Apartment with Kitchen*

Glenda & Tim Udy
52 Anders Road,
Palmerston North

Tel (06) 354 1722
or 027 440 9299
kiwitim@clear.net.nz
www.udysonanders.co.nz

Double/Twin $130
Single $110
(Full breakfast)
Children $20
Dinner negotiable
Visa MC accepted
Children welcome
1 Queen 1 Double (1 bdrm)
Bathrooms: 1 Ensuite

We offer superior accommodation. An elegantly furnished self-contained apartment, own lounge and full kitchen. Quiet country location, huge lawn, edge of town, 7 minutes to CBD. Plexipave tennis court, beautiful mediterranean courtyard and large games room for our guests to make use of. Cleanliness, attention to detail and great hospitality are our priorities. We are well travelled and love meeting people. Enjoy your own space or get to know us. So... come, relax, enjoy. Tariff includes full breakfast. Apartment is smoke-free. Dinner by arrangement.

Waitarere Beach *14 km NW of Levin*

B&B Approved

Dunes *B&B Homestay*

Robyn & Grant Powell
10 Ngati Huia Place,
Waitarere Beach 5510

Tel (06) 368 6246
or 027 285 3643
sand.dunes@xtra.co.nz
http://waitarere.dunes.googlepages.com

Double/Twin $135
Single $100
(Continental breakfast)
Dinner $30
Visa MC accepted
2 Queen (2 bdrm)
Bathrooms: 2 Ensuite

Robyn & Grant Powell welcome you to our absolute beachfront retreat. Enjoy beach walks and magnificent views of Kapiti and Mounts Taranaki and Ruapehu. We offer 2 queen-size bedrooms with own private entrance and deck areas, ensuites, own living areas with TV, tea/coffee making facilities - continental breakfast provided. Situated 14km north west of Levin, approximately 1 and a half hours from Wellington and 35 minutes from Palmerston North. Laundry facilities, off-street parking, non-smoking. Dinner by arrangement.

Levin *1 km NE of Levin*

Fantails *B&B Cottage with Kitchen Self-contained cottages*

Heather Watson
40 MacArthur Street,
Levin 5510

Tel (06) 368 9011
Fax (06) 368 9011
fantails@xtra.co.nz
www.fantails.co.nz

Double/Twin $130-$160
Single $120-$135
(Special breakfast)
Dinner by arrangement
Self-contained cottages $110-$150
Visa MC accepted
Children and pets welcome
1 King 2 Queen 1 Twin
4 Single (4 bdrm)
Bathrooms: 3 Ensuite 1 Private

Fantails offers a choice of self contained Cottages or Bed & Breakfast in two acres of botanical gardens. Certified organic food and home baking will tantilise your taste buds. Gluten free, dairy free/all specialities. Our friendly staff will make your stay memorable. Our unique location offers outdoor pursuits - 6 beaches all within a 30 minute drive. Travel packages available, either tramping or travelling to the famous Kapiti Bird Sanctuary. View our Activities page for more information. Memories are made here.

Levin *5 km S of Levin*

Ardo Highland Haven *B&B Farmstay*

Malcolm & Rachel Phillips
170 McLeavey Road,
RD 20, Levin 5570

Tel (06) 368 7080
or 021 506 990
Fax (06) 368 7080
info@ardohighlandhaven.co.nz
www.ardohighlandhaven.co.nz

Double/Twin $130
Single $100 (Full breakfast)
Dinner by arrangement $35 inc. wine
Should you require twin beds please use both rooms!
Visa MC accepted
2 Queen 1 Single (3 bdrm)
Our guest rooms are upstairs and are sunny and private.
Bathrooms: 1 Private
We host one party only at a time.

Travelling to or from Wellington? A warm welcome awaits you at Ardo, our country home on 10 acres,5km south of levin. Upstairs is for you alone as we host one party only at a time. We have a dairy farming background, and now breed highland cattle and friendly sheep. Hosting is wonderful - such interesting guests from many countries. Mandy, our Australian Terrier enjoys our guests, and Lola, our tabby cat, may put in an appearance! Please take time to read our Guest Reviews.

Levin *3 km NE of Levin*

Annandale Manor *B&B Farmstay Feijoa Orchard*

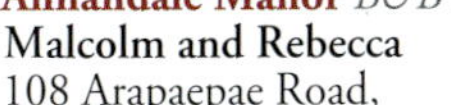

Malcolm and Rebecca
108 Arapaepae Road,
SH 57, Levin, 5510

Tel 0800 201 712
or (06) 368 5476
Fax (06) 368 5473
annandalemanor@xtra.co.nz
www.annandalemanor.co.nz

Double/Twin $135-$150
Single $100-$120
(Continental breakfast)
Children under 12 years half price
Dinner Two course $35,
Three Course $55 per person
Cooked Breakfast $10 Spa Pool
Children and pets welcome
1 Queen 1 Double 1 Twin (3 bdrm)
Bathrooms: 1 Guest share

Look no further you will find it here colonial elegance infused with peace, serenity and abundant hospitality. Prepare to be charmed by the grand old lady that is Annandale Manor. The gardens and orchard with bird song and ambience. You will find activities to energise or slumber to revitalise, with hunting and rafting to beaches and bush walks. Its all here now just waiting for you. The Horowhenua experience that you will not want to miss. As we do not have visa and or eftpos facilities we request our guests to note that we only take cash as full payment at check out times. Thank you.

~

Levin *2 km N of Levin*

Blueberry Art B&B *B&B Farmstay Apartment with kitchen Blueberry Orchard*

Maggie & Joe Kieninger
7 Heatherlea East Road, Levin

Tel (06) 367 3648
or 027 422 5489
Fax (06) 368 3651
info@blueberryart.co.nz
www.blueberryart.co.nz

Double/Twin $100 -$120
Single $80-$100
(Breakfast by arrangement)
Children welcome by arrangement
Long term by arrangement
Visa MC Eftpos accepted
2 Queen (2 bdrm)
Bedsofa in each unit
Bathrooms: 2 Ensuite - new facilites

Our self-contained accommodation is surrounded by park-like gardens with alpacas and a fruit and nut orchard. Two completely renovated flats with fully equipped kitchen and cosy woodburner are waiting for you to relax and enjoy the friendly atmosphere. Freeview TV is installed as well as Internet access to keep you entertained and informed. Take a walk through the farm and feed the friendly alpacas. Stroll at the near beach or tramp in the Tararura Ranges. Joe & Maggie, artists in residence, English/German speaking..

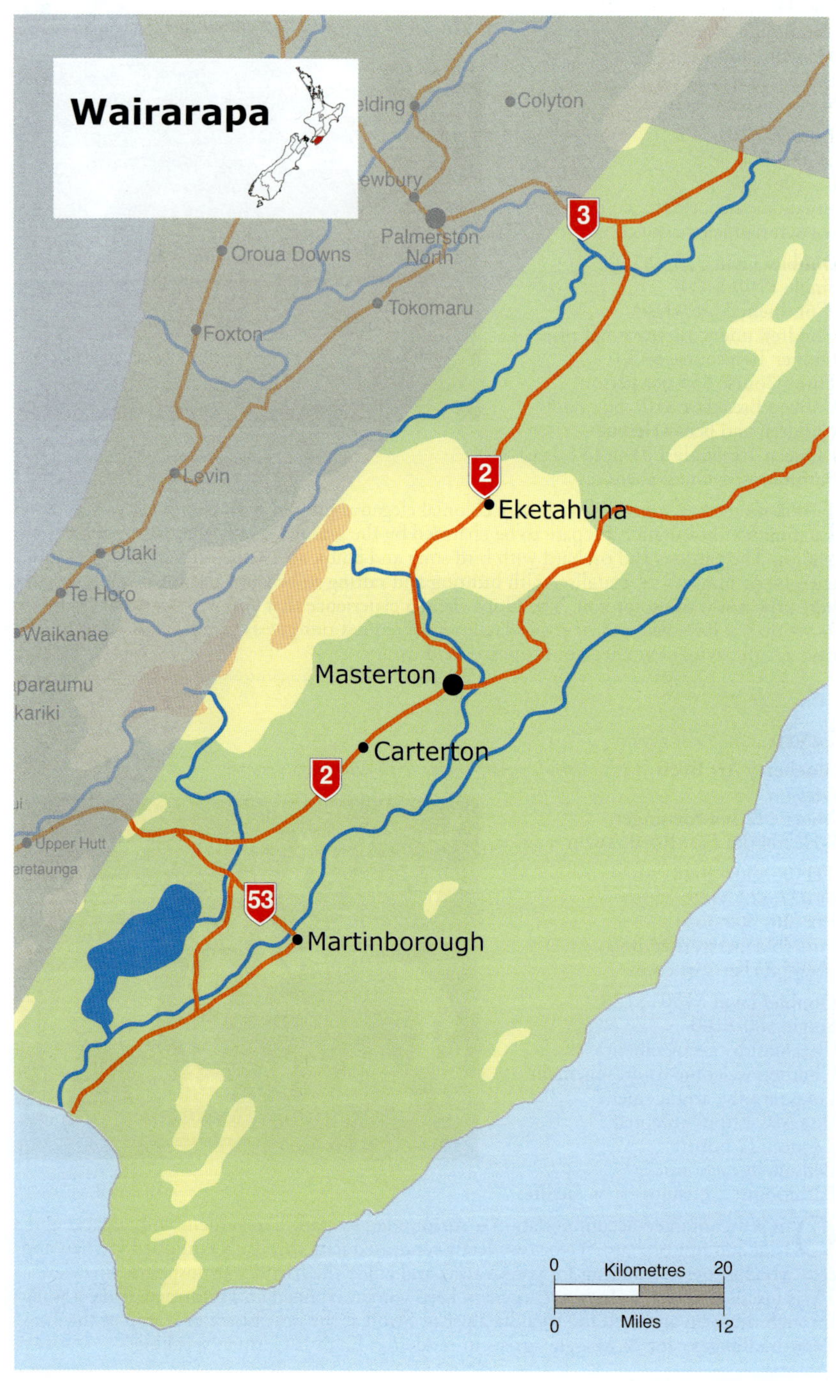
Wairarapa
Colyton
Palmerston North
Oroua Downs
Tokomaru
Foxton
Levin
Eketahuna
Otaki
Te Horo
Waikanae
Masterton
Carterton
Upper Hutt
Martinborough
3
2
2
53
0
Kilometres
20
0
Miles
12

Eketahuna *45 km N of Masterton*

Brookfields Lodge *B&B Licensed restaurant and separate self catering cottage*

Terry and Corinna Carew
31 Alfredton Road, Eketahuna, 4900
Tel 06 375 8686
or 021 214 7039
or 021 145 5947
terry@brookfieldslodge.co.nz
www.brookfieldslodge.co.nz

Double/Twin $120-$140
Single $120-$120 (Full breakfast)
Dinner available in
the attached restaurant
Cottage price on application
Visa MC Eftpos accepted
Children welcome
3 Queen (3 bdrm)
Stylish, relaxing en suite
accommodation
Bathrooms: 3 Ensuite
1 bathroom in self catering

Brookfields is ideally situated halfway between Wellington and Napier providing the discerning traveller with a relaxed friendly place to stay overnight or longer. Originally built as a 3 bedroom villa in 1910, this grand old home has been tastefully restored to provide comfortable en-suite accommodation in the heart of the Tararua District. The emphasis is on good food, comfortable surroundings and pleasant company.

Masterton *3 km W of Masterton*

Harefield *B&B Farmstay Cottage with Kitchen*

Marion Ahearn
147 Upper Plain Road,
Masterton
Tel (06) 377 4070
Fax (06) 377 4070

Double/Twin $90
Single $45-$50
(Full breakfast)
Children half price
Self-contained flat for 2 $60
Children welcome
1 Double 1 Single (1 bdrm)
Double & single in flat,
double & single in house.
Bathrooms: 2 Private
1 in flat, 1 private in house

A warm welcome awaits you at Harefield, a small farmlet on the edge of town. A quiet country garden surrounds the cedar house and self-contained flat. The flat has 1 bedroom with double and single beds. 2 divan beds in living area. Self-cater or have breakfast in our warm dining room. Convenient for restaurants, showgrounds, vineyards, schools, tramping. 1.5 hour drive to Picton Ferry. We enjoy meeting people, aviation, travel, reading, art, farming and tramping. Baby facilities available. Smoke-free.

Masterton *10 km W of Masterton*

Tidsfordriv *B&B Homestay*

Glenys Hansen
54 Cootes Road,
Matahiwi,
RD 8,
Masterton 5888

Tel (06) 378 9967
Fax (06) 378 9957
ghansen@contact.net.nz

Double/Twin $95-$100
Single $60 (Full breakfast)
Children half price
Dinner $25 by arrangement
includes pre-dinner drink
Visa MC accepted
Children welcome
1 Queen 2 Single (2 bdrm)
1 Queen room, 1 twin room
Bathrooms: 1 Private

A warm welcome awaits you at 'Tidsfordriv' - a 64 acre farmlet - seven kilometres off the main bypass route. Enjoy the comforts of a modern home set in parklike surroundings with large gardens & lakes. Bird watch with ease and enjoy the peaceful serenity of this 'Rural Retreat'. Glenys invites you to join her for dinner and enjoy good conversation about gardening, conservation and travel. A friendly Labrador is the outdoor pet. Enjoy visits to Pukaha Mount Bruce Wildlife Centre, and other Wairarapa attractions.

Masterton *1 km E of Masterton*

B&B Approved

Mas des Saules *B&B Homestay*

Mary & Steve Blakemore
35A Pokohiwi Road,
Homebush, Masterton

Tel (06) 377 2577
or 027 620 8728
or 021 027 23828
Fax (06) 377 2578
mas-des-saules@wise.net.nz

Double/Twin $125
Single $85
(Full breakfast)
Children $40
Dinner $40
Visa MC accepted
Children and pets welcome
2 Queen (2 bdrm)
Bathrooms: 1 Guest share

Hidden down a tranquil country lane, discover our authentic French Provencal farmhouse with its landscaped garden, stream, and courtyard. Swimming and trout fishing in nearby river. Our children have departed, leaving us with two cats, our small dog, and cattle on our small farm. Guest lounge and bathroom with bath and shower. Open fire and central heating. Enjoy farmhouse cooking with fresh vegetables from our large country garden, barbecues and picnic lunches. We are a well-travelled couple who enjoy helping guests discover the unspoilt Wairarapa.

Masterton *1 km W of Urban Boundary*

Llandaff *B&B Farmstay*

B&B Approved

Elizabeth & Robin Dunlop
183 Upper Plain Road Masterton

Tel (06) 378 6628
or 021 359 562
Fax (06) 378 6628
llandaff@xtra.co.nz
www.wairarapa.co.nz/llandaff

Double/Twin $110-$130
Single $70-$120 (Full breakfast)
Children $25
Dinner $30-$35
Children welcome
1 King 2 Queen 1 Double
1 Twin (5 bdrm)
Decorated in the style of the historic house
Bathrooms: 1 Ensuite 3 Guest share
Ensuite shower only

Elegantly restored, the homestead boasts beautiful native NZ timbers throughout, wood panelled rooms, polished floors, old pull-handle toilets, a 'coffin' bath, open fireplaces and cosy woodburning kitchen stove. Explore the historic hayloft and stables, washhouse, produce shed, gardener's shed, pavilion and dove cote. See the vintage farm machinery. Relax in the majestic garden beneath 120 year old trees, or wander the farm and feed the animals. Bike riding, croquet and petanque are available to guests. Enjoy a cooked breakfast with dinner available on request.

Masterton *8 km E of Masterton*

Vista Homestay *B&B Homestay*

B&B Approved

Carol and Quenten Hansen
339A Te Ore Ore Settlement Road,
RD 6,
Masterton 5886

Tel (06) 370 8919
or 027 360 6499
cqhansen@xtra.co.nz

Double/Twin $95
Single $65
(Special breakfast)
Children $25
Dinner $25 per adult includes pre dinner drink
Visa MC accepted
Pet free home
Children welcome
1 Queen 2 Single (2 bdrm)
One queen room, one twin room
Bathrooms: 1 Private
1 party per booking

More than just stunning views, Vista Homestay is situated in a tranquil environment where you will be welcomed by the smell of fresh flowers home baking and good coffee. Our modern home and garden are for you to enjoy along with a private spa pool. To make your visit memorable we would love you to join us for dinner.

Carterton *1 km N of Carterton*

Homecroft *B&B*
Christine & Neil Stewart
Somerset Road,
RD 2,
Carterton

Tel (06) 379 5959
homecroft@xtra.co.nz

Double/Twin $100-$110
Single $60
(Full breakfast)
Dinner $30pp by arrangement
1 Queen 1 Double 1 Twin (3 bdrm)
Queen & twin in house,
double ensuite seperate from house
Bathrooms: 1 Ensuite 1 Private

Homecroft is surrounded by our country garden. Handy to the vineyards, crafts, antiques, and golf courses of the Wairarapa. Wellington and the inter-island ferry are 90 minutes away. Guest accommodation is in a separate wing of the house with small lounge, the bedrooms open onto a deck. The double room with ensuite, The Croft, is separate from the house. All bedrooms overlook the garden. A leisurely breakfast at Homecroft is an enjoyable experience. We look forward to making your stay with us happy and relaxing.

~

Carterton *3 km S of Masterton*

Pinnacle Grove *Homestay*
Alma & Ad van der Tol
240 Norfolk Road,
RD 1
Carterton, 5791

Tel 06 370 3309
or 021 682 216
avdt@pinnacle-grove.walnuts.co.nz

Double/Twin $120
Single $100
(Continental breakfast)
Visa MC accepted
Children welcome
2 King (2 bdrm)
Bathrooms: 1 Guest share

Pinnacle Grove Homestay is situated in Carterton District at a short distance from Masterton township on the road to the Tararua Forest Park and Mt Holdsworth recreation area. Jessie, our Jack Russel terrier will welcome you enthusiastically and so will Alma and Ad in our modern, comfortable home situated on 28 acres of walnut plantation in a relaxed and friendly atmosphere. Linger and relax on the verandah, walk in the Tararua Forest Park or enjoy the wine, arts and craft of the Wairarapa.

Martinborough *0.5 km NW of Martinborough*

B&B Approved

Oak House *B&B*

Polly & Chris Buring
45 Kitchener Street,
Martinborough

Tel (06) 306 9198
Fax (06) 306 8198
chrispolly.oakhouse@xtra.co.nz
http://buringswines.co.nz

Double/Twin $120-$140
Single $60-$70
(Special breakfast)
Children by arrangement
Dinner by arrangement
Visa MC accepted
Children welcome
2 Queen 2 Single (3 bdrm)
Bathrooms: 1 Ensuite 1 Guest share

Our characterful 80 year old Californian bungalow offers gracious accommodation. Our spacious lounge provides a relaxed setting for sampling winemaker Chris's wonderful products. Our guest wing has its own entrance, bathroom (large bath and shower) and separate toilet. Our new bedroom has ensuite facilities. Bedrooms enjoy afternoon sun and garden views. Breakfast features fresh croissants, home-preserved local fruits and conserves. Creative cook Polly matches delicious dishes (often local game) with Chris's great wines. Tour our onsite winery with Chris. Meet our multi-talented cats.

Martinborough *1 km W of Martinborough*

B&B Approved

The Old Manse *B&B Homestay*

Sandra & John Hargrave
Corner Grey & Roberts Streets,
Martinborough

Tel (06) 306 8599
or 0800 399 229
Fax (06) 306 8540
info@oldmanse.co.nz
www.oldmanse.co.nz

Double/Twin $170-$190
(Full breakfast)
Visa MC Diners
Amex Eftpos accepted
Not suitable for children
5 Queen 1 Twin (6 bdrm)
Bathrooms: 6 Ensuite

In the heart of the wine district, a beautifully restored Presbyterian Manse, built 1876, has been transformed into a boutique homestay. Spacious, relaxed accommodation in a quiet, peaceful setting. 1 twin, 5 queen-size bedrooms all with their own ensuites. All day sun. Off-street parking, open fireplace. Amenities include spa pool, petanque, billiards. Enjoy breakfast or wine overlooking vineyard. Walking distance to Martinborough Square with selection of excellent restaurants. Close to vineyards, antique and craft shops, adventure quad bikes and golf courses. Qualmark 4+

Martinborough *1 km S of Martinborough Village Square*

The Martinborough Connection *B&B*

B&B Approved

David & Lorraine Murray
80 Jellicoe Street,
Martinborough, 5711

Tel (06) 306 9708
or 027 438 1581
Fax (06) 306 9706
martinboroughconnection@xtra.co.nz
www.martinboroughconnection.co.nz

Double/Twin $130-$140
Single $110-$115 (Full breakfast)
Children in room with extra bed $15
Additional adult in room
with extra bed $30
Visa MC Eftpos accepted
Pet free home Children welcome
4 Queen 1 Single (4 bdrm)
One room has a sofa bed
in addition to queen
Bathrooms: 4 Ensuite

Bed & breakfast accommodation situated within the Martinborough wine village. Originally built in 1889 the property has been fully restored retaining its original character. Open your bedroom door to a sunny verandah & garden. Start the day with a scrumptious breakfast, before visiting Martinboroughs wineries,or Cape Palliser with its spectacular coastline,lighthouse,& furseal colony. Relax at the end of the day in the guest lounge with its open fire or outside in the lovely gardens. We look forward to hosting you.

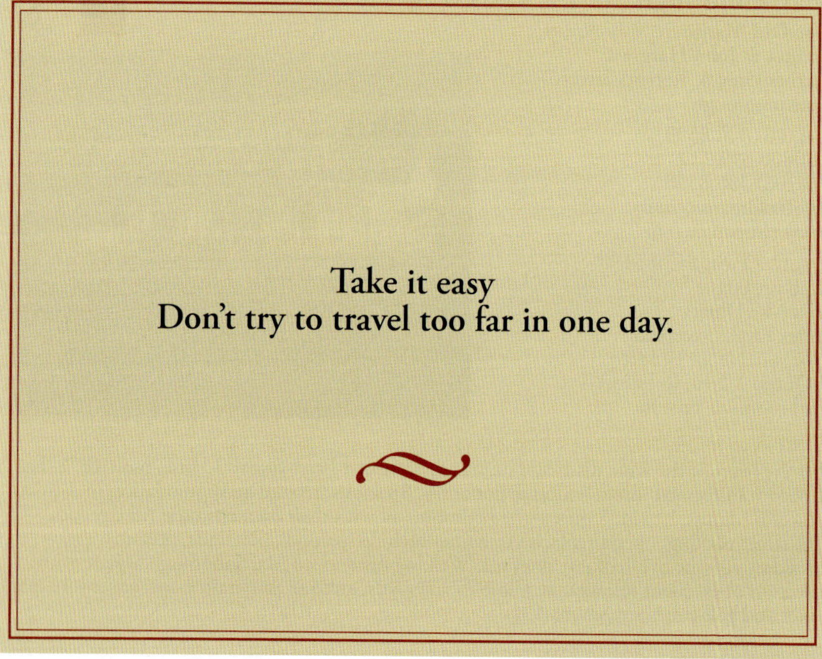

Wellington
Kapiti Island
Kapiti Coast
Otaki
Te Horo
Waikanae
Paraparaumu
Raumati
Plimmerton
Paremata
Tawa
Upper Hutt
Stokes Valley
Lower Hutt
Petone
Wainuomata
Eastbourne
1
2
See Wellington City next page
0 Kilometres 10
0 Miles 6

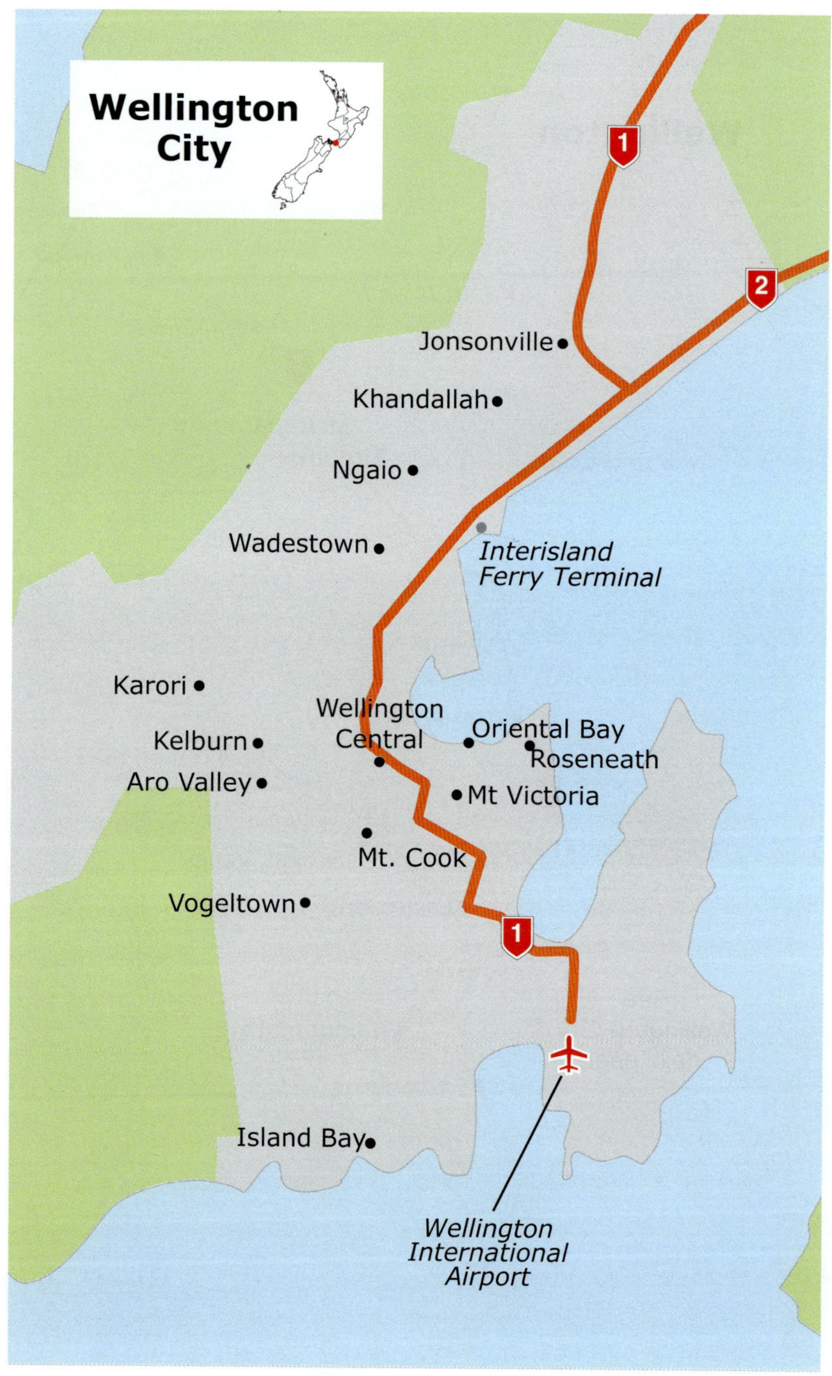
Wellington
City
1
2
Jonsonville
Khandallah
Ngaio
Wadestown
Interisland
Ferry Terminal
Karori
Wellington
Central
Kelburn
Aro Valley
Oriental Bay
Roseneath
Mt Victoria
Mt. Cook
Vogeltown
1
Island Bay
Wellington
International
Airport

Te Horo *7 km N of Waikanae*

Pateke Lagoons Wetlands *B&B Farmstay Separate Suite*

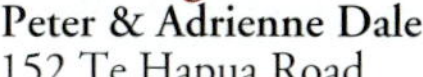

Peter & Adrienne Dale
152 Te Hapua Road,
Te Horo, RD 1,
Kapiti Coast

Tel (06) 364 2222
or 0275 439 661
Fax (06) 364 2214
peterdale@xtra.co.nz
www.pateke-lagoons.co.nz

Double/Twin $195
Single $195 (Special breakfast)
Dinner $65 including wine
Visa MC accepted
Not suitable for children
2 Queen 1 Single (2 bdrm)
2 en suite bedrooms
Bathrooms: 2 Ensuite 1 Private
Wheelchair bathroom

Pateke Lagoons overlooks a private 50 acre wetland and waterfowl refuge on the Kapiti Coast. It offers peace and quiet in tranquil rural surroundings. 2 guest rooms, each with ensuite and private courtyard. Large lounge with wildfowl and wetland ecology library. Beautiful views of farmland, sea and wetland. Easy 30 minute walking tracks through native bush and wetland. Fresh seafood is our specialty with garden fresh vegetables. Special breakfast using local products. Close to Ruth Pretty Cooking School. Open wetlands are unsuitable for children.

Waikanae *1 km E of Waikanae*

Country Patch *Apartment with Kitchen Cottage with Kitchen*

Sue & Brian Wilson
18 Kea Street,
Waikanae

Tel (04) 293 5165
or 027 457 8421
or 027 296 3716
Fax (04) 293 5164
stay@countrypatch.co.nz
www.countrypatch.co.nz

Double/Twin $160-$240
(Full breakfast provisions)
Children $30
Visa MC Eftpos accepted
Children welcome
2 King/Twin 1 Queen
2 Single (3 bdrm)
Bathrooms: 3 Ensuite

Two delightful self-contained accommodation sites. Country patch studio with its own entrance and deck has a queen bed with ensuite and twin beds on the mezzanine floor of the kitchen lounge. Country patch villa has an open fire and a large verandah with magic views. It is wheelchair accessible and the 2 bedrooms (each with ensuite) have king beds that unzip to twin. We warmly invite you to share our patch of the country.

Waikanae Beach *5 km W of Waikanae*

Konini Cottage & Homestead *B&B Separate Suite Cottage with Kitchen*

Maggie & Bob Smith
26 Konini Crescent, Waikanae Beach, Kapiti Coast

Tel (04) 904 6610 or 027 260 6492
Fax (04) 904 6610 konini@paradise.net.nz
www.konini.co.nz

Double/Twin $130-$160 Single $100-$150
(Breakfast by arrangement)
Children $15 under 13yrs. Dinner Cafes/Restaurants within walking
Extra Adult $25 Visa MC Amex accepted Children welcome
2 Queen 2 Single (3 bdrm)
Bathrooms: 1 Ensuite 1 Private

Bob and Maggie welcome you to the haven of KONINI. You can enjoy a walk or swim at the endless sandy ocean beach, have a game of golf on the adjoining golf links, or simply sit on the veranda and enjoy the peace and tranquillity of the large garden. Being only 1 hours drive from the Interisland ferries it is the perfect stop off. Both the Homestead and the Cottage are of Lockwood solid timber construction. Bob, a cabinetmaker, has crafted all the furniture. Maggie has developed the large garden.

THE HOMESTEAD SUITE: A traditional B&B in its own wing of the main house. The suite comprises Queen bedroom, an adjoining guests sitting room overlooking the garden & private ensuite bathroom. Guests may have breakfast(included in tariff) in their suite or join us in our dining room.

THE COTTAGE: Self contained & situated in the garden. Tastefully furnished offering a spacious 70 Sq Meters of self-catering accommodation with fully equipped kitchen. Two bedrooms (one Queen & one Twin), lounge with cable TV, Shower room, & laundry facilities. Breakfast can be provided by arrangement.

Directions: Turn off SH1 at traffic lights to the Beach. 4 km to automotive garage. Take right fork then next right. 1km to Konini Cres.

Waikanae *6 km E of Waikanae*

RiverStone *B&B Cottage with Kitchen*
Paul & Eppie Murton
111 Ngatiawa Road,
Waikanae
Tel (04) 293 1936
riverstone@paradise.net.nz
www.riverstone.co.nz

Double/Twin $130
Single $90 (Full breakfast)
Children $45
Visa MC accepted
1 Queen 1 Twin (2 bdrm)
Bathrooms: 1 Private

Birdsong, the sound of the river and complete privacy. Peace and quiet with a scrumptious breakfast and comfortable accommodation. Riverstone has scenic views a garden with river walks and local pottery and cafe. Waikanae, 5 minutes by car, has cafes, shops, boutiques, Lindale Farm Park, the Southward Car Museum, Nga Manu Bird Sanctuary, golf courses and beautiful beaches. Pick up from train or bus. Laundry facilities. Smoke-free. Internet available.

Waikanae Beach *6 km NE of Waikanae Beach*

(Helen's) Waikanae Beach B&B *B&B Homestay*
Helen Anderson
115 Tutere Street,
Waikanae Beach,
Kapiti Coast 5036
Tel (04) 902 5829
or 021 259 3396
or 0800 897 143
Fax (04) 902 5840
waikanaebeachbandb@paradise.net.nz
www.waikanaebeachbandb.net

Double/Twin $140-$160
Single $120-$140 (Full breakfast)
Children negotiable
Visa MC accepted
Pet free home
2 Queen 1 Single (2 bdrm)
Fold-down/roll-away bed available for Seaview Room
Bathrooms: 1 Ensuite 1 Private

Needing time out to relax and unwind? Then come and experience Helen's warm, friendly hospitality by the sea. Direct access to a long sandy beach. Kick off your shoes and paddle barefoot in the shallows as you leisurely walk the beach. Marvel at beautiful sunsets, wonderful views of Kapiti Island, the Tararua Ranges, not to mention the night skies. All-cotton bed linen, bath robes, electric blankets, and tea-making facilities in guest rooms. Cable TV main lounge only. Tasty home-cooked food. Cafes/Restaurants close by.

Waikanae *45 km N of Wellington*

Waimoana *B&B Homestay*
Elizabeth and Bryan Couchman
63 Kakariki Grove,
Waikanae 5036,
Kapiti Coast
Tel (04) 293 2005
or 021 0222 0217
relax@waimoana.co.nz
www.waimoana.co.nz

Double/Twin $150
Single $120
(Continental breakfast)
Visa MC accepted
1 Queen (1 bdrm)
Bathrooms: 1 Ensuite

Waimoana was purpose built as a quality homestay. Enjoy majestic sea views over Kapiti from the sundeck or pool. Living rooms radiate from a glass-roofed atrium featuring an indoor swimming pool, garden and waterfall. Our guest room has its own private entrance, parking and ensuite facilities. Local activities include native bush walks, beaches, first-class restaurants and cafes, craft and mosaic shops, bird sanctuaries and golf courses. A warm welcome awaits you from our three sons and cat Tabitha.

Waikanae *1 km E of Waikanae*

Te Rimu B & B *B&B*
Barbara Baylis
11 Hira Street,
Waikanae 5036
Tel (04) 293 2535
or 021 118 9845
enquiries@terimu.co.nz
www.terimu.co.nz

Double/Twin $120-$150
Single $80-$100
(Full breakfast)
Dinner by prior arrangement
Visa MC accepted
Pet free home
Not suitable for children
1 King/Twin 1 Double (2 bdrm)
1 King/twin room, 1 double room
Bathrooms: 1 Guest share

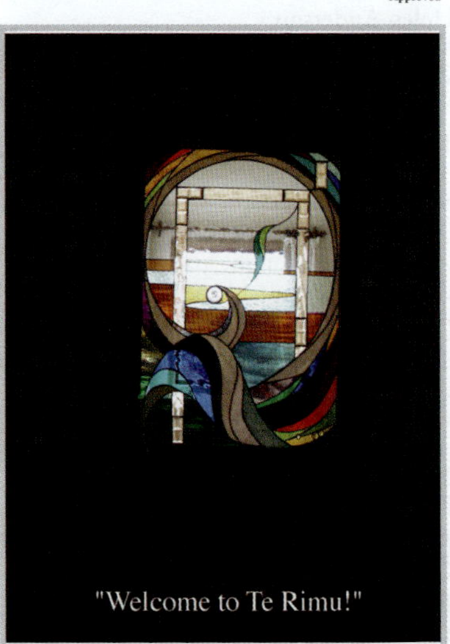

Join me in my beautiful home set among trees, tuis and tranquility on the eastern slopes of the hill in Waikanae.I enjoy good company and good food and will endeavour that you do also. As I work away from home forward bookings would be appreciated, so I can give you great hospitality.

Raumati Beach *3 km SW of Paraparaumu*

B&B Approved

Sea Haven *B&B Homestay*

Jan & Laurie Bason
325 Rosetta Road,
Raumati Beach,
Paraparaumu

Tel (04) 902 0047
or 021 0279 8803
jan-laurie@paradise.net.nz

Double/Twin $110
Single $95
(Continental breakfast)
Visa MC accepted
Not suitable for children
1 Queen (1 bdrm)
1 single blowup bed if required
Bathrooms: 1 Private

Welcome to our spacious smoke-free home. Our guest room opens to a small garden, with seating amongst native trees. Private access to the beach. 250 metres from village shops, restaurants, swimming pool, bowling green and Marine Gardens. Kapiti Miniature Railway is situated at Marine Gardens with various locomotives running on Sunday afternoons. Golf courses in the area. Laurie, a railway enthusiast, has a miniature locomotive and collection of railway memorabilia. We enjoy overseas travel, and around NZ in our Motorhome. Elderly shy cat in residence.

Plimmerton *6 km N of Porirua*

B&B Approved

Aquavilla Seaside Self-contained B&B *B&B Cottage with Kitchen*

Graham & Carolyn Wallace
16 Steyne Avenue,
Plimmerton,
Porirua

Tel (04) 233 1146
or 027 231 0141
aquavilla@paradise.net.nz
www.aquavilla.co.nz

Double/Twin $180
Single $160 (Special breakfast)
Children $50
Dinner $50
Extra adults $50
Visa MC accepted
Children welcome
1 Queen 1 Single (1 bdrm)
Bathrooms: 1 Private

In the gorgeous garden of our seaside villa, your architecturally-designed accommodation features courtyard, kitchenette, barbeque and comfort-plus. Guests love the pure cotton sheets, flowers,homemade biscuits and artistic touches. Explore Wellington easily by car or rail, or enjoy the forest and beach walks, cafes and restaurants, golfing, galleries, shopping and windsurfing close by. Scrumptious breakfast menu has light or full cooked options: homemade muesli or blueberry pancakes and sweetcorn fritters, etc. Warm and widely-travelled, we're art and nature lovers and very welcoming! Safe parking.

Paremata *5 km N of Porirua*

Cottage on the Inlet *Self Contained Cottage*

B&B Approved

Michelle & Mike
300a Paremata Road,
Paremata,
Wellington
Tel (04) 234 1699
or 021 305 342
Fax (04) 234 8817
mdykes@dykesassoc.co.nz
www.cottageontheinlet.co.nz

Double/Twin $160
Single $160
(Full provisions supplied)
Dinner not provided
Children & pets welcome
1 Queen 2 Single (2 bdrm)
Bathrooms: 1 Private

Are you looking for a private peaceful retreat? Located just north of Wellington on the Pauatahanui Inlet with unrestricted views of the water, the Cottage on the Inlet could be just what you need. The self contained cottage is nestled in an old fruit orchard and is part of a larger property built in the early 1900s. The cottage has recently been renovated and is spacious yet cosy whilst still retaining that 'country cottage' feel. Come and enjoy your retreat today.

All our B&Bs are non-smoking unless stated otherwise in the text.

Tawa *15 km NW of Wellington CBD*

Perry B&B Homestay *B&B Homestay Homestay B&B*

B&B Approved

Jocelyn & David Perry
5 Fyvie Avenue,
Tawa,
Wellington 5028

Tel (04) 232 7664
djperry@actrix.co.nz
www.perryhomestay.co.nz

Double/Twin $100
Single $65
(Special breakfast)
Children Under 15 $30
Dinner by arrangement
Visa MC accepted
Children welcome
1 Double 1 Twin 1 Single (3 bdrm)
Bathrooms: 1 Guest share
1 Family share

We are a retired couple. Together with our cat "Boots" we welcome you to stay with us. There is a 5 minute walk to the suburban railway station with a half hourly service into the city (15 minutes) and north to the Kapiti Coast. Alternatively you can drive north to the coast, enjoying sea and rural views before sampling tourist attractions in this area. We are happy to provide transport to and from the Interisland ferry. Laundry facilities available.

Upper Hutt *45 km N of Wellington*

Tranquility Homestay *B&B Homestay*

Elaine & Alan
136 Akatarawa Road,
Birchville, Upper Hutt

Tel (04) 526 6948 or 027 675 8341
or FreePhone 0800 270 787
Fax (04) 526 6968
tranquility@xtra.co.nz
www.tranquilityhomestay.co.nz

Double/Twin $90-$130
Single $75-$130
(Continental breakfast)
Children negotiable
Dinner $30 by prior arrangement
Airport pick up
Visa MC Diners accepted
Children and pets welcome
1 King/Twin 1 Queen 1 Double 1 Single (4 bdrm)
Queen and Double have Ensuites, King twin or King super
Bathrooms: 2 Ensuite 2 Family share - Luxury Queen Ensuite with spa bath

Tranquility Homestay. The name says it all. Escape from the stress of city life approx 25 minutes from Wellington off SH2. Close to Upper Hutt - restaurants, cinema, golf, racecourse, leisure centre (swimming), bush walks. We are near the confluence of the Hutt and Akatarawa Rivers which is noted for its fishing. 13km to Staglands. Country setting, relax, listen to NZ tuis, watch the fantails or wood pigeons, or simply relax and read. Comfortable, warm and friendly hospitality.

Lower Hutt *1 km N of Lower Hutt Centre*

Judy & Bob's Place *Homestay*
Judy & Bob Vine
11 Ngaio Crescent,
Woburn, Lower Hutt

Tel (04) 971 1192
or 021 510 682
or 0274 500 682
Fax (04) 971 6192
bob.vine@paradise.net.nz
www.bobvine.gen.nz

Double/Twin $130
Single $65
(Full breakfast)
Dinner $35
Visa MC Diners Amex accepted
Pet free home
1 Queen 2 Single (2 bdrm)
Bathrooms: 1 Private
Limit: 1 booking a time to obviate bathroom sharing

Located in Woburn, a picturesque and quiet central city suburb of Lower Hutt, known for its generous sized houses and beautiful gardens. Within walking distance of the Lower Hutt downtown, 15 minutes drive from central Wellington, its railway station and ferry terminals; airport 25 minutes; 3 minutes walk to Woburn Rail Station. Private lounge and TV. Love to entertain and share hearty Kiwi style cooking with good New Zealand wine. Laundry facilities. Transfer transport available. High speed Internet connections.

Lower Hutt *3 km E of Hutt City*

Casa Bianca *B&B Apartment with Kitchen long term stays available*
Jo & Dave Comparini
10 Damian Grove,
Lower Hutt, Wellington

Tel (04) 569 7859
or 027 357 4395
Fax (04) 569 7859
casabiancanz@xtra.co.nz
http://Casa Bianca NZ.

Double/Twin $95-$120
Single $75-$100
(Continental breakfast provisions)
Longterm stays available
Visa MC accepted
Pet free home
Not suitable for children
1 King 1 Single (1 bdrm)
1 large king & single in the lounge
Bathrooms: 1 Private

Our B&B is close to Hutt City. A short hop to the Open Polytech, Hutt Hospital, and Waterloo station. Wellington is 20 minutes away. We have a lovely self-contained apartment with double bedroom. bathroom, large lounge, fully equipped kitchen, laundry and a single bed in the lounge. Breakfast provisions provided in apartment. Stays long or short term. If you are relocating call us first. Enjoy our special hospitality. Broadband, Safe off-street parking. Not suitable for children. Non smoking please.

Lower Hutt *0.5 km SE of Lower Hutt*

Rose Cottage *B&B Homestay*

Maureen & Gordon Gellen
70A Hautana Street,
Lower Hutt,
Wellington

Tel (04) 566 7755
or 021 481 732
Fax (04) 566 0777
gellen@xtra.co.nz

Double/Twin $110-$125
Single $95-$110
(Full breakfast)
Dinner $35 by arrangement
For 1 night stay, $10 surcharge
Visa MC accepted
Not suitable for children
1 King/Twin 1 Queen (2 bdrm)
Bathrooms: 1 Ensuite 1 Family share

Relax in the comfort of our cosy home which is just a 5 minute walk to the Hutt City Centre and 15 minutes to ferries. Originally built in 1910 the house has been fully renovated. Interests,travel,sports and live theatre. As well as TV in guest room there's coffee and tea-making facilities. Breakfast will be served in our dining room at your convenience. Unsuitable for children. We look forward to welcoming you into our smoke-free home which we share with Scuffin our cat.

Lower Hutt - Harbourview *1.5 km W of Lower Hutt*

Harbourcity View B & B *B&B Homestay*

Mary Quayle
14 City View Grove,
Harbourview,
Lower Hutt 5010

Tel (04) 586 0557
or 027 688 3306
harbourcityview@xnet.co.nz

Double/Twin $115-$150
Single $70-$120
(Full breakfast)
Dinner $25 pp by arrangement
Visa MC accepted
Not suitable for children
1 Single (3 bdrm)
2 Super King
Bathrooms: 1 Ensuite 1 Family share

Welcome to my home situated on the edge of a bush reserve with panoramic views of Wellington harbour and Hutt River. 15-minutes to Ferry, Westpac Stadium and Parliament. 20-minutes to Te Papa, Botanical Gardens and Karori Bird Sanctuary. Hike in the Regional Parks; fish the Hutt River or Golf on nearby courses. At the end of the day relax in secluded bush surrounded garden with a view of the sea. Guest tea/coffee facilities and laundry available. Sightseeing tours arranged, transfers and off street parking.

Lower Hutt *1 km SE of Lower Hutt i-site*

Hallcroft Homestay *B&B Homestay*

Lynley Hall
2 Miro Street,
Woburn,
Lower Hutt 5010

Tel (04) 938 1686
or 021 253 4131
lyndavid@paradise.net.nz

Double/Twin $60-$120
Single $60-$60
(Continental breakfast)
Children By arrangement
Cash or NZ cheque only
Children and pets welcome
1 Queen 2 Twin (2 bdrm)
Bathrooms: 1 Guest share

A smoke free, wheelchair accessible home and facilities. Off road parking. One queen bedroom. One twin bedroom. Shared Guest Bathroom. Cot and high chair available. Radio, TV and hairdryers, tea & coffee making facilities in rooms. Continental breakfast. 3 mins walk to railway station, 20 mins by train to Wellington station. Easy walk to local eating places. One small dog lives inside.

Lower Hutt - Stokes Valley *15 km N of Lower Hutt*

Rambling Brook *Cottage with Kitchen*

Mal & Nina
30 Tawhai Street,
Stokes Valley,
Lower Hutt

Tel 04 563 8716
malboandnina@yahoo.co.nz

Double/Twin $130-$160
Single $120-$135
(Breakfast by arrangement)
Children $35
Gluten & dairy-free breakfasts available
Short & long term rates
Children welcome
1 Queen (1 bdrm)
Double pullout couch in lounge
Bathrooms: 1 Ensuite

Welcome to Rambling Brook B&B.Come and enjoy our hospitality while relaxing in our private garden beside the stream, with birds singing during the day and the sounds of moreporks and frogs in the evening.We offer a private self contained cottage with off street parking. We have a range of DVD movies to watch and board games to play. 20 minutes to Lower Hutt or Upper Hutt. Close to Golf Course and driving range. Our three cats will also love to meet you.

Lower Hutt - Stokes Valley *08 km S of upper hutt*

B&B Approved

Myrian House *B&B Homestay*

Myra Moon & Ian Lawson
435 Stokes Valley Road,
Stokes Valley,
Lower Hutt 5019
Tel (04) 938 1143
or 021 159 4441
myrianhouse@paradise.net.nz

Double/Twin $120-$130
Single $70-$80
(Full breakfast)
Pet free home
Not suitable for children
2 Queen (2 bdrm)
Bathrooms: 1 Guest share

Myra & Ian welcome you to Myrian House @ 435 Stokes Valley rd; with complimentary Devonshire tea on arrival. .Surrounded by bush and birdsong ,you will feel relaxed and comfortable. Only a short drive from CBD,Kapiti coast or wine country. Whether you enjoy a game of golf,bushwalks,beach ,theatre or shops we have it all. Free wireless internet, cable/sky TV, dinner by arrangement. As your hosts we are committed to make your stay with us memorable.

Lower Hutt - Belmont *2 km W of Lower Hutt*

B&B Approved

MusicHaven *Homestay*

Ruth Birnie & Gerard Hudson
56 Park Road,
Belmont,
Lower Hutt, 5010
Tel (04) 565 3432
or 027 451 5486
info@musichaven.co.nz
www.musichaven.co.nz

Double/Twin $90-$110
Single $80-$100
(Continental breakfast)
Visa MC accepted
Not suitable for children
1 Queen 1 Double (2 bdrm)
Bathrooms: 1 Guest share

Private and secluded with bush to the rear. Decking around our dining room and lounge has harbour views making the outside as enjoyable and accessible as the indoor living spaces. Our two cats love company. The separate lounge is available for reading, relaxing, playing music or watching TV. Wireless internet available. We love music, food, wine and our vibrant region. Only a 5 minute drive from Lower Hutt city. We can pick up guests from airport, railway or bus stations.

Moores Valley - Wainuiomata *8 km SE of Lower Hutt*

Moores Valley Retreat *B&B Farmstay Cottage with Kitchen*
Chuni & Jaya Govan
303 Moores Valley Road,
Wellington, 5373

Tel (04) 564 7504
or 021 986 504
Fax (04) 5647508
mooresvalley@ihug.co.nz

Double/Twin $120-$150
Single $95
(Continental breakfast provisions)
Children $30
Visa MC accepted
Pet free home
Children welcome
2 Queen 1 Single (3 bdrm)
Bathrooms: 1 Private

Welcome to our idyllic countryside homestay, set in 10 beautiful acres of farmland. Located only 30mins drive from Wellington's CBD, and minutes from the local village. This private and comfortable homestay has spacious guest rooms, a fully equipped kitchen, laundry and bathroom. You'll enjoy access to our very own private and natural stream with bridge. Located close to Rimataka reserve, and many other scenic bush walks and local golf courses. This is the perfect rural holiday retreat located within easy reach of the capital.

~

Eastbourne - York Bay *3 km N of Eastbourne*

Bush House *Homestay*
Belinda Cattermole
12 Waitohu Road,
York Bay,
Eastbourne

Tel (04) 568 5250
or 027 408 9648
Fax (04) 568 5250
belindacat@paradise.net.nz

Double/Twin $100
Single $80
(Special breakfast)
Dinner by arrangement
1 Double 1 Single (2 bdrm)
Bathrooms: 1 Private 1 Family share

Come and enjoy the peace and tranquility of the Eastern Bays. You will be hosted in a restored 1920's settler cottage nestled amongst native bush and looking towards the Kaikoura mountains of the South Island. My love of cordon-bleu cooking and the pleasures of the table are satisfied through the use of my country kitchen and dining room. Other attractions: A Devon Rex cat. Eastbourne is a small seaside village across the harbour from Wellington City with a range of attractions.

Eastbourne - Days Bay *12 km E of Wellington*

FernTree Hideaway *B&B Apartment with Kitchen Boutique*

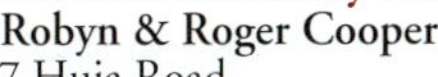

Robyn & Roger Cooper
7 Huia Road,
Days Bay, Eastbourne
Tel (04) 562 7692
or 027 616 9826
Fax (04) 562 7690
relax@ferntreehideaway.co.nz
www.ferntreehideaway.co.nz

Double/Twin $175-$205
Single $155-$185
(Continental breakfast provisions)
Children $30
Extra adults $45
Visa MC accepted
Children welcome
1 King (1 bdrm)
1 king bedroom, 2 sofabeds in lounge
Bathrooms: 1 Private

Ride our private cable car through native bush to FernTree Hideaway, a secluded romantic retreat overlooking Wellington harbour. Enjoy sparkling sea views; wake to bellbird song; breakfast on your garden patio; relax with books, Sky TV, DVDs. Open plan lounge/dining/kitchenette, luxury bath/shower, phone, wireless internet. 200 metres to beach, cafes, galleries. Days Bay ferry to Central Wellington (20 minutes) berths near Te Papa and The Stadium. Inter-island ferry 20 minutes. 'This place is Dreamland - a Kiwi Shangri-la.' Self-catering optional.

Eastbourne - Lowry Bay *14 km N of Wellington*

Lowry Bay Homestay *B&B Homestay*

Pam & Forde Clarke
35 Cheviot Road,
Lowry Bay,
Eastbourne,
Wellington
Tel (04) 568 4407
or 0508 266 546
Fax (04) 568 4408
homestay@lowrybay.co.nz
www.lowrybay.co.nz

Double/Twin $165-$195
Single $135-$165
(Full breakfast)
Children negotiable
Visa MC Diners Amex accepted
Pet free home
Children welcome
1 King/Twin 1 Queen 1 Single (2 bdrm)
Bathrooms: 1 Private

Warm, restful, peaceful, yet close to Wellington and Hutt Cities, transport, restaurants and art galleries. Play tennis on our court, stroll to the beach, walk in the bush, sail on our 28 foot yacht, or relax under a sun umbrella on the deck. Native birds abound. Our sunny, elegant bedrooms have garden views, TV, tea/coffee and central heating. We share with our 2 grown up daughters, Isabella and Kirsty, interests in sailing, skiing, tennis, ballet and theatre. Laundry. From SH2 follow Petone signs then Eastbourne.

Eastbourne *20 km E of Wellington*

B&B Approved

The Anchorage *B&B*
Bet & Wal Louden
107 Marine Parade,
Eastbourne,
Wellington

Tel (04) 562 8310
or 021 049 5169
or 021 329 993
betandwal@paradise.net.nz

Double/Twin $140
Single $110
(Continental breakfast)
Extra guests $60
Visa MC accepted
Children welcome
1 Queen 1 Single (2 bdrm)
1 queen,1single/lounge-sofa bed
Bathrooms: 1 Private

Welcome to our waterfront property, wonderful views of Wellington Harbour and city. One minute walk to Eastbourne Village and wharf, supermarket, cafes, restaurants, pub, antique shops and art gallery. We offer for the more adventurous a choice of guided bush walks from an easy 2 hours to a demanding 7 hours (bookings essential; Mon-Friday only), outstanding beech, northern rata and podocarp forests. Coastal walks (mountain bike rides) to Pencarrow Lighthouse. Kayak trips also available. Labrador, Splash on property.Wireless broadband.Single party bookings only.

Eastbourne *2 km S of Eastbourne Village*

B&B Approved

The Walnut Tree *B&B*
Jasmin & Alan Macdonald
335 Muritai Road,
Eastbourne, Wellington, 5013

Tel (04) 562 8768
or 027 439 3886
Fax (04) 562 8763
jasmin@thewalnuttree.co.nz
www.thewalnuttree.co.nz

Double/Twin $160 Single $120
(Full breakfast) Children $30
Not suitable for mobile pre schoolers
Dinner $30 pp by arrangement
Hosts day tour of Wellington incl. transport (bpa)
Visa MC Eftpos accepted
1 Queen 2 Twin 1 Single (3 bdrm)
1Queen & kitchenette, 1Twin, 1Single
Only 1 party at a time
Bathrooms: 1 Private semi-ensuite

Enjoy glorious views, birdsong and total privacy from the top storey of our renovated multi-level country character home. We offer delicious food, three charming Bedrooms, a sumptuous upstairs Lounge with widescreen tv, garden balcony and outdoor spa. Easy stroll to the beach and bush, or cafes and boutiques in Eastbourne village. The Wellington bus stops right at the front gate.Our two teenagers and two spoilt Siamese cats live with us too. The welcome mat is out, the croissants are hot- we'd love your company!

Eastbourne - Days Bay *10 km S of Petone*

Ruru Lane Bed & Breakfast *B&B*

Les Maiden & Nicky Long
12 Korimako Road,
Days Bay, 5013

Tel Landline (04) 562 8970
or Mobile 021 628 617
info@rurulane.co.nz
www.rurulane.co.nz

Double/Twin $160-$180
Single $140-$160
(Continental breakfast)
Visa MC Amex accepted
Not suitable for children
1 King 1 Double (2 bdrm)
Rooms have sofas, writing tables, tea and coffee facilities
Bathrooms: 1 Private
Single party bookings only

Ruru Lane is a large, gracious house with luxurious accommodation surrounded by an abundance of trees, ferns and flowering plants.Two generous bed sitting rooms adjoin the guest entrance hall. Both rooms have sofas, writing tables, tea and coffee making facilities and delightful views. Enjoy the spacious bathroom with clawfoot bath, shower and a generous range of toiletries. Breakfast is continental with fresh juices, seasonal fruit, organic yoghurt, homemade cereal and preserves. Choose from a range of breads or items from the bakery.

Wellington - Johnsonville *8 km N of Wellington*

Paparangi Homestay *B&B Homestay*

Joy and Autry Kawana
145 Helston Road,
Johnsonville,
Wellington

Tel (04) 478 1747
or 027 485 6432
or 027 478 1747
autry.joy@xtra.co.nz

Double/Twin $100-$110
Single $60-$70
(Full breakfast)
Children negotiable
Dinner with family $25
Children welcome
1 Queen 1 Double
1 Twin 1 Single (2 bdrm)
Bathrooms: 1 Ensuite 1 Family share

Paparangi Homestay is a 100 year old restored cottage set in 1 acre of peaceful cottage gardens with abundant birdlife. Bedrooms have TV/Radio, heaters, electric blankets and garden views. We are 10 min from ferry and city and 2km from train station which takes you straight to stadium and city. Bus stop at top of drive to city. Free wireless internet access. Homemade muesli, bread, preserves and free range hens. Autry and Joy enjoy the company of all nationalities and our home is your home while you are with us.

Wellington - Johnsonville *8 km N of Wellington*

Cherswud *B&B Homestay*
David & Marilyn McDonald
121 Helston Road, Johnsonville, Wellington, 6037
Tel (04) 477 6767 or 021 060 7815
stay@cherswud.com
www.cherswud.com

Double/Twin $120 Single $80 (Special breakfast)
Dinner 3 courses $35, by prior arrangement
Gluten-free options
Discounts available for stays longer than 3 nights
Visa MC accepted Pet free home
2 Queen 1 Twin (3 bdrm)
Maximum of 2 parties at one time
Bathrooms: 2 Private

We're delighted to welcome you to Cherswud, our fully-restored 1919 home, with two lounges, conservatory and sunny deck overlooking a lovely sheltered garden. Our accommodation has two queen rooms, which are warm and bright with very comfortable beds, electric blankets, feather duvets, and well-stocked bookcases. Each room has its own private bathroom, one with a spa bath and massage shower.

A twin room is also available if required. We host a maximum of two parties at one time.We offer warm hospitality with delicious meals, including home-made bread and gluten-free options. Help yourself to tea and coffee in the kitchen at any time. Dinner (pre-arranged) is served with New Zealand wine, although several restaurants are within 12 minutes' walk.

Free broadband internet access plus free transfer of photos from digital cameras to CD. Ten easy minutes from the inter-island ferry and two minutes off State Highway 1 at the Johnsonville exit.

Wellington - Khandallah *7 km N of Wellington*

B&B Approved

Clothier Homestay *Homestay*

Sue & Ted Clothier
22 Lohia Street,
Khandallah,
Wellington
Tel (04) 479 1180
or 027 246 6158
sclothier@xtra.co.nz

Double/Twin $110
Single $90
(Continental breakfast)
Not suitable for children
1 Twin (1 bdrm)
Bathrooms: 1 Ensuite

This is a lovely, sunny and warm open plan home with glorious harbour and city views. A quiet easily accessible street just 10 minutes from the city and 5 minutes from the ferry. Close to Khandallah Village where you can make use of the excellent local restaurant, cafe or Monteiths pub. We are a non-smoking household. Another family member is an aristocratic white cat called Dali. We enjoy sharing our home with our guests.

~

Wellington - Khandallah *7 km N of Wellington*

B&B Approved

The Loft in Wellington *B&B Separate Suite*

Phillippa & Simon Plimmer
6 Delhi Crescent,
Khandallah,
Wellington
Tel (04) 938 5015
or 021 448 491
plimmers@paradise.net.nz

Double/Twin $120
Single $95
(Continental breakfast provisions)
Visa MC accepted
Pet free home
Not suitable for children
1 Queen (1 bdrm)
Bathrooms: 1 Ensuite

The Loft in Wellington offers comfort and style in a beautifully appointed self-contained studio (no cooking facilities). Enjoy complete privacy with your own entrance. Cable TV, off-street parking, laundry and internet access available. 10 minutes from downtown Wellington. Close to ferry terminal. 300 metres to local train and bus. 15 minutes train ride direct to Westpac Stadium. 500 metres from Khandallah Village and local restaurants. Studio not suitable for pets. We have 3 young children.

Wellington - Ngaio *7 km NW of Wellington*

Ngaio Homestay *B&B Homestay Apartment with Kitchen*
Jennifer & Christopher Timmings
56 Fox Street, Ngaio, Wellington

Tel (04) 479 5325
Fax (04) 479 4325 enquiries@ngaiohomestay.co.nz
www.ngaiohomestay.co.nz

Double/Twin $160-$180 Single $100-$140 (Continental breakfast)
Children negotiable Dinner $35pp by arrangement
Self-contained $160-$180 double, extra person $45
Weekly rates available Visa MC accepted
1 Queen 1 Double/Twin 2 Twin 3 Single (5 bdrm)
Bathrooms: 3 Ensuite 1 Private
Shower & bath in apartments, shower in ensuite B&B

Welcome to Wonderful Wellington! Share your visit with us and enjoy helpful personal hospitality! Our unusual multi-level open plan character home [built1960] is in the suburb of Ngaio.Guests may leave their car here and take the train to CBD [10 minutes] We are 5 minutes by car to InterIsland Ferry terminal.

Our double room has tea/coffee facilities, quality bedding, tiled ensuite and french doors opening onto a deck and private jungle garden. Breakfast is continental. Evening meals an optional extra.

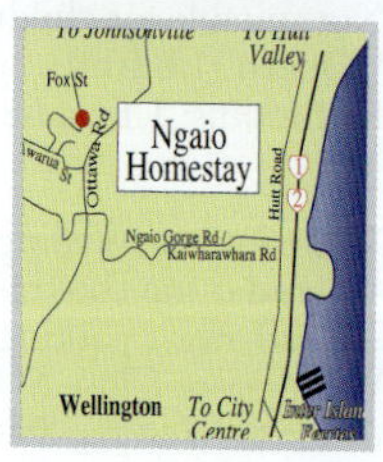

2 self-contained apartments, 1 queen, 1 twin, adjacent to our property, are comfortable, convenient, tastefully furnished and recently re-decorated. Each apartment also has a couch with a fold-out bed in lounge, fully equipped kitchen, shower, bath, laundry facilities, cable TV, phone and internet [small fee] There is a large garden with trees, birds and views. Perfect for business, holiday or relocating.

Jennifer plays harp at home and live piano music daily in NZ's top department store.

Compliment from guest: "This is a home where there is beautiful music, art and love."Do come and share! Please phone before 11am or after 3pm or fax or email. Bookings essential.

Wellington - Wadestown *2.5 km NW of Wellington*

The Nikau Palms Bed & Breakfast *B&B*

Diane & Bill Boyd
95 Sar Street,
Wadestown,
Wellington 6012

Tel (04) 499 4513
or 027 674 0644
Fax (04) 499 4517
thenikaupalms@xtra.co.nz
www.thenikaupalms.co.nz

Double/Twin $180-$200
Single $125-$130
(Continental breakfast)
Suitable for children 10 and over
Visa MC accepted
2 Queen 1 Single (2 bdrm)
One upstairs, one downstairs
Bathrooms: 2 Ensuite

You are invited to share our spectacular views of Wellington Harbour overlooking the city, Interisland ferry and Westpac Stadium, all within walking distance. Our home is a few minutes drive from Wellington's attractions, Historic Thorndon's restaurants, shops and Heritage Trail and Katherine Mansfield's birthplace. The bedrooms include ensuites, one with private sunroom. Continental breakfast provided. Tea and coffee making facilities and refrigerator in bedrooms. Off-street parking provided.

Wellington - Wadestown *2 km N of Wellington*

Harbour Lodge Wellington *B&B*

Lou & Chris Bradshaw
200 Barnard Street,
Wadestown,
Wellington

Tel (04) 976 5677
or 021 032 6497
lou@harbourlodgewellington.com
www.harbourlodgewellington.com

Double/Twin $180-$270
(Continental breakfast)
Children negotiable
Visa MC Amex accepted
Children welcome
4 King (4 bdrm)
Bathrooms: 4 Ensuite

Let your stresses be gently lulled away in the luxurious comfort of this beautiful lodge. Admire the fabulous views of Wellington Harbour from the large sunny deck. Take a spa. Laze in the comfort of a large guest lounge with stunning harbour views. All this is only a few minutes drive from central Wellington, ferry terminal or Wellington Stadium. Children of all ages welcome, no pets please.

Wellington - Wadestown *2.3 km N of Central Wellington*

Annaday Homestay *B&B Homestay*

Anne & David Denton
39 Wadestown Road,
Wellington 6012

Tel (04) 499 1827
Fax (04) 472 1190
annaday@tavis.co.nz
www.tavis.co.nz/annaday

Double/Twin $130-$200
Single $90-$150
(Full breakfast)
Children $20-$50
Dinner $25-$35
Sauna $5
Children and pets welcome
2 King/Twin 2 King
1 Queen 2 Twin (4 bdrm)
5 rooms: can alter bed configuration
Bathrooms: 1 Ensuite 1 Private
1 Guest share 1 Family share

Excellent facilities. Great Views. Fast internet. Hospitality adapted to suit you. Start with courtesy pickup, enjoy our free orientation tour of the city, borrow a book, join us for dinner or try the local takeaways or cafes. On the bus route, close to the city, ferries, train & we will take you to the airport. Near stadium & Bowen Hospital. Our dog and grandson stay out of guest areas but make friends if you choose. Discounts/negotiable rates for longer stays and groups.

Wellington - Wadestown *2 km NW of information centre*

Ahu Mairangi *B&B*

James and Helen
128 Weld Street,
Wadestown

Tel landline (04) 473 7157
or freephone 0800 678 031
or James mob 0274 504 818
james.quinn@xtra.co.nz

Double/Twin $120-$150
Single $100-$120
(Continental breakfast)
Neg.rates for longer stays
Pet free home
Not suitable for children
1 Queen 1 Double (2 bdrm)
1 with ensuite and
1 with own bathroom
Bathrooms: 1 Ensuite 1 Private

Welcome to "Ahu Mairangi"Located high up on the hills above Wellington City for awesome views and maximum sun. Our recently modernised home has a large guest bedroom with ensuite which has both bath and shower. Also a second double bedroom with adjoining bath room and separate w.c. Both rooms have peaceful bush views so come and enjoy a relaxing stay in our beautiful city. As we adjoin the town belt there are some great walks for the fitter guests. .Dinner optional extra

Wellington - Karori *5 km W of Wellington*

Campbell Homestay *Homestay*
Murray & Elaine Campbell
23 Parkvale Road, Karori 6012, Wellington
Tel (04) 476 6110 or 0274 535 080
Fax (04) 476 6593 ctool@ihug.co.nz

Double/Twin $110 Single $70 (Continental breakfast)
Children half price (under 12) Dinner $35 b/a
Visa MC Eftpos accepted Children and pets welcome
1 Queen 1 Twin 1 Single (2 bdrm)
Bathrooms: 1 Guest share
Separate toilet, full bathroom/shower next to bedrooms

Welcome to our home right in the village of Karori, but only ten minutes from the central city.Dine with us, or eat out at the local taverns, cafes, enjoy our local village shopping centre,library, Post Office and other amenities all within a few minutes walking distance. As we are on the main bus route, guests,can park their car off street and take the bus into the city. We are happy to pick you up from ferry, train, bus or airport terminals and of course make sure you do not miss your onward connection.We are situated close to the Karori Wildlife Sanctuary, Botanic Gardens and Otari-Wilton's Bush, Cable Car, historic Thorndon's boutique shopping centre and restaurants, Katherine Masefield's birthplace, the Westpac Stadium

"Absolutely Positively Wellington" is a dynamic ever changing compact city making it easy to walk from one place to the next and with simply the most friendly helpful people. Take advantage of Wellington's cultural events: orchestra, ballet, opera, galleries and theatres. Visit our fabulous modern museum Te Papa or take a shuttle ferry across the harbour.

We have two guest bedrooms, 1 Queen and 1 Twin which can also be a single.Guests have the sole use of a separate toilet and a full sized bathroom next door to the bedrooms.Relax and make yourself at home - use our laundry, garden, lounge, email/internet facilities. Meet Charlie our border collie dog. Children of all ages welcome. Our home is perfect for business folk or families relocating as it is so close to all the village amenities and schools.Weekly rates on application Evening meals are an optional extra, $35.00 per person. From the motorway, when coming into Wellington from the north, take the Hawkestone Street/Karori exit off the motorway and follow the signs up past the Botanic gardens, through the tunnel, up the hill past the Marsden shops and down to the Karori village. Turn right at the lights into Parkvale Road (first turn past the Shopping Mall), then turn left down the drive to No 23 where a big welcome awaits you.

Wellington - Karori *4 km W of Wellington CBD*

Bristow Place *B&B Apartment with Kitchen*

Helen & Tony Thomson
8 Bristow Place,
Karori,
Wellington

Tel (04) 476 6291
or 021 656 825
Fax (04) 476 6293
h.t.thomson@xtra.co.nz

Double/Twin $160-$200
(Breakfast by arrangement)
Dinner by arrangement
Long stay or self-catered b/a
Visa MC accepted
Children welcome
1 Queen 1 Double (1 bdrm)
Separate bedroom (queen)
plus fold-out double in lounge
Bathrooms: 1 Private

We offer a private, fully self-contained apartment, able to sleep up to 4, that can be enjoyed either as a regular B&B facility or on a self-catered, self-serviced basis. Enjoy Sky TV, electric blankets, bathrobes, heated towel rails, etc. Full laundry facilities. Share coffee and conversation with us; we enjoy music, theatre, travel, sports and bridge. German spoken. Inner suburb location with ample parking, good transport and local shops and restaurants. Internet and fax at small charges.

Wellington - Karori *2 km N of the central city*

B&B and Homestay *B&B Homestay Separate Suite*

Judit & Julian Farquhar
15 Nottingham Street,
Wellington, 6005

Tel (04) 976 8144
or 021 1810 8064
Fax (04) 976 8144
judit.farquhar@gmail.com
http://farquharsbedandbreakfast.blogspot.com/

Double/Twin $120-$130
Single $80-$90
(Full breakfast provisions)
Children welcome at lower rates
Dinner by arrangement $20-$35
Major currencies accepted
Children welcome
1 Queen 2 Single (1 bdrm)
Bathrooms: 1 Private

Welcome to our 100-year-old eco colonial home in the Wellington suburb of Karori with a beautiful mature organic garden, 5 minutes from the central city. We are a well-travelled Hungarian-Kiwi couple with our 9-year-old daughter. There is music, art and technology inside. Good transport, local shops and restaurants. We offer a separate guest-room for 2-4 people with its own WC and washbasin. There is also a self-contained, private apartment with kitchen to accomodate up to 4 people for longer period, by arrangment.

Wellington - Kelburn *1 km W of Wellington*

Kelburn House Bed & Breakfast *Luxury B&B*

Margie & Greg du Bern
27 Glen Road,
Kelburn, Wellington 6012

Tel (04) 475 7950
or 021 0205 8577
info@kelburnhouse.co.nz
www.kelburnhouse.co.nz

Double/Twin $195-$225
Single $130-$180 (Full breakfast)
Dinner by prior arrangement
Special diets catered for
Visa MC Diners Amex
Eftpos accepted
Pet free home
Not suitable for children
1 Queen 1 Single (2 bdrm)
1 Queen with ensuite, own entrance / 1 single
Bathrooms: 1 Ensuite 1 Family share

Great Location! Within easy walk of CBD, University, Stadium, Te Papa, Botanical Gardens and Cable Car.Handy to public transport, cafes and restaurants. Warm and friendly upmarket B & B in quiet street with free off street parking. Sumptuous gourmet breakfast with home baking and complimentary refreshments. High speed wirelessbroadband internet access. Guest lounge with SKY TV & DVD. Your hosts Margie & Greg are keen travellers and will make every effort to ensure your stay is comfortable and enjoyable.

Wellington - Kelburn *1 km W of city centre*

Above Town Bed and Breakfast *B&B*

Maria and Michael Phelan
23 Rimu Road,
Kelburn,
Wellington 6012

Tel (04) 971 5737
abovetownbnb@paradise.net.nz
www.abovetownbnb.co.nz

Double/Twin $140-$170
Single $120-$150
(Full breakfast)
Visa MC accepted
1 King/Twin 1 Double (1 bdrm)
Guest room
Bathrooms: 1 Ensuite

Enjoy our spacious guest room situated in a quiet street above the city centre. Nearby Wellington's cable car to central city locations and the harbour. Walk to Victoria University and Botanic Gardens. Te Papa, downtown entertainments and Stadium are easily reached. Knowledgeable hosts, Maria and Michael, can provide information to help you explore Wellington. Then relax in your stylish room with sitting area, TV, coffee/tea making, airconditioning and fridge. Double futon for extra guests; quality linen; separate entrance and roadside parking. Friendly pet dog in residence.

Wellington - Aro Valley *2 km SW of Information Centre*

Millie's Bed & Breakfast *B&B Homestay*

Miriam Busby
33 Holloway Road,
Aro Valley, Wellington 6021

Tel (04) 381 2968
or 021 254 7308
Fax (04) 381 2969
miriam.busby@paradise.net.nz
www.milliesbb.co.nz

Double/Twin $130
Single $90 (Full breakfast)
Children $40
Dinner $25 for Colonial cottage cuisine
Children welcome
No credit card facilities,
cash or cheque only
1 Double 1 Single (2 bdrm)
1 double/ queen sized bed and one single room available
Bathrooms: 1 Family share
One bath & shower available for guests to use

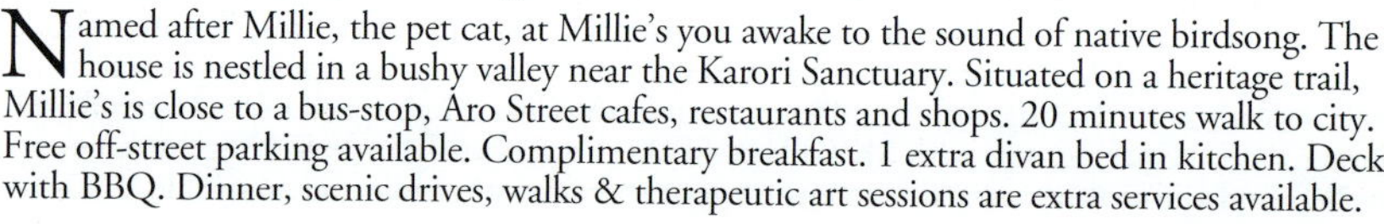

Named after Millie, the pet cat, at Millie's you awake to the sound of native birdsong. The house is nestled in a bushy valley near the Karori Sanctuary. Situated on a heritage trail, Millie's is close to a bus-stop, Aro Street cafes, restaurants and shops. 20 minutes walk to city. Free off-street parking available. Complimentary breakfast. 1 extra divan bed in kitchen. Deck with BBQ. Dinner, scenic drives, walks & therapeutic art sessions are extra services available.

Wellington - Mt Cook *2 km SE of Wellington*

Apartment One *B&B Homestay*

Jim & Colleen Bargh
1/2 King Street,
Mt Cook,
Wellington

Tel (04) 385 1112
or 027 247 8145
or 027 275 0913
apartmentone@yahoo.co.nz

Double/Twin $130-$140
Single $90-$100
(Full breakfast)
Visa MC accepted
Pet free home
Not suitable for children
2 Queen (2 bdrm)
Bathrooms: 2 Ensuite

Experience apartment living in the city. We moved off the farm into our converted warehouse to try city life. We love its ever-changing beauty and the people are simply the best. Come try it for yourself. Buses depart every few minutes. 2 minutes walk to the Basin Reserve and 10-15 minutes walk to Courtenay Place (Wellington's restaurant, cafe and theatre district). Less than 10 minutes drive to the ferry terminal and airport. We serve a deluxe breakfast to get you through your eventful day.

Wellington

Please let us know how you enjoyed your B&B.
There are comment forms at the end of the book.

Wellington - Oriental Bay *1 km E of Wellington CBD*

Crescent Guest House *Luxury B&B Outdoor Living*

Sue and Brad Ilg
10 The Crescent,
Roseneath,
Wellington

Tel (04) 970 9811
or 027 491 6411
stay@10thecrescent.co.nz
www.10thecrescent.co.nz

Double/Twin $175-$250
Single $175-$250
(Continental breakfast provisions)
Children call to enquire suitabity
Dinner available on request
Visa MC accepted
Children and pets welcome
1 King (1 bdrm)
King bed in gorgeous bay window room
Bathrooms: 1 Private
Glass-tiled feature wall and standalone bath, rain shower

Where else can you lie in bed and enjoy the city and harbour views, and see the sailboats and shipping traffic go by? Whether you are with us on business or for pleasure, the Crescent Guest House a wonderful place to relax, and recharge. Luxury, privacy, views, and fantastic location!

Wellington - Mt Victoria *0.5 km E of Central Wellington*

Villa Vittorio *B&B Homestay*

Annette & Logan Russell
6 Hawker Street, Mt Victoria, Wellington
Tel (04) 801 5761 or 027 432 1267
Fax (04) 801 5762
villa@villavittorio.co.nz
www.villavittorio.co.nz

Double/Twin $195-$220 Single $135 (Full breakfast)
Dinner by arrangement
Visa MC Diners Amex accepted
1 Double/Twin (1 bdrm)
Bathrooms: 1 Private

WELCOME TO VILLA VITTORIO. Centrally located close by Courtenay Place. Short walk to restaurants, theatres, shopping, conference centres, Te Papa Museum, Parliament & Stadium. Guest bedroom with TV, tea & coffee facilities. Adjoining sitting room with balcony overlooking city. Bathroom with show- and bath.

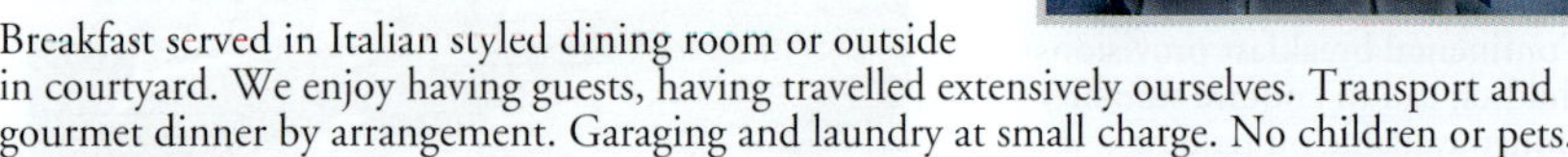

Breakfast served in Italian styled dining room or outside in courtyard. We enjoy having guests, having travelled extensively ourselves. Transport and gourmet dinner by arrangement. Garaging and laundry at small charge. No children or pets.

Directions: phone, fax, email or write.

Wellington - Mt Victoria *0.5 km E of Courtenay Place*

B&B Approved

Austinvilla *B&B Apartment with Kitchen*

Zarli & Mark
11 Austin Street,
Mt Victoria,
Wellington

Tel (04) 385 8334
info@austinvilla.co.nz
www.austinvilla.co.nz

Double/Twin $160-$220
(Continental breakfast)
Visa MC Eftpos accepted
Not suitable for children
2 Queen (2 bdrm)
Bathrooms: 2 Ensuite

Top location: Set amongst beautiful gardens in one of Mt Victoria's elegant turn-of-the-century villas, Austinvilla is within minutes walk of theatres, restaurants, Oriental Bay and Te Papa. Close to public transport and short drive to airport, ferries, and Westpac Stadium.2 self-contained apartments with individual entrances come equipped with queen bed, ensuite (bath and shower), kitchen, living/dining area, cable TV, phone and wireless internet access. Both offer privacy, sun and city views with one having its own patio/garden. Laundry facilities and off-street parking available.

~

Wellington - Roseneath *2 km E of Central city*

B&B Approved

Panorama *B&B*

Peg Mackay
1 Robieson Lane,
Roseneath

Tel (04) 801 8691
or 021 801 869
pegmackay@hotmail.com
www.wellingtonpanorama.co.nz

Double/Twin $140-$170
Single $100-$120
(Continental breakfast)
Children by arrangement
Evening meals by arrangement
Long term rates on application
2 Queen (2 bdrm)
2 Queen with harbour views
Bathrooms: 1 Private 1 Guest share
1 Guest bath

Enjoy the panorama of ships, ferries and tugs and the sun, peace and privacy of our warm modern home above Oriental Bay. You have your own deck and sitting room with TV and refreshments. 5 min walk up to Mt Victoria or 15-20 minute walk down to Oriental Bay, the city, theatres, galleries and Te Papa: the Museum of New Zealand. Taste NZ in the many nearby cafes and restaurants. Ferry/Airport 10 minutes, city 5 minutes drive. AND you can park right at our door!

Wellington - Roseneath *3 km E of Wellington Central*

Harbourview Homestay and B&B *B&B Homestay*

Hilda & Geoff Stedman
125 Te Anau Road,
Roseneath,
Wellington

Tel (04) 386 1043
or 021 0386 351
h.stedman@hotmail.com
http://nzhomestay.co.nz/harbourview_homestay

Double/Twin $130-$170
Single $100-$150
(Full breakfast)
Dinner from $40
Visa MC accepted
Children welcome
1 Double 2 Single (2 bdrm)
Bathrooms: 2 Private

Five minutes drive from Wellington city, 10 minutes drive from the airport and on the No. 14 bus route. The house offers comfortable hospitality and elegance. Each bedroom opens to a wide deck, offering expansive views of Wellington harbour. Pleasantly decorated rooms quality beds and linen, separate guest's bathroom with shower and spa bath. Harbourview is situated in a peaceful setting close to the city, catering for business people, tourists and honeymooners. A surcharge will be added if paying by credit card. The property is not suitable for wheelchair access.

~

Wellington - Roseneath *1 km E of Wellington CBD*

Maida Vale *B&B*

Bessie Sutherland
6 Maida Vale Road,
Roseneath,
Wellington

Tel 027 332 1570
or (04) 970 5184
bess.sutherland@clear.net.nz
www.maidavalebnb.co.nz

Double/Twin $150-$180
Single $60
(Continental breakfast)
Children negotiable
Weekly rates negotiable
Visa MC Amex accepted
Children welcome
1 King 1 Single (2 bdrm)
Main room is spacious with harbour views
Bathrooms: 1 Ensuite

Our centrally located home has spectacular views across the harbour to the city centre. The larger room has an ensuite. Both rooms are on the ground floor and have their own entrance (our family lives above). The city centre, restaurants, theatres and museums are a 5 minute drive away or, alternatively, a 20 minute walk along the waterfront. The airport and ferry terminals are 10-15 minutes away. The family will greet you with a warm welcome as will Zoe, the Jack Russell terrier.

Wellington - Roseneath *2 km E of Central City*

Crescent Point *B&B*

Bobbi & John Gibbons
18 The Crescent,
Roseneath,
Wellington 6011

Tel (04) 972 3464
or 027 485 0846
Fax (04) 972 3465
gibbonsjg@paradise.net.nz
www.crescentpoint.co.nz

Double/Twin $180
Single $100
(Full breakfast)
Dinner by arrangement
Visa MC accepted
Children and pets welcome
1 Queen (1 bdrm)
Bathrooms: 1 Private
Ensuite with spa bath

We welcome you to sunny Crescent Point,a spacious modern home with panoramic views overlooking the harbour above Oriental Bay. We offer two bedrooms with ensuites, cable TV. One with kitchenette, own entrance and carpark, the other a spa bath. Take a 5 min bush walk to Oriental Bay beach, then a pleasant 10 min walk to the City entertainment area, with restaurants, theatres and Te Papa. 10-15 min drive to Central City and Ferry. 10 mins to Wellington Airport. There is a cat in residence.

~

Wellington - Roseneath *1 km N of Wellington*

Carlton Gore *Luxury B&B*

Brent & Janice Davies
17 Carlton Road,
Roseneath,
Wellington

Tel (04) 385 8508
or 027 284 0983
Fax (04) 385 8548
janibrent@xtra.co.nz
www.carltongore.co.nz

Double/Twin $140-$250
(Full breakfast)
Visa MC accepted
Children welcome
4 Queen (4 bdrm)
Bathrooms: 2 Ensuite
1 Private 1 Guest share

Location, Location.Welcome to our luxury character 1900's home with all the modern conveniences, sea, sun and views (ground floor). We offer central heating, sky TV (ensuite rooms only), DVD, wireless internet access, continental or full breakfast, quality linen, own entrance, lounge and dining room to relax in. On-site parking, take a five minute ride to central city from the bus stop at door or fifteen minute scenic walk along Oriental Bay. Ten minutes to Wellington airport.

Wellington - Vogeltown (South Mt Cook)

3 km S of Wellington CBD

Finnimore House *B&B Homestay*
Willie & Kathleen Ryan
2 Dransfield Street,
Vogeltown, Wellington
Tel (04) 389 9894
Fax (04) 389 9894
w.f.ryan@xtra.co.nz
www.finnimorehouse.co.nz

Double $100-$130
Single $90-$110 (Full breakfast)
Children $30 Twin $120-$140
Extra person $30
Seaonal rates vary
Visa MC accepted
Children welcome
3 Queen 2 Single (3 bdrm)
Bathrooms: 1 Guest share

Welcome to our historical manor 5 minutes drive from downtown Wellington. Your hosts, Willie and Kathleen Ryan, offer warm Irish hospitality, spacious Victorian rooms with tea/coffee/fridge facilities, full cooked breakfast at your convenience. As a service to guests, Willie offers enthusiastic guidance to Wellington√??s attractions. Our location is close to: airport, ferries, restaurants, Basin Reserve, hospital, zoo, Massey University, National School of Dance and Drama. Secure private parking on-site, convenient public transport. Laundry facilities free if staying 3 nights or more (otherwise a charge applies).

Wellington - Island Bay *4 km S of Courtenay Place*

Buckley Homestay *B&B Homestay Separate Suite*
Mrs Wilhelmina Muller
51 Buckley Road, Melrose,
Island Bay, Wellington
Tel (04) 934 7151
or 021 112 3445
Fax (04) 934 7152
willy.muller@paradise.net.nz
www.buckleyhomestay.co.nz

Double/Twin $120-$140
Single $110
(Continental breakfast)
Children negotiable
Dinner by arrangement
Visa MC accepted
Pet free home
Children and pets welcome
1 King/Twin 1 Queen 3 Single (3 bdrm)
Bathrooms: 2 Private 1 Family share

Large 2 storey sunny home with spectacular scenery and beautiful views over Wellington. New tastefully decorated, private entrance, 1 bedroom, self-contained suite with private balcony, TV, conservatory. Handy to hospitals. We are interested in food, wine, travel, relaxing and meeting people. Willy is a nurse, enjoys cooking, gardening and speaks Dutch. No pets or children at home. Off-street parking, complimentary refreshments, dinner by arrangement. On bus route. Handy to all tourist attractions, and airport.

Wellington - Island Bay *6 km S of Wellington City Central*

B&B Approved

The Lighthouse & The Keep *Self-contained*

Bruce Stokell
326 The Esplanade & 116 The Esplanade,
Island Bay,
Wellington

Tel (04) 472 4177
or 027 442 5555
bruce@thelighthouse.net.nz
www.thelighthouse.net.nz

Double/Twin $180-$230
(Full breakfast provisions)
Visa MC accepted
Not suitable for children
1 Double/Twin (1 bdrm)
Bathrooms: 1 Private

Island Bay - 10 minutes city centre, 10 minutes airport, 20 minutes ferry terminal.

The Lighthouse is on the south coast and has views of the island, fishing boats in the bay, the beach and rocks, the far coastline, the open sea, the shipping and, on a clear day, the South Island. There are local shops and restaurants.

The Lighthouse has a basic kitchen and bathroom on the first floor, the bedroom/sitting room on the middle floor and the lookout on the top. Romantic.

The Keep is a stone tower just 2 minutes from The Lighthouse. It has a lounge/basic kitchen on 1 level and a bed with ensuite on the next level. Also a spa bath in the bedroom. It is very cosy and has excellent views of the sea, especially in a storm. Stairs from the bedroom lead to a hatch which opens on to the roof.

Wellington - Island Bay *3 km S of Courtenay Place*

B&B Approved

Ma Maison *B&B Boutique B&B*

Margo Frost
9 Tamar Street, Island Bay, Wellington
Tel (04) 383 4018 or 027 2429 827
Fax (04) 383 4018
bedandbreakfast@paradise.net.nz
www.nzwellingtonhomestay.co.nz

Double/Twin $140
Single $120 (Full breakfast)
Visa MC accepted
2 Queen (2 bdrm)
Bathrooms: 1 Ensuite 1 Private

Luxury in a warm, comfortable home at a realistic price, our 1920s home is decorated with a French flavour. Drive to door, lovely garden.

The brown guest room has it's own entrance and ensuite, the blue room has private bathroom. Both rooms have queen posturepedic beds and are equipped with everything to make your stay as comfortable as possible.

Island Bay is a popular seaside suburb with excellent local restaurants. We are 8 minutes by car to the city and very handy to great bus service.

A full delicious breakfast is served at a time to suit you. Resident family cat.

Wellington - Island Bay *7 km S of Wellington City Central*

Nature's Touch Guest House *Luxury B&B Separate Suite*

Maarten & Natsuko Groeneveld
25A Happy Valley Road, Owhiro Bay, Wellington
Tel (04) 383 6977 or 027 559 0966
info@naturestouchguesthouse.com
http://naturestouchguesthouse.com

Double/Twin $130-$170
Single $110-$140 (Full breakfast)
Children $15-$45 per child
Japanese Dinner $40pp, European Dinner $35pp
Wireless broadband available,
bring your own computer |
Visa MC accepted
Children welcome
1 King 2 Double/Twin (2 bdrm)
Bathrooms: 1 Private

"Warm welcome & delightful hospitality in beautiful craftman-built home. Spacious, comfortable suite with stunning views. Convenient location. Superb cuisine, both Western & Japanese. A true gem." Margaret, Australia

"Nature's Touch Guest House was the best B&B that we experienced in New Zealand during our trip in March 2008. ...the food was amazing. The breakfasts outdid any other B&B by a long shot, and the Japanese meal was great. Thank-you Natsuko and Maarten for making our vacation memorable with a stay at your home" Don and Julie, Canada

A warm welcome from us and baby Lina and friendly dog, Lucky! We are nautical themed B&B and just a short stroll to the beach. Only 10 minutes drive to the city, 15 minute drive (almost straight line) to the ferry terminal and the airport driving along the coast. Upper Boat Bedroom (Luxury suite) is for you to enjoy whole of upstairs and elevated views as well as privacy. Enjoy tranquillity.

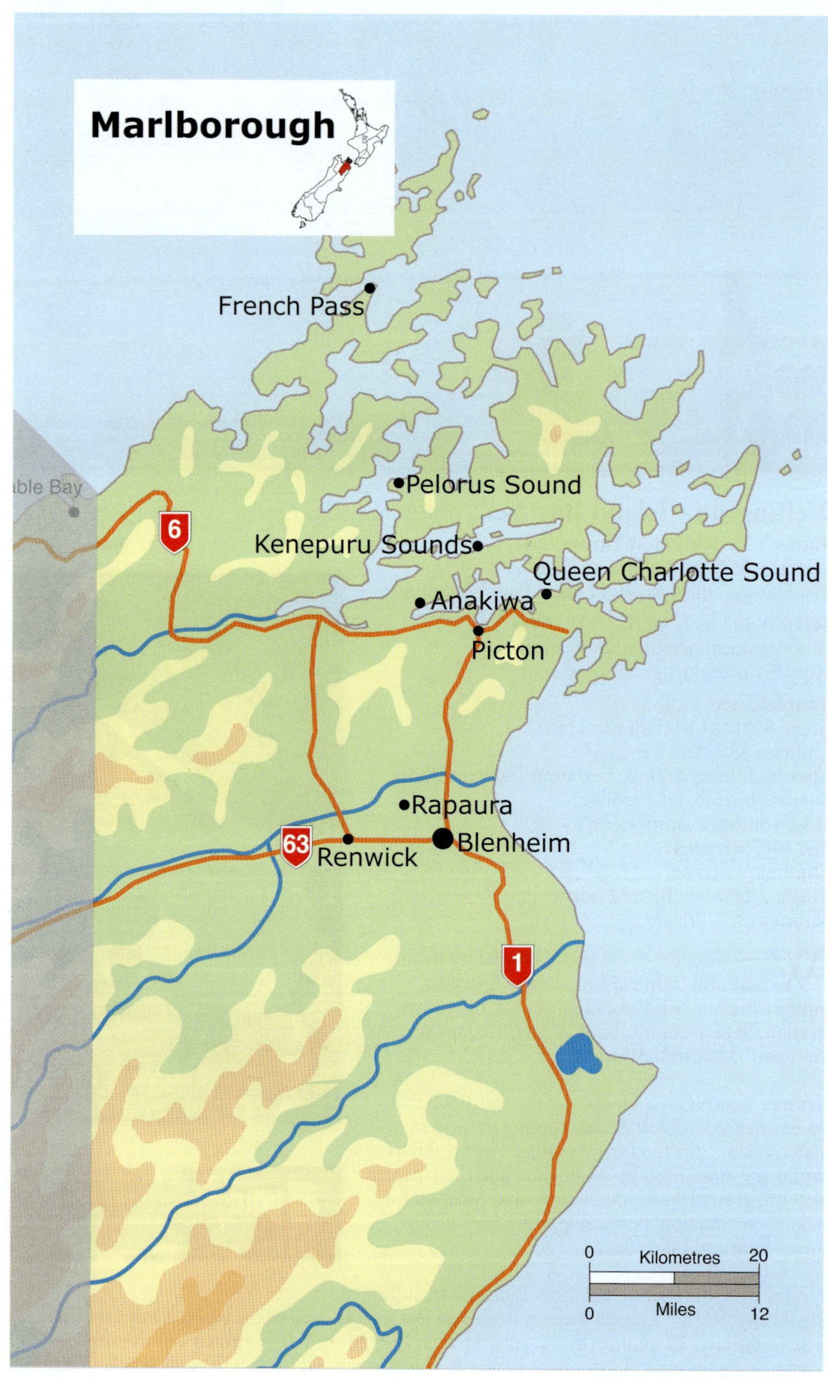
Marlborough
French Pass
Pelorus Sound
Kenepuru Sounds
Queen Charlotte Sound
Anakiwa
Picton
Rapaura
Blenheim
Renwick
6
63
1
0
Kilometres
20
0
Miles
12

Picton *1 km E of Picton Central*

Retreat Inn *B&B Homestay*
Alison & Geoff
20 Lincoln Street,
Picton 7220

Tel (03) 573 8160
or 021 143 2224
Fax (03) 573 8160
alisonandgeoff@retreat-inn.co.nz
www.retreat-inn.co.nz

Double/Twin $130-$140
(Special breakfast)
Room rate $130-$140
Not suitable for children
2 Queen 2 Single (2 bdrm)
(Either a Queen or twin room upstaris)
Bathrooms: 1 Ensuite 1 Private

Set in peaceful bush surroundings, Retreat Inn Homestay/B&B offers you comfort & rest, with a yummy breakfast! A choice of guest bedrooms - ground floor queen room (ensuite, bath and shower)with outside access to fern/seating area. Upstairs - queen(or twin)room, private bathroom. Marlborough province is diverse, unforgettable - come stay 2 or 3 nights and explore what we have to offer. Flat off-street parking. A happy 2 person/1 cat/1 hen household!

Picton *0.5 km SE of Picton Central*

Grandvue *B&B Homestay Apartment with Kitchen*
Rosalie & Russell Mathews
19 Otago Street, Picton 7220

Tel (03) 573 8553
or 0800 49 1080
or 027 249 1080
Fax (03) 573 8556
enquiries@grandvuepicton.co.nz
www.grandvuepicton.co.nz

Double/Twin $125-$140
Single $70-$100
(Continental breakfast)
Children $40
Visa MC accepted
Pet free home Children welcome
2 Queen 1 Twin 1 Single (3 bdrm)
1 in Apartment, 2 in homestay
Bathrooms: 1 Ensuite 1 Family share

On the hills above Picton, Grandvue is a quiet haven in a secluded garden with a grand-view. It's a 5 minute walk to the shopping area, restaurants, the waterfront & bushwalks. Russell, retired, enjoys boating, fishing & gardening. Rosalie an enthusiastic quilter, loves cooking & gardening. Both enjoy meeting people. The accommodation is spacious, warm, quality & self-contained with kitchen & ensuite. Other rooms available in our home. Feast on magnificent views from our conservatory while enjoying a wholesome breakfast. Courtesy transport, parking & laundry facilities

Picton *0.25 km SE of Picton*

Rivenhall *B&B Homestay*
Nan & Malcolm Laurenson
118 Wellington Street,
Picton,
Marlborough 7220

Tel (03) 573 7692
rivenhall@kol.co.nz
www.rivenhall.co.nz

Double/Twin $140
Single $100
(Full breakfast)
Visa MC accepted
Pet free home
Children welcome
1 Queen 1 Double (2 bdrm)
Bathrooms: 2 Private

Up the rise, on the left, at the top of Wellington Street, is Rivenhall. A gracious home with all the warmth, comfort and charm of days gone by, overlooking the town of Picton with its background of surrounding hills. Yet it is a gentle stroll to the centre of town or the ferry's beyond. Courtesy pick up from the ferry, bus or train. The Marlborough Sounds start at the bottom of our street.

Picton - Kenepuru Sounds *80 km NE of Havelock*

B&B Approved

The Nikaus *B&B Farmstay*
Alison & Robin Bowron
86 Manaroa Road,
Waitaria Bay, RD 2,
Picton 7282

Tel (03) 573 4432
or 027 454 4712
Fax (03) 573 4432
info@thenikaus.co.nz
www.thenikaus.co.nz

Double/Twin $130
Single $65
(Full breakfast)
Dinner $35
Visa MC accepted
1 Queen 4 Single (3 bdrm)
1 Queen & 2 twin
Bathrooms: 1 Guest share

The Nikaus sheep & cattle farm is situated in Waitaria Bay, Kenepuru Sound, 2 hours drive from Blenheim or Picton. We offer friendly personal service in our comfortable spacious home. Large gardens contain rhododendrons, roses, Camellia, lilies and perennials, big sloping lawns and views out to sea. House pets Minny (Jack Russel-cross)Honey (Lab)+ 4cats, Other animals include the farm dogs, donkeys, pet wild pigs, turkeys, hens and peacocks. Country meals, home-grown produce. Operators available for fishing trips, launch charters, golf and various walks.

Picton - Queen Charlotte Sounds *16 km W of Picton*

Tanglewood *B&B Homestay Separate Suite Apartment with Kitchen*

Linda & Stephen Hearn
1744 Queen Charlotte Drive,
The Grove,
RD 1,
Picton

Tel (03) 574 2080
or 027 481 4388
Fax (03) 574 2044
tanglewood.hearn@xtra.co.nz

Double/Twin $145-$165
Single $95-$120
(Full breakfast)
Dinner $40
Self-contained $195
Visa MC accepted
2 King/Twin 1 Queen 2 Single (4 bdrm)
Bathrooms: 4 Ensuite

Modern architectural home nestled amongst the native ferns overlooking Queen Charlotte Sounds. Enjoy our luxury Super King/Twin ensuite rooms with balcony and views; or a self contained guest wing which includes Queen and two Single beds (with ensuites), lounge, kitchen and sunny balcony/BBQ area. Relax in our jacuzzi surrounded by beautiful native garden and birds or view the glow-worms. Substainal breakfast provided before your day's pursuits, swimming, fishing, kayaking, walking the Queen Charlotte Walkway or exploring Marlborough Wineries. Fifth generation Kiwi hospitality at its best.

~

Pelorus - Mahau Sound *33 km W of Picton*

Ramona *B&B Homestay*

Phyl & Ken Illes
460 Moetapu Bay Road,
Mahau Sound, Marlborough

Tel (03) 574 2215
or 027 247 6668
illes@clear.net.nz

Double/Twin $120
Single $85 (Continental breakfast)
We can accomodate 3 children
3 course dinner served with
local wine by arrangement
Tea & coffee available
in conservatory
Visa MC accepted
Pet free home Children welcome
1 Queen 2 Twin (2 bdrm)
All beds have electric blankets
Bathrooms: 1 Private Hair dryer in bathroom

Our waterfront home on the beautiful Mahau Sound has been designed for you to share. Our guest floor has its own conservatory, here you can view the passing water traffic. Awake to the call of bellbirds and tuis, and after breakfast stroll around our large garden, or fossick on the beach. In the evening, see our glowworms. Phyl's interests include quilting, gardening and oilpainting. Ken is a retired builder. Visits to local craft studios can be arranged. We host only 1 party at a time.

Picton - Queen Charlotte Sound *11 km W of Picton*

Waterfront Bed & Breakfast *B&B Homestay*

Vicki & David Bendell
Queen Charlotte Drive,
2383 Little Ngakuta Bay,
RD 1,
Picton

Tel (03) 573 8584
or 027 748 4172
waterfront@farmside.co.nz
www.picton.co.nz/waterfront

Double/Twin $165-$185
(Full breakfast)
Dinner with notice $50pp
BBQ or fish followed by cheese platter
Diners accepted
Children welcome
2 Queen (2 bdrm)
Bathrooms: 1 Ensuite 1 Private

Our waterfront accommodation is as close to the water as you can get. Seperate from our cottage are the aptly named and themed Boatshed and Pacific rooms with ensuite, private bathroom and Italian cotton linens. A long jetty outfront is ideal for swimming, fishing or an evening stroll to see the water fluoresce. Please join us for a meal on the deck over-looking the water. We have a young family and dog - not just another B&B but an accommodation experience with a NZ family.

~

Picton *0.5 km E of Picton*

Glengary *B&B*

Glenys & Gary Riggs
5 Seaview Cresent,
Picton

Tel (03) 573 8317
or 027 498 6388
g.riggs@xtra.co.nz
www.glengary.co.nz

Double/Twin $130-$140
Single $70
(Continental breakfast)
Pet free home
Not suitable for children
2 King/Twin 2 Queen (3 bdrm)
Bathrooms: 2 Ensuite 1 Private

Located a short drive from Picton Ferry Terminal and a few minutes walk to the town centre. Inner harbour across the road. Whether you are interested in visiting wineries, fishing, bush walking, cruising, sea kayaking or simply relaxing in idyllic surroundings Glengary Bed & Breakfast is ideally located to explore the Marlborough area. Your friendly hosts will provide you with the best service to ensure your stay in the beautiful Marlborough Sounds is relaxing and enjoyable.. Ferry pick up. 2 night stay recemended..

Marlborough

Picton *3 km NE of Picton*

B&B Approved

Michiru *B&B*
Rosemary & Paul Royer
247B Waikawa Road, Waikawa, Picton
Tel (03) 573 6793 or (mob) 021 212 1689
Fax (03) 573 6793
relax@michiru.co.nz
www.michiru.co.nz

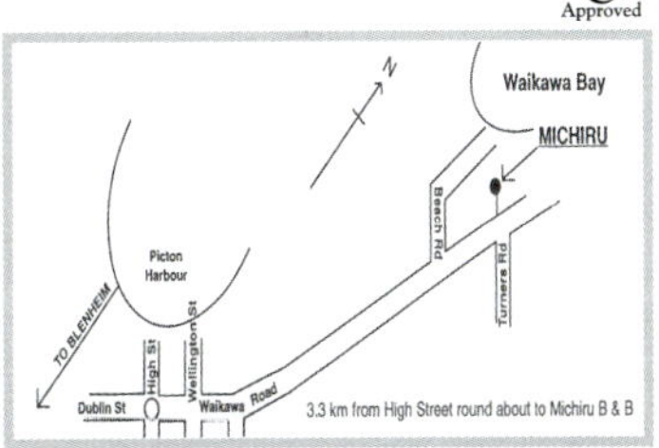

Double/Twin $140-$160 Single $90
(Special breakfast)
Dinner $50 by arrangement
Visa MC accepted Children welcome
1 King 1 Queen 2 Single (3 bdrm)
Bathrooms: 1 Ensuite 2 Private

We only have one aim - to give you the finest and most memorable experience that we are able to provide. We overlook Waikawa Bay and the beautiful Queen Charlotte Sounds so you can watch the ferries and cruise ships pass while enjoying breakfast: and all of this is only 3km from Picton town centre.

The bright and sunny rooms are all located on the ground floor with a lovely private guest lounge and garden patio. Guests have the use of laundry facilities. We invite you to join us for Rosemary's delightful 3 course dinners with a glass of wine (by arrangement). We will of course meet or drop you at the ferry terminal, especially if you are walking the Queen Charlotte Track and don't have your own transport. There is a waterside restaurant and a cafe/bar within 5 minutes walk of the house. You'll love this location!

Walk the Queen Charlotte Track, kayak or sail the Queen Charlotte Sounds, take half or whole day winery tours, daily dolphin watch tours, re-live The Edwin Fox experience (she's the world's ninth oldest ship), visit the fascinating Seahorse World, and finally our favourite place Karaka Point historical site. Superb accommodation for the discerning guests!

Picton *0.25 km SW of Post Office*

Marineland Heritage House B & B *B&B Guest House*

Rosemary Baxter & Peter Broad
28 Waikawa Road, Picton, 7250

Tel (03) 5736 429
or Freephone: 0800 616 429
Fax (03) 5737 634
marineland@xtra.co.nz
www.marinelandaccom.co.nz

Double/Twin $90-$120
Single $75-$120
(Continental breakfast)
Dinner by arrangement during winter only
Visa MC Diners Amex
Eftpos accepted
Not suitable for children under 13
1 King 1 Queen 5 Double
3 Twin 1 Single (11 bdrm)
Bathrooms: 5 Ensuite 6 Guest share

Enjoy Marineland Heritage House B & B, built in 1925 for the local Doctor. All downstairs rooms have ensuites, upstairs rooms have shared bathrooms. Rooms have electric blankets & tea/coffee making facilities. A comfortable lounge with Broadband Internet access & SKY TV. Adjacent to the lounge is the breakfast room for our "Picton Breakfast", a wheat & gluten free option is available. We offer a laundry & parking. In-ground swimming pool. We are a few minutes walk from town centre & water front.

Picton- Queen Charlotte Sound - Anakiwa *22 km W of Picton*

Queens View B&B *B&B Separate Suite Apartment with Kitchen*

Ann & John McGuire
259G Anakiwa Rd,
Anakiwa - Picton, RD1

Tel (03) 574 2363
or 021 0229 2864
enquiries@queensview.co.nz
www.queensview.co.nz

Double/Twin $145-$180
Single $90-$120
(Full breakfast)
Dinner by arrangement -
BBQ Facilities Available
Local Hotel 6 mins drive
Visa MC accepted
Pet free home
Children welcome
2 Queen 1 Twin (3 bdrm)
Bathrooms: 1 Ensuite 2 Private

Our elevated deck over the top of the Punga trees offers guests argueably some of the best views off the Queen Charltte Sound. The shoreline no more than a 3 min walk. The Queen Charlotte Track (10 mins walk),the holiday town of Picton (30 mins), the marina & mussel town of Havelock (25 mins)and the winery district of Blenheim (40 mins). So if your holiday is walking, swimming, boating, fishing, kayaking or exploring the many wineries then Queensview BnB is the ideal central location.

Picton *0.2 km N of Picton*

Echo Lodge *B&B Homestay*

Sharon & Russell Hooker
5 Rutland Street,
Picton

Tel (03) 573 6367
or 0274 988 544
or 0274 213 359
Fax (03) 573 6387
echolodge@xtra.co.nz
www.echolodge.co.nz

Double/Twin $120-$140
Single $80
(Continental breakfast)
Twin from $120
Pet free home
Children welcome
2 Queen 1 Twin 1 Single (3 bdrm)
Bathrooms: 3 Ensuite

Overlooking the Picton Marina, Echo lodge is an easy 5 minute stroll from the town centre with its many cafes, restaurants and tour operators and a 2 minute walk from the many bush and waterfront walks in the area. Come and enjoy our home comforts, including a continental breakfast featuring fresh bread, locally made jams and homemade yoghurt served in our guest lounge.A large garden offers many areas to sit and relax. Courtesy transfer from Picton airport, bus train or Ferry Terminals.

Picton *0.5 km SE of Picton*

Palm Haven B&B *B&B*

Denise Heaps
15 A Otago Street,
Picton, 7220

Tel (03) 573 5644
or 027 475 5178
Fax (03) 5735648
palmhaven@xtra.co.nz
www.palmhaven.co.nz

Double/Twin $135-$145
Single $85
(Continental breakfast)
Visa MC Eftpos accepted
Pet free home
Not suitable for children
2 Queen 1 Twin 1 Single (3 bdrm)
One triple, one double, one twin
Bathrooms: 2 Ensuite 1 Private

Palm Haven is a modern purpose built home designed for your comfort and convenience. Overlooking Picton and Mt Freeth, it is just a few minutes walk to the shopping center,cafes, restaurants and waterfront where guided walks, kayaking and a variety of boating, fishing and winery tours are available. Guest rooms, two with ensuites and one with private bathroom, accomodating triple, double or single occupancy all have tea and coffee making facilities, TV and bar fridge. Courtesy pickup from ferry, bus or train is provided.

Picton *9.1 km NE of Picton*

Charlotte House *B&B*
Peter Hill
432 Port Underwood Road,
Picton
Tel (03) 573 8969
charlothouse@kol.co.nz
www.charlottehousemarlboroughsounds.co.nz

Double/Twin $150
(Continental breakfast)
Visa MC accepted
Pet free home
Not suitable for children
1 Queen (1 bdrm)
Bathrooms: 1 Ensuite

Enjoy the magnificence of the Queen Charlotte Sounds from your secluded, private suite where a uniquely tranquil and restful environment awaits you. A private deck runs the full length of the suite, with its own private entrance, air conditioned comfort with amazing sea views from every room. Lazy boy chairs, LCD TV, CD and DVD players with a selection of disks, wool underlay on bed. A home away from home. As one of our guests put it "An absolutely beautiful haven, wish were staying longer".

Blenheim - Rapaura *12 km NW of Blenheim*

Thainstone *Homestay Cottage with Kitchen*
Vivienne & Jim Murray
120 Giffords Road, RD 3, Rapaura
Tel (03) 572 8823
Fax (03) 572 8623
thainstone@xtra.co.nz
www.thainstone.co.nz

Double/Twin $140
Single $75
(Full breakfast)
Dinner $45
Self catering housc $130-$190,
(sleeps 2-4) no breakfast
Visa MC Amex accepted
Not suitable for children
1 King 2 Queen 2 Twin (5 bdrm)
3 bedrooms in homestay, 2 in cottage
Bathrooms: 1 Ensuite
1 Private 1 Guest share

Our large home is surrounded by vineyards and within walking distance of the Wairau River and several wineries. In our home there are 3 upstairs bedrooms and a guest lounge. The self-catering house has 2 bedrooms and is fully equipped for longer stays. The indoor swimming pool is heated during the summer months. We are widely travelled and some interests are bird watching, trout fishing, woodworking and cards. Evening meals, by prior arrangement, are served with Marlborough wines.

Blenheim *1 km W of Blenheim Central*

Beaver B&B *Homestay Cottage with Kitchen*
Jen & Russell Hopkins
60 Beaver Road,
Blenheim

Tel (03) 578 8401
or 021 626 151
Fax (03) 578 8401
rdhopkins@xtra.co.nz
http://marlborough.co.nz/beaver/

Double/Twin $100
Single $60
(Continental breakfast)
Visa MC accepted
Not suitable for children
1 Queen (1 bdrm)
Bathrooms: 1 Ensuite

Our self-contained unit has its own entrance and off-street parking-5 minutes drive from central Blenheim and 10 minutes drive from the wineries and the Aviation Heritage Centre.The bed is queen-size.The mini-kitchen has a microwave,small sink and fridge containing items for a self-serve continental breakfast to have at your leisure.The bathroom has a large bath and a separate shower and toilet.2 cats live with us and we have bikes for hire.

Blenheim *2.5 km N of Blenheim*

Philmar *B&B Homestay*
Wynnis & Lex Phillips
9 Maple Close,
Springlands,
Blenheim

Tel (03) 577 7788
Fax (03) 577 7788
philmar9@xtra.co.nz

Double/Twin $80-$100
Single $60-$80
(Continental breakfast)
Dinner $20pp by arrangement
2 Queen 1 Twin (3 bdrm)
Bathrooms: 1 Ensuite 1 Guest share

Welcome to our home 2.5 km from the town centre. Guests can join us in our spacious sunny living areas. We both enjoy all sports on TV and our other interests include wood turning, handcrafts and the Lions organisation. Blenheim has many wineries, parks, craft shops, art galleries and golf courses. Not far from Picton, Nelson & Kaikoura whale watching. We share our home with our pets, Lucy-Lu and Louie. Smoking is not encouraged. Just phone to be picked up at airport, bus or train.

Blenheim *2 km N of Blenheim*

The Willows *B&B Homestay*

Millie Amos
6 The Willows,
Springlands,
Blenheim
Tel (03) 577 7853
Fax (03) 577 7853

Double/Twin $112
Single $70
(Continental breakfast)
Payment by cash or cheque
1 Queen 2 Twin (2 bdrm)
Bathrooms: 1 Private

Only 2km from the centre of town. The Willows is a spacious and modern home in close proximity to shops, restaurants and wineries. Peaceful location surrounded by lovely gardens. I welcome you to my home, so please phone first.

~

Blenheim *1 km N of Blenheim Central*

Maxwell House *Homestay*

John and Barbara Ryan
82 Maxwell Road,
Blenheim
Tel (03) 577 7545
Fax (03) 577 7545
mt.olympus@xtra.co.nz

Double/Twin $140
Single $100
(Full breakfast)
Visa MC accepted
Children welcome
1 Queen 1 Twin (2 bdrm)
Bathrooms: 2 Ensuite

Welcome to Marlborough. We invite you to stay at Maxwell House, a grand old Victorian residence. Built in 1880 our home has been elegantly restored and is classified with the Historic Places Trust. Our large guest rooms are individually appointed with ensuite, lounge area, television and tea & coffee making facilities. Breakfast will be a memorable experience, served around the original 1880's kauri table. Set on a large established property Maxwell House is an easy ten minute walk to the town centre. Non-smoking.

Blenheim *30 km S of Picton*

ParkView B&B *B&B*

B&B Approved

Geoff & Shirley Cant
30 Solway Drive,
Blenheim, Marlborough
Tel (03) 578-4492 or 0800 784 492
or 021 299 1705 or 021 141 7660
Fax (03) 578 4492
parkviewbb@xtra.co.nz
www.parkviewbb.co.nz

Double/Twin $120-$130
Single $100-$100
(Continental breakfast)
Children $45
Cooked breakfast by arrangement
Visa MC accepted
Pet free home Children welcome
3 Queen 1 Single (3 bdrm)
En-suited bedroom overlooks park
Bathrooms: 1 Ensuite 1 Private 1 Family share Bath & shower in en-suite

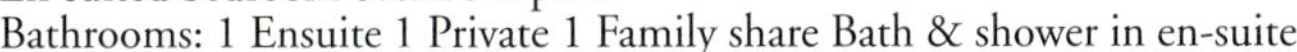

ParkView is a modern quality residence in a quiet Blenheim suburb adjacent to Harling Park & Japanese Garden and Wither Hills Farm Park.You can enjoy walking or cycling in Harling Park and the magnificent Wither Hills Farm Park and borrow our cycles and visit some of the many local wineries. Relax on ParkView's verandah overlooking the Japanese Garden with a glass of local wine. We offer free of charge:Wireless broadband internet Laundry & BBQComplimentary transfer service to airport, bus, train or restaurant.

~

Blenheim *0.1 km W of central Blenheim*

Henry Maxwell's B&B *Luxury B&B*

B&B Approved

Diana and Graham Westenra
28 Henry Street, Blenheim
Tel (03) 578 8086 or 0800 436 796
or 027 477 4808 or 027 485 5142
graymere@xtra.co.nz
www.henrymaxwells.co.nz

Double/Twin $110-$140
Single $80-$90 (Full breakfast)
Children price depending on age
Visa MC Eftpos accepted
Children welcome
3 Queen 1 Double 1 Twin
2 Single (5 bdrm)
3 large comfortable rooms,
one small single, 1 small double
Bathrooms: 4 Ensuite 1 Private
Bath in the large bathroom

Welcome to Henry Maxwell's Bed & Breakfast and Accommodation. A gracious 80 year old home,under new management. Guests have spacious quiet rooms, 4 with ensuites, 1 with a private bathroom. Comfortable beds and chairs, TV, tea, coffee, and complimentary port.Breakfast in the unique dining room (maps and charts)is memorable, kitchenette facilities. Guest laundry, wireless, library. 5 minutes stroll to town, restaurants, shops, theatre. Off-street parking.Very suitable for extended stays,conference and wedding parties. Discounts. Affordable luxury.

Blenheim *7 km N of Blenheim*

Blue Ridge Estate Vineyard Homestay *B&B Homestay*

Lesley & Brian Avery
50 O'Dwyers Road,
RD 3,
Blenheim

Tel (03) 570 2198
stay@blueridge.co.nz
www.blueridge.co.nz

Double/Twin $200-$250
Single $200-$250
(Full breakfast)
Visa MC accepted
Not suitable for children
2 Queen 2 Twin (3 bdrm)
Bathrooms: 1 Ensuite 2 Private

Set on a 20 acre vineyard, Blue Ridge Estate, 2002 Marlborough Master Builders' "House of the Year", enjoys a rural setting with stunning views across vineyards to the Richmond Range and is close to many of Marlborough's fine wineries, restaurants and gardens. Our home has proven popular with all visitors. Share our home with Bella our friendly labrador, where comfort and privacy will ensure your Marlborough visit is indeed a memorable one. Wireless Internet access available. This property is not suitable for children

Blenheim *9 km NW of Blenheim*

Stonehaven Vineyard Homestay *B&B Homestay*

Paulette & John Hansen
414 Rapaura Road, RD 3, Blenheim

Tel (03) 572 9730 or 027 682 1120
Fax (03) 572 9730
stay@stonehavenhomestay.co.nz
www.stonehavenhomestay.co.nz

Double/Twin $225-$250
Single $145-$230 (Full breakfast)
Children suitable 10 years and over
Three course dinner $68pp
by arrangement wine available
Guest bike hire $30 pp
Visa MC accepted
1 King 1 Queen 1 Twin (3 bdrm)
Vineyard and mountain views
from all guest rooms
Bathrooms: 2 Ensuite 1 Private
Twin room private bathroom is downstairs

Stonehaven is surrounded by beautiful gardens in a Sauvignon Blanc vineyard in the premium grape growing area of Marlborough. Spacious and comfortable, our home commands exquisite views over vineyards to the Richmond Ranges. Close by are some of NZ's most outstanding wineries. Our delicious breakfasts are often served in the summerhouse overlooking the pool.Dinner is available by arrangement. Wireless internet access available. We have a cat and labrador. We look forward to making your stay as relaxing or as active as you choose.

Blenheim *3 km S of Blenheim*

Redwood Heights *Luxury B&B*

Kathy & Mike Besley
245 Redwood Street,
Blenheim, 7201

Tel 0800 733 001
or (03) 578 0143
or 027 680 3125
Fax (03) 578 0143
redwoodheights@xtra.co.nz
www.redwoodheights.co.nz

Double/Twin $115-$175
Single $90
(Full breakfast)
Visa MC accepted
Children welcome by arrangement
1 King 1 Queen 2 Single (3 bdrm)
1 king, 1 queen, 2 singles
Bathrooms: 1 Ensuite 2 Private

Relax in modern, private quality accommodation. Enjoy extensive views and a country atmosphere. Stream Reserve Room is spacious, with ensuite and refreshment making facilities. Separate guest lounge and balcony. Close to wineries, restaurants, 3km to town centre. Adjacent to Wither Hills walkways and bike tracks. A perfect base for day trips to Picton, Marlborough Sounds, Kaikoura or Nelson. one friendly cat, Wireless, internet available and free laundry. Room photos and information on website.

Blenheim Central *1.5 km SW of Post Office*

Radfield House *Luxury B&B*

Bill & Jayne Telford
126 Maxwell Road,
Blenheim, 7201

Tel (03) 578 8671
or 021 357 038
jaynebill@xtra.co.nz
www.radfieldhouse.co.nz

Double/Twin up to $150
(Continental breakfast)
Children welcome by arrangement
Dinner $40-$50 by arrangment
House trained pets welcome
by arrangement
Visa MC Eftpos accepted
2 Queen 1 Twin (3 bdrm)
Twin is for children - bunk beds
Bathrooms: 1 Ensuite 1 Private
Private bathroom as shower and spa bath

Enjoy luxury Bed and Breakfast accommodation at Radfield House, one of Blenheim's more gracious properties. We provide courtesy transfers to/from Picton ferry terminals or the local airports. Free tea, coffee and juice also free use of mountain bikes to tour the vineyards. Our main aim is to make your stay as comfortable and memorable as possible. Bill and Jayne look forward to meeting you as do Tess our dog and BeeJay our Birman cat.

Blenheim Central *0.1 km E of Blenheim*

Brickweld House *B&B*
Julie Yonge
5 Weld Street, Blenheim

Tel (03) 577 9915
or 027 686 5891
info@brickweldhouse.co.nz
www.brickweldhouse.co.nz

Double/Twin $140-$160
Single $70-$100
(Full breakfast)
Dinner by arrangement
Visa MC accepted
Not suitable for children
2 King/Twin 2 Queen (3 bdrm)
Queen with ensuite; twin king single queen
Bathrooms: 1 Ensuite 1 Private
1 Guest share

Your sanctuary after discovering the treasures Marlborough has to offer. Enjoy the convenience of a 10 minute stroll to the town centre where you will find many dining options or dine in by arrangement (24 hours notice required). In a peaceful garden setting, relax in the friendly atmosphere; sleep under the luxury of pure silk duvets; breakfast in the garden. Tea and coffee making facilities in rooms; separate guest lounge. Famous wineries just minutes away. Off-street parking. Join me for a glass of world acclaimed Marlborough Sauvignon blanc at the end of your day of adventure. You will also meet Lizzie, my very affectionate cat.

Blenheim *5 km SW of Blenheim*

B&B Approved

Ashwood Bed & Breakfast *B&B Homestay*
Maureen & Reg Sagar
17 Ashwood Drive
Blenheim 7201

Tel (03)579 1700 or 027 313 0125
maureen.reg@xtra.co.nz
www.ashwoodbnb.co.nz

Double/Twin $115 Single $78
(Continental breakfast)
Children: 3-12 $30, Under 3 Free
Dinner $35pp with 24 hours notice
Children welcome
Cooked breakfast extra, by request
1 Queen 2 Twin (2 bdrm)
Bathrooms: 1 Guest Share

Reg and Maureen welcome you to Ashwood Bed and Breakfast in our warm, modern home adjacent to the foothills of the Wither Hills Farm Park. We offer a continental breakfast,or cooked by arrangement, served in our dining room looking out to the beautiful Richmond Ranges. You can be assured of a good nights sleep in comfortable beds in a quiet neighbourhood. 5 Minutes drive from the centre of Blenheim, we are also near the Provincial Museum, the Aviation Centre and many local wineries.

Blenheim - Riverlands *6.5 km S of Blenheim*

B&B Approved

Riverlands B & B *B&B*
Cathryn & Colin White
42 Hardings Road,
Riverlands,
Blenheim 7274
Tel (03) 577 6733
or 021 036 1091
Fax (03) 577 6733
cathryn.colin@xtra.co.nz

Double/Twin $120-$150
Single $90-$90
(Continental breakfast)
Dinner by arrangement
Not suitable for children
3 Queen 1 Single (3 bdrm)
3 double rooms with queen beds
Bathrooms: 1 Private 1 Guest share

Warm friendly hospitality awaits you at our sunny, comfortable, modern home located only 6.5 km from Blenheim, opposite Montana Brancott Winery. We offer quiet rural accommodation, with panoramic views over the Wairau Valley and nearby vineyards. Share our spacious lounge, or relax in the guest lounge, or have a soak in our luxury outdoor spa. We share our lovely home with our son Dlyan and our cat Sid.We offer free of charge: Broadband internet Laundry, BBQ, Spa

Renwick *10 km W of Blenheim*

B&B Approved

Clovelly *B&B Homestay*
Don & Sue Clifford
2A Nelson Place,
Renwick,
Marlborough 7204
Tel (03) 572 9593
or 027 695 1614
Fax (03) 572 7293
clifford@actrix.co.nz
www.clovelly.co.nz

Double/Twin $140
Single $100
(Special breakfast)
Visa MC accepted
Children welcome
1 King/Twin 1 Queen (2 bdrm)
Bathrooms: 2 Private

Our colonial style home is set in lovely private grounds in the heart of vineyard country. We overlook organic orchards and out to the Richmond Range. Complimentary tea and coffee with home made baking.Visit the quaint local English pub. Dine in the village or vineyard restaurants. We are close to a number of prestigious vineyards. Complimentary bicycles are available for guests to cycle the vineyards and surrounds. Don, Sue and our Scottish terriers Chloe and Phoebe and cat Sophie, will welcome you most warmly.

Renwick *10 km W of Blenheim*

Olde Mill House B&B & Cycle Hire *B&B Homestay*

Diane Sutton
9 Wilson Street,
Renwick, Marlborough

Tel (03) 572 8458
or 0800 653 262 (0800 Old BNB)
Fax (03) 572 8458
info@oldemillhouse.co.nz
www.oldemillhouse.co.nz

Double/Twin up to $140
Single up to $100
(Continental breakfast)
Children under 12yrs $40
Extra adult in room $70
Visa MC Amex Eftpos accepted
Children welcome
2 King/Twin 1 Queen (3 bdrm)
Room can be king or twin single
Bathrooms: 3 Ensuite Heritage room ensuite with bathtub

Welcome to our elevated character bungalow, refurbished for your comfort whilst retaining its olde world charm. Our property consists of an extensive spa/bbq, garden area for you to relax in and enjoy views to the Richmond Ranges. We provide complimentary cycles for you to enjoy the local wine trail, a complimentary transfer service to local vineyard restaurants for evening dining. We also provide a wireless broadband internet service. We both enjoy gardening, motorcycling and our Border Collie dogs Rosie & Vinnie.

Near French Pass - Pelorus Sounds *110 km NE of Nelson*

Ngaio Bay Eco-homestay and B&B *B&B Homestay*

Jude & Roger Sonneland
Ngaio Bay, French Pass Road,
Pelorus Sounds

Tel (03) 576 5287
Fax (03) 576 5287
welcome@ngaiobay.co.nz
www.ngaiobay.co.nz

Double/Twin $175
Single $130 (Special breakfast)
Children 3-12 years $80,
Under 2 $30 all inclusive
Dinner $35pp, children 3-12 years $15
Lunch $20pp, picnic $15 pp,
$8 per child 3-12 years
Visa MC Eftpos accepted
2 King 3 Single (2 bdrm)
comfortable, sunny, private, own decks
Bathrooms: 2 Private R and D selfcontained, Garden Cottage bathroom in main house

Ngaio Bay, 2 hours scenic drive from Nelson or Blenheim, with private beach, is an authentic Kiwi experience.Near awesome waters of French Pass. The Garden Cottage and Rose & Dolphin are comfortable and private, overlooking beach, garden and bush. A honeymooners favourite. Guests linger at dinner enjoying scrumptious food and good conversation, open fire for cool evenings. Organic vegetable and flower garden and orchard, eco-composting toilets. Swim, walk, boat, relax; your choice.! Private fireheated bath on beach. special. Children welcome. 2 loveable labradors.

French Pass *116 km NE of Nelson*

French Pass Sea safaris & Beachfront Villas *Apartment with*

Kitchen Cottage with Kitchen

Danny and Lyn Boulton
RD3 French Pass, Marlborough Sounds

Tel (03) 576 5204 or (03) 576 5204
adventure@seasafaris.co.nz
www.seasafaris.co.nz

Double/Twin $164-$212
Single $52-$190 (Continental breakfast)
Children under 12yrs $35 to $55
Dinner - Scrumptious, organic salads & vegetables where possible served to your villa or barbecue patio
Visa MC Eftpos accepted
Pet free home Children welcome
3 Queen (5 bdrm)1 queen, 1 bunkroom in each villa, 1 queen cottage
Bathrooms: 3 Private
Private bathroom with shower in each Villa & Cottage

Breathtaking drive, stunning seascapes, Exquisite Qualmark 4 star waterfront accommodation. Barbecue patio and infra-red sauna. Relax, rejuvenate and revitalize. For adventure take a wildlife discovery tour, island walk or swim with seals and dolphins. For the sportfisher let us cook your catch for a taste of real kiwi living. Watch the moon rise from the sea and the sun set behind an island paradise. Dolphins from your balcony. Scrumptious home cooked meals, fresh organic salads, wonderful hospitality. Members Nelson's Sustainable Tourism Charter and active environmentalists.

Just as we have a variety of B&Bs you will also be offered a variety of breakfasts, and they will always be generous.

Nelson,
Golden Bay
Pakawau
Collingwood
Parapara
Takaka
60
Abel Tasman
National Park
Marahau
Kaiteriteri
Motueka
Motueka Valley
Ruby Bay
Atawhai
Mapua
Upper
Moutere
6
Nelson
Richmond
Wakefield
Brightwater
0
Kilometres
20
0
Miles
12
6
63
Murchison
65
Nelson
Lakes
St Arnaud

Nelson - Atawhai *6 km NE of Nelson*

B&B Approved

Mike's B&B *B&B Homestay*

Mike Cooper & Lennane Cooper-Kent
4 Seaton Street,
Nelson

Tel (03) 545 1671
mikecooper@actrix.co.nz
www.bnb.co.nz/hosts/kent

Double/Twin $80-$90
Single $80-$85
(Full breakfast)
Dinner $45 pp with prior notice
Visa MC accepted
2 Queen (2 bdrm)
Two double
Bathrooms: 2 Ensuite
Showers in ensuite bathroom

Five minutes NE of Nelson City we welcome you to our comfortable home in a quiet neighbourhood with extensive views out over Tasman Bay to the mountains beyond. Our guests' accommodation is almost self contained and includes ensuite bedrooms, a kitchenette with a fridge/freezer, microwave and complimentary tea and coffee making facilities, a small lounge with TV and part of our collection of books. Laundry facilities, internet access and off street parking are available. Our interests include travel, education, and volunteer work abroad.

Nelson *2 km SW of Central Nelson*

B&B Approved

Harbour View Homestay *B&B or Self-contained house (By arrangement)*

Judy Black
11 Fifeshire Crescent,
Nelson

Tel (03) 548 8567
or 027 247 4445
Fax (03) 548 8667
harbourview-homestay@xtra.co.nz

Double/Twin $145-$160
Single $125-$145
(Continental breakfast)
Enquire about available discounts
Visa MC accepted
2 Queen 2 Single (3 bdrm)
Bathrooms: 2 Ensuite 1 Private

Our home is above the harbour entrance. Huge windows capture spectacular views of beautiful Tasman Bay, Haulashore Island, Tahunanui Beach, across the sea to Abel Tasman National Park and mountains. Observe from the bedrooms, dining room and decks, ships and pleasure craft cruising by as they enter and leave the harbour. If you can tear yourself away from our magnificent view, within walking distance along the waterfront there are excellent cafes and restaurants. Judy, David and Possum the cat welcome you for a memorable stay.

Nelson *5 km SW of Nelson*

Arapiki *B&B Apartment with Kitchen B&B Self-contained Homestay Units*

Kay & Geoff Gudsell
21 Arapiki Road,
Stoke,
Nelson

Tel (03) 547 3741
bnb@nelsonparadise.co.nz
www.nelsonparadise.co.nz

Double/Twin $90-$120
Single $70-$90
Continental breakfast optional $7.50pp
Visa MC accepted
1 Queen 1 Double 1 Single (2 bdrm)
Bathrooms: 2 Ensuite

Enjoy a relaxing holiday in the midst of your trip. The 2 quality smoke-free units in our large centrally located home offer comfort, privacy, offstreet parking and Wireless Internet Access. The larger Unit 1 in a private garden setting opens on to a deck with outdoor furniture. It has an electric stove, microwave, TV, auto washing machine and phone. Unit 2 has a balcony with seating to enjoy sea and mountain views. It has a microwave, hotplate, TV and phone. We have two Tonkinese cats.

Nelson *3 km E of Nelson*

Brooklands *B&B Homestay*

Lorraine & Barry Signal
106 Brooklands Road,
Atawhai,
Nelson

Tel (03) 545 1423
Fax (03) 545 1423
barry.lori@xtra.co.nz

Double/Twin $120-$160
Single $75-$100
(Full breakfast)
Children by arrangement
Dinner $50
Visa MC accepted
Pet free home
Children welcome
1 King 1 Queen 1 Double
1 Twin (3 bdrm)
Bathrooms: 1 Ensuite 1 Guest share spa bath

Spacious, luxurious 4 level home with superb sea views. Spacious well furnished king room on top level. Next level has 2 bedrooms sharing large bathroom with spa bath for 2. 1 bedroom has a private balcony. Spacious indoor/outdoor living areas. We enjoy sports, travel and outdoors. Lorraine makes dolls and bears and enjoys crafts, gardening and cooking. We are close to Nelson's attractions - beaches, crafts, wine trails, national parks, lakes and mountains. We enjoy making new friends. Smoke-free. Courtesy transport available.

Nelson *0.75 km SW of Nelson Central*

B&B Approved

Peppertree B&B *B&B Separate Suite*

Richard Savill & Carolyn Sygrove
31 Seymour Avenue,
Nelson 7010

Tel (03) 546 9881
or (03) 021 074 6540
Fax (03) 546 9881
c.sygrove@clear.net.nz

Double/Twin $120
(Continental breakfast)
Children $20
Dinner $30-$40 by arrangement
Extra adult $35
Visa MC accepted
Children welcome
1 Queen 1 Double 1 Single (1 bdrm)
Separate master bedroom
adjoining private lounge
Bathrooms: 1 Ensuite

Enjoy space and privacy in our heritage villa, only 10 minutes riverside walk from Nelson's city centre. The master bedroom has an ensuite bathroom and walk-in wardrobe. Your private adjoining rooms include a large lounge with double innersprung sofabed, single bed, heat pump, Sky TV, fridge, microwave, kettle etc. Also sunroom with cane setting and private entrance. Email/internet/fax facilities and off-street parking available. We have 2 daughters aged 15 and 13. Children are welcome.

~

Nelson *2 km SW of Nelson*

B&B Approved

Beach Front B&B *B&B*

Oriel & Peter Phillips
581 Rocks Road,
Nelson

Tel (03) 548 5299
or 021 063 9529
Fax (03) 548 5299
peterp@tasman.net
www.bnb.co.nz

Double/Twin $125-$135
Single $100
(Full breakfast)
Visa MC accepted
Not suitable for children
1 Queen 1 Double (2 bdrm)
Bathrooms: 1 Ensuite 1 Private

As recommended by The Rough Guide. Our home is situated overlooking Tahunanui Beach, Haulashore Island and Nelson waterfront-amazing daytime mountain views-magnificent sunsets. Enjoy a wine out on the deck with your hosts. Excellent restaurants and cafes within walking distance, stroll to beach or 5 minute drive to city. Golf course, tennis courts and airport nearby. 1 hour drive to Abel Tasman. Both rooms have ensuite/private facilities, quality beds, electric blankets, fridge, TV, tea & coffee making facilities, heaters, iron and hairdryers. Kiwi Host. House Cat Rufus.

Nelson *0.5 km S of Information Centre*

Grampian Villa *B&B*

John & Jo Fitzwater
209 Collingwood Street, Nelson

Tel (03) 545 8209
or 021 459 736 (Jo), 021 969 071 (John)
Fax (03) 548 7888
Stay@GrampianVilla.co.nz
http://GrampianVilla.co.nz

Double/Twin $250-$350
Single $250-$350 (Full breakfast)
Children POA Dinner POA
Visa MC Eftpos accepted
Pet free home Not suitable for children
2 King/Twin 1 King 1 Queen 1 Single (4 bdrm)
Bathrooms: 4 Ensuite

Grampian Villa is a Grand Historic Villa from the Victorian Period. Located in the Historic precinct of Nelson City Centre, the Villa is a pleasant 5 minute walk to cafes, restaurants, parks, art galleries and museums.

Grampian Villa offers 4 spacious ensuites (3 SuperKing, 1 Queen w/clawfoot bath and shower) each have french doors opening onto the spacious verandahs with views of Nelson City and out to sea.

Grampian Villa Facilities: spacious tiled showers with heated floors and large heated towel rails. Wireless DSL internet access. Writing desk in all rooms. TV, DVD, in-house movies etc. available in all bedrooms Complimentary tea/coffee, port, local chocolates, cookies. An ever changing mouth watering breakfast is included.TV, VCR, CD, DVD, Stereo & SKY available in Lounge Children under the age of 12 years, by arrangement only.

To check for availability and/or make a reservation please go online to:
http://art.globalavailability.com/guests/guest-main.php?pid=271

Nelson - Tahunanui *4.5 km SW of Nelson*

B&B Approved

Lamont B&B *B&B*

Pam & Rex Lucas
167A Tahunanui Drive,
Tahunanui,
Nelson

Tel (03) 548 5551
or 0274 351 678
Fax (03) 548 5501
rexpam@xtra.co.nz

Double/Twin $125
Single $95 or by arrangement
(Full breakfast)
Children welcome by arrangement
Dinner (2 courses) $30
(24 hrs. notice required.)
Visa MC accepted
1 Queen 1 Double (2 bdrm)
Bathrooms: 1 Private 1 Guest share

We are in a position to offer high standard accommodation having 2 double bedrooms with own toilet and bathroom facilities. Our house is on a private property in Tahunanui Drive opposite the Nelson Surburban Club where it is possible to get an evening meal. A 2 minute drive to Tahuna Beach and 5 minutes to a number of waterfront restaurants gives plenty of variety and choice. We are a few minutes from the airport. Pick-up from airport and bus if required. 1 cat in residence.

Nelson *1 km E of Nelson Cathedral*

B&B Approved

Te Maunga - Historic House *B&B Homestay & Apartment with Kitchen*

Anne Kolless
15 Dorothy Annie Way
@ 82 Cleveland, Nelson City

Tel (03) 548 8605
or 021 201 2461
temaungahouse@xtra.co.nz
www.nelsoncityaccommodation.co.nz

Double/Twin $90-$135
Single $75-$90
(Continental breakfast)
Children negotiable
Self-catered $140
Visa MC accepted
Pet free home Children welcome
2 Double 1 Twin 1 Single (3 bdrm)
All with great views & comfort
Bathrooms: 2 Private 1 Guest share
Showers & tub-shower

Anne welcomes you to her family's 1930's registered Heritage House. Only 5 mins to downtown this stunning unique Arts & Crafts style, native woods example is mostly original with modern facilities. Te Maunga sits on a knoll, in rambling gardens, giving commanding views over Nelson, sea and valleys. Your special continental style breakfast includes local produce, home-made breads, and preserves. Relax and enjoy your aperitif, while taking in the amazing views. Self-catered unit next door! NZQA Food Safety Cert. Wireless Broadband link.

Nelson - Atawhai *4 km N of Nelson*

A Culinary Experience B&B at Sea Watch Estates

Luxury B&B Homestay

Kay & Joe Waller
15 Seawatch Way, Atawhai, Nelson
Tel (03) 545 1886 or 0800 891 886
or 027 445 1886 Fax (03) 545 1869
stay@a-culinary-experience.com
www.a-culinary-experience.com

Double/Twin $210-$325 Single $195-$310 (Special breakfast)
Not suitable for young children
Join your hosts for a 3-course gourmet dinner
Cooking Classes and Therapeutic Massage can be booked
Visa MC accepted Pets welcome
2 King/Twin 2 King (2 bdrm)
Bathrooms: 2 Ensuite

Welcome to our lovely home filled with laughter, amazing views, original art and fabulous food. Completed in June, 2009 this purpose-built Luxury Bed and Breakfast was designed with the discerning traveler in mind. Joe, a Naturopathic Doctor, provides therapeutic massage. Kay, cookbook author and former cooking school owner, provides delightful dinners or cooking classes. Let us pamper you! Indulge yourself with a soak in the spa, relax in the infrared sauna, have a massage and feel rejuvenated.

Enjoy the sea views from your private balcony or patio, the vineyard or olive and lavender garden or feed our lovely alpacas. Sip a complimentary glass of wine served with yummy appetizers to celebrate sensational sunsets, exquisite bay & mountain views. Read in the sculpture garden and quaff the aroma of fresh herbs, fruit, and organic produce that we grow for our gourmet meals. Book one of our luxurious rooms: king-size beds, heated tile ensuites (bathrooms) with 2 person shower or double spa bath, tea facilities, refrigerators and Wifi. Guest computer and media centre are located in the guest lounge. With so much to do in the region, a stay of 3 or more nights is recommended. Arrive as guests - leave as treasured friends.

Nelson *1 km E of Nelson Central*

Sussex House Bed & Breakfast *B&B*

home NEW ZEALAND
B&B Approved

Victoria & David Los
238 Bridge Street,
Nelson

Tel (03) 548 9972
Fax (03) 548 9975
reservations@sussex.co.nz
www.sussex.co.nz

Double/Twin $150-$180
Single $110-$150
(Full breakfast)
Visa MC Amex Eftpos accepted
Children welcome
5 Queen 3 Twin 3 Single (5 bdrm)
Bathrooms: 4 Ensuite 1 Private

Experience the peace and charm of the past in our fully restored circa 1880s B&B, one of Nelson's original family homes. Situated beside the beautiful Maitai River, Sussex House has retained all the original character and romantic ambiance of the era. It is only minutes' walk from central Nelson's award-winning restaurants and cafes, the Queens Gardens, Suter Art Gallery and Botanical Hill (The Centre of NZ) and many fine river and bushwalks.

The five sunny bedrooms all have TVs and are spacious and charmingly furnished. All rooms have access to the verandahs and complimentary tea and coffee facilities are provided. Breakfast includes a variety of fresh and preserved fruits, hot croissants and pastries, home-made yoghurts, cheeses and a large variety of cereals, rolls, breads and crumpets.

Other facilities include: wheelchair suite; free email/internet station; fax; courtesy phone; laundry facilities; separate lounge for guest entertaining; complimentary port; tea & coffee facilities; very sociable cat (Riley). We have lived overseas and have travelled extensively. We speak French fluently.

Nelson - Atawhai *5 km N of Nelson on SH6*

Strathaven Lodge *B&B Homestay*

Julie & Hugh Briggs
42 Strathaven Place,
Atawhai, Nelson

Tel (03) 545 1195
or 027 243 5301
Fax (03) 545 1195
strathavenlodge@xtra.co.nz
www.strathavenlodge.com

Double/Twin $125-$200
Single $100-$125
(Full breakfast)
Children $50
Dinner $40pp
Visa MC Diners accepted
Pet free home Children welcome
1 King 1 Queen 1 Single (3 bdrm)
3 (2 suites)Bathrooms: 2 Private

Relax in terrace spa, enjoy beautiful sea and mountain views, spectacular sunsets. Listen to melodious songs of tuis and bellbirds. Sleep deeply in very comfortable beds, in suites each with private bathrooms, robes, TV's and hairdryers. Wireless Internet access or free use of host's Internet. Bar fridge and tea-making in hall. Families welcome. Savour Hugh's generous breakfasts! Enjoy this slice of Nelson's paradise! Share travel experiences with your well travelled hosts, over a complimentary glass of local wine or beer and nibbles.

Nelson *3 km N of Nelson*

Havenview Homestay *B&B Homestay*

Shirley & Bruce Lauchlan
10 Davies Drive,
Nelson, 7010

Tel (03) 546 6045
or 027 420 0737
or 0800 546 604
havenview@paradise.net.nz
www.havenview.co.nz

Double/Twin $130-$150
(Full breakfast)
Dinner Two course with
a glass of wine $35 pp
Visa MC accepted
Not suitable for children
2 Queen (2 bdrm)
Large Queen ensuite sea view
other Queen room garden view
Bathrooms: 1 Ensuite 1 Private
Ensuite has shower; private shower and double spabath

Built for the magnificent views, our sunny modern home is on the northern entrance to Nelson, and only three minutes to the city. Relax with a complimentary wine while enjoying panoramic views overlooking the Miyazu Gardens and Tasman Bay. Enjoy dinner with us, or dine at a local restaurant; then relax in our lounge with Sky TV /Internet available. We are well travelled New Zealanders; play golf, and feel sure we can make your stay a pampered experience.

Nelson - Enner Glynn *5 km SW of Nelson*

home NEW ZEALAND   B&B Approved

Double View *B&B*

Judy Sisam
142 Panorama Drive,
Enner Glynn, 7011

Tel (03) 547 7292
or 027 411 8594
Fax (03) 547 7638
judy@doubleview.co.nz
www.doubleview.co.nz

Double/Twin $160
Single $140 (Special breakfast)
Dinner by prior arrangement
Visa MC Eftpos accepted
Pet free home
1 King 1 Queen (2 bdrm)
Beautifully appointed
Superior & Junior Suite.
Bathrooms: 1 Ensuite
Junior Suite shares ensuite

Double View has spectacular views over Tasman Bay located 5 minutes from Nelson Airport and 10 minutes from Nelson township. The Superior Suite is well appointed with spacious luxury Super King accommodation. The Junior Suite shares ensuite facilities. Guests are welcome to use laundry. Host Judy previously owned a cooking school and provides a great gourmet selection for breakfast. Dinner available by prior arrangement. Judy welcomes you to Double View to use as your base while exploring the region.

Nelson East *0.7 km E of Cathedral*

B&B Approved

Annick House *B&B Separate Suite*

Ann and Nick James
29 Cleveland Terrace,
Nelson, 7010

Tel (03) 548 0554
or 021 134 2808
Fax (03) 548 0505
nick.james@xtra.co.nz
www.annickhouse.co.nz

Double/Twin $180-$220
Single $140-$180
(Full breakfast)
Children over 12 are charged full rate
Dinner by arrangement only
Visa MC accepted
Children welcome
3 King/Twin 1 Single (3 bdrm)
Three super king bedrooms
Bathrooms: 3 Private

Annick house offers two private self contained studio units and a tradional bed and breakfast suite in a secluded garden setting eight minutes walk to the city centre. Our Out of Africa unit is 50sq/m. The A Touch Oriental unit is 40sq/m and has a separate lounge. Both are tastefully furnished and have a private entrances and bathrooms. They are equipped with kitchen facilities, cooking essentials and a BBQ. We offer a continental or cooked breakfast tray. Expect a welcome from our two Tokinese cats.

Richmond *0.5 km E of Richmond*

B&B Approved

Hunterville *Homestay*

Cecile & Alan Strang
30 Hunter Avenue,
Richmond,
Nelson

Tel (03) 544 5852
Fax (03) 544 5852
strangsa@clear.net.nz

Double/Twin $100
Single $70
(Full breakfast)
Children half price
Dinner $30 by arrangement
Children and pets welcome
1 King 1 Twin 1 Single (3 bdrm)
Bathrooms: 1 Private 1 Family share

Experience a family welcome in a real Kiwi home with drinks poolside in summer, or a cuppa and home-made biscuits. Our home is up a short driveway where we enjoy bird-song from surrounding trees. We are enroute to Golden Bay and Able Tasman park but just 15 minutes from Nelson City. We travel frequently so appreciate travellers needs;comfortable beds, laundry, generous breakfasts, dinner with local food and wine. Our interests: music, reading, bridge, our friendly Dalmatian(Coco) and the company of guests.

Richmond *1 km E of Richmond*

B&B Approved

Antiquarian Guest House *B&B*

Robert & Joanne Souch
12A Surrey Road,
Richmond,
Nelson

Tel (03) 544 0253
or (03) 544 0723
or 021 417 413
Fax (03) 544 0253
souchebys@clear.net.nz
http://souchebys@clear.net.nz

Double/Twin $95-$125
Single $80
(Full breakfast)
Children $10
Visa MC accepted
Children and pets welcome
1 King 1 Queen 1 Twin (3 bdrm)
Bathrooms: 1 Ensuite 1 Guest share

Bob & Joanne Souch welcome you to their peaceful home only 2 minutes from Richmond (15 minutes drive south of Nelson) - excellent base for exploring National Parks, beaches, arts/crafts, ski fields etc. Relax in the garden, beside the swimming pool or in our large TV/guest lounge. Tea/coffee facilities, home-baking and memorable breakfasts. Our family pet is Gemma (friendly border collie). As local antique shop owners we know the area well.

Richmond *12 km SW of Nelson*

Idesia *B&B*
Jenny & Barry McKee
14 Idesia Grove,
Richmond,
Nelson

Tel (03) 544 0409
or 0800 361 845
Fax (03) 544 0402
idesian@xtra.co.nz
www.idesia.co.nz

Double/Twin $100-$140
(Full breakfast)
Dinner $40 by arrangement
Visa MC accepted Pet free home
1 King/Twin 1 Queen (2 bdrm)
Bathrooms: 1 Ensuite 1 Private

You are assured of a warm welcome and quality service at Idesia Bed & Breakfast. Our home, elevated for sun and views is in a quiet grove easily accessible from State Highway 6. Breakfast is served with fresh seasonal fruits and a sizzling cooked selection. Join us for dinner, however Richmond's restaurants are close by. We offer broadband wireless network, off-road parking, information/booking Abel Tasman National Park. With our proven B&B experience we aim to give service and hospitality so you enjoy our regions attractions.

Richmond *12 km S of Nelson*

Lansfield Bed & Breakfast Homestay *B&B*
Dianne & Malcolm Tillier
6 Hugh Brown Place,
Richmond,
Nelson

Tel (03) 544 8166
or 021 131 3415
Fax (03) 544 8165
stay@lansfieldbedandbreakfast.co.nz
www.lansfieldbedandbreakfast.co.nz

Double/Twin $130-$150
Single $120
(Full breakfast)
Dinner $30
1 King/Twin 1 Queen (2 bdrm)
Quality linen, garden viewsBathrooms: 2 Ensuite

Situated in the foothills of Richmond, a suburb of Nelson, our home offers commanding views of the Waimea Plains and Tasman Bay. Expect a warm welcome, home baking and a wonderful breakfast. We use chemical free ENJO cleaning fibres throughout our home which reduce asthma and allergy reactions. our interests include Tango, classic cars and gardening. We have a friendly Burmese cat, Pheobe. Close by are vineyards and restaurants, and you are welcome to join us for a meal if arranged prior.

Brightwater *10 km NW of Richmond*

Westleigh *B&B Homestay Farmstay Separate Suite*

B&B Approved

John and Dell
Westleigh, Waimea West Road,
Brightwater,
Nelson, 7091

Tel (03) 542 3654
westleigh@paradise.net.nz
www.westleigh.co.nz

Double/Twin $130-$130
Single $100-$100
(Full breakfast)
Dinner 3 course with wine $35pp
Visa MC accepted
1 Queen 1 Twin (2 bdrm)
1 queen with ensuite, 1 twin
Bathrooms: 1 Ensuite 1 Guest share

Country home in 27 acres of privacy. House dates from c1860, now updated. 10 minutes to Richmond, golf and beach. Good local restaurants, but most guests eat with us,- more sociable and the food is ok too. A place for RnR, and central to all Nelson attractions. One cat. Directions: From Nelson, R6 past Richmond, turn off right at Brightwater, stay on that road c 5K. Westleigh sign prominent lhs. Or phone!

Wakefield *16 km S of Richmond*

Bushwalk B&B & Homestay *B&B Homestay*

B&B Approved

Bruce & Sandra Monro
15 Hunt Terrace,
Wakefield,
Nelson 7025

Tel (03) 541 9615
s_bmonro@bushwalk.co.nz
http://bushwalk.co.nz

Double/Twin $140-$160
Single $70-$80 (Full breakfast)
Children $50-$60 per child
3 course dinner b/a $40pp
Single room rates are per person
Visa MC accepted
Children welcome
1 King 1 Double 1 Twin (3 bdrm)
Three large double rooms
Two have access onto decks
Bathrooms: 1 Ensuite 1 Family share
Ensuite has shower, family share bathroom

Our home is in the trees adjacent to Faulkner's Bush Reserve surrounded by Totara, Beech, Pungas and ferns. It is only a ten minute stroll through the bush to the local shops and restaurants. Relax on the elevated deck or the courtyard with Missy the cat and the native birds. With a pottery and workshop on site you can be taught how to make a pot on the wheel, with your host, Bruce. Our interests are travel, music, singing, art, golf, pottery and furniture making.

Mapua - Nelson *30 km W of Nelson*

Hartridge *B&B*

Sue & Dennis Brillard
103 Aranui Road,
Mapua, Nelson

Tel (03) 540 2079
or 021 189 7622
stay@hartridge.co.nz
www.hartridge.co.nz

Double/Twin up to $150
Single up to $110
(Full breakfast)
Dinner $45pp discounts for 2 nights or more
Visa MC accepted
Not suitable for children
1 King/Twin 1 Queen (2 bdrm)
2 ensuite rooms
Bathrooms: 2 Ensuite

Delightful 1915 home,listed with Historic Places Trust, between Nelson City 40mins and fabulous Abel Tasman 40mins. Quiet elevated position in coastal Mapua Village. Secluded mature gardens. Recent upstairs accommodation spacious,private and sunny. Every effort made for that vital good night's sleep. Sue's beautifully presented gourmet breakfasts include daily baking,preserves,organic vegetables, local fruit, great coffee/teas. Private parking, stroll to restaurants, shops, charming wharf area.Beach 20min walk.Experienced hosts with local knowledge.Broadband.Picton 2 1/2hours,Westcoast 3 1/2 hours.

Mapua *30 km W of Nelson*

Accent House B&B *Luxury B&B Bed & Breakfast*

Wayne & Jacqui Rowe
148 Aranui Road,
Mapua Village, Nelson 7005

Tel (03) 540 3442
or 027 540 3442
Fax (03) 540 3442
info@accentbnb.co.nz
www.accentbnb.co.nz

Double/Twin $185
Single $165
(Full breakfast)
Visa MC Amex Eftpos accepted
Pet free home
1 King/Twin 2 King (3 bdrm)
Designed for you comfort and pleasureBathrooms: 3 Ensuite
Heated white fluffy towels and heated undefloor tiles.

Welcome to our new award winning home set on 1.5 acres overlooking our lagoon rich with local birdlife and drenched in Tasman Bay sunshine. Stroll to Mapua Village, cafes and local restaurants. Check out the local arts and crafts studios and the many local wineries all within a few minutes drive. Easy drive to Nelson City and Abel Tasman National Park. Private guest entrance, Guest lounge with outdoor access & tea/coffee making facilities, laundry. TV's in all suites and access to our gardens.

Mapua *4 km S of Mapua*

Kimeret Place Boutique B&B *Luxury B&B Apartment with Kitchen Cottage with Kitchen*

Gill & Ian Knight
78 Bronte Road East (off SH60),
Near Mapua,
Nelson

Tel (03) 540 2727
Fax (03) 540 2726
stay@kimeretplace.co.nz
www.kimeretplace.co.nz

Double/Twin $210-$350
Single $185-$320
(Special breakfast)
2 bedroom cottage $400
Visa MC Eftpos accepted
Children welcome
4 King/Twin (4 bdrm)
2 luxury suites, 1 apartment and 1 studio
Bathrooms: 4 Ensuite Suites have jacuzzi baths

A tranquil coastal setting in the heart of the wine & craft region with stunning views, heated swimming pool and spa. Just 4km to restaurants and 40 minutes to Abel Tasman National Park. A range of accommodation all with ensuite facilities, (2 with spa-baths), TV, DVD, Hi-fi, tea/coffee, fridge, sitting area and views from either balcony or deck. The 2 bedroom cottage also has a kitchenette and dining area. Light meals,laundry and internet are also available. Dog-lovers may wish to meet our golden retriever Alice

---

Ruby Bay *20 km W of Nelson*

Broadsea B&B *B&B*

Rae & John Robinson
42 Broadsea Avenue,
Ruby Bay,
Nelson

Tel (03) 540 3511
Fax (03) 540 3511
raer@clear.net.nz

Double/Twin $130-$135
Single $110-$120
(Full breakfast)
Not suitable for children
1 Queen (1 bdrm)
Tastefully furnished with queen size bed.Bathrooms: 1 Ensuite 1 Private

Beach front accommodation, with lovely walks on beach and reserve; cafes and tavern close by, as are wineries and restaurants. We are 15 minutes from Richmond and Motueka, 30 minutes from Nelson and the airport. Abel Tasman and Kaiteriteri are within 40 minutes drive. We want our guests to feel at home and have their privacy in a peaceful and private setting. Coffee, tea and old fashioned home-made biscuits available. Our Birman cat Bogart will greet you when you arrive.

Ruby Bay *32 km W of Nelson*

B&B Approved

Sandstone House *B&B*

John and Jenny Marchbanks
30 Korepo Road, Ruby Bay, Nelson
Tel (03) 540 3251
or 027 514 0652
Fax (03) 540 3251
sandstone@rubybay.net.nz www.rubybay.net.nz

Double/Twin $250 Single $220 (Full breakfast)
Visa MC accepted Not suitable for children
2 Queen (2 bdrm)
Bathrooms: 2 Ensuite

Welcome to Sandstone House - the ideal place to relax, stay a few days and explore this delightful region. We enjoy a maritime and semi-rural situation, ideally situated midway between Nelson and Motueka. We are handy to all the fine attractions that this region has to offer - National Parks, wineries, award winning restaurants, beaches, arts and crafts, the famous Mapua Wharf and lots lots more. We have 35 years local knowledge and are happy to assist you to make the most of your holiday and can help with any other forward bookings or reservations you may require. We are keen for you to have the best stay and trust you will enjoy our relaxed and homely atmosphere - our place is your place. Feel free to enjoy a drink, snack or a BBQ on either the front deck or the back verandah - depending on the weather, and if its winter time, enjoy some time out by the fire. Feast on the fabulous views anytime. We offer delicious homemade breakfasts with fresh free range eggs, baking, jams and preserves, and other local seasonal produce. Internet and laundry facilities are complimentary, and there is plenty of off street parking available. We hope you have a safe journey and look forward to sharing a "welcome" drink with you when you arrive.

Upper Moutere *30 km W of Nelson*

Kotare Estate Boutique Accommodation *Boutique B&B Accommodation*

Beverley and John Mockett
1270 Moutere Highway,
RD 1 Upper Moutere, 7173
Tel (03) 543 2425 or 027 497 1611
enquiry@kotareestate.co.nz
www.kotareestate.co.nz

Double/Twin $200-$250
(Special breakfast)
Children under 12 years $80
12 years and over $100
Hosted dinner by arrangement $60
includes local wine Afternoon teas
Children's meals by arrangement
Visa MC accepted Pet free home
Children welcome
1 King 2 Single (1 bdrm)
Spacious, luxurious with doors to decks, gardens and valley
Bathrooms: 1 Ensuite

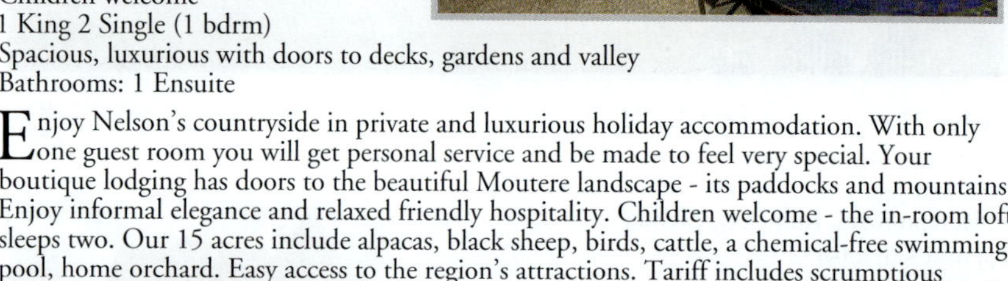

Enjoy Nelson's countryside in private and luxurious holiday accommodation. With only one guest room you will get personal service and be made to feel very special. Your boutique lodging has doors to the beautiful Moutere landscape - its paddocks and mountains. Enjoy informal elegance and relaxed friendly hospitality. Children welcome - the in-room loft sleeps two. Our 15 acres include alpacas, black sheep, birds, cattle, a chemical-free swimming pool, home orchard. Easy access to the region's attractions. Tariff includes scrumptious breakfasts. Hosted dinners available.

Motueka Valley *20 km SW of Motueka*

Vistara Bed & Breakfast *B&B Homestay*

Bruce & Guruvati Dyer
2035 Motueka River Valley,
RD 1 Motueka, 7196
Tel (03) 526 8288 h
or 021 079 7919
or 021 027 28008
or (03) 548 7284 wk
Fax (03) 526 8288
info@vistara.co.nz
www.vistara.co.nz

Double/Twin $95 Single $75
(Continental breakfast)
Children $15 Dinner $15
Visa MC accepted
Children and pets welcome
1 Queen 1 Double 2 Single (3 bdrm)
Polished floors & charming decor
Bathrooms: 2 Guest share

We welcome you to Vistara a relaxed peaceful haven situated on our 7 acre property adjacent to the Motueka River. Attractions include great river swimming, native birds and bush, a beautiful garden, mountain scenery and Jess our Jack Russell dog. Bedrooms feature polished floors and charming decor. Guests have their own lounge, tea and coffee facilities and are welcome to use the meditation room. Enjoy a delicious breakfast of home-made preserves, yoghurt, muesli and fresh organic fruit. Meals are organic, vegetarian and lovingly prepared.

Motueka Valley *25 km S of Motueka*

The Kahurangi Brown Trout *B&B Farmstay Apartment with Kitchen*

David Davies & Heather Lindsay
2292 Westbank Road, Pokororo, RD 1, Motueka
Tel (03) 526 8736 or 021 141 0717
Fax (03) 526 8736
enquiries@kbtrout.co.nz   www.kbtrout.co.nz

Double/Twin $150 Single $120 (Full breakfast)
Child in your room $25 $100 for extra room
Dinner $50/head, includes salad, fresh bread, wine, dessert
Our gardens are 100% organic
Visa MC accepted Children and pets welcome
2 King/Twin 3 King 3 Single (3 bdrm)
3 rooms with courtyard entrances and mini kitchen facilities
Bathrooms: 3 Ensuite
We also have an outdoor wood fired bath

Enjoy the sound of the beautiful Motueka River. Step across the road for trout fishing, a refreshing swim or even the thrill of an inner-tube float. Come "home" for a delicious meal made with our home grown organic fruit and vegies. Enjoy the unique garden with its pizza oven, fish pond, ducks and the wood fired bush bath. Comments from last years visitors book say it all: We remember you, Heather and David, not as hosts, but as new friends. Really glad we found you. What a beautiful spot. Good food, good company, amazing garden. Very relaxed, peaceful and invigorating place to stay. It's a pleasure to eat fresh homegrown food with a good glass of wine. Quite an inspiring way to live. It was like a second honeymoon. The breakfast with the duck eggs was fantastic. A wonderful relaxing time. The food, surroundings and sleep were all great, and the best blueberries we've ever had. Your hospitality has been the best. Love your unique style What a gift of peace and relaxation it has been to spend time here with you both. Enjoyed the unique house and beautiful gardens. A good place to unwind. I will have to return next trip. We aim for a relaxing atmosphere with time to socialize with our guests. Meals are timed to fit into your schedule as much as possible. Avi the Border Terrier assists with entertaining visitors. We are a little off the beaten track, and central to the Abel Tasman, Kahurangi and Nelson Lakes National Parks. You will want to stay a few days to fit it all in.

Motueka Valley *26 km S of Motueka*

Doone Cottage Country Homestay *B&B Homestay*

Glen & Stan Davenport
2281 Motueka Valley Highway,
Rural District No 1,
Motueka 7196

Tel (03) 526 8740
Fax (03) 526 8740
doone-cottage@xtra.co.nz
www.doonecottage.co.nz

Double/Twin $110-$190
Single $110-$160
(Full breakfast)
Dinner by arrangement,
nearest restaurants 5/20 minutes away
Visa MC accepted
Not suitable for children
2 King/Twin 1 Queen (3 bdrm)
Bathrooms: 3 Ensuite

Charming 130yr old cottage welcoming guests for 25 years. Secluded native flora & flower gardens in mountain setting overlooking Motueka River Valley. 5 Trout rivers - Guiding available. In-house Guestrooms plus Private Garden Chalet. Enjoy countrystyle B & B, homemade breads, preserves, free range eggs etc. Sheep, chickens, ducks, donkeys. Weaving/Woolcraft Studio. Short distance Abel Tasman, Kahaurangi, Nelson Lakes. Or just relax & soak up the country atmosphere of yesteryear in this special place. Nelson 45 mins. Picton 2.1/2 hours Westcoast 3 hours.

Motueka *1.4 km E of Motueka*

Williams B&B *B&B Homestay Apartment with Kitchen*

Rebecca & Ian Williams
186 Thorp Street,
Motueka

Tel (03) 528 9385
Fax (03) 528 9385
info@Motueka-Homestay.co.nz
www.motueka-homestay.co.nz

Double/Twin $130
Single $75
(Full breakfast)
Children $20
Dinner by arrangement
Apartment with Kitchen $200
Visa MC accepted
3 Queen 1 Double 2 Single (4 bdrm)
2 Bedroom Apartment with Kitchen,
Sleeps 4 or 5
Bathrooms: 2 Ensuite

We only look expensive. We are 1.4km to Motueka shopping centre and 1.2km to 18 hole golf course. Each bedroom has own ensuite. The guest lounge has tea & coffee making facilities and fridge. Motueka is the stop-over place for visitors to explore Abel Tasman and Kahurangi National Parks. Golden Bay and Kaiteriteri golden sands beach is 10km away. We have a Jack Russell dog. Visa and Mastercard accepted.

Motueka *2 km S of Motueka*

B&B Approved

Grey Heron - The Italian Organic Homestay *B&B Homestay*

Sandro Lionello & Laura Totis
110 Trewavas Street, Motueka 7120
Tel (03) 528 0472 or 021 0229 3547
Fax (03) 528 0472 sandro@greyheron.co.nz
www.greyheron.co.nz

Double/Twin $100-$130 Single $60-$80 (Continental breakfast)
Dinner $28pp Main + dessert
or $40pp typical 3course Italian dinner Children welcome
3 Queen 1 Single (4 bdrm)
Bathrooms: 1 Ensuite 1 Private 1 Guest share

We are a couple from Northern Italy, much travelled and keen on tramping, mountaineering and motorbiking. We welcome you to our private hideaway and birdwatchers' paradise on the tidal estuary.

Pleasant beach-walks at the door-steps, far enough from the noise of the main road and yet only 5 mins drive to shops and restaurants. Or you can relax here after your exploring day, join us for dinner and taste our italian organic cuisine overlooking a beautiful sunset behind the mountains and enjoying Sandro's huge collection of Jazz records.

The Abel Tasman NP is 25 mins drive; 45 mins drive to the alpine, easy accessible, Kahurangi NP and to Nelson city. The Guest Accommodation includes both ensuite/private and shared-facilities with toilet room and bathroom each separate (4-5 guests max capacity in the shared area). Basic tea-coffee facilities and secure off-street parking.

We serve a generous Continental breakfast including home-made breads and jams, fresh fruit and juice, yogurt and muesli. As keen walkers and mountaineers we can give helpful hints to maximize your exploration of the area. We also offer guided walks thanks to Sandro's experience as geologist and to our interest in the local flora and fauna. Rock-climbing and Italian Language lessons by arrangements.

Water-Taxi ticketing service and Kayak Tours booking service available. We are conveniently located just around the corner from the reliable and well-known "Sea Kayak Company". "Benvenuti tutti gli amici italiani!"

Motueka *10 km S of Motueka*

Motueka River Hills Bed & Breakfast *B&B*

B&B Approved

Anthea Garmey & Andrew Claringbold
394 Westbank Road,
RD1, Motueka

Tel (03) 528 8979
or 027 208 3106
Fax (03) 528 8979
stay@motuekariverhills.co.nz
www.motuekariverhills.co.nz

Double/Twin $140-$160
Single $130
(Full breakfast)
Portacot available for young children
Dinner available by arrangement
Children welcome
1 King/Twin (1 bdrm)
Bathrooms: 1 Ensuite

Motueka River Hills is nestled on the foothills of the Kahurangi National Park above the Motueka River. We have stunning views over rural Motueka, Tasman Bay and out to D'Urville Island. Listen to Morepork while you relax and unwind in the steaming hot outdoor bath. Awake to a gorgeous sunrise and the chorus of native birds. Enjoy a large breakfast with homemade muffins. We share our home with daughters Hannah and Isabel as well as Basil, the cat.

~

Motueka *2 km SW of Motueka*

The Queen Vic *B&B Separate Suite Orchardstay*

B&B Approved

Clare and Graham Ryder
199 Queen Victoria Street,
Motueka, 7120

Tel Landline (03) 528 8963
or Mobile 027 449 9180
or 0800 307 757
Fax (03) 528 8963
clare@motuekabedandbreakfast.co.nz
http://motuekabedandbreakfast.co.nz

Double/Twin up to $135
(Full breakfast)
Visa MC accepted
1 Queen (1 bdrm)
Large room with ensuite
Bathrooms: 1 Ensuite

You will be assured of a warm welcome when you stay at The Queen Vic. Your room, separate from the house and overlooking the orchard, is private and spacious with it's own ensuite. Soak in the spa pool in the garden, pick fruit fresh off the trees and sample our own apple juice. A continental or cooked breakfast and delicious home baking is provided, and on arrival, a complimentary small bottle of New Zealand wine. 20 mins to the Abel Tasman National Park and beaches.

Kaiteriteri *10 km N of Motueka*

Bracken Hill B&B *Luxury B&B*

B&B Approved

Grace & Tom Turner
293 Riwaka-Kaiteriteri Road
RD2, Motueka

Tel (03) 528 9629
graceturner@xtra.co.nz
www.bnb.co.nz/brackenhillbb.html

Double/Twin $140-$150
Single $110-$120
(Continental breakfast)
Not suitable for children as unsafe
Fine restaurants available, close by
Out door Spa, sea-view over Tasman Bay
Visa MC accepted Pet free home
1 King/Twin 2 Queen (3 bdrm)
Comfortable sized beds and
glorious sea-views
Bathrooms: 3 Private

Stunning Coastal Views. Welcome to our spacious modern home.All rooms have superb sea views over Tasman Bay.Enjoy mountains, native bush, sunrises,& stars! A sundeck leads to a natural rock garden,and outdoor Spa.Guests' TV lounge,guest laundry.Experience Kaiteriteri Beach, Abel Tasman National Park,kayaking,water taxis, and great scenic easy walking tracks,and golden swimming beaches. Excellent Restaurants close by.We can supply Brochures and information on all Kaiteriteri and Golden Bay activities.Interests: travel, Lions Clubs & Miniature Shoes.

Nelson Golden Bay

Kaiteriteri *12 km N of Motueka*

Bayview *B&B*

B&B Approved

Tim Rich
2 Bayview Heights,
Kaiteriteri, RD 2,
Motueka 7197

Tel (03) 527 8090
or 027 454 5835
Fax (03) 527 8090
book@kaiteriteribandb.co.nz
www.kaiteriteribandb.co.nz

Double/Twin $165-$195
(Full breakfast)
Visa MC accepted
Pet free home
Not suitable for children
1 King/Twin 1 King 1 Twin (2 bdrm)
Spacious rooms purpose built
with en suites
Bathrooms: 2 Ensuite

Welcome to a piece of paradise. This modern house has huge windows with outstanding sea views overlooking Kaiteriteri Beach out to Abel Tasman National Park. Large, beautifully furnished guest rooms have every convenience you could want. Enjoy delicious home cooked breakfast in the dining room with your host who has an intimate knowledge of the area. Laundry, wireless broadband and booking facilities for boat trips, walking and kayaking are available. A two day minimum stay in this unique area recommended.

Kaiteriteri *13 km N of Motueka*

Everton B&B *B&B*

Martin & Diane Everton
Kotare Place,
Little Kaiteriteri,
RD 2 Motueka

Tel (03) 527 8301
or 021 527 830
Fax (03) 527 8301
everton@xtra.co.nz
www.evertonbandb.co.nz

Double/Twin $140-$160
Single $100-$120
(Continental breakfast)
Wireless Internet
Visa MC accepted
Pet free home
1 King/Twin 1 King 1 Queen 1 Twin (3 bdrm)
Bathrooms: 1 Ensuite 2 Private

With wonderful sea views we are 2 minutes walk from beautiful Little Kaiteriteri Beach. Continental breakfast may include fresh bread or muffins. Nearby are excellent restaurants for evening dining. Our interests include Rotary, Toastmasters, golf, tennis, music, travel, and boating. The Abel Tasman National Park is right here where you can kayak, walk and water taxi. Martin is licensed to take you on a personalised trip in our boat. We offer email access and wireless internet. We have no pets and are non-smokers.

Kaiteriteri - Tapu Bay *12 km N of Motueka*

Maison Luc *B&B Cottage with Kitchen*

Angie & Martin Lucas
Tapu Bay,
410 Riwaka-Kaiteriteri Road,
RD 2, Motueka

Tel (03) 527 8247 or 0800 468 815
or 021 022 03196
Fax (03) 527 8347
info@maisonluc.co.nz
www.maisonluc.co.nz

Double/Twin $100-$130
Single $115-$120
(Continental breakfast)
Cottage Single $115 Double $140
Extra guest $15
Visa MC accepted
Children welcome
1 King/Twin 2 Queen 1 Double (4 bdrm)
2 in B and B, 2 in cottage
Bathrooms: 2 Ensuite 1 Private

Maison Luc is centrally located to the Abel Tasman National Park and 1km to the golden sands of beautiful Kaiteriteri beaches. Relax by our sun trapped pool or walk 2 mins to local beaches. We have a fully self contained cottage set in a peaceful organic fruit garden. We offer a choice of two B&B rooms with ensuites and private entrance. (Complementary tea, coffee & homebaking). Enjoy wholesome breakfasts on our deck which overlooks the bay.We offer a relaxed family atmosphere and genuine kiwi hospitality. Angie, Martin and Lu (dog).

Kaiteriteri *12 km N of Motueka*

Kaiteriteri Heights *Luxury B&B Separate Suite Apartment with Kitchen*

Mary & Richard Shee
28 Cederman Drive,
Kaiteriteri Heights,
Motueka

Tel (03) 527 8662
or 027 229 1698
Fax (03) 527 8662
info@KaiteriteriHeights.com
www.kaiteriteriheights.com

Double/Twin $130-$160
Single $110-$110
(Full breakfast)
Visa MC Eftpos accepted
Not suitable for children under 12
2 King/Twin 1 Queen
1 Double 2 Single (2 bdrm)
Also one rollaway bed
Bathrooms: 1 Ensuite 1 Private

Kaiteriteri's Premier Bed & Breakfast located in the hills overlooking Tasman Bay and the Riwaka Estuary. On the doorstep of the magnificent Abel Tasman National Park. Take the gentle 5-minute stroll down to Little Kaiteriteri beach, with its golden sands and safe swimming. Full privacy, or interact as part of the family. Shared facilities include the outdoor deck with barbeque area, coffee/tea facilities, spa pool, the main lounge area with TV with Sky.

Abel Tasman National Park - Marahau *18 km NW of Motueka*

Abel Tasman Bed & Breakfast *B&B Cottage with Kitchen*

George Bloomfield
Abel Tasman National Park,
Marahau, Nelson Region

Tel (03) 527 8181
Fax (03) 527 8181
abel.tasman.stables.accom@xtra.co.nz
www.abeltasmanstables.co.nz

Double/Twin $110-$150
Single $80-$100
(Continental breakfast)
Dinner by prior arrangement
Cottage $150 (sleeps 4)
Visa MC accepted
Pet free home
Children welcome
3 Queen 2 Double 4 Single (6 bdrm)
B&B 2 bedrooms, cottage 2 bedrooms, one in each motel
Bathrooms: 5 Ensuite 1 Private 1 Family share Showers

Great views, hospitality, peaceful garden setting are yours at Abel Tasman Stables accommodation. Closest ensuite facility to Abel Tasman National park. Guests comments include: 'I know now that hospitality is not just a word', TH, Germany. 'Wonderful place, friendly hospitality. The best things for really special holidays. We leave a piece of our hearts', P&M, Italy. 'The creme-de-la-creme of our holiday. What a view', MN & JW, England. Homestay bed & breakfast or self-contained options. Cafe close by.

Abel Tasman National Park *17 km NW of Motueka*

B&B Approved

Split Apple Rock Homestay *B&B Homestay*

Thelma & Rodger Boys
116 Tokongawa Drive,
Split Apple Rock,
RD 2,
Motueka

Tel (03) 527 8182
splitapplerock@hotmail.com
www.splitapplerock.com

Double/Twin $140-$165
Single $120-$150
(Full breakfast)
Dinner $40 pp by arrangement
Visa MC accepted
Children welcome
1 Queen 1 Twin (2 bdrm)
Bathrooms: 2 Ensuite

Enjoy 180 degree panoramic sea views of Tasman Bay and Abel Tasman National Park. Our Eco-log home rooms have private entrances and decking. We are within walking distance of golden sand beaches, 5 minutes drive to Marahau and the start of Abel Tasman National Park where walking, kayaking, boating, swimming and more are available. 2 cats in residence. Directions: on the Marahau/Kaiteriteri Road take the Tokongawa Drive turn-off, 1.2km up Tokongawa Drive the "Split Apple Rock Homestay" sign is on your right.

Takaka - Patons Rock Beach *10 km W of Takaka*

B&B Approved

Patondale *Cottage with Kitchen*

Vicki & David James
177 Patons Rock,
RD 2,
Takaka 7182

Tel (03) 525 8262
or 0800 306 697 (NZ only)
or 0274 936 891
Fax (03) 525 8262
patondale@xtra.co.nz
www.patonsrockbeachvillas.co.nz

Double/Twin up to $150
Single $130
(Breakfast provisions first night)
Children $20
Visa MC accepted
Pet free home
Children welcome
4 King 8 Single (8 bdrm)
All units 2 bedroom,1 king & 2 single
Bathrooms: 4 Private

Four sunny, spacious, deluxe self-contained units, own attached carports. 2 bedrooms. Peaceful rural setting at the seaward end of our dairy farm yet only a few minutes walk to beautiful Patons Rock Beach. Central location, approx. 5mins to Mussell Inn. Simply the Best. Your Kiwi hosts, David & Vicki invite you to be our guests.

Takaka - Tata Beach *15 km NE of Takaka*

The Devonshires *B&B Homestay*

a home NEW ZEALAND

B&B Approved

Brian & Susan Devonshire
32 Tata Heights Drive,
Tata Beach,
RD 1,
Takaka,
Golden Bay

Tel (03) 525 7987
Fax (03) 525 7987
devs.1@actrix.co.nz

Double/Twin $100
Single $70
(Full breakfast)
Children not suitable
Dinner $25-$30 by arrangement
Visa MC accepted
1 Queen (1 bdrm)
Bathrooms: 1 Ensuite

The Devonshires live at Tata Beach and invite you to enjoy their comfortable home and stroll to the nearby beautiful golden beach. A tranquil base for exploring the truly scenic Golden Bay, the Abel Tasman Walkway, Kahurangi National Park, Farewell Spit, amazing coastal scenery, fishing the rivers or visiting interesting craftspeople. Brian, an educator, wine and American Football buff is a keen fisherman. Susan enjoys crafts, painting, gardening and practising her culinary skills. Charlie Brown and Hermione are the resident cats. Longer visits welcomed.

~

Parapara *20 km NW of Takaka*

Hakea Hill House *B&B*

B&B Approved

Vic & Liza Eastman
PO Box 35,
Collingwood 7054

Tel (03) 524 8487
Fax (03) 524 8487
vic.eastman@clear.net.nz

Double/Twin $130
Single $90
(Full breakfast)
Children $50
Family dinner by arrangement
Visa MC accepted
Children and pets welcome
2 Queen 6 Single (3 bdrm)
Two bedrooms have large balconies
Bathrooms: 2 Guest share
Bathtub and shower

Hakea Hill House at Parapara has views from its hilltop of all Golden Bay. The 2 story house is modern and spacious. Two guest rooms have large balconies; the third for children has bunk beds and a cot. American and New Zealand electric outlets are installed. Television, tea or coffee, telephone and broadband lines are available in rooms. Vic is a practising physician with an interest in astronomy. Liza is a quilter and cares for outdoor dogs. Please contact us for reservations and directions.

Collingwood *25 km N of Takaka*

Heron's Rest *B&B Cottage with B&B + cooking facilities*

Maureen & Angus Scotland
23 Gibbs Road,
Collingwood Township,
Golden Bay

Tel (03) 524 8987
Fax (03) 524 8987
be@herons-rest.co.nz
www.herons-rest.co.nz

Double/Twin $100-$120
Single $70-$90 (Special breakfast)
Children Negotiable
Visa MC accepted
1 Queen 1 Double
1 Twin 2 Single (3 bdrm)
Nicely appointed, with ensuites
Bathrooms: 2 Ensuite 1 Family share
Bath available

Travelling towards the tip of the South Island, your journey is rewarded by spectacular sea, mountain and estuary views, all visible from Heron's Rest. We're situated between the Abel Tasman and Heaphy Tracks and surrounded by superb sandy beaches, being a short bush-walk (or drive) away from Farewell Spit Tours and Collingwood eateries.Welcoming hosts offer relaxation, comfort and lasting memories served up with home-made and locally-produced foods plus complimentary drinks. Potter's studio, internet, hairdryer, BBQ, laundry available. Directions: Website and Lewis Street signboard along estuary.

Pakawau *9 km N of Collingwood*

Twin Waters Lodge *Luxury Lodge*

Trish & Mike Boland
PO Box 33,
Collingwood

Tel (03) 524 8014
Fax (03) 524 8054
twin.waters@xtra.co.nz
www.twinwaters.co.nz

Double/Twin $200-$250
Single $175-$200
(Full breakfast)
Dinner by arrangement
Visa MC accepted
Not suitable for children
1 King/Twin 3 Queen (4 bdrm)
Bathrooms: 4 Ensuite

Nestled harmoniously beside a tidal estuary and just fifty metres from a sandy beach, Twin Waters features curved timber ceilings, panoramic windows and multilevel decks. The elegant interior has ample space for guests to enjoy its charm and tranquility. Waking to tuis singing, breakfasting in the sun, sipping wine on the decks overlooking the estuary, or savouring a delicious dinner, there's sure to be a special moment to remember. Trish and Mike and their feline companions look forward to welcoming you at Twin Waters.

Nelson Lakes - St Arnaud *85 km S of Nelson*

Nelson Lakes Homestay *Homestay*

Approved

Gay & Merv Patch
RD 2,
State Highway 63,
Nelson 7072

Tel (03) 521 1191
Fax (03) 521 1191
Home@Tasman.net
www.nelsonlakesaccommodation.co.nz

Double/Twin $145
Single $110
(Full breakfast)
Visa MC accepted
2 King/Twin 1 Queen (2 bdrm)
Bathrooms: 2 Ensuite

Nestled on the sunny slopes of the St Arnaud Mountain Range, Nelson Lakes National Park, our spacious modern home is designed for the comfort and convenience of our guests. Spacious ensuite rooms, with doors opening on to our garden, large comfortable lounge and terrace to relax on at the end of the day and admire the magnificent mountain views. Laundry facilities are available. We have a house cat. Directions: State Highway 63, 4km east of St Arnaud.

~

Murchison *0.2 km N of Murchison*

Murchison Lodge *B&B*

Approved

Shirley & Merve Bigden
15 Grey Street,
Murchison

Tel (03) 523 9196
or Freephone 0800 523 9196
info@murchisonlodge.co.nz
www.murchisonlodge.co.nz

Double/Twin $150-$210
Single $125-$185
(Full breakfast)
Children over 12 welcome
Free wireless broadband,
use of bicycles & golf clubs
Visa MC accepted
1 King/Twin 2 Queen 1 Twin (4 bdrm)
Bathrooms: 3 Ensuite 1 Private

Warm and quiet timber Lodge with comfortable beds and hearty BBQ breakfasts, using our own eggs and fruit. Our four acres support various animals (including a friendly dog) and accesses the Buller River and its swimming holes. Trees and mountains surround us, yet Murchison's cafes are within five minutes walk. A great base to explore three National Parks; fly-fish, raft or play golf. Return home to a cold beer on the sunny verandah or a wine in front of the log fire. WI-FI throughout

West Coast
Karamea
67
Carters Beach
Cape Foulwind
Westport
6
Charleston
69
Punakaiki
Reefton
Barrytown
7
Greymouth
Hokitika
Ruatapu
0
Kilometres
60
0
Miles
36
6
Whataroa
Franz Josef
Fox Glacier
6

Reefton *0.1 km S of Reefton Central*

Reef Cottage B&B and Cafe *B&B Cottage with Kitchen*

Susan & Ronnie Standfield
51-55 Broadway, Reefton

Tel (03) 732 8440 or 0800 770 440
or 027 319 5490 Fax (03) 732 8440
info@reefcottage.co.nz
www.reefcottage.co.nz

Double/Twin $100-$150
Single $90-$135 (Full breakfast)
Dinner by arrangement $10-$35
Visa MC Diners Amex
Eftpos accepted
Children welcome
1 King/Twin 1 Queen
2 Double (4 bdrm)
Rooms have TVs, radio alarm,
electric blankets, heating.
Bathrooms: 2 Ensuite 2 Private Queen suite has bath

Built in 1887 this former Barrister and Solicitors office has been carefully renovated to its former glory. Elegantly decorated and fully self contained the house features 4 charming rooms with ensuites and private bathrooms, guest lounge, Kitchen and laundry, central heating plus guests private deck and garden. Complimentary continental and cooked breakfast is served next door in Reef Cottage Cafe (circa 1876) featuring open fire, elegant surroundings and the best espresso coffee in town. Reef Cottage is unrivalled as the finest hosted accommodation in town.

Reefton *.1 km N of Reefton Central*

Quartz Lodge *B&B*

Paddy & Alan Rainey
78 Shiel Street,
Reefton, West Coast

Tel (03) 732 8383
or 0800 302 725
Fax (03) 732 8083
quartz-lodge@xtra.co.nz
www.quartzlodge.co.nz

Double/Twin $90-$130
Single $70-$95
(Full breakfast)
Children $25
Dinner $15-$30
Visa MC accepted
Children and pets welcome
1 King 1 Queen 1 Twin
1 Single (3 bdrm)
Bathrooms: 1 Ensuite 1 Private 1 Guest share

A friendly welcome awaits you when you arrive at Quartz Lodge superior accommodation in the heart of Reefton. Guests only entrance will take you upstairs to rooms with huge picture windows, luxurious beds, quality linen, robes and so much more. Complimentary coffee and a selection of teas are available in your spacious private lounge/dining area. Laundry service and Internet is also available upon request.We pride ourselves on making you feel at home. Quality and comfort says it all!

Karamea *84 km N of Westport*

Beachfront Farmstay B&B *B&B Farmstay*

Dianne & Russell Anderson
3578 Karamea Highway,
RD3, Karamea

Tel (03) 782 6762
or 027 249 8827
Fax (03) 782 6762
farmstay@xtra.co.nz
www.WestCoastBeachAccommodation.co.nz

Double/Twin $160-$180
Single $140
(Special breakfast)
Children negotiable
Dinner $70
Visa MC accepted
Pet free home
Children welcome
1 King 1 Queen (2 bdrm)
Bathrooms: 2 Ensuite

Our 500 cow dairy farm has 2.5kms of coastline, a 2min walk and you will be on a sandy beach usually all to yourself. Relax in elegant rooms with your own private deck. Special farmhouse breakfasts,home preserving, tasty whitebait, bacon and egg dishes, espresso coffee. Join us for delicious country cuisine, farm grown meat, fresh fish, organic vegetables, homemade desserts served with NZ wine. Inquire about a BBQ and bonfire on the beach,a unique Kiwi tradition,(weather permitting) or a fishing experience with Russell and his Kentiki Torpedo.

Westport - Cape Foulwind *11 km SW of Westport*

Steeples Cottage, Studio & B&B *Studio B&B, Self Contained cottage with Kitchen*

B&B Approved

Pauline & Bruce Cargill
48 Lighthouse Road,
Cape Foulwind, Westport

Tel (03) 789 7876 or 0800 670 708
or 021 663 687
thesteeples@xtra.co.nz
www.steeplescottage.co.nz

Double/Twin $100-$120
Single $60-$90
(Continental breakfast)
Children $20
Whitebait meal by arrangement
Self-contained cottage $120 double
Studio B/B $100
4 Queen 1 Single (4 bdrm)
1 in cottage 1 in studio 2 in house
Bathrooms: 3 Ensuite 1 Guest share
1 cottage ensuite studio ensuite and share B/B

Enjoy our peaceful rural accommodation, lovely gardens, magnificent sea views, rugged coastline, beautiful beaches & tranquil sunsets. Great swimming, surfing, fishing kayaking. Walk the popular seal colony walkway, dine at The Bay House Restaurant or friendly Star Tavern. Local attractions includes golf course, Coaltown Museum, jet boating, horse riding, underworld & white water rafting, bush walks unimog trips & Punakaiki National Park. We have a Jack Russell and cat.Laundry and off-street parking.Self Contained Cottage and Queen ensuite studio also available. Whitebait meals by arrangment. Internet available.

Westport *0.01 km N of Westport Central*

B&B Approved

Havenlee Homestay *B&B Homestay*

Jan & Ian Stevenson
76 Queen Street,
Westport

Tel (03) 789 8543
or 0800 673 619
Fax (03) 789 8502
info@havenlee.co.nz
www.havenlee.co.nz

Double/Twin $110-$160
Single $100
(Continental breakfast)
Children negotiable
Visa MC accepted
Children welcome
2 Queen (2 bdrm)
Two double rooms with a queen sized bed in each
Bathrooms: 1 Private 1 Guest share

Peace in Paradise - this is Havenlee: a welcoming, relaxed, spacious, quality homestay where you will feel at home right away. Centrally located, an idyllic base from which to explore the environmental wonderland, share local knowledge or just to take time out. Check out the adventure experiences and local attractions. Soak up the nature, rest and restore body and soul in the peace and quiet of a garden oasis. Generous continental-plus breakfast. Laundry facilities available. Denniston Heritage site is a "must see"

Westport - Carters Beach *3 km S of Westport*

B&B Approved

Bellaville *B&B Separate Suite*

Marlene & Ross Burrow
No 10 State Highway 67 A,
Carters Beach,
PO Box 157, Westport

Tel (03) 789 8457
or 0800 789 845
or 027 6131 689
bellaville@xtra.co.nz

Double/Twin $100-$120
Single $70-$80
(Full breakfast)
Children $15
Extra Adult $25
Pet free home
1 Queen 1 Single (1 bdrm)
Extra large room with rollaway available
Bathrooms: 1 Ensuite 1 Private
Spa Bath With separate shower

Hear the sound of waves pounding our safe swimming beach. Ouiet sunny extra large, studio room, private entrance, parking at door. No steps, no traffic noise. Private ensuite, large bathroom spa bath, shower separate toilet. Ideal family unit. Electric blankets, TV, fridge, tea & coffee and home-baking. Laundry available. Close to all activities, coastal walks, seal colony. 3mins walk to licensed cafe/bar, golf course, playground. Have travelled extensively overseas & in NZ. Don't rush, stay a day or two, you will be glad you did.

Westport - Carters Beach *4 km S of Westport*

Carters Beach B&B *B&B*

Sue & John Bennett
Main Road Carters Beach,
On State Highway 67A,
Westport

Tel (03) 789 8056
or 0800 783 566
or 027 589 8056
cartersbeachaccom@xtra.co.nz
www.bnb.co.nz/cartersbeachbb.html

Double/Twin $100-$120
Single $70-$80
(Continental breakfast)
Pet free home
Children welcome
2 Queen 1 Twin (3 bdrm)
Very spacious
Bathrooms: 1 Ensuite 1 Private

Carters Beach - a lovely relaxed atmosphere, Situated only 4km south of Westport. 3 minute walk to our beach, with fully licenced resturant/cafe and bar. Golf links, world famous seal colony and Bay House Cafe within a few minutes drive. Our rooms are very spacious with TV and tea/coffee making facilities. Own private entrance-ways with sun decks. Laundry facilities available by arrangement. Ideal accommodation for couples travelling togeather. We look forward to meeting and sharing our local knowledge with you. Cheers, Sue and John Bennett.

Charleston *35 km N of Punakaiki*

Birds Ferry Lodge & Ferry Mans Cottage
Luxury B&B or Lakeside Cottage

Alison & Andre Gygax
Birds Ferry Road,
8KM North Charleston, off SHW 6,
Just North of Punakaiki

Tel 0800 212 207
or 021 337 217
info@birdsferrylodge.co.nz
www.birdsferrylodge.co.nz

Double/Twin $200-$390
Single $200-$390 (Full breakfast)
Cottage suitable for children
Dinner our speciality - be sure to book
We are a short drive from Punakaiki
Visa MC accepted
1 King/Twin 1 King 3 Queen
1 Double 2 Twin 2 Single (5 bdrm)
3 double rooms in Lodge + 2 bedroomed cottage
Bathrooms: 3 Ensuite 1 Ensuite is purpose built for wheelchair use

Relax and unwind with some pampering at Birds Ferry Lodge. We are located 4-5 hrs from The Glaciers and Abel Tasman. Guests enjoy fabulous meals prepared in the Lodge kitchen as well as on site Holistic Massage Therapy. Ferry Man's Cottage is 300m from the Lodge and enjoys the same spectacular views. Close by is Punakaiki & numerous coastal and forest walks or you can visit an exhibition gold mine or take the Charleston Nile River Forest Train.

Punakaiki - Barrytown *27 km N of Greymouth*

Golden Sands Homestay *Homestay*

Sue & Tom Costelloe
4 Golden Sands Road,
Barrytown
RD1,
Runanga 7873

Tel (03) 731 1115
Fax (03) 731 1116
goldensands@paradise.net.nz

Double/Twin $95-$105
Single $55
(Continental breakfast)
Children by arrangement
Dinner by arrangement
Visa MC accepted
Children welcome
2 Queen 1 Twin (3 bdrm)
Bathrooms: 1 Ensuite 2 Private

Nestled between the paparoa range and tasman sea on the corner of golden sands road barrytown and greymouth-westport scenic highway,we offer a warm welcome with a cuppa, fresh baking,friendly atmosphere and comfortable rooms.handy to punakaiki,pancake rocks and national park 15 minutes north, with greymouth 25 minutes south.stunning views and wonderful sunsets,a cosy fire in the winter and jasper the cat. we have local knowledge on walking tracks and activities. enjoy breakfast with rural and sea views

Punakaiki - Barrytown *20 km N of Greymouth*

Kallyhouse *B&B Homestay Apartment with Kitchen*

Kathleen & Alister Schroeder
13 Cargill Road,
Runanga, RD 1, 7873,
Westland

Tel (03) 731 1006
Fax (03) 731 1106
kallyhouse@xtra.co.nz
www.kallyhouse.co.nz

Double/Twin $115-$140
Single $75
(Continental breakfast)
Visa MC accepted
Pet free home
Children welcome
3 Queen 1 Twin (4 bdrm)
Bathrooms: 1 Ensuite 1 Guest share
1 Spa Bath

We have a new spacious home on a quiet rear section, a garden setting, native bush backdrop and sea views. We offer a self-contained flat downstairs, with queen room and twin beds in spacious living area. Kitchen, bathroom, washing machine, parking and separate entrance. Also 2 queen rooms upstairs. Breakfast with host. Punakaiki Pancake Rocks and adventure activities in Paparoa National Park, 10-minutes north. Greymouth 20 minutes south. Turn at Allnations Hotel, past 3 houses on left, up lane, house on left. Licensed Restaurant handy.

Punakaiki - Greymouth *14 km N of Greymouth*

Breakers Boutique Accommodation *B&B Boutique*

Jan Macdonald
Nine Mile Creek,
State Highway 6,
Greymouth

Tel (03) 762 7743
Fax (03) 762 7733
stay@breakers.co.nz
www.breakers.co.nz

Double/Twin $200-$330
(Full breakfast)
Dinner $75 pp
(48 hours prior notice required)
Visa MC accepted
Children welcome
2 King 2 Queen 2 Twin (4 bdrm)
All with fantastic sea views
Bathrooms: 4 Ensuite

Stunning views overlooking the Tasman Sea with 2 acres of native bush and gardens, Breakers is a great place to finish your day or base yourself while exploring the Coast. Walk on the beach or sit back and relax, enjoy the view with the sound of breaking waves rocking you to sleep. Private and peaceful, yet close enough to all the activities the Coast has to offer, Pancake Rocks, Paparoa National Park and the best stretch of coastline in NZ. Two friendly dogs on site.

Greymouth *0.5 km N of Greymouth Central*

Ardwyn House *Homestay*

Mary Owen
48 Chapel Street,
Greymouth

Tel (03) 768 6107
Fax (03) 768 5177
ardwynhouse@hotmail.com

Double/Twin $85-$90
Single $55
(Full breakfast)
Children half price
Visa MC accepted
Children welcome
2 Queen 3 Single (3 bdrm)
Bathrooms: 1 Guest share

Ardwyn House is 3 minutes walk from the town centre in a quiet garden setting offering sea, river and town views. The house was built in the 1920s and is a fine example of an imposing residence with fine woodwork and leadlight windows, whilst being a comfortable and friendly home. Greymouth's ideally situated for travellers touring the West Coast being central with good choice of restaurants. We offer a courtesy car service to and from local travel centres and also provide off-street parking.

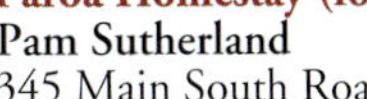

Greymouth *6 km S of Greymouth*

Paroa Homestay (formerly Pam's Homestay) *Homestay*

Pam Sutherland
345 Main South Road,
Greymouth

Tel (03) 762 6769
or 027 323 3118
Fax (03) 762 6765
paroahomestay@xtra.co.nz
www.paroahomestay.co.nz

Double/Twin $110-$140
Single $100-$110
(Continental breakfast)
Children negotiable
Visa MC accepted
2 King 1 Double (3 bdrm)
Also 1 Super King Bed
Bathrooms: 1 Ensuite 1 Private
1 Guest share

Relax on terraces overlooking the sea and watch incredible sunsets. 3 minutes walk to the beach. Towering trees, native bush surrounds spacious classic home with luxurious guest lounge. Excellent restaurants nearby. Experience superb continental breakfast as baking and cooking is Pam's forte (previously owning Greymouth's busiest cafe/bar). Pam has NZQA Food Hygiene qualifications. West Coast born, Pam's local knowledge is invaluable. Pam enjoys hospitality, antiques, organic gardening and bush walking. Pam has welcomed guests for 13 years. Guest comments "Best breakfast in NZ" "incredible hospitaliy".

Greymouth *3.5 km S of Greymouth*

Maryglen Homestay *Homestay Bed and Breakfast*

Allison & Glen Palmer
20 Weenink Road,
Karoro, Greymouth

Tel 0800 627 945
or (03) 768 0706
Fax (03) 768 0599
mary@bandb.co.nz
www.bandb.co.nz

Double/Twin $115-$140
Single $90-$125
(Continental breakfast)
Children negotiable
Dinner Snack $20-full $45
Full dinner (pre-notice)
Visa MC accepted
Children welcome
2 King/Twin 1 Queen 1 Single (3 bdrm)
1 family room - sleeps 3-4, 2 double rooms
Bathrooms: 3 Ensuite all private

Large Native ferns and bush surround our hillside home overlooking the sea. Our guests comment- amazing location. The sound of the surf will lull you to sleep. Off the main road, quiet location, 2 rooms have own deck entrance. Amazing sunsets, Complimentary transport available from bus/train. Let us share our wonderful coast with you as we help you plan your days-scenic tours, bush walks, Argo Bike tours, Trans-scenic train (a must), Shantytown History Village, Punakaiki Pancake Rocks. Your home away from home.

Greymouth *6 km S of Greymouth*

Sunsetview *B&B Homestay Apartment with Kitchen*

Russell & Jill Fairhall
335 Main South Road,
Greymouth 7805,
South Island

Tel (03) 762 6616
Fax (03) 762 6616
sunsetview@xtra.co.nz

Double/Twin $100-$140
Single $90-$120
(Full breakfast)
Children by arrangement
Dinner by arrangement
Lunch by arrangement
Visa MC accepted
Children and pets welcome
2 King/Twin 1 King 1 Queen (4 bdrm)
Bathrooms: 2 Ensuite 1 Private

Jill & Russell welcome you to our sunny modern home with amazing sea and mountain views. We offer well-appointed superior bedrooms. Sky TV in rooms. Home-cooked meals available on request. Outdoor areas, pool and barbecue. Short walk to beach, shop approx 5 to 10 minutes walk Courtesy car available to local resturants, travel centres. Off-street parking. Downstairs apartment has two bedrooms (either can be king double or single beds) bathroom with wardrobe/dressing room. Kitchen with dining/lounge area. Own entrance with undercover parking.

Greymouth *15 km S of Greymouth*

Chapel Hill *B&B Homestay Farmstay*

Joy & John Ruesink
783 Rutherglen Road,
Paroa,
Greymouth

Tel (03) 762 6662
info@chapelhill.co.nz
www.chapelhill.co.nz

Double/Twin $90-$115
Single up to $90
(Full breakfast)
Visa MC accepted
Children welcome
2 King/Twin 1 King 2 Queen (3 bdrm)
Bathrooms: 2 Private 1 Guest share

Touch the ferns out your window! Spectacular architect-designed country stay in a rainforest setting, ONLY 15 minutes south of Greymouth on the Christchurch-Glaciers Highway. Huge logfire for those cooler evenings, wireless internet, big comfy beds with electric blankets. Hearty country breakfasts included. Home-grown food. 40 minutes to Pancake Rocks & Hokitika Gorge, 60 minutes to Arthurs Pass. Non-smoking inside. Pets, farm and wildlife on the property. Unusual multi-level design is unsuitable for toddlers or disabled. Inquire about block or group bookings.

Greymouth *2 km S of Greymouth Post Office*

Jivana Retreat *Luxury B&B Private Chalet*

B&B Approved

Sandie
8 Leith Crescent,
Greymouth

Tel (03) 768 6102
Fax (03) 768 6108
sandie@jivanaretreat.co.nz
www.JivanaRetreat.co.nz

Double/Twin $135-$145
Single $125
(Special breakfast)
Children negotiable
Dinner $40
Private Chalet $160
Visa MC accepted
Children welcome
1 King 2 Queen 1 Twin (3 bdrm)
Bathrooms: 1 Ensuite 1 Private
1 Guest share plus bush bath

Jivana Retreat is a serene, affordable, quality haven. Sandie spoils you with a homemade organic breakfast menu of your choice, served indoors in the sunny conservatory, or lush outdoors. Special diets catered for.Fun games, musical instruments, and great library.Pamper yourself with a, massage, reflexology or relaxing yoga session while you stay. Purification/Detox Health programs on request.Beaches, lakes, and rivers are all nearby. A stunning location & tranquil oasis in this mad world! Beautiful hospitality, which refreshes the soul B Jones.

Greymouth *12 km S of Greymouth*

New River Bluegums B & B *B&B Farmstay Cottage with Kitchen*

@home New Zealand · B&B Approved

Sharon & Michael Pugh
985 Main South Road,
New River, Greymouth

Tel (03) 762 6678
or 027 4385 324
or 027 6644 265
Fax (03) 762 6678
mail@bluegumsnz.com
www.bluegumsnz.com

Double/Twin $135-$185
Single $100-$145
(Full breakfast)
Children $25
Dinner by arrangement
Visa MC accepted
1 King 2 Queen 2 Double
2 Single (3 bdrm)
Bathrooms: 3 Ensuite

The Pugh family welcome you to the comfort of their log and stone home on a small farm. The homestead offers an ensuite king room. Two superbly appointed self-contained cottages. Tennis court. Laundry facilities. Wireless Broadband. Feed the sheep and cattle or play with Coco (labrador). 15 min walk to beach & 5 min drive to Shantytown. "Beautiful setting! Delightful home! Your relaxed and welcome manner made us feel like we were somewhere special and we certainly were, thank you!" G&K Guestbook.

Hokitika *2 km N of Hokitika*

Hokitika Heritage Lodge *Luxury B&B Homestay Cottage with Kitchen*

Dianne & Chris Ward
46 Alpine View, Hokitika
Tel (03) 755 7357 or 0800 261 949 or 027 437 1254
Fax (03) 755 7357 hokitikaheritage@xtra.co.nz
www.hokitikaheritagelodge.co.nz

Double/Twin $195-$250 Single $195-$210 (Full breakfast)
Children: Enquire, Dinner by arrangement,
Visa MC accepted
1 King/Twin 1 King 3 Queen 1 Single (5 bdrm)
3 bedrooms in Bank House; 2 bedrooms in Gatehouse Cottage
Bathrooms: 3 Ensuite 1 Private
3 ensuites in Bank House; 1 private in Gatehouse Cottage

Dianne (Literacy Teacher) and Chris (Property Consultant and Rotarian) warmly welcome you to our Lodge (B&B) and Gatehouse Cottage (self-contained holiday home) situated in a quiet location overlooking Hokitika, Tasman Sea and Southern Alps, including Mount Cook. Bank House B&B offers a stylish lounge with huge windows providing magnificent views; relaxation in the bush-setting spa; or outside terrace. Heritage themed bedrooms "Gold, Jade and Heritage" reflecting the West Coast History provide comfort and views. All guest rooms are spacious with high-quality bedding. They are quiet; have ensuites; superb views; tea/coffee making, TV; Broadband Internet and wireless network are available. Gatehouse Cottage is self-catering holiday home and includes 2 beautiful bedrooms with private bathroom; lounge with TV, dining and full kitchen, laundry. Stay and explore Lake Kaniere; Hokitika Gorge; Glow-worm Dell; craft-galleries; bush and history walks; restaurants; or visit the Glaciers (1.5hours); or Punakaiki (1.25hours). Take a scenic flight. All arrangements we can help you with. Guests comments: "Outstanding hospitality and facilities; superb accommodation; beautiful house; warm welcome; best cooked breakfast; the BEST night that we have had in NZ" Directions: Find us by following "Lodge" signs from the main road to the airport, along Tudor Street, turning left into Airport Drive. Turn right at the top of the hill into Alpine View. Travel to the end of the street, turning left into our drive. Follow the road around the house to the parking area and main entrance.

Hokitika *3 km S of Hokitika*

B&B Approved

Meadowbank *Rural Homestay*
Alison & Tom Muir
Takutai Road,
RD 3,
Hokitika
Tel (03) 755 6723
Fax (03) 755 6723

Double/Twin $90
Single $60
(Full breakfast)
Children half price
Dinner by arrangement
Children welcome
1 Double 2 Single (2 bdrm)
Bathrooms: 1 Guest share

Tom and Alison welcome you to their lifestyle property, situated just minutes south of Hokitika. Our large home, which we share with 2 cats, is modern, sunny and warm, and has a large garden. Nearby we have the beach, excellent golf-links, Lake Mahinapua, paddleboat, river, and of course Hokitika, with all its attractions. Directions: travel south 2km from south end of Hokitika Bridge on SH6, turn right - 200 metres on right. North-bound traffic - look for sign 1km north of Golf-links and Paddleboat.

Hokitika - Upper Kokatahi *28 km E of Hokitika*

B&B Approved

Sheridan Farmstay *Farmstay Cottage with Kitchen*
Trish & Terry Sheridan
31 Middle Branch Road,
Upper Kokatahi RD 1,
Hokitika 7881
Tel (03) 755 7967
tpsheridan@farmside.co.nz

Double/Twin $120
Single $70
(Full breakfast)
Children negotiable
Dinner $35 by arrangement
Self-contained cottage from $95
Children welcome
2 Queen 2 Double 2 Twin (6 bdrm)
Clean, warm, all beds have electric blankets
Bathrooms: 1 Ensuite 2 Guest share 1 Family share

Welcome to our 1000 acre dairy farm at the top of Kokatahi Valley 28km east of Hokitika. Numerous day walks, 3 rivers with trout fishing and kayaking and Lake Kaniere are all minutes away. Share our home with our three lovely cats or stay in our self-contained unit. We enjoy meeting people and love travelling. Terry enjoys current affairs and all sports while Trish is happy in the kitchen or garden. Enjoy dining with us in peaceful surroundings.

Hokitika *2 km E of Hokitika*

Woodland Glen Lodge *Luxury B&B*
Janette & Laurie Anderson
96 Hau Hau Road,
Blue Spur,
Hokitika

Tel (03) 755 5063
or 0800 361 361 (NZ Only)
or 027 201 6126
Fax (03) 755 5063
l.anderson@xtra.co.nz
www.hokitika.net

Double/Twin $180-$220
Single $150-$180
(Full breakfast)
Visa MC Diners Amex
Eftpos accepted
Not suitable for children
5 Queen 2 Twin 2 Single (5 bdrm)
Bathrooms: 3 Ensuite 1 Guest share

Our 6500 square foot lodge is located on 21 acres and is surrounded in native kahikatea trees providing quiet and privacy. A great place for a retreat or time out. Most guests base themselves in Hokitika for visits to the glaciers and Punakaiki, allow 2 nights. We welcome you to Woodland Glen Lodge, we are widely travelled and have many experiences to share with you. Laurie is a retired police officer and now commercial pilot, Janette is a health professional with a keen interest in quilting.

Hokitika *1 km N of Hokitika*

Top View B&B *B&B*
Lin & Colin Jackson
24 Whitcombe Terrace, Hokitika

Tel (03) 755 7060
or 027 7381 7206
or 027 733 9627
Fax (03) 755 7060
topview24@clear.net.nz
www.topview.co.nz

Double/Twin $110-$140
Single $80
(Breakfast by arrangement)
Children price depending age
Reduced rates for longer stays
Visa MC accepted
Pet free home Children welcome
2 Queen 2 Twin (3 bdrm)
Clean and comfortable, electric blankets
Bathrooms: 2 Ensuite 1 Guest share

We offer you a place to relax with a superb view of mountains, sea and sunsets from the lounge/breakfast room. Colin and Lin are retired farmers with many interests including Lions, Diabetes Societies, outdoor activities. Can provide Whitebait nets, Fishing Rods. We look forward to your company. From the main road north, turn at the Airport sign on Tudor Street, take the next left into Bonar Drive to the top of the hill on to Whitcombe Terrace, turn left.

Hokitika Central *1 km E of Post Office*

Amberlea B & B *B&B*

B&B Approved

Sharyn & Butch Symons
146 Gibson Quay,
Hokitika, 7810

Tel (03) 755 7346
or 027 697 1130
Fax (03) 755 7349
rpsmsymons@hotmail.com

Double/Twin $120-$140
Single $100-$120
(Full breakfast)
Children under 5yrs $10
Children under 12yrs $30
Children and pets welcome
3 Queen 1 Twin (4 bdrm)
All upstairs
Queen beds in ensuite rooms
Bathrooms: 2 Ensuite 1 Guest share
All bathrooms have showers

Sharyn and Butch along with their Bichons and cats invite you to their quiet friendly home situated beside the Hokitika River. Relax in the lovely gardens or watch the sunsets over the Tasman Sea and the Southern Alps. We are a five minute walk from the town centre and all of its tourist attractions, resturants and beach. Visit the Hokitika Gorge. Visit our great greenstone, paua, gold and ruby rock shops or relax at the beach or lakes enjoying the clean air.

Ruatapu *12 km S of Hokitika*

Berwick's Hill *B&B Homestay*

B&B Approved

Eileen & Roger Berwick
Ruatapu,
106 Ruatapu-Ross Road,
State Highway 6, RD 3,
Hokitika

Tel (03) 755 7876
Fax (03) 755 7870
berwicks@xtra.co.nz
www.berwicks.co.nz

Double/Twin $100-$130
Single $60-$80
(Full breakfast)
Dinner $40 by arrangement
Visa MC accepted
2 King/Twin 1 Queen (2 bdrm)
Heater in bedrooms
Bathrooms: 1 Ensuite 1 Private
1 bath in ensuite

Welcome to Berwick's Hill. We offer you a friendly and relaxed stay in our comfortable home. Magnificent views of the Tasman Sea and the Southern Alps are seen from the main living areas. Experience the sunsets and sunrises. We are close to Lake Mahinapua, bush walks, Mananui Bush and Beach walk ,golf course. On our lifestyle farm we have sheep, Belted Galloway cattle and a farm dog also hens. We and our cat look forward to meeting you

Whataroa *35 km N of Franz Josef*

Matai Lodge *Farmstay*

Glenice & Jim Purcell
Whataroa, 7668,
South Westland

Tel (03) 753 4156
or 0800 787 235
or 021 395 068
Fax (03) 753 4156
jpurcell@xtra.co.nz

Double/Twin $150-$180
Single $120
(Full breakfast)
Dinner $40pp
1 King/Twin 1 King 2 Single (3 bdrm)
Bathrooms: 1 Ensuite 1 Private

When your coming to the Glaciers, walk in the world heritage park or visit the White Heron Bird Sanctuary we warmly welcome you to share our spacious home, this tranquil rural valley retreat. 20 minutes from Franz Josef Glacier. Upstairs is a suite of 2 bedrooms, conservatory and private bathroom. Downstairs a king-size ensuite. You're welcome to join us for a home-cooked dinner with NZ wines. Our motto is: A stranger is a friend we have yet to meet. Glenice speaks Japanese, is a keen golfer, and has taught felting, weaving and spinning in Japan.

Whataroa - South Westland *13 km N of Whataroa/10 mins*

Mt Adam Lodge *B&B Homestay Farmstay*

Dale & Stephanie Bowater
State Highway 6,
Tetaho,
Whataroa,
South Westland

Tel (03) 753 4030
or 0800 675 137 NZ only
mtadamlodge@paradise.net.nz
www.mountadamlodge.co.nz

Double/Twin $125-$150
Single $105-$115
(Continental breakfast)
Fold-away bed $25extra
Visa MC Eftpos accepted
Children welcome
2 Queen 1 Double 2 Twin
2 Single (7 bdrm)
Bathrooms: 5 Ensuite 2 Guest share

If you're wanting to escape the crowds in the busy tourist centres then we are an ideal place for you to stay. Just a short 35 minute drive north of Franz Josef Glacier. We are situated on our farm at the foot of Mt Adam surrounded by farmlands and beautiful native bush. Our lodge offers comfortable accommodation and a fully licensed restaurant. You can stroll along the river bank and the farm tracks meeting our variety of animals along the way.

Franz Josef *5 km N of Franz Josef Glacier*

Ribbonwood Retreat *Luxury B&B Cottage with Kitchen*

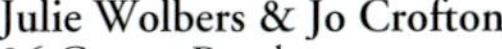

Julie Wolbers & Jo Crofton
26 Greens Road,
Franz Josef Glacier

Tel (03) 752 0072
ribbon.wood@xtra.co.nz
www.ribbonwood.net.nz

Double/Twin $180-$275
(Full breakfast)
A variety of restaurants in Franz Josef village
Free Wifi
Visa MC accepted
Children welcome
1 King 3 Queen 1 Single (3 bdrm)
3 rooms queen beds, cottage king plus single
Bathrooms: 2 Ensuite 1 Private
Luxurious tiled bathrooms, private bathroom next to room

Relax in our modern home or cottage, enjoying panoramic views of the forests, glaciers and mountains of Westland National Park. Our grounds are landscaped to provide habitat for native birds.Jonathan is a wildlife ranger and Julie an international school teacher. We are keen hikers and bird enthusiasts. We cater for just a few guests because we want you to feel completely at home.Breakfast includes homemade foods; fresh fruit salad, crepes, free range egg dishes and freshly baked bread. Enquire now about our discounts

Fox Glacier *20 km S of Franz Josef*

Roaring Billy Homestay *B&B Homestay*

Kathy
PO Box 16,
21 State Highway 6,
Fox Glacier

Tel (03) 751 0815
Fax (03) 751 0815
billy@xtra.co.nz

Double/Twin $105-$135
Single $105-$135
(Special breakfast)
Visa MC accepted
Not suitable for children
1 King/Twin 1 Double
1 Twin (2 bdrm)
Bathrooms: 1 Private 1 Guest share

Welcome to the comfort, warmth and hospitality of our 2 storey home. Our livingroom, kitchen, diningroom and veranda are upstairs and lined with local timbers, with 360-degree views of glacier valley, mountains, farms and the township. We're the closest homestay to the glacier and 2 minutes walk to all eating and tourist facilities. We are happy to book your local activities. The bus goes past our home. We offer a special cooked vegetarian breakfast. We have 1 cat, 1 small dog.

Fox Glacier *0.5 km W of Fox Glacier*

B&B Approved

The Homestead *B&B Farmstay*

Noeleen & Kevin Williams
PO Box 25, Cook Flat Road, Fox Glacier
Tel (03) 751 0835
Fax (03) 751 0805
foxhomestead@slingshot.co.nz

Double/Twin $140-$180
(Full breakfast)
Cooked breakfast $7pp
Pet free home
Not suitable for children
1 King/Twin 1 King 1 Queen (3 bdrm)
Bathrooms: 2 Ensuite 1 Private

Kevin and Noeleen, welcome you to our 2200 acre beef cattle and sheep farm. Beautiful native bush-clad mountains surround on 3 sides, and we enjoy a view of Mt Cook.

Our spacious 105 year old character home, built for Kevin's grandparents, has fine stained glass windows. The breakfast room overlooks peaceful pastures to the hills, and you are served home-made yoghurt, jams, marmalade, scones etc, with a cooked breakfast if desired.

We are very well travelled internationally and enjoy discussing and learning of other countries, trips, etc. Kevin has a wealth of knowledge of farming and local family history; a descendant of the two pioneering families. He loves talking to farmers from other countries.

The guest lounge, with its beautiful wooden panelled ceiling, has an open fire for cool autumn nights. A rural retreat within walking distance of village facilities, with Matheson (Mirror Lake) and glacier nearby. It is our pleasure to help you with helihikes, helicopter scenic flights and glacier walks.

Unsuitable for small children. Bookings recommended. Smoke-free.

Directions: On Cook Flat Road, fifth house on right, 400 metres back off road before church.

Fox Glacier *.5 km W of Fox Glacier*

B&B Approved

Fox Glacier Homestay *Homestay*

Eunice & Michael Sullivan
58 Cook Flat Road,
Fox Glacier

Tel (03) 751 0817
Fax (03) 751 0817
euni@xtra.co.nz

Double/Twin $90-$120
Single $80-$90
(Continental breakfast)
Children and pets welcome
1 Queen 1 Double 1 Twin
1 Single (4 bdrm)
Bathrooms: 1 Family share

Eunice and Michael are third generation farming and tourism family. We have 3 grown children and 3 cats (Bushy Tail, Sabrina & Tig). Our grandparents were founders of the Fox Glacier Hotel. We are a couple who enjoy meeting people and would like to share the joys of living in our little paradise (rain and all). Our home is surrounded by a large garden and has views of the mountains and Mt Cook. A 5 minute walk from township.

Fox Glacier *.2 km N of Fox Glacier*

B&B Approved

The White Fox B&B *B&B Homestay*

Jane Wellard & Gary Scott
4 State Highway 6,
PO Box 82, Fox Glacier

Tel (03) 751 0717
or 027 306 6759
or 027 738 7452
Fax (03) 751 0717
thewhitefox@slingshot.co.nz
www.thewhitefoxbandb.co.nz

Double/Twin $140-$170
Single $120-$150
(Continental breakfast)
Children negotiable by age
Visa MC accepted
Children and pets welcome
1 Queen 1 Single (1 bdrm)
Queen bed/single rollaway
Bathrooms: 1 Ensuite

Relax & enjoy the warmth & hospitality of a genuine NZ family home. Gary is a 4th generation local & we have considerable knowledge to assist our guests. We offer an easy to find location. Your room has a super comfortable bed, quality linen, electric blanket, TV & modern ensuite. Wake to the aroma of freshly baked bread & enjoy a generous Continental breakfast. We share our home with 2 young daughters Meghan-6 & Isla-4, Jess the Border Collie & Irish the Tabby Cat.

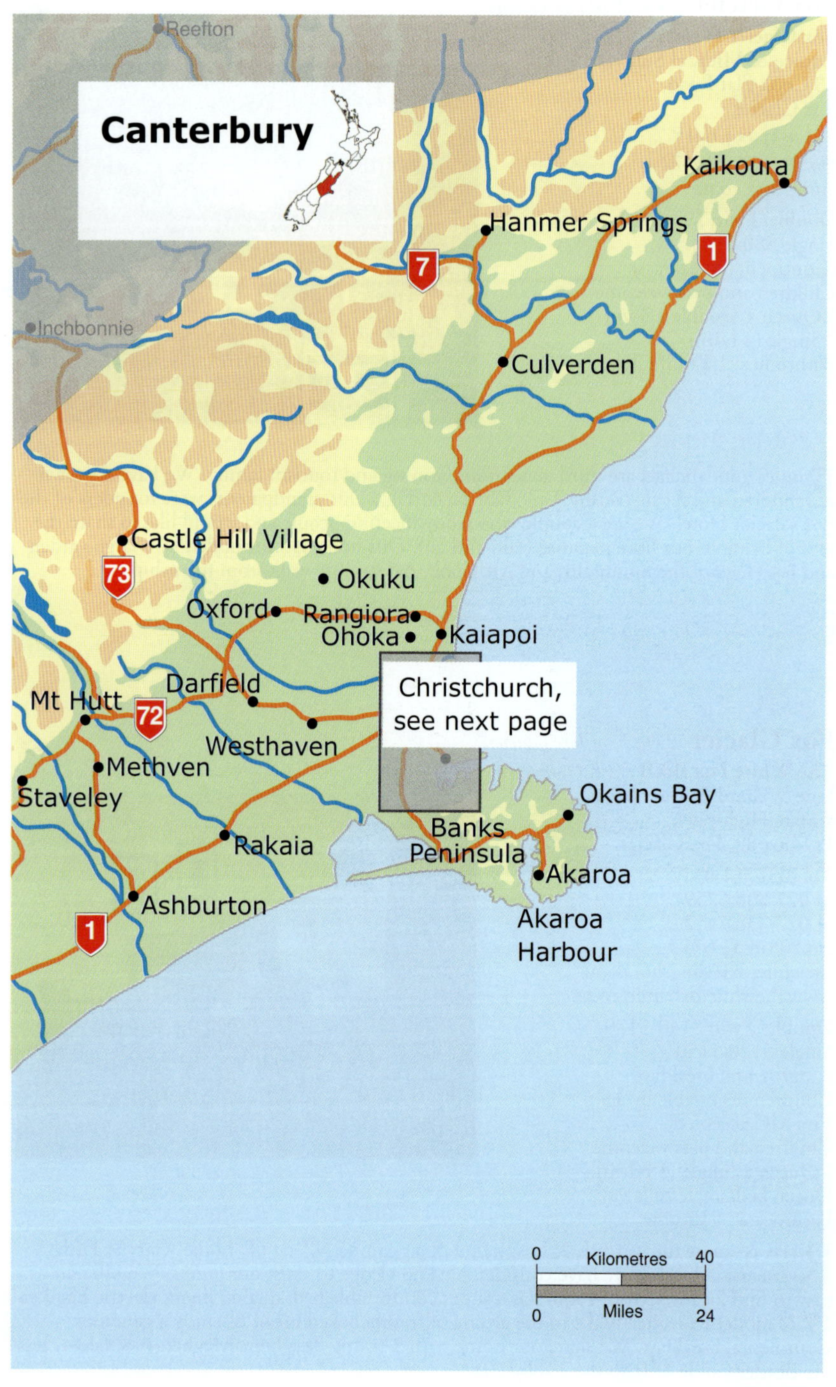
Canterbury
Reefton
Inchbonnie
Kaikoura
Hanmer Springs
1
7
Culverden
Castle Hill Village
73
Okuku
Oxford
Rangiora
Ohoka
Kaiapoi
Darfield
Mt Hutt
72
Westhaven
Christchurch, see next page
Methven
Staveley
Okains Bay
Banks Peninsula
Rakaia
Akaroa
Ashburton
1
Akaroa Harbour
0
Kilometres
40
0
Miles
24

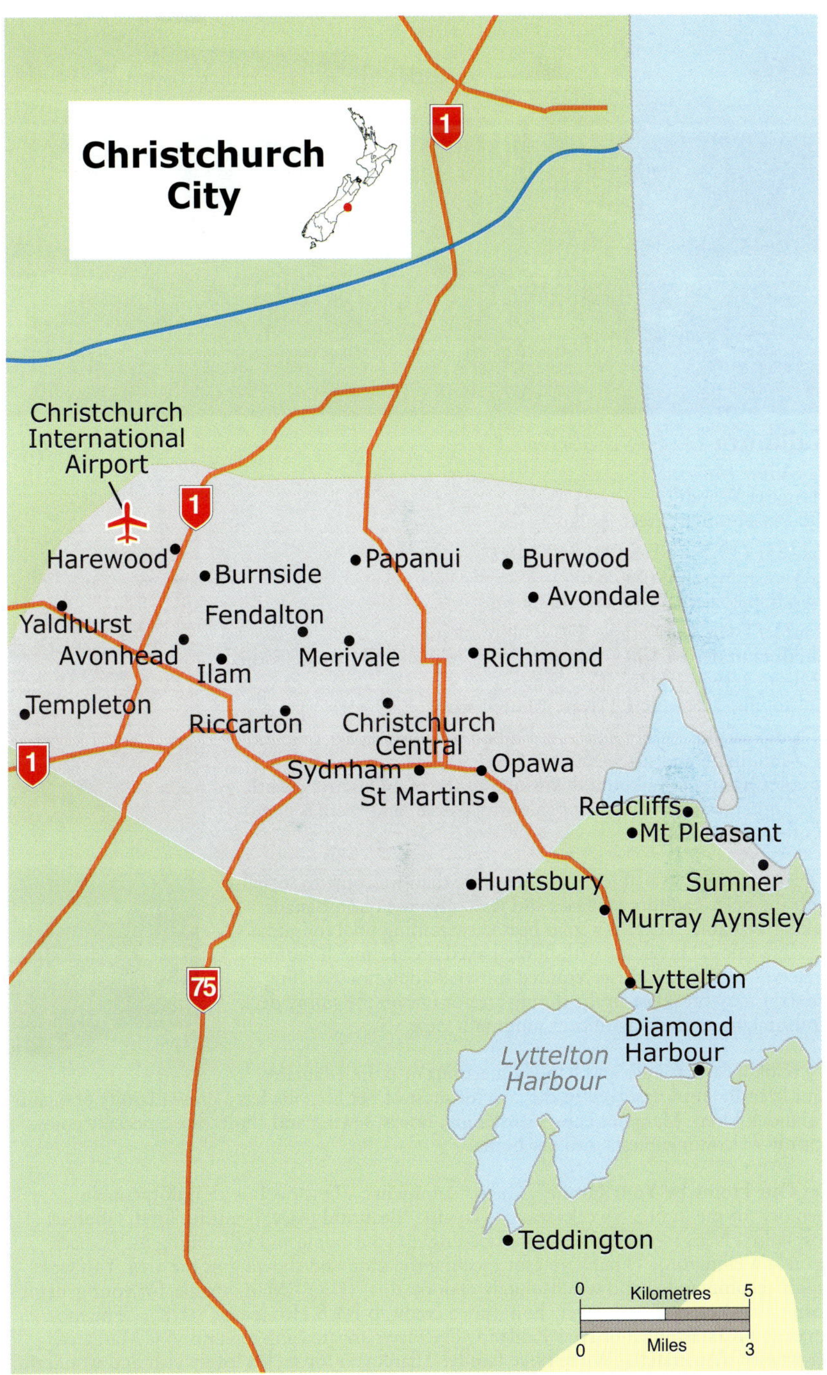

Christchurch City
1
Christchurch International Airport
1
Harewood
Burnside
Papanui
Burwood
Avondale
Yaldhurst
Fendalton
Avonhead
Ilam
Merivale
Richmond
Templeton
Riccarton
Christchurch Central
1
Sydnham
Opawa
St Martins
Redcliffs
Mt Pleasant
Sumner
Huntsbury
Murray Aynsley
Lyttelton
75
Diamond Harbour
Lyttelton Harbour
Teddington
0 Kilometres 5
0 Miles 3

Kaikoura *130 km S of Blenheim*

Bay-View *Homestay*
Margaret Woodill
296 Scarborough Street, Kaikoura

Tel (03) 319 5480 Fax (03) 319 7480
bayviewhomestay@xtra.co.nz
www.bnb.co.nz/bayviewkaikoura.html

Double/Twin $120 Single $70 (Full breakfast)
Children under 14 $30 Dinner $30 Children and pets welcome
1 Queen 1 Twin 1 Single (3 bdrm)
Bathrooms: 1 Ensuite 1 Private 1 Guest share

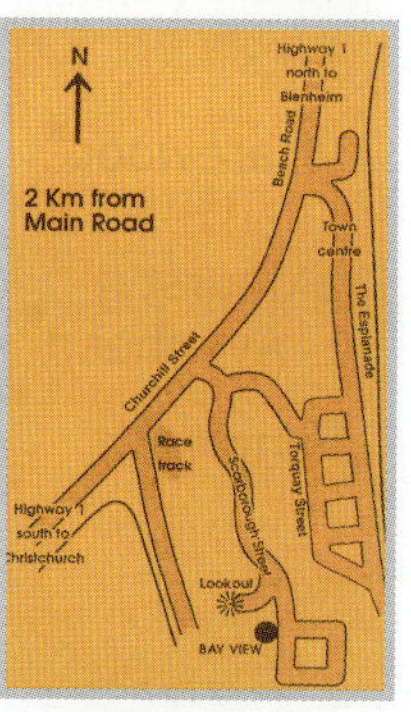

Our spacious family home on Kaikoura Peninsula has splendid mountain and sea views and is exceptionally quiet. Only 5 minutes from the Kaikoura township, off the main highway south. The house nestles in an acre of colourful garden and there is plenty of off-street parking.

A guest lounge is available or you are more than welcome to socialise with the host. Laundry facilities and tea/coffee with home-made baking available. There is a solar heated swimming pool for guests use. Traditional breakfast with home-baked bread, muesli, home preserves, available early as required for whale/dolphin watching guests. Enjoy breakfast in the dining area or out on the sunny deck whilst taking in the magnificent mountain view.

We book local activities and happily meet bus or train. Margaret, your friendly host, has lived in the area for most of her life. She has a grown family of 4, and 7 grandchildren. Margaret enjoys gardening, bowls, sewing and choir. She especially enjoys warmly welcoming guests into her home.

"Let Our Home be Your Home". Guests comments: "This B&B is an unforgettable memory for me in NZ 5 weeks travel" (Japan). "Beautiful place, beautiful food, fabulous hospitality, Margaret. Thank you for opening up your home and welcoming us. Be back again" (Wellington). "Thank you for meeting the train and showing us the area. You were highly recommended and we absolutely endorse this" (UK). "Many thanks for your generous hospitality. You and your lovely home are a credit to B&B Homestays" (UK). "The most amazing breakfast in all of New Zealand. The views are amazing too and so is Margaret's hospitality" (Australia). "We felt like family! Thank you for such a lovely visit and wonderful, delicious meals. We thank you a million!" (USA).

Kaikoura - Oaro *22 km S of Kaikoura*

Waitane Homestay *B&B Homestay Cottage with Kitchen*

Kathleen King
38 Waitane Road,
Oaro
RD 2,
Kaikoura

Tel (03) 319 5494
Fax (03) 319 5524
kathleen.king@xtra.co.nz

Double/Twin $85-$95
Single $50
(Full breakfast)
Children $25
Dinner $25 by arrangement
Visa MC accepted
Children and pets welcome
1 Double 4 Single (3 bdrm)
1 in B&B, 2 in cottage
Bathrooms: 2 Private

Waitane is 48 acres, close to the sea and looking north to the Kaikoura Peninsula. Enjoy coastal walks to the Haumuri Bluff with bird watching, fossil hunting etc, or drive to Kaikoura along our beautiful rocky coast. This is a mild climate and we grow citrus and sub-tropical fruits, mainly feijoas. Guest room in house has 2 single beds. Self-contained unit has 2 bedrooms, sleeps 4. 1 friendly cat lives here. Join me for dinner - fresh vegies, home preserves and home-made ice cream.

Kaikoura *1 km N of Kaikoura Central*

Bendamere House *B&B*

Kerry and Julie Howden
37 Adelphi Terrace,
Kaikoura

Tel (03) 319 5830
or 0800 107 770
Fax (03) 319 7337
bendamerehouse@xtra.co.nz
www.bendamere.co.nz

Double/Twin $150-$200
Single $130-$170
(Continental breakfast)
Children negotiable
Visa MC Diners Eftpos accepted
2 King 3 Queen 2 Twin
3 Single (5 bdrm)
All ensuite rooms
Bathrooms: 5 Ensuite

Kaikoura's Bendamere House B&B offers you 5 quality ensuite rooms all with private balconies where you can enjoy the breathtaking ocean and mountain views. Relax in our expansive lawns and rose gardens or take a short stroll into the Kaikoura township .All rooms have sleepyhead beds, silent fridges,heat pumps, tea/coffee/bathrobes and more. Free wireless Internet and laundry facilities as well as secure offstreet parking.

Kaikoura *4 km NE of Kaikoura town centre*

The Point *B&B*

Peter & Gwenda Smith
85 Fyffe Quay,
Kaikoura
Tel (03) 319 5422
Fax (03) 319 7422
pointsmith@xtra.co.nz
www.pointbnb.co.nz

Double/Twin $100-$135
Single $80-$95
(Continental breakfast)
Visa MC accepted
2 Queen (2 bdrm)
Bathrooms: 2 Ensuite

We offer a warm and friendly welcome to our home, which we share with our two daughters Sarah and Kate. Enjoy the quiet, unique location of our farmhouse built in the late 1800's. Our 90 acres of farmland is part of the Kaikoura Peninsula, on the waterfront with spectacular views of the sea and Kaikoura Mountains. Ideally situated for walking around Kaikoura Peninsula and the Seal Colony. Short walk to top Kaikoura restaurants. We run daily Sheep Shearing Shows; have farm dogs and a cat.

Kaikoura *183 km N of Christchurch*

Nikau Lodge *B&B*

Lilla Fitzwater
53 Deal Street,
Kaikoura Central
Tel (03) 319 6973
or 021 332 076
Fax (03) 319 6973
stay@NikauLodge.com
www.NikauLodge.com

Double/Twin $165-$225
Single $95-$195
(Full breakfast)
Visa MC Eftpos accepted
Pet free home
Not suitable for children
1 King/Twin 5 Queen 1 Single (7 bdrm)
Bathrooms: 6 Ensuite 1 Private

Conveniently located in the heart of Kaikoura close to SH1 with magnificent hilltop views of sea and mountains, Nikau Lodge offers high quality affordable B&B accommodation. 5 minutes walk takes you to Kaikoura's main street where you can enjoy local rock lobster. Relax in the hot-tub or garden with a glass of wine and gaze at the stars and snow-capped mountains. Internet access, Sky/TV, complimentary tea/coffee, in-room TV/movies. We welcome the opportunity to make your stay enjoyable and memorable.

Kaikoura *1 km NW of Kaikoura Central*

Driftwood Villa B&B *B&B Deluxe B&B*

Suzy & Chris Valkhoff
166A Beach Road, Kaikoura

Tel (03) 319 7116 or 0272 217 675 Fax (03) 319 7116
stayatdriftwoodvilla@xtra.co.nz www.driftwoodvilla.co.nz

Double/Twin $140-$180 Single $95-$125 (Full breakfast)
Children 2 years and under free, $10 up to 15 years.
Full use of kitchen
Visa MC accepted Children welcome
1 King 3 Queen 1 Twin 4 Single (4 bdrm)
Bathrooms: 4 Ensuite

Bed and Breakfast with a difference! Our Qualmark 4 star Villa is set up specifically for Guests enjoyment. The use of all the facilities in the home: including a large kitchen and living areas, internet access and outdoor spa pool.

Many of our guests have commented how wonderful and relaxed a stay they have had having use of the entire house, and not having to worry about intruding on the owners privacy.

Our rooms have:
- Powerful showers
-Good beds with fine linen
- Bathrobes, TV / Alarm Clock
- Tea, Coffee, Biscuits & sweets!

Villa facilities:
- Cooked and/or continental breakfast
- Spa with mountain views
- Wireless & internet connection
- Petanque/Boulles
- Comfortable Guest Lounge
- Full use of kitchen
- Complimentary Pick up & Drop Off

Your hosts: Chris, Suzy and daughters Annabelle 4, Sophie 2 plus the cat. (We live in a separate house at the back of the Villa!)

Kaikoura *130 km S of Blenheim*

B&B Approved

Churchill Park Lodge *B&B Separate Suite*

Gordon & Priscilla Wright
34 Churchill Street, Kaikoura, Marlborough
Tel (03) 319 5526 or 0800 363 690
cplodge@ihug.co.nz
www.churchillparklodge.co.nz

Double/Twin $130 Single $100 (Continental breakfast)
Children by arrangement
Extra guests Add $30 per night
Visa MC accepted
1 Queen 1 Double/Twin 1 Twin (2 bdrm)
Bathrooms: 2 Ensuite

Churchill park lodge is conveniently located in central Kaikoura on SHWY1 (Churchill street) on the hill capturing the magnificent Kaikoura mountain and sea views.

We welcome you to our purpose built, self contained upstair units with ensuite bathrooms (the double ensuite is compact but well appointed). We get many guests comment on how comfy the beds are. The units have T.V., fridge, lounge settee, dining suite, balcony table and chairs, heating and electric blankets with tea and coffee making facilities including plunger coffee. There is also off street parking and a private guest entrance with laundry facilities available. We serve a continental breakfast to your room for you to enjoy at your leisure. We believe the sea and mountain views from your room are unbeatable in Kaikoura.

Our B&B is only 5 minutes walk through Churchill park to the town centre. Where you will find shops, restaurants, cafes, the information centre and beach.

Cilla & Gordon are a down to earth "Kiwi" couple who are keen fishermen. You are welcome to join us on any trips we have planned, checking the lobster pots, catching a fish by boat or surfcasting from the beach. Also the local stream has many brown trout which are very challenging to catch.

We have two friendly dogs (who do not have access to the guest area) "Miss Spanky" a fun Bichon/Tibetan terrier X and "Xena" an aging pointer. We can book local activities or tours, and will happily meet you at the bus or train.

Kaikoura *5 km N of Kaikoura*

B&B Approved

Ardara Lodge *B&B Cottage with Kitchen*

Winnie & Phil Hood
233 Schoolhouse Road, RD 1, Kaikoura
Tel (03) 319 5736 or 0800 226 164
ardara@xtra.co.nz
www.ardaralodge.com

Double/Twin $110-$150
Single $110-$140 (Continental breakfast)
Children by arrangement
Cottage $165-$250
Visa MC accepted
Children welcome
7 Queen 3 Twin 4 Single (7 bdrm)
Bathrooms: 5 Ensuite 1 Private

After and exhilarating day exploring the natural splendours of Kaikoura unwind in the tranquility of Ardara Lodge.

You will enjoy a relaxed and peaceful stay in a beautiful rural setting near the magnificent Kaikoura mountains. Relax on the decks and enjoy Winnie's colourful garden which complements the panoramic veiw. Enjoy the outdoor hot tub (spa), veiw the Kaikoura mountains by day and the stars by night or read a book in the guest lounge.

The cottage has an upstairs bedroom with a queen and two single beds. Downstairs there is a bedroom with a queen bed, a bathroom with a shower and a lounge, kitchen, dining room. The deck is private with a great veiw of the Mountains. It has been very poplular with groups, families and honeymoon couples.The house has ensuite bathrooms with queen beds, plus a two bedroom unit, all with t.v, fridge, settee and coffee/tea facilities. You have you own private entrance and you are welcome to come and go as you please. We offer laundry facilities, off street parking and a courtesy car from the bus/train. There is an excellent restaurant, Donnegal House, within walking distance.

Phil owns a construction company based in Blenheim and Winnie was an office assistant before purchasing Ardara Lodge. Phil's hobbies are fishing, diving, motor racing, squash and harriers. Winnie's hobbies include gardening, lace making, embroidery and fishing. We like meeting people and look forward to your company.

Directions: Driving North, 4kms from Kaikoura on State Highway 1, turn left into Schoolhouse Road and continue 1.5kms until our sign.

Kaikoura *130 km S of Blenheim*

A Rest-n-Kai *B&B*
Carmel Tindall
5 Fyffe Ave,
Kaikoura

Tel (03) 319 7330
cartin@slingshot.co.nz
www.arestnkai.co.nz

Double/Twin $110-$120
Single $40-$65
(Full breakfast)
Children $20
Babies $10
Pet free home
Children welcome
1 Queen 1 Single (2 bdrm)
1 Queen/ 1 Single
Bathrooms: 1 Ensuite 1 Family share

Welcome to my home where I offer a Rest-n-Kai. Kai meaning food in Maori. I am a retired nurse and still enjoy caring for people. The home is new and comfortable, with lovely mountain views from the main rooms and external access from the large bedroom. A short walk into the township and other attractions including Whalewatch and Dolphin Encounter. I am happy to assist guests with directions and bookings. Many complimentary comments in visitors book indicate satisfaction with A Rest-n-Kai.

Kaikoura - Mangamaunu *15 km N of Kaikoura*

B&B Approved

Surfwatch Village *B&B Separate Suite Cottage with Kitchen*
Lynn & David Robinson
1137 State Hwy One,
Kaikoura, 7340

Tel (03) 319 6611
or 027 616 2903
or (03) 319 6658
Fax (03) 319 6658
bnb@ofu.co.nz
www.surfwatchbnb.com

Double/Twin $140-$250
Single $140-$250
(Breakfast by arrangement)
Visa MC accepted
Children welcome
1 King 1 Queen 1 Single (2 bdrm)
1 Ensuite, 1 Cottage
Bathrooms: 1 Ensuite 1 Private

The views here say it all. Five acres of tranquil rural country setting with stunning views overlooking the Pacific Ocean. Quiet and relaxing, melt away the city hustle-bustle in our spacious lawn and gardens. From the OceanView Ensuite you can watch dolphins play while Sharkeys Cottage is nestled in the garden. Both have kitchenettes, private entrances, parking, and are uniquely decorated with local wood and stone. Enjoy breakfast at your leisure. Wireless broadband. Lynn, David, Jessica and dogface Layla look forward to meeting you.

South Bay - Kaikoura *130 km S of Blenheim*

Ann's B & B *B&B Homestay*

Ann and Brent Fearnley
28 Moa Road,
Kaikoura, 7300

Tel (03) 319 5586
or 0274 521 075
Fax (03) 319 5584
brent.fearnley@xtra.co.nz

Double/Twin $120
Single $70
(Continental breakfast)
Children welcome
1 Queen 1 Twin (2 bdrm)
Spacious and comfortable,
Queen and King Single Beds
Bathrooms: 1 Guest share

We have a great location very close to the beginning of the stunning Peninsula Walk Track and beach walks. Our lounge and dining areas offer excellent views of the mountains and the sea. We are a friendly couple with 4 grown children; 2 daughters currently at home and 1 ginger cat. We have spacious guest rooms, comfortable beds and a new guest bathroom. We offer a Continental Breakfast. We are keen to help make your stay enjoyable, can advise on local activities and cuisine and assist with bookings.

Hanmer Springs *5 km SW of Hanmer Springs*

Mira Monte *B&B Countryhomestay*

Anna & Theo van de Wiel
324 Woodbank Road,
Hanmer Springs

Tel (03) 315 7604
or 021 050 5863
Fax (03) 315 7604
relax@miramonte.co.nz
www.miramonte.co.nz

Double/Twin $140-$150
Single $100-$110
(Special breakfast)
Children negotiable
Visa MC accepted
Children welcome
2 King 1 Single (2 bdrm)
Luxury comfortable large bed-rooms
Bathrooms: 2 Ensuite

Close to the thrills of Hanmer Springs, at the foot of the mountains, lies our peaceful home. Our guest rooms have been tastefully decorated to make your stay special. Relax in your own sitting room or join us. We make a great espresso! We are here to pamper you. There is a grand piano and our large garden has a swimming pool. We speak Dutch and German. Mindy, our Jack Russell is part of the family. Come as a Stranger! Leave as a Friend!

Canterbury

Hanmer Springs *1 km SW of Hanmer Springs*

Albergo Hanmer Lodge & Alpine Villas *Luxury B&B Separate Suite Apartment with Kitchen Cottage with Kitchen B&B & Self-contained*

Bascha & Beat Blattner
88 Rippingale Road, Hanmer Springs
Toll-Free 0800 342 313 **Ph/fax** (03) 315 7428
albergo@paradise.net.nz www.albergohanmer.com
Check web for packages

Double/Twin $160-$250 Single $120 (Special breakfast)
Dinner by prior arrangement Villa $260-$525
Visa MC Diners Amex Eftpos accepted
Pet free home Children welcome
3 King/Twin 1 King 1 Queen 2 Single (4 bdrm)
Bathrooms: 4 Ensuite

BREAKFAST - WELLNESS - CUISINE

Arrive at Albergo to blitz your senses in the fresh n' fun eclectic interiors with whimsical touches. **Dramatic alpine views** from all windows. **Stretch out on super king beds**, with TV/fridge/tea & coffee, and spacious ensuites (great water pressure) - choose the spa one for that bubble bath delight! European comforts for all seasons: u/floor heat, double glaze, aircon. Relax in cosy corners or wander out to the sunken Feng Shui courtyard, with soothing waterfall & fragrant lavenders galore. **Privacy & all day sun:** 2 minutes from Hot Pools, shops & cafes, or via new scenic walkway. **Ask about pamper package delights, Reiki healing & motivational readings by Bascha.**

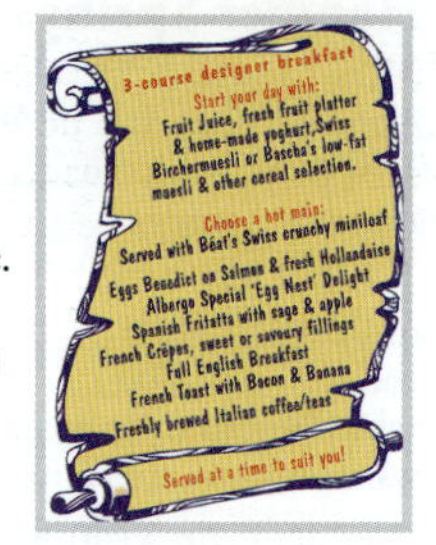

For privacy plus choose one of the stand alone Alpine Villas, with self-catering options. The awesome cinema & DVD library compliments the superb American king bedroom with large ensuite, boasting 'wow' views from the high panorama window, while you shower! Slip on a fluffy bathrobe, wander out to the split-level courtyard with private Jacuzzi and soak up Hanmer's starry night skies.

Go WOW over Albergo's renowned 3-course breakfast, served at a time to suit you, offering over 10 choices: Creative fruit platters or Swiss Birchermuesli, followed by the wafting smell of **homemade Swiss breads, & fine Italian coffee.** This perfect fusion of NZ & Swiss cuisine features: Salmon Eggs Benedict, French fluffy omelets, wafer-thin crepes, 'Albergo Egg Nests' or 'Full English', with crispy bacon. Fondue dinners by prior arrangement.
'Best breakfasts ever and Gold award for porridge' Sheila Bennett, NYC. *'Loved the milk jug containing cow - the decor and food was divine'* Charlotte, UK. *'Your quirky decors are a feast for the eyes, what an accommodation experience'* Gavin & Kerrie, Brisbane

DIRECTIONS: At junction before main village, 300m past Caltex Garage, take Argelins Rd (Centre branch), take 2nd road left Rippingale Rd. Albergo Hanmer is 800m down on the left (Sign at drive entrance).

Hanmer Springs *0.1 km E of in Hanmer village*

Cheltenham House *Luxury B&B Cottage No Kitchen Boutique Heritage B&B*

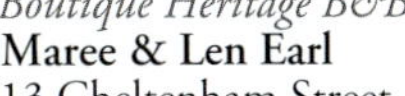

Maree & Len Earl
13 Cheltenham Street,
Hanmer Springs

Tel (03) 315 7545
Fax (03) 315 7645
enquiries@cheltenham.co.nz
www.cheltenham.co.nz

Double/Twin $220-$260
Single $190-$230
(Special breakfast)
Children by arrangement
Extra person $40
Visa MC Diners Eftpos accepted
Children and pets welcome
2 King/Twin 5 Queen 1 Single (6 bdrm)
Four house suites & two cottage garden suites
Bathrooms: 5 Ensuite 1 Private

Located on a quiet street, 200 metres from the Thermal Pools, restaurants & forest walks, we renovated this gracious 1930's home with the guests' comfort paramount. The four spacious, sunny suites in the house and two cottage suites in the park-like garden, are centrally heated. Enjoy a gourmet breakfast served in your own suite and complimentary wine in the billiard room in the evening. Star-gaze from the garden spa. Free wireless internet. Together with our sociable siamese & labrador, we look forward to meeting you.

~

Hanmer Springs *005 km N of village centre*

Hanmer View *Luxury B&B*

Margaux & Paul Delamain
8 Oregon Heights,
Hanmer Springs, 7334

Tel (03) 315 7947
or 027 431 9620
Fax (03) 3157947
hanmerview@xtra.co.nz
www.hanmerview.co.nz

Double/Twin $180-$240
Single $150-$190
(Full breakfast)
Visa MC accepted
Not suitable for children
1 King/Twin 1 King 1 Queen (3 bdrm)
Ensuited with views and
balcony access

Hanmer View adjoining the forest and Conical Hill walkway enjoys stunning panoramic views of the village and Hanmer Basin. Enjoy a tranquil stay in air-conditioned ensuited rooms with views and balcony. Margaux and Paul with their cats and dog have pleasure in welcoming you and ensuring you have an enjoyable stay at Hanmer View. We are happy to help you choice and enjoyment of the activities Hanmer Springs and its environs offer. Stroll to the village centre and pools. Special packages and wireless internet available.

Culverden *3 km S of Culverden*

Ballindalloch *Farmstay*

Diane & Dougal Norrie
Longplantation Road,
Culverden,
RD 2,
North Canterbury 7392

Tel (03) 315 8220
or 027 437 3184
Fax (03) 315 8220
norrie@amuri.net

Double/Twin $130
Single $80
(Full breakfast)
Children $35
Dinner $35 by arrangement
Children welcome
1 Queen 2 Single (2 bdrm)
Bathrooms: 1 Guest share

Welcome to "Ballindalloch"a family farming enterprise with 3 family members farming on their own behalf on 4,000 acre irrigated farms, now milking 3,000 cows. We are just over 1 hour north of Christchurch, half an hour to Hanmer Springs, 1 1/2 hours to Kaikoura Whale Watch. Culverden is situated between 2 excellent fishing rivers. Having travelled extensively overseas we appreciate relaxing in a homely atmosphere - this we extend to our guests. We look forward to welcoming you to our home.

Rangiora *2 km E of Rangiora*

Coldstream House *Luxury B&B Farmstay Cottage No Kitchen*

Rupert Ward
11 Coldstream Road, Rangiora, 8254

Tel (03) 310 6006
or 021 039 6016
Fax (03) 310 6007
rupertward@hotmail.com
www.coldstreamhouse.co.nz

Double/Twin $120-$140
Single $100-$120 (Full breakfast)
Children welcome - our second casual bedroom is great for 2 children
Dinner not offered but cafes and restaurants nearby
1 Queen (1 bdrm)
Separate cottage & ensuite, verandah, second casual bedroom
Bathrooms: 1 Ensuite
Ensuite spacious bathroom with shower

Coldstream House is an original Canterbury Homestead. Rupert Ward and his three children offer a very friendly welcome. The "Copper Cottage" guest cottage is 130 years old and has a pretty country bedroom with ensuite and private verandah with farm view. Coldstream has a beautiful living and dining room for guests use overlooking 130 year old tranquil formal gardens and tenniscourt surrounded by beautiful trees and a wild flower garden.We have a second casual bedroom which is great for kids.

Rangiora - Fernside *5 km W of Rangiora*

Petes Farm Stay B&B *B&B Farmstay*

B&B Approved

Gaye & Peter Hurst
45 Mairaki Road,
Rangiora RD 1, 7471

Tel (03) 313 5180
or 027 221 8989
Fax (03) 313 5182
petesfarm@xtra.co.nz
http://petesfarm.co.nz

Double/Twin $120-$140
Single $80-$100
(Continental breakfast)
Children half price
Dinner $40 per person
Visa MC accepted
Children welcome
1 King/Twin 1 Queen
1 Double 2 Single (3 bdrm)
Large spacious and great views
Bathrooms: 2 Private

Welcome to Pete's Farm B&B.We are situated 25 minutes from Christchurch Airport & City. Also just seconds off Inland Scenic Route 72.See a sheep shearing and dog demo. Relax in our new home and experience first hand the quietness and great views we get from every room in the house.

Okuku-Rangiora *12 km N of Rangiora*

Serenada Country Lodge *Luxury B&B Farmstay Separate Suite*

B&B Approved

Lyn & Mark Malcolm
Foothills Road,
Okuku,
Rangiora 7474

Tel (03) 313 2263
Fax (03) 313 2264
info@serenada.co.nz
www.serenada.co.nz

Double/Twin $295-$340
(Full breakfast)
Visa MC Eftpos accepted
Children and pets welcome
4 King/Twin (4 bdrm)
Superking Luxury Suites
Bathrooms: 4 Ensuite

Luxury accommodation 12 klm from Rangiora.
Serenada Country Lodge is also the home of "Riarma" Quarter Horse Stud. We have our own heated swimming pool - spa. Sauna - gym and 9 hole golf course. Restaurant and bar. Relax and enjoy the peace and quiet of Serenada. 4 X large Beautiful luxury accommodation Suites with king size beds and spa bath in each. Friendly atmosphere. A holiday to remember.

Oxford *60 km W of Christchurch*

Country Life *B&B Apartment with Kitchen*
Helen Dunn
137 High Street,
Oxford,
North Canterbury 7430

Tel (03) 312 4167

Double/Twin $75-$90
Single $45-$50
(Full breakfast)
Dinner $20 by arrangement
Children and pets welcome
4 Twin (2 bdrm)
Self Contained Unit - 2 Twin beds, kitchen & Ensuite,
2 Twin in house - bathroom handy
Bathrooms: 1 Ensuite 1 Family share

Country life has been operating since 1987, the house is 80 years old and has a spacious garden, warm and sunny. Helen enjoys meeting people from far and wide - whether overseas visitors or those wanting a peaceful break away from Christchurch - all are welcomed at Country Life. High Street is left off the Main Road. Sign outside the gate.

Oxford *54 km W of Christchurch Airport*

Hielan' House *B&B Homestay Countrystay*
Shirley & John Farrell
74 Bush Road, Oxford,
North Canterbury

Tel (03) 312 4382
or 0800 279 382 (freephone)
or 0274 359 435 Fax (03) 312 4382
hielanhouse@ihug.co.nz
www.hielanhouse.co.nz

Double/Twin $150-$175
Single $120-$140 (Full breakfast)
Children price on application
Dinner by arrangement
Visa MC accepted
Children and pets welcome
1 King/Twin 1 Queen
1 Twin 1 Single (2 bdrm)
1 King/Twin Room, 1 Queen
Bathrooms: 2 Ensuite

Quality upstairs guest rooms with relaxing areas, ensuites, separate entrance. TV/DVD, tea/coffee facilities, fridges, hairdryers, bathrobes, slippers. Complimentary laundry, internet, sauna, spa, outdoor swimming pool, golf clubs to use. Safe parking. Enjoy John's breakfasts, dinners with home-grown meat/vegetables. Relax, unwind on 6 acres in peaceful, rural Oxford or stay longer and make us your base for day trips to Arthurs Pass, Hamner, Akaroa. Situated 3 mins from Inland Scenic Route 72, via Bay/Bush Roads. We enjoy meeting people and look forward to spoiling you.

Ohoka *6 km W of Kaiapoi*

Oakhampton Lodge *B&B*

Angus & Jackie Watson
24 Keetly Place,
Ohoka,
Kaiapoi RD2, 7692

Tel (03) 312 6413
or 021 502 313
Fax (03) 3126314
info@oakhampton.co.nz
www.oakhampton.co.nz

Double/Twin $150-$180
(Full breakfast)
Not suitable for young children
Dinner available on request $35
Visa MC accepted
1 King 1 Queen 1 Twin (2 bdrm)
All bedrooms have views or access to large country garden.
Bathrooms: 2 Ensuite

Set amongst 4 acres of lawns, mature trees and herbaceous borders, Oakhampton Lodge is the perfect place to unwind and experience a slice of country life. Ideal for weekend stays or as a stopover while travelling around New Zealand. Heading north from Christchurch on the Northern Motorway (SH1) take second Kaiapoi/Ohoka turnoff over Waimakariri River, follow signs to Ohoka. Keetly Place is 6 kms along Mill Rd, on right, just before Ohoka Hall and Service Station. No 24 is on your right.

Kaiapoi *15 km N of Christchurch*

Morichele *B&B*

Helen & Richard Moore
25 Hilton Street,
Kaiapoi

Tel (03) 327 5247
morichele@xtra.co.nz

Double/Twin $100
Single $70
(Full breakfast)
Children negotiable
Dinner by arrangement
1 Double 1 Twin (2 bdrm)
Comfortable
Bathrooms: 1 Guest share

Helen & Richard+ Sooky the cat provide comfortable accommodation in a beautiful garden setting, close to rivers, beaches, golf course and walks. With off-street parking, own entrance, sitting/dining area with fridge, tea and coffee making facilities, TV and video. Cafes and restaurants within walking distance alternatively, if you prefer, you are welcome to bring back takeaways or barbeque in the garden. Ski fields, Hanmer Springs themal reserve, Akaroa (home of the Hector's Dolphin) and Kaikoura (whale watching)are less than two hours away.

Kaiapoi - Mandeville *20 km N of Christchurch*

Ohoka Meadows B&B / Gatehouse Cottage *B&B Farmstay Cottage with Kitchen*

Mary and Graeme Chisnall
49 Ohoka Meadows Drive,
RD 2, Kaiapoi, 7692

Tel (03) 313 1781
or 0274 311 979
ohokameadows@xtra.co.nz
www.ohokameadows.co.nz

Double/Twin $130-$150
Single $100-$110 (Full breakfast)
Child price on application
Dinner by arrangement
Children welcome
1 King 1 Queen 1 Twin (2 bdrm)
2 in B&B, 1 in cottage
Bathrooms: 3 Ensuite

Graeme and Mary welcome you into their home.Enjoy privacy and peace while staying in modern B&B rooms with your own facilities, our luxurious fully equipped Gatehouse Cottage with full kitchen or enquire about our apartment in the Christchurch city. Take Chester and Devon, the alpacas for a walk or feed the other animals. Enjoy 4 acres of landscaped grounds and admire the mountains. Only 22 kms to Christchurch International Airport and Shopping Malls. Our interests include model engineers, jetboating, teaching and entertaining guests.

Christchurch - Harewood *7.5 km N of Christchurch Centre*

St James B&B *Luxury B&B*

Margaret & David Frankish
125 Waimakariri Road,
Harewood, Christchurch 8005

Tel (03) 359 6259
or 027 455 3554
or 0274 320 996
Fax (03) 359 6299
dj.frankish@xtra.co.nz
www.stjamesbnb.com

Double/Twin $120-$180
Single $95-$120
(Full breakfast)
Children $40
Visa MC accepted
Children welcome
1 King 1 Queen 1 Single (2 bdrm)
Bathrooms: 1 Ensuite 1 Private

Located 5 minutes from Christchurch Airport, 10 minutes from city. Begin/ end your South Island trip in our warm, modern home with its tranquil garden setting, and the horses who share our 3 acre property. Our lovely guest rooms include private lounges, ensuite bathroom and private spa/bathroom upstairs. Rooms have tea/coffee facilities and TV. Internet access is available. Our beautiful spoodle collects the daily newspaper. Close by are golf courses, excellent restaurants, shopping, Wildlife Reserve, McLeans Island Recreation Area and Antarctic Centre.

Christchurch - Harewood *4 km N of Central Post Office*

Belmont on Harewood *B&B Botique Accommodation*

Alan and Jan Taylor
37 Harewood Road,
Papanui, Christchurch, 8053

Tel (03) 354 6890
or (021) 479 920
Fax (03) 354 6895
janalltd@paradise.net.nz
www.belmontbnb.co.nz

Double/Twin $120-$295
Single $90-$220 (Full breakfast)
Children in parents room $25
Dinner $15 plus quality restaurants within 4 min walk
Visa MC accepted Children welcome
1 King/Twin 3 Queen 1 Single (5 bdrm)
Large and warm with quality furniture
Bathrooms: 2 Ensuite 1 Private 1 Guest share
Platinum suite has a two person spa bath

Heritage home seven minutes from Airport. Our large sunny open lounge and dining room are where you can meet for wines, tea, coffee and chats. Close to restaurants, city and major tourist attractions. A range of accommodation choices with ensuites and non facility rooms. Disabled facilities and off street parking. Wireless internet. LCD TV's and DVD's. @ HOMENZ and regularly inspected. Quality furnishings. Central heating, all year round comfort. Continental or full breakfasts. Fire alarm. Free pickup from Plane, Rail or Bus. Try us!

Christchurch - Yaldhurst *8 km W of Christchurch Central*

Gladsome Lodge *B&B Homestay*

Stuart & Sue Barr
314 Yaldhurst Road,
Avonhead, Christchurch 8042

Tel (03) 342 7414
or 0800 222 617 or 021 278 6982
Fax (03) 342 3414
sue@gladsomelodge.com
www.gladsomelodge.com

Double/Twin $100-$130
Single $95-$110
(Continental breakfast)
Children 0-5 free, 5-12 $20
Dinner $25 by arrangement
Cooked breakfast available
Visa MC Diners Amex accepted
Children welcome
3 Queen 1 Double 1 Twin 2 Single (5 bdrm)
Bathrooms: 2 Ensuite 3 Guest share

Located close to airport with easy access to key attractions. Be assured of professional, attentive hosting in a friendly environment. Enjoy our tennis court, swimming pool or sauna. Guest wireless internet access available. We are able to accommodate couples travelling together. Have knowledge of Maori history and culture. Our house is centrally heated. On bus route to city. On route to ski fields and West Coast Highway.Outside friendly dog. Hosts Sue and Stuart, New Zealanders who have travelled and have a wide variety of interests.

Christchurch - Avonhead *10 km W of Christchurch Central*

Russley 302 *B&B*
Helen & Ron Duckworth
302 Russley Road,
Avonhead, Christchurch 8042

Tel (03) 358 6510
or 021 662 016
Fax (03) 358 6470
haduck@xtra.co.nz
www.ducksonrussley.co.nz

Double/Twin $120-$150
Single $80-$120
(Full breakfast)
Evening meal (with local wines) b/a
Comp. airport transfers day or night
Visa MC accepted
1 King 1 Queen 1 Twin
1 Single (4 bdrm)
Bathrooms: 1 Ensuite 2 Private

Located on main north/south highway near Christchurch airport Russley 302 provides complimentary airport transfers and excellent hospitality for guests arriving and departing the "garden city". All guest rooms are very attractively furnished, and comfortable. Each double room is well equipped with private bathroom, tea/coffee facilities, refrigerator, television, electric blanket, clock/radio, hair dryer. Email/fax facilities available if required. Dinner is available by prior arrangement. Our "garden city" has much to offer and is an ideal location for daily excursions to Canterbury's hinterland.

Christchurch - Avonhead *6 km NW of City Centre*

Maidstone Bed & Breakfast *B&B*
Paul and Angela Cossey
155 Maidstone Road,
Avonhead,
Christchurch 8042

Tel (03) 358 5442
or 027 326 6511
panda@snap.net.nz
www.maidstonebedandbreakfast.com

Double/Twin $120
Single $110
(Continental breakfast provisions)
Children by arrangement
1 Queen (1 bdrm)
Private guestroom with ensuite
Bathrooms: 1 Ensuite

You'll enjoy our comfortable guestroom giving you a relaxed and private stay. We're just minutes from the airport and Botanical Gardens and City Centre. There's so much to do in Christchurch and you can also plan day trips to Akaroa or escape to the ski-fields. See our website for more ideas of what you can see and experience while in Christchurch. Private entrance and off-street parking and courtesy pickup from airport.

Christchurch - Burnside *7 km W of Christchurch*

B&B Approved

Stableford Airport B&B *B&B*

Margaret & Tony Spowart
2 Stableford Green,
Burnside,
Christchurch 8053

Tel (03) 358 3264
or 021 883 804
stableford@xtra.co.nz
www.stableford.co.nz

Double/Twin $140
Single $130
(Full breakfast)
Visa MC accepted
2 Queen 1 Twin (3 bdrm)
Bathrooms: 2 Ensuite 1 Private

Welcome to Stableford, the closest B&B to the Christchurch Airport, making it ideal for arriving or departing visitors. City bus-stop at door. We are situated adjacent to the prestigious Russley Golf Club. Let us know if you require a tee booking at the Russley Golf Course. Stableford is new, clean and comfortable with a separate guest lounge. Good restaurants nearby. Our interests are travel, sport, music, & antiques. Cat in residence. Ask about our winter rates.

Christchurch - Burnside *8 km NW of City Centre*

B&B Approved

Blossom Tree Homestay *B&B Homestay*

Lorna Watson
29 O'Connor Place,
Burnside,
Christchurch 8053

Tel (03) 358 2635
Fax (03) 358 2665
blossomtree@xtra.co.nz

Double/Twin $100-$120
Single $60-$80
(Continental breakfast)
Children welcome $20
1 Queen 1 Double 2 Single (3 bdrm)
Bathrooms: 2 Private 1 Guest share

Located 5 minutes from Christchurch Airport, free transfer to and from airport, car hire depots very close, 15 minutes from City Centre. Good bus services closeby. Russley Golf Course and a variety of excellent restaurants and cafes nearby. Modern 7 year old home, along with it's owners, Lorna & Lyndsay and lovely cat Emma, welcomes bed & breakfast guests. Enjoy lovely surroundings and a generous continental breakfast. Off-street parking and laundry facilities available. We look forward to welcoming you.

Christchurch - Ilam *7.5 km NW of Christchurch*

Anne & Tony Fogarty Homestay *B&B Homestay*

Anne & Tony Fogarty
7 Westmont Street,
Ilam,
Christchurch 8041

Tel (03) 358 2762
Fax (03) 358 2767
tony.fogarty@xtra.co.nz

Double/Twin $100
Single $60
(Continental breakfast)
Dinner $30 by arrangement
Visa MC accepted
4 Single (2 bdrm)
Bathrooms: 1 Guest share
1 Family share

Our home is in the beautiful suburb of Ilam, only minutes from Canterbury University and Canterbury University College of Education. Close to Christchurch Airport (7 minutes by car) and the railway station (10 minutes). A bus stop to the central city, with its many attractions is 50 metres from our home. Willing to arrange transport from airport or train.Excellent local information. Guests are welcome to use our laundry. Complimentary tea and coffee at any time. Stay with us and get value for money.

Christchurch - Papanui *5 km E of Christchurch Airport*

Heatherston Boutiqe Bed & Breakfast *Luxury B&B*

Jan and Murray Binnie
46 Searells Road,
Christchurch, 8052

Tel (03) 355 3239
or 027 418 8961
Fax (03) 355 3259
enquiries@heatherston.co.nz
www.heatherston.co.nz

Double/Twin $120-$150
Single $120
(Full breakfast)
Not suitable for children
2 King/Twin 1 Queen 1 Single (3 bdrm)
Bathrooms: 3 Ensuite

Comfortable, convenient and quiet. A superbly situated, purpose-built, modern house with every convenience, only ten minutes from the Airport, and ten minutes from Central Christchurch. Heatherston has a sunny guests' kitchenette/lounge, bedrooms with comfortable beds, refreshment facilities, and television. Ensuites have heated towel rails, hairdryers and toiletries. Heatherston is close to shops and restaurants, and is conveniently located for sight-seeing in the city, or travelling to wineries, walking tracks, golf courses, and skifields. Heatherston is the perfect tranquil retreat!

Christchurch - Fendalton *5.0 km NW of Christchurch city centre*

B&B Approved

Glenveagh B&B *B&B*

Alison & Ian Boyd
230C Clyde Road,
Fendalton, Christchurch

Tel (03) 351 4407
or 0800 000 107
Fax (03) 351 4406
boyd45@xtra.co.nz
www.glenveagh.co.nz

Double/Twin $120-$190
Single $120-$150
(Continental breakfast)
Children by arrangement
Visa MC Eftpos accepted
1 King/Twin 1 Queen 1 Twin
2 Single (3 bdrm)
King/twin/triple/ queen/twin/single
Bathrooms: 1 Ensuite 1 Private

Ian & Alison welcome you to our beautiful home in a quiet area of Fendalton, Christchurch. Just off airport,city road. We have three guest rooms, upstairs and downstairs a lounge, courtyard. Tralee: King/twin/triple with ensuite and TV. Erigal: Twin with private bathroom and TV. Galway: Queen with private bathroom and TV. Restaurants within walking distance. Off-street parking. Courtesy car from airport, bus, train. Five minutes by car to central city, bus at gate.Wirelessinternet. Continental breakfast. No smoking inside. Look forward to your company.

Christchurch - Riccarton *6 km E of Christchurch Central*

B&B Approved

Sunrise *B&B Homestay*

Ella and Kamal
9 Main South Road,
Upper Riccarton, Christchurch

Tel (03) 981 3807
or 0800 526 924 or 0274 808 955
Fax (03) 981 3809
stay@sunrisebnb.co.nz
www.sunrisebnb.co.nz

Double/Twin $65-$75
Single $55-$60
(Breakfast by arrangement)
Children negotiable
Family room sleeps three $90
Visa MC accepted
Children welcome
2 Queen 4 Twin 1 Single (5 bdrm)
Bathrooms: 2 Guest share

Sunrise BnB welcomes you to the Garden City. We are a caring, comfortable and affordable accommodation with room only options. Walking distance to University, shopping areas & 6am to midnight super market. Sunrise has a homely atmosphere & offers warm sunny rooms, independent kitchen, lounge, laundry, parking. We have courtesy pick up from airport, rail, and bus (by arrangement) and offer excellent weekly and long term rates. Your hosts: Ella, Kamal & family including Gypsy, affectionate German Shepherd. We look forward to see you soon.

Christchurch - Riccarton *6 km W of City centre*

Thistle Guest House *B&B Guest House*
John and Alison Goodfellow
21 Main South Road,
Church Corner,
Upper Riccarton,
Christchurch, 8042

Tel (03) 348 1499
or 0800 93 21 21
Fax (03) 348 1577
stay@thistleguesthouse.co.nz
www.thistleguesthouse.co.nz

Double/Twin $86-$96
Single $55-$78
(Continental breakfast)
Visa MC Amex Eftpos accepted
Children welcome
1 King 4 Queen 3 Twin
4 Single (10 bdrm)
Bathrooms: 1 Ensuite 3 Guest share

A small friendly guest house offering quality homestyle accommodation. 10 private bedrooms with fridge, tea/coffee facilities and wireless internet access for laptops. Fully equipped guest kitchen, lounge, off-street parking and attractive garden. Laundry facilities and guest telephone also available. Handy to Canterbury University and College of Education and two minutes walk to shops, restaurants and supermarket. On good bus route to city (15 mins) and 10 minutes drive from airport. Courtesy pick-up by arrangement. Weekly rates and tariffs excluding breakfast also available.

Christchurch - Merivale *2 km N of Christchurch*

Leinster B&B *B&B Homestay*
Kay and Brian Smith
34B Leinster Road,
Merivale,
Christchurch

Tel (03) 355 6176
or 027 433 0771
Fax (03) 355 6176
brian.kay@xtra.co.nz
www.leinsterbnb.co.nz

Double/Twin $150-$175
Single $120
(Full breakfast)
Children negotiable
Visa MC accepted
Children welcome
1 Queen 1 Double 1 Single (2 bdrm)
Bathrooms: 1 Ensuite 1 Private

At Leinster Bed & Breakfast we pride ourselves on creating a relaxed friendly atmosphere in our modern sunny home. Only 5 minutes to city centre (art gallery, museum, botanical gardens, Cathedral Square, casino, town hall etc), 10 minutes from the airport. For evening dining convenience there are excellent restaurants just a leisurely stroll away at Merivale Village. Laundry, email, fax and off-street parking facilities makes us your home away from home. Bedrooms have TV, electric blankets, heaters, tea/coffee. Well behaved puss & pooch in residence.

Christchurch - Richmond *2 km E of CBD*

B&B Approved

Avon Grove Villa Bed & Breakfast *B&B*

Janice and Ian Cundall
273 River Road,
Christchurch, 8013
Tel (03) 381 7099
or 027 442 3076
enquiries@avongrovevilla.co.nz
www.avongrovevilla.co.nz

Double/Twin $140-$160
Single $90-$110
(Full breakfast)
Visa MC accepted
Children welcome
2 Queen 1 Single (3 bdrm)
Bathrooms: 2 Ensuite 1 Private

This 1900's Villa is situated beside the Avon River, in a quiet location, and is close to the CBD, being only 5 minutes by car or a 30 minute walk along the river. Two large, comfortably appointed double guest rooms, each with original fireplace and bay windows, are available. Each room has an ensuite, TV, and tea and coffee facilities. There is also a single room with a separate private bathroom. A full cooked breakfast is served in the dining room.

Christchurch - Burwood *4 km N of Christchurch City*

B&B Approved

Finlay Banks B&B *B&B*

Fay & Lindsay Turner
7 Banks Avenue,
Burwood,
Christchurch
Tel (03) 385 1012
or 027 485 1015
Fax (03) 385 1014
finlaybanks@xtra.co.nz
www.finlaybanks.co.nz

Double/Twin $150-$200
Single $110-$150
(Full breakfast)
Children POA
Dinner POA
Visa MC accepted
2 Queen
Bathrooms: 2 Ensuite

In the heart of picturesque garden city is your home away from home - 'Finlay Banks'. Our smoke free location is central to all that the city has to offer yet peaceful and private in its rose garden surroundings. Offering 2 well-appointed sun drenched en-suite guest rooms with single sofa bed, serviced daily. Your host is an enthusiastic cook who will treat you to a delicious continental or cooked breakfast. Evening meals and picnic baskets also available upon request, along with courtesy pickup and drop off.

Christchurch - Avondale *8 km NE of Christchurch Central*

B&B Approved

Hulverstone Lodge *B&B*

Diane & Ian Ross
18 Hulverstone Drive, Avondale, Christchurch
Tel (03) 388 6505 or 0800 388 650 (NZ only)
Fax (03) 388 6025
hulverstone@caverock.net.nz
www.hulverstonelodge.co.nz

Double/Twin $120-$160 Single $100-$120
(Full breakfast)
Triple (queen + single) $200
Visa MC accepted
Pet free home Not suitable for children
3 King/Twin 1 Queen 1 Single (4 bdrm)
Bathrooms: 2 Ensuite 1 Private 1 Guest share 1 Family share

Gracing the bank of the Avon River in a quiet suburb, yet only 10 minutes from the city centre, stands picturesque Hulverstone Lodge. From our charming guest rooms watch the sun rise over the river, catch glimpses of the Southern Alps or enjoy views of the Port Hills. Delightful riverside walks pass the door. A pleasant stroll along the riverbank leads to New Brighton with its restaurants, sandy Pacific Ocean beach and pier. Numerous golf courses and the QEII Leisure Complex are close at hand.

Located just off Christchurch's Ring Road system, Hulverstone Lodge offers easy access to all major tourist attractions, while frequent buses provide convenient transport to the city. An ideal base for holidays year-round, Hulverstone Lodge is only a couple of hours from quaint Akaroa, Hanmer Springs' thermal pools, Kaikoura's Whalewatch, and several ski fields.

You are guaranteed warm hospitality and quality accommodation at Hulverstone Lodge. All our rooms are decorated with fresh flowers from our garden. A delicious breakfast, either cooked or continental, is included in the tariff. We also offer: - complimentary pick up; - king, queen or twin beds;- 'francais parle', Deutsch gesprochen. Come and experience the ambience of Hulverstone Lodge.

Windsor Hotel
BED & BREAKFAST

Christchurch City *.5 km NW of Christchurch CBD*

B&B Approved

B&B Hotel *B&B Hotel*

Carol Healey & Don Evans
52 Armagh Street, Christchurch 8013
Tel (03) 366 1503 or 0800 366 1503 Fax (03) 366 9796
reservations@windsorhotel.co.nz www.windsorhotel.co.nz

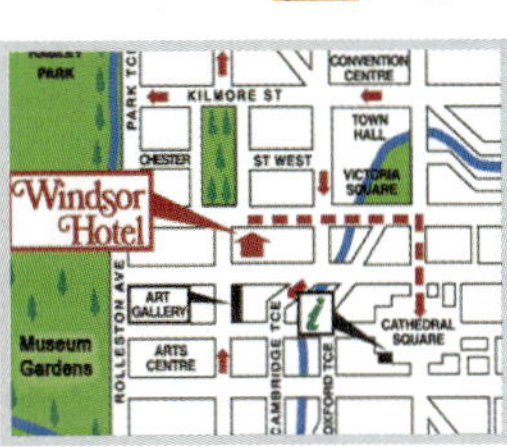

Double/Twin $140 Single $98 (Full breakfast)
Triple $180, Quad/Family $200
Visa MC Diners Amex Eftpos accepted
12 Double/Twin 18 Twin 10 Single (40 bdrm)
Bathrooms: 24 Guest share

Looking for Bed & Breakfast in Christchurch, then try The Windsor. Built at the turn of the century this inner city residence is located on the Tourist Tram Route and is within 5-10 minutes walk of the city centre, restaurants, convention centre, casino, galleries, museum and botanical gardens. Guests are greeted on arrival by our pet dachshund, Miss Winnie and shown around our charming colonial style home. Often described as traditional, this family operated bed & breakfast hotel prides itself on the standard of accommodation that it offers. The warm and comfortable bedrooms are all decorated with a small posy of flowers and a watercolour by local artist Denise McCulloch.

The shared bathroom facilities have been conveniently appointed with bathrobes provided, giving warmth and comfort in the bed & breakfast tradition. Such things as "hotties" and "brollies" add charm to the style of accommodation offered, as does our 1928 Studebaker sedan.

Our generous morning breakfast (included in the tariff) offers fruit juice, fresh fruits, yogurt and cereals followed by bacon and eggs, sausages, tomatoes, toast and marmalade, and is served in the dining room each morning between 6.30 and 9.00. The 24 hour complimentary tea & coffee making facilities allow guests to use them at their own convenience. "Supper" (tea, coffee and biscuits) is served each evening in the lounge at 9.00.

As part of our service the hotel offers "Free" broadband internet / wireless access, coin operated laundry, luggage lift, off-street parking and bicycle and baggage storage.

QUOTE THIS BOOK FOR 10% DISCOUNT

Christchurch City *0.8 km N of Christchurch Cathedral Square*

Home Lea B&B *B&B Homestay*
Pauline & Gerald Oliver
195 Bealey Avenue,
Christchurch

Tel (03) 379 9977
or 0800 355 321
Fax (03) 379 4099
homelea@xtra.co.nz
www.homelea.co.nz

Double/Twin $145-$190
Single $95-$135
(Special breakfast)
Children negotiable
Dinner by arrangement
Extra adult $35
Visa MC Amex Eftpos accepted
Children welcome
1 King 2 Queen 4 Single (4 bdrm)
Bathrooms: 2 Ensuite 2 Private

Home Lea offers the traveller a comfortable and enjoyable stay. Built in the early 1900s, Home Lea has the charm and character of a large New Zealand home of that era: rimu panelling, leadlight windows, and a large lounge with a log fire. Off-street parking. Wireless/broadband internet available for guests. Special diets catered for. Pauline and Gerald are happy to share their knowledge of local attractions and their special interests are travel, sailing and music.

Christchurch City *1.2 km N of Christchurch Central*

Eliza's Manor on Bealey *Luxury B&B*
Ann Zwimpfer & Harold Williams
82 Bealey Avenue,
City Central, Christchurch

Tel (03) 366 8584
or 0800 366 859
Fax (03) 366 4946
info@elizas.co.nz
www.elizas.co.nz

Double/Twin $195-$295
Single $175-$275 (Full breakfast)
Visa MC Diners Amex
Eftpos accepted
Pet free home
Not suitable for children
4 King 4 Queen 1 Single (8 bdrm)
All with ensuites -
Heritge and Classic Rooms
Bathrooms: 8 Ensuite Large tiled walk in showers

Eliza's is a beautifully restored Victorian mansion, built in 1861. The original architecture includes a magnificent staircase in the foyer, lead light windows and wood panelling. The tariff includes a full continental and cooked breakfast. It is a short drive from the airport and a 15 minute level walk to the Arts centre, botanical gardens, art gallery, museum, city centre, golf course and restaurants. Free parking and internet access is available to guests. We are a day trip to Hanmer Springs, Akaroa, and Kaikoura.

Christchurch City *0.1 km NW of Christchurch CBD*

B&B Approved

The Devon B&B *B&B*

Sandra & Benjamin Humphrey
69 Armagh Street,
Christchurch

Tel (03) 366 0398
Fax (03) 366 0392
stay@thedevon.co.nz
www.thedevon.co.nz

Double/Twin $145-$180
Single $125-$145
(Full breakfast)
Children under 15 years $30
Extra adults $40
Visa MC Diners Amex
Eftpos accepted
1 King 7 Queen 12 Single (11 bdrm)
Bathrooms: 9 Ensuite 1 Private

The Devon is a personal guest house located in the heart of beautiful Christchurch City, which offers elegance and comfort in the style of an olde worlde English manor. Just 5 minutes walk to Christchurch Cathedral, Town Hall, and Convention Centre, casino, museum, art gallery, hospital and botanical gardens in Hagley Park. TV lounge, tea & coffee making facilities. Off-street parking. Free broadband internet/wireless access and luggage storage.

~

Christchurch City *.5 km SW of Information Centre*

B&B Approved

Slingerland Green Stay *B&B*

Catherine Slingerland
25 Cambridge Terrace,
Christchurch 8013

Tel (03) 379 7632
Fax (03) 379 7632
caseo@xtra.co.nz
www.slingerland.co.nz

Double/Twin $120
Single $100
(Special breakfast)
Children $20
Extra person $20
Lacto-ovo Vegeterian Breakfast
Children and pets welcome
1 Queen 1 Double 1 Single (2 bdrm)
One with queen bed and ensuite
The other sleeps three
Bathrooms: 1 Ensuite 1 Family share

Relax in front of the picture window in the sunny & spacious lounge, watch the ducks swimming in the Avon River and people embarking on a punt ride through the Botanic Gardens. Many other attractions are within a short walk: The Canterbury Museum,Arts Centre, Tramway & Cathedral Square. Start your day with a healthy vegetarian breakfast of a fresh fruit smoothie, a variety of cereals and breads, plus a hot "English breakfast".

Canterbury

Christchurch City *.5 km N of Centre*

The Grange Guesthouse / Motel *B&B Apartment with Kitchen*

Des & Tracey Ramsay
56 Armagh,
Christchurch, 8013

Tel (03) 366 2850
or 0800 932 850
Fax (03) 374 2470
reservations@thegrange.co.nz
www.thegrange.co.nz

Double/Twin $140-$180
Single $120-$160
(Full breakfast)
Visa MC Diners Amex
Eftpos accepted
Children welcome
2 King/Twin 14 Queen (16 bdrm)
Bathrooms: 16 Ensuite

The Grange is a category II listed historic mansion built in 1874 now tastefully refurbished offering 8 bnb ensuite rooms full of character and original features , or 8 stylish studio and 1 bedroom motel rooms over looking our private courtyard.Being within the Cultural Precinct its just a short stroll to the Botanic Gardens Art Gallery and Cathedral Sq Free Parking , broadband internet / wireless .

Christchurch - Westhaven *10 km N of City central*

Granita B & B *Luxury B&B*

Juanita & Graeme Wilson
17 Lytham Green,
Christchurch, 8061

Tel (03) 385 2343
or 027 205 5807
Fax (03) 385 2343
wilson@granita.co.nz
www.granita.co.nz

Double/Twin up to $185
Single up to $165
(Full breakfast)
Visa MC accepted
Not suitable for children
2 Queen (2 bdrm)
Bathrooms: 2 Private
One shower room, one bath room

Granita B & B is located in a quiet suburb close to the airport, beaches, shops and restaurants, yet only 10 minutes drive to the city centre. The accommodation has two queen bedrooms attractively decorated, each have a private bath room and there is guests lounge/dining. A full breakfast is provided. We provide courtesy transfers, laundry facilities, and internet access.We would look forward to sharing with you our love of our country, travel, gardening, cars, food and wine and of course our beloved cats.

Christchurch - Templeton *3 km S of Hornby*

Cedarview Farm Homestay B&B *B&B Homestay Farmstay*

Carol & Terrance White
33 Barters Road, Templeton
RD 8, Christchurch

Tel (03) 349 7491 or 0274 335 335
Fax (03) 349 7755
cedarviewfarm@xtra.co.nz
www.cedarviewhomestay.com

Double/Twin $135-$175
Single $100-$135 (Full breakfast)
Children - family room options, please ask for rates giving childs ages
High quality accomodation in a very convenient location
Visa MC accepted
Pet free home Children welcome
1 King 1 Queen 2 Single (3 bdrm)
All three of our bedrooms are bright, modern & warm
Bathrooms: 1 Ensuite 1 Private

Cedarview Farm Homestay B+B is ideally situated for visitors to Christchurch. Our modern smoke free home is close to the Airport, highways, shopping, bars, restaurants. An easy 15-20 minute drive into the central city.Our rooms are bright, well appointed and have lovely views out over our small farm where we keep cattle, sheep, hens, a farm cat called Alfie and Labrador called Ruby. We moved to New Zealand from the UK in 1986.Our lifestyle is quiet and relaxed. Enquiries are welcome.See you soon.

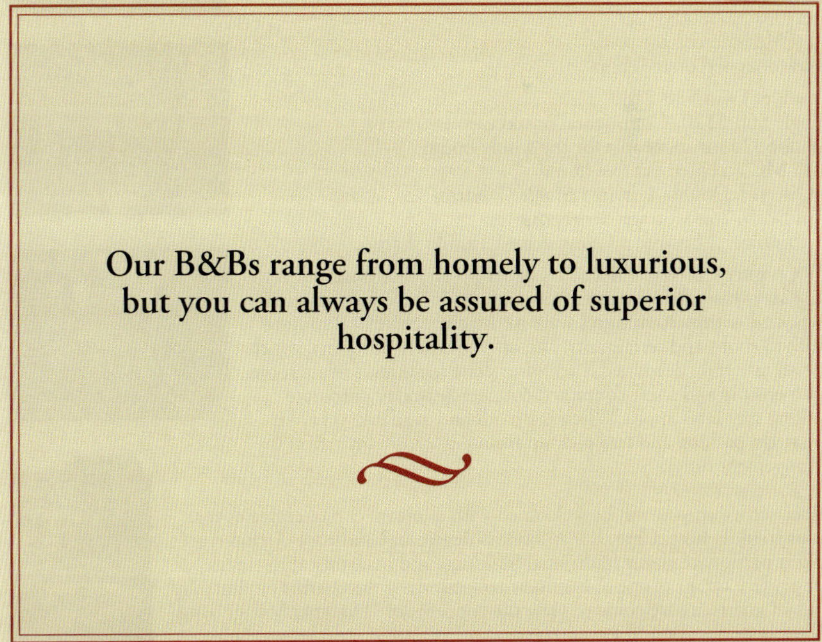

Christchurch - Sydenham *1.8 km S of Christchurch City Square*

B&B Approved

Designer Cottage, Villa & Designer 55

B&B Homestay Cottage with Kitchen

Chet Wah
53 Hastings Street West,
Sydenham, Christchurch City

Tel 0800 161 619
or (03) 377 8088
or 021 210 5282
Fax (03) 377 8099
stay@designercottage.co.nz
www.designercottage.co.nz

Double/Twin $80-$180
Single $60-$120 (Continental breakfast)
$100-$320 for six people for the whole house
Visa MC accepted Pet free home
4 Queen 1 Double 1 Twin 1 Single (7 bdrm)
4 in B&B, 2 in Cottage, 1 sleepout
Bathrooms: 2 Ensuite 3 Guest share 1 Family share

Designer Cottage, Villa & Designer 55 are charming places to stay. Just off Colombo Street situated in peaceful surroundings, and within 20 minutes walk to the city centre or 2 minute walk to shops and restaurants. We offer a variety of rooms, which are all tastefully decorated, including share facilities, private room with ensuite and a self-contained cottage. Seasonal, corporate & long stay rates apply. Wireless Broadband available. There is off-street parking and free pick up from city centre on arrival (by arrangement only).

Once settled in you will be welcomed with a 'mean' cup of coffee or tea. Your friendly host, Chet, has an honors degree in Landscape Architecture and is passionate about traditional buildings and his landscaping ideas. Designer Cottage is one of his finest collections of the charms of yesterday and all guests are welcome to view the concepts of "Designer Village" and hear his stories about these cottages.

Christchurch - St Martins *3 km S of Christchurch City Centre*

Kleynbos B&B *B&B Separate Suite Apartment with Kitchen*

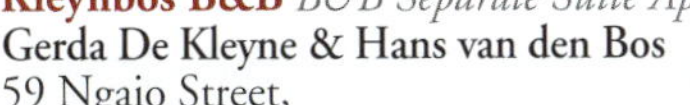

Gerda De Kleyne & Hans van den Bos
59 Ngaio Street,
Christchurch

Tel (03) 332 2896
KLEYNBOS@xtra.co.nz
www.kleynbos.co.nz

Double/Twin $80-$100
Single $70-$80
(Continental breakfast)
Children are welcome, cot available
Apartment $ 100-$130
Visa MC accepted
2 Queen 2 Double 2 Single (4 bdrm)
Large Ensuite rooms
Bathrooms: 2 Ensuite
1 Private 1 Guest share

Quality accommodation with a personal touch, since 1991. We are 3km to city centre, in an easy to find, friendly, tree-lined street. Your large ensuite rooms are $100 with microwave, fridge and jug. A computer is available to keep in contact with friends and family. Self-catering options are available in the apartment, which sleeps 5 for $100-$130. The children are 19 and 16 years old. Directions; SH74 Barbadoes Street, Waltham Road, Wilsons Road, right into Gamblins Road, first left is Ngaio Street.

Christchurch- Opawa *4 km S of Christchurch city*

Riverelm Lodge *B&B*

Peter & Rita Green
5 Locarno Street,
Opawa,
Christchurch, 8024

Tel (03) 981 3402
or 021 131 7177
riverelm_lodge@paradise.net.nz
www.riverelmlodge.com

Double/Twin $160-$185
Single $120-$140
(Continental breakfast)
Visa MC Eftpos accepted
Pet free home
Not suitable for children
2 Queen 1 Single (3 bdrm)
2 queens + 1 single
Bathrooms: 3 Ensuite

Let us welcome you to our riverside property along side the banks of the Heathcote River in this tree lined suburb. Your hosts Peter and Rita welcome you to stay in one of our rooms which comprise of 2 queen and 1 single all with thier own ensuite, central heating, TV & DVD, heated blankets, hairdryers and wireless internet. Your own lounge, microwave,fridge, tea/coffee making facilities and outside balcony area. Gorgeous fresh continental breakfast served in guest dining room. Close to all amenities.

Christchurch - Murray Aynsley *4 km SE of City Centre Information*

Pool House *B&B Separate Suite*

Jill and Richard Entwistle
57 Aynsley Terrace,
Murray Aynsley,
Christchurch, 8022

Tel (03) 337 0380
or 021 131 6441
poolhouse@slingshot.co.nz

Double/Twin $135
Single $95
(Continental breakfast)
Children by arrangement
Visa MC accepted
Children welcome
1 King/Twin (1 bdrm)
1 king/twin bedroom +
sofabed in lounge area
Bathrooms: 1 Ensuite

The Pool House offers quiet and comfortable, private self-contained accommodation with separate living and sleeping areas, bathroom en-suite. Ample self-serve continental breakfast provided. Children by arrangement, on a sofa-bed. Outdoor swimming pool. Hansen Park and the Heathcote River offer gentle riverside walks and a children's playground. Central Christchurch and the Port of Lyttelton are 10 minutes by bus or by car. Local sandy beaches are 10-15 minutes by car.

Christchurch - Redcliffs *10 km E of Cathedral Square*

B&B Approved

Pegasus Bay View *B&B Separate Suite*

Denise & Bernie Lock
121A Moncks Spur Road,
Redcliffs,
Christchurch

Tel (03) 384 2923
or 021 254 2888
pegasusbay@slingshot.co.nz
www.pegasusbayview.co.nz

Double/Twin $130-$150
Single $110-$120
(Continental breakfast)
Visa MC accepted
1 Queen 1 Double (2 bdrm)
1 bedroom and sofa bed in lounge
Bathrooms: 1 Private

Enjoy spectacular views over the South Pacific and across the city to the Southern Alps from our modern home. Your private guest suite has its own entrance and is tastefully furnished, with spacious bedroom, separate lounge (which can converted to a second double bedroom for additional family/friends) and private bathroom. Relax over a delicious breakfast, served outside on warm days, while enjoying the stunning panorama. Close to beach and restaurants and just 15 minutes drive from Christchurch City centre. We offer free wireless broadband access.

Christchurch - Mt Pleasant *8 km E of Christchurch*

B&B Approved

Mt Pleasant Bed & Breakfast *B&B Separate Suite with full-size private kitchen*

Nicola & Paul Kristiansen
14 Hobday Lane, Mt Pleasant, Christchurch
Tel (03) 384 9220
Fax (03) 384 9235
Kristiansen@xtra.co.nz
http://mtpleasantbandb.co.nz

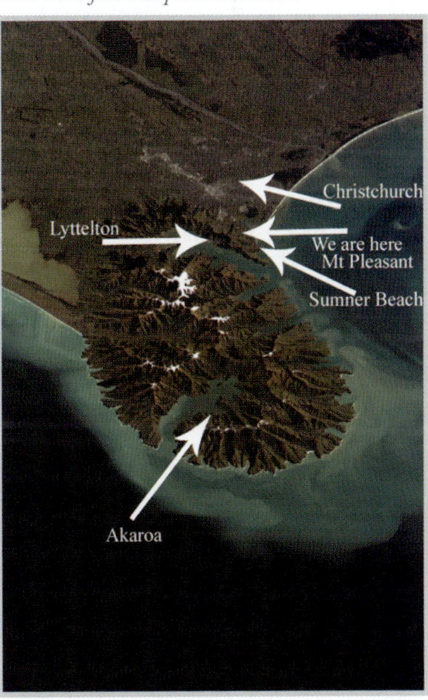

Double/Twin $110
(Continental breakfast,
includes bacon & eggs)
Big size lounge
Private Kitchen
Visa MC accepted
Pet free home
Children welcome
1 Queen (1 bdrm)
Bathrooms: 1 Ensuite
Private sauna holds six

This unique home offers a friendly and relaxed stay in your private suite. Enjoy your spacious and comfortable queen bedroom, ensuite bathroom with vintage cast-iron bath (such bliss our guests tell us!)

Sitting room with private entrance leading to deck and sauna. Own kitchen facilities. Explore the huge rambling garden facinating with waterwheel, plentiful trees and abundant bird life.

Conveniently situated 15 minutes from city, 10 minutes to popular Sumner Beach, 5 minutes to windsurfing, gondola, walking and bike tracks. You'll love it!

Christchurch - Sumner *12 km E of Cathedral Square*

Villa Alexandra *B&B Separate Suite Self Contained Studio & S/C Beach Front Apartment.*

Wendy & Bob Perry
1 Kinsey Terrace,
Clifton Hill,
Sumner,
Christchurch 8081

Tel (03) 326 6291
Fax (03) 326 6096
villa_alexandra@xtra.co.nz
www.villaalexandra.co.nz

Double/Twin $120-$140
Single $90-$100
(Full breakfast)
Children under 12 $15
Apartment - $150 P/N
Children welcome
1 Queen 1 Double 1 Twin 1 Single (3 bdrm)
Bathrooms: 2 Ensuite 1 Private

Enjoy the warmest hospitality in our spacious turn of the century villa overlooking Sumner Bay. Our home retains the graciousness of a bygone era while offering all modern comforts. In winter enjoy open fires, cosy farmhouse kitchen and on sunny days the verandah and turret. Spectacular sea views from Sumner to the Kaikouras. We enjoy food, wine, music, gardening, tramping, travel. 5 minutes walk to beach; off-street parking; laundry. Also self-contained beach front apartment, 2 double bedrooms, $150 per night, minimum 3 nights.

~

Christchurch - Sumner Beach *12 km E of Cathedral Square*

Cave Rock Bed & Breakfast *B&B*

Gayle & Norm Eade
16 Esplanade, Sumner, Christchurch

Tel (03) 326 6844
or 027 436 0212 or (03) 326 5600
Fax (03) 326 5600
eade@chch.planet.org.nz
www.caverockguesthouse.co.nz

Double/Twin $140-$150
Single $105-$115
(Continental breakfast provisions)
Children $20
Corporate Rates available
Visa MC Amex Eftpos accepted
Pet free home Children welcome
3 Queen 1 Double (4 bdrm)
Spacious queen rooms each with ensuite bathroom
Bathrooms: 4 Ensuite One with spa bath ensuite

The Cave Rock B&B - Sumner's ultimate Beachfront accommodation opposite Sumner's Cave Rock. Hosts Gayle & Norm Eade enjoy meeting people from overseas and within NZ. Large spacious double rooms with sea views, TV, heating and ensuite bathrooms, can sleep up to 4. Kitchen facilities. Sumner - the ideal holiday location, 15 minutes from Ch.Ch City, excellent bus service - cafe/bars, shops, cinema, within walking distance. Hill and cliff walks close by, safe sandy beach across the road. We have a friendly dalmatian dog.

Christchurch - Sumner *13 km E of Christchurch Cathedral Square*

B&B Approved

Abbott House Sumner Bed & Breakfast *Self-contained suite with kitchen, & self-contained studio*

Janet & Chris Abbott
104 Nayland Street,
Sumner, Christchurch

Tel (03) 326 6111
or 0800 020 654
or 021 654 344 Fax (03) 326 7034
info@abbotthouse.co.nz
www.abbotthouse.co.nz

Double/Twin $120-$140
Single $100-$120
(Breakfast provisions first night)
Children $10 per extra child/night
(Max $30pw)
Weekly discounts (seasonal)
Visa MC accepted
3 King/Twin (3 bdrm)
Bathrooms: 1 Ensuite 1 Private

Your hosts, Chris and Janet Abbott welcome you to our historic restored 1870s villa in Christchurch's unique seaside village. Our home is one block from the beach, and an easy ten-minute walk along the beach to Sumner's many cafés, restaurants, boutique shops and cinema. Both suite and studio have king-sized beds, own kitchen areas, TV, DVD and internet access. Off-street parking. Laundry facilities (suite only). Home-baked bread. Wonderful base for many walks, swimming, surfing, mountain biking and road biking.

Christchurch - Sumner *15 km E of Cathedral Square*

B&B Approved

Scarborough-Heights *Luxury B&B*

Barbara and Brian Hanlon
21 Godley Drive,
Scarborough,
Christchurch 8081

Tel (03) 326 7060
or 027 229 7312
Fax (03) 326 7061
stay@scarborough-heights.co.nz
www.scarborough-heights.co.nz

Double/Twin $180
Single $120 (Full breakfast)
Children $50 (5-12years)
Dinner $50 by arrangement
Visa MC accepted Children welcome
1 King 1 Queen 3 Single (2 bdrm)
1 king or twin beds, 1 queen bed
Bathrooms: 1 Ensuite 1 Private
Private bathroom has bath and shower.

Scarborough-Heights is a large, modern architecturally designed home set in an award winning garden, high on Scarborough Hill and offering luxurious bed & breakfast accommodation. All rooms offer spectacular views of the Southern Alps, Christchurch City and South Pacific Ocean. We provide friendly hospitality in peaceful, quiet surroundings yet are only 20 minutes from the city centre and 5 minutes from the trendy and popular seaside village of Sumner with its many cafes, specialty shops and cinema. We share our home with two cats.

Lyttelton *9 km E of Christchurch*

The Rookery *B&B Homestay*

Angus & Rene Macpherson
9 Ross Terrace,
Lyttelton, 8082
Tel (03) 328 8038
rooks@amma.co.nz
http://therookery.co.nz

Double/Twin $131-$148
Single $84
(Full breakfast)
2 Queen 1 Single (3 bdrm)
Bathrooms: 1 Ensuite 1 Family share

The Rookery is one of Lyttelton's oldest cottages with delightful panoramic views over the harbour. To capture the character of the Victorian era we as designers have paid particular attention to the colours and finishes that ensure our visitors' enjoyment during their stay. Rooms are double glazed with underfloor heating and electric blankets. Only 15 minutes from the Garden City we are ideally located for exploring the Banks Peninsula. Angus, Rene and our cat Cleopatra offer you a warm and friendly welcome.

Teddington - Lyttelton Harbour *20 km S of Christchurch*

Bergli Hill Farmstay *Farmstay*

Rowena & Max Dorfliger
265 Charteris Bay Road,
Teddington, RD 1 Lyttelton
Tel (03) 329 9118
or 027 482 9410
Fax (03) 329 9118
farmstay@bergli.co.nz
www.bergli.co.nz

Double/Twin $135-$160
Single $95-$120 (Full breakfast)
Dinner from $40 b/a
Woolcrafts and children's activites b/a
Visa MC accepted
Children and pets welcome
1 King/Twin 1 Queen 1 Double
3 Twin 9 Single (3 bdrm)
In our log house, views of harbour
Bathrooms: 2 Ensuite 1 Family share

Enjoy panoramic views of Lyttelton Harbour from our custom-built log house. Stretch your legs with a climb up Bergli Hill, feed our friendly Sheep, Alpacas and Chickens then unwind in the spa. By prior arrangement we offer woolfun workshops, children's activity days and home cooked meals on request. Golf, horse-trekking and swimming are nearby as well as easy access to the walking and cycle tracks of the Port Hills and Lyttelton Crater Rim.Ideally situated for sightseeing in Christchurch (30mins), Akaroa (1hr10mins) and Banks Peninsula.

Banks Peninsula - Okains Bay *18 km N of Akaroa*

Kawatea *Farmstay*
Judy & Kerry Thacker
1048 Okains Bay Road, Okains Bay, Banks Peninsula
Tel (03) 304 8621 Fax (03) 304 8621 kawatea@xtra.co.nz
www.kawateafarmstay.co.nz

Double/Twin $120-$155 Single $80-$155 (Full breakfast)
Children by arrangement Dinner $35 Visa MC accepted
3 Queen 2 Single (3 bdrm)
Bathrooms: 1 Ensuite 1 Private 1 Guest share
Bath, Shower, Separate Toilet

Experience the grace and charm of yesteryear, while enjoying the fine food and wine of NZ today. Revel in the peace of countrylife, but still be close to sights and activities. Welcome to Kawatea, an historic homestead set in spacious gardens, and surrounded by land farmed by our Irish ancestors since the 1850s. Built in 1900 from native timbers, the carefully renovated house features stained glass windows and handcrafted furniture.

Linger over your choice of breakfast in the conservatory. Join us in the evening for creative country fare and seafood from the Bay whilst sharing experiences with fellow travellers.

Explore our 1400 acre farm and feed the pet sheep. Enjoy Okains Bay's unspoilt swimming beach, observe the birdlife on the estuary, or walk along the scenic coastline to secluded bays and a seal colony with excellent photographic opportunities. Learn about Maori culture and the life of early settlers at the acclaimed Okains Bay Museum.

Visit Akaroa with its French influence and galleries. Sample local wines and watch traditional cheese making. Golf, kayak, take a cruise or swim with the rare Hector Dolphins.

We have been hosting since 1988, and offer thoughtful personal attention and friendly hospitality in a relaxed atmosphere. Directions: Take Highway 75 from Christchurch through Duvauchelle. Turn left at signpost marked Okains Bay. Kawatea is 11km on right.

Akaroa - Paua Bay *12 km E of Akaroa*

Paua Bay Farmstay *B&B Farmstay*
Murray & Sue Johns
Postal: C/- 113 Beach Road, Akaroa, Banks Peninsula
Tel (03) 304 8511 or 021 133 8194
Fax (03) 304 8511
info@pauabay.com
www.pauabay.com

Double/Twin $120-$150 (Full breakfast)
Dinner $40 Children welcome
1 Queen 1 Twin (2 bdrm)
Bathrooms: 1 Ensuite 1 Guest share

Time spent at Paua Bay is a truely unique experience. Not only will you be able to enjoy the wonderful surroundings but also you will join a traditional NZ farming family sharing their daily endeavors.

Set in a private bay our 900 acre sheep, cattle & deer farm is surrounded by spectacular coastline, native bush & streams.You are spoilt for choice, walk to the beach, enjoy seals and extensive birdlife, join in seasonal farm activities.

The farmhouse is surrounded by a wonderful garden and around each corner in the path is a new surprise, a secluded moonlight bath.....a hammock....a sculpture. The guest room has wooden floors, a clawfoot bath, fresh flowers and from the queensize bed you can watch the sun rise out of the South Pacific.

In the evening take the opportunity to enjoy the company of our 6th generation farming family. Share a generous meal of fresh farm produce with relaxed conversation around the large kitchen table. New Zealand wines & beers are included.

The nearby historic French settlement of Akaroa offers guests world renouned harbour cruises and its Hector dolphins. Quiet wanderings exploring this village allows guests time to reflect on days gone by.

Akaroa *5 km N of Akaroa*

B&B Approved

LeLievre Farmstay *Homestay Farmstay*

Hanne & Paul LeLievre
Box 4 Akaroa,
154 Takamatua Valley Road,
Banks Peninsula

Tel (03) 304 7255
Fax (03) 304 7255
Double.L@Xtra.co.nz
www.sealtours.co.nz

Double/Twin $140
Single $90
(Full breakfast)
Dinner $35
Children welcome
1 Queen 1 Double 1 Single (2 bdrm)
Both with ensuites
Bathrooms: 2 Ensuite

Our home is situated 1.5km up Takamatua Valley and 5km from Akaroa. We farm sheep, cattle deer and usually have a menagerie of orphaned pets etc. Our interests include golf and bridge. We invite you to enjoy some good old fashioned country hospitality. A trip to the Akaroa Seal Colony, which featured on the TV programmes A Flying Visit,Totally Wild and The Great Outdoors,is a must do. Safari includes a scenic drive, through, a working farm, with the farmer.

Akaroa *80 km SE of Christchurch*

B&B Approved

The Maples *B&B*

Lesley & Peter Keppel
158 Rue Jolie,
Akaroa

Tel (03) 304 8767
Fax (03) 304 8767
maplesakaroa@xtra.co.nz
www.themaplesakaroa.co.nz

Double/Twin $150
Single $120
(Full breakfast)
Visa MC accepted
3 Queen 1 Single (3 bdrm)
Bathrooms: 3 Ensuite

The Maples is a charming historic 2 storey home built in 1877. It is situated in a delightful garden setting, 3 minutes walk from the cafes and waterfront. We offer 2 queen bedrooms with ensuites upstairs and a separate garden room with a queen and single bed also ensuite. You can relax in the separate guests' lounge where tea and coffee is available. Our delicious continental and cooked breakfasts include freshly baked croissants and home made jams.

Akaroa *80 km SE of Christchurch*

Wilderness House *Luxury B&B*

Jim & Liz Coubrough
42 Rue Grehan,
Akaroa

Tel (03) 304 7517
or 021 669 381
Fax (03) 304 7518
info@wildernesshouse.co.nz
www.wildernesshouse.co.nz

Double/Twin $290
Single $290
(Full breakfast)
Visa MC Eftpos accepted
Not suitable for children
1 King/Twin 3 Queen (4 bdrm)
Bathrooms: 3 Ensuite 1 Private

Treat yourself to a memorable experience in one of Akaroa's gracious historic homes. Built in 1878 our home is set in a one acre garden including a petite vineyard. Rooms have free wireless internet, harbour/valley views and feature gorgeous linen, garden flowers, a selection of teas, coffee and home-baking. Linger over our special breakfasts. Secluded and private we are just a short stroll to the village. Join us for a glass of our wine each evening. Unwind, relax and enjoy! Resident cat George.

Akaroa Harbour - French Farm *70 km SE of Christchurch*

B&B Approved

Bantry Lodge *B&B Cottage with Kitchen*

Dolina Barker
French Farm,
RD 2,
Akaroa

Tel (03) 304 5161
or 027 313 2406
Fax (03) 304 5162
barker.d@xtra.co.nz
www.bantrylodge.co.nz

Double/Twin $130-$150
(Full breakfast)
Dinner $40 by arrangement
Self-contained cottage sleeps 4
Visa MC Diners Amex accepted
Children and pets welcome
2 Queen 2 Double (3 bdrm)
2 in B&B, 2 in Cottage
Bathrooms: 2 Private 1 Guest share

This historic home has views across Akaroa Harbour 50 metres away. Groundfloor queen room has french doors to verandah and sea views, private bath. Upstairs queen room with balcony overlooks harbour , private bath. Coffee, tea facilities provided with home-baking. The comfortable sitting room is for relaxing or joining me for a drink. Full breakfast is served in the elegant dining room. Tranquillity and space. A self-contained cottage sleeps 4. Linen, breakfast ingredients supplied. 1 shy cat.

Akaroa - Barry's Bay *15 km W of Akaroa*

B&B Approved

Bayfield B&B *B&B Separate Suite*

Bob & Robin Jones
5447 Christchurch Akaroa Road,
Barry's Bay

Tel (03) 304 5752
info@bayfieldbnbnz.com
http://bayfieldbnbnz.com

Double/Twin $160-$175
Single $150-$165
(Full breakfast)
Dinner 3 courses by prior arrangement $40 pp
Snack platter by prior arrangement $45
Visa MC accepted
Pet free home
Not suitable for children
1 Double (1 bdrm)
1 self contained room with separate entrance
Bathrooms: 1 Ensuite

The spacious room has antiques in the sitting and sleeping areas and also contains a kitchenette and ensuite.

Your hosts are retired professionals who arrived in New Zealand in 2000 after sailing from the eastern United States. We look forward to sharing the spectacular view with our guests along with our interest in different cultures, photography, fishing, and 4WD.

Only one hour from Christchurch International Airport, we're a great first stop for overseas visitors and would happily help you plan your Kiwi adventure.

Akaroa *80 km SE of Christchurch*

B&B Approved

Mulberry House *B&B Homestay Cottage with Kitchen Guest House*

Anne Craig & Jack Clark
9 William Street, Akaroa 8161
Tel (03) 304 7778 or 021 610 456
Fax (03) 304 7778
anneandjacknz@yahoo.com
www.mulberryhouse.co.nz

Double/Twin $125-$165 Single $90 (Special breakfast)
$10 surcharge 1 night stay
Children welcome
3 King 1 Queen 1 Twin 4 Single (7 bdrm)
Bathrooms: 2 Ensuite 1 Private 2 Guest share

Experience the very best in homestyle accommodation and delight in the setting of Mulberry House, which accommodates up to thirteen guests. All rooms are beautifully decorated and feature quality beds and fine linen. There is a choice of double rooms, with or without ensuite, and a twin room which will delight children.

The romantic poolside summerhouse has its own kitchen, ensuite and garden to provide total privacy if desired. We also have a beautifully furnished,self contained cottage with full kitchen.

Breakfasts are a specialty and feature a choice of American, European, English, and New Zealand styles. Champagne breakfasts and other meals by arrangement. Meals can be served outside in the summer months overlooking the pool.

Your hosts: Well travelled and semi retired Anne Craig and Jack Clark offer unparalleled hospitality. Fussy about food, both Anne and Jack love to cook: Anne preserves and bakes, and Jack adds his American expertise to breakfasts of pancakes, waffles, omelettes, fresh fruits, and delicious coffee from the espresso machine.

Guest Comments - Desmond Balmer (LondonGuardian/Observer Travel) recommends Mulberry House as amongst New Zealand's Top Twenty. Featured on Sydney's channel 7 "Ernie Dingo's Getaway" as "the place to stay "in Akoroa. Featured in Autumn 2000 European "Wining and Dining.

Akaroa *80 km SE of Christchurch*

B&B Approved

La Belle Villa *B&B*

Alice & Paul Hewitson
113 Rue Jolie,
Akaroa

Tel (03) 304 7084
or 021 045 9156
Fax (03) 304 7084
bookings@labellevilla.co.nz
www.labellevilla.co.nz

Double/Twin $140-$160
Single $120-$140
(Special breakfast)
Visa MC accepted
Children welcome
1 King/Twin 2 King 1 Queen (4 bdrm)
Bathrooms: 4 Ensuite

A warm welcome awaits you. Relax in the surroundings of a bygone era and appreciate the antiques in our much photographed historic villa. Built in the 1870's La Belle Villa is set in beautiful, mature grounds,with a trickling stream, it offers indoor/outdoor living including separate guest lounge. Our special alfresco breakfast which includes fresh local produce, homebaking and espresso coffee has won universal praise. Located in close proximity to restaurants, shops and cinema makes us the ideal place to stay in Akaroa.

Highcountry Canterbury - Castle Hill *33 km W of Springfield*

B&B Approved

The Burn Alpine B&B *B&B Homestay*

Bob Edge & Phil Stephenson
11 Torlesse Place,
Castle Hill Village, Canterbury

Tel (03) 318 7559
Fax (03) 318 7558
theburn@xtra.co.nz
www.theburn.co.nz

Double/Twin $160-$180
Single $90-$100
(Continental breakfast)
Children under 13 half price
Dinner home cooked dining $35 p/p
Dinner, Bed & Breakfast $125 p/p
Visa MC accepted Children welcome
3 Queen 1 Twin (4 bdrm)
Bathrooms: 2 Guest share
Two bathrooms with showering facilites and seperate toilets

1 hour west of Christchurch, a carefree atmosphere prevails at The Burn. Nestled in the heart of the Southern Alps, it's arguably New Zealand's highest B&B. We designed and built our alpine lodge to maximise mountain vistas. Centered in the mystic Castlehill Basin, surrounded by native forest, this is a fantastic place to return after a days activity or just kick back and relax on the sunny deck. A host of outdoor sports include ski/snowboarding, hiking, mountain biking, and flyfishing. Professional flyfishing guiding available.

Darfield *4 km W of Darfield*

The Oaks Historic Homestead *B&B Homestay*

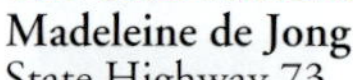

Madeleine de Jong
State Highway 73,
Corner of Clintons Road,
Darfield

Tel (03) 318 7232
or 027 241 3999
Fax (03) 318 7236
theoaks@quicksilver.net.nz
www.theoakshomestead.co.nz

Double/Twin $175-$275
Single $150
(Full breakfast)
Dinner $65 pp on request
Visa MC Eftpos accepted
Children and pets welcome
3 Queen 1 Single (4 bdrm)
Bathrooms: 1 Ensuite 2 Private

One of Canterbury's oldest homesteads, restored to its former glory. Located amidst stunning scenery of the Southern Alps to the Westcoast, with ski fields, golf courses and tourist attractions on its doorstep. The Oaks features: guest rooms with ensuite/private bathrooms, a guest dining and living room featuring stunning open fires, a traditional large homestead kitchen, beautiful verandas for outdoor entertaining. Children welcome. Pets on request. Your Host Madeleine speaks 5 languages and is a keen cook. Wherever possible I try to use fresh organic produce.

Mt Hutt - Methven *6.4 km E of Methven*

Pagey's Farmstay *B&B Farmstay Kitchen - new*

Shirley & Gene Pagey
663 Methven-Chertsey Road,
RD 12, Rakaia

Tel (03) 302 1713
Fax (03) 302 1714
pageysfarmstay@clear.net.nz
www.tourism.net.nz

Double/Twin $120
Single $90
(Full breakfast)
Children under 12 half price
Dinner $30pp
Spa pool
Pet free home
Children welcome
1 King 1 Queen 4 Single (3 bdrm)
Large with quality beds
Bathrooms: 2 Private - new, large showers

Enjoy hospitality warmth and freedom in our lovely expansive home with new kitchen, bathrooms, large redorated bedrooms with luxurious beds, set amidst aged oak trees and large rose garden. Watch our 47" TV . Enjoy a pre-dinner drink, wine, crystal clear mountain water and home-grown cuisine. Star gaze in our luxurious massaging spa. Surrounding activities include breathtaking bush walks, 2 superior golf courses, ballooning and skiing. Short notice is our speciality. Directions from Methven town centre, turn down Methven Chertsey Road, 6km signposted.

Mt Hutt - Methven *11 km W of Methven*

Glenview Farmstay *B&B Farmstay Cottage No Kitchen*

B&B Approved

Helen & Mike Johnstone
142 Hart Road, Methven
Tel (03) 302 8620
Fax (03) 302 8620
helenmikejohnstone@yahoo.com

Double/Twin $110 Single $80 (Full breakfast)
Children $25
Dinner $25
Children welcome
2 Queen 2 Double/Twin 1 Twin 2 Single (5 bdrm)
Bathrooms: 1 Ensuite 1
Guest share Ensuite in unit

Glenview Farmstay is situated at the base of Mt Hutt Ski Field, with the house designed to look at the mountains and down the Canterbury Plains to the Port Hills.

We farm cattle and sheep on our 1200 acre farm. We have several working farm dogs and a very friendly cat and a pet dog.

There is a peaceful unit in the garden which is suitable for a couple or a family. It has two bedrooms, one with 1 queen bed and the other with 1 double and 1 single bed, ensuite, TV, tea & coffee facilities and wonderful views. The rooms in the house have separate access, good heating and are non-smoking. Dinner by arrangement. Free farm tours on request.

Methven is only 10 minutes away and we are very close to good fishing, golf, ballooning, horse treking, bush walks and jet boating. Free transfers to local walkways. One hour from Christchurch and we are on the way to Queenstown along Highway 72.

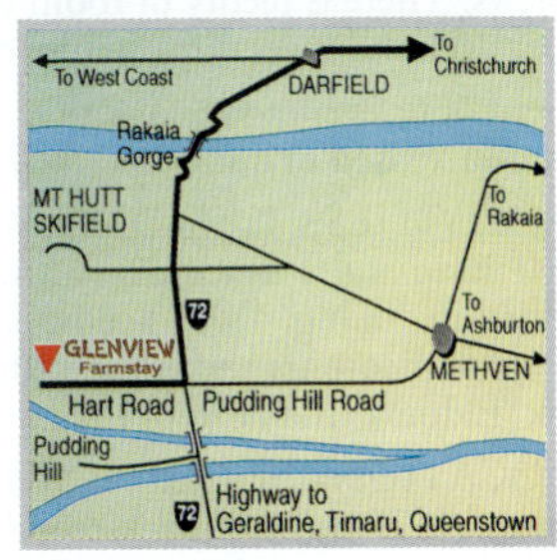

Mt Hutt - Methven *4 km NW of Methven - Mt Hutt Village*

Green Gables Deer Farm *B&B Farmstay*

Irene & Mike Harris
185 Waimarama Road, Methven-Mt Hutt Village

Tel (03) 302 8308
or New Zealand (0800 466 093)
Fax (03) 302 8309
greengables@xtra.co.nz   www.nzfarmstay.com

Double/Twin $140-$180 Single $110-$140
(Special breakfast)
Children $55 Dinner $50 pp by arrangement
Visa MC accepted Children welcome
2 King 2 Twin (3 bdrm)
Bathrooms: 2 Ensuite 1 Private

Set in tranquil surroundings at the foot of Mt.Hutt, Green Gables Deer Farm is within easy reach of Christchurch (1hr), Kaikoura for Whale Watching and Dolphins (3hrs), Mt.Cook (3.5hrs) and Queenstown (approx 5.5hrs).

Our stylish rooms have all the comforts you will require with your own private entrance opening out onto the garden with a backdrop of graceful deer wandering in the paddocks and the ever changing colours of the mountain views. There is plenty of room to stroll, maybe feed the pet deer and meet our friendly dogs or just relax and unwind.

Start your evening meal with a complimentary pre-dinner drink and enjoy the fresh local produce used in our home cooked meals and desserts.

ACTIVITIES:- Try out the many summer and winter activities close by - Golf courses at Methven and Terrace Downs (club & cart hire available), Fishing, Hot Air ballooning, Jet Boating, Skiing, 4WD Scenic Tours (available by arrangement), Horse Trekking, Scenic Flights, Ecotours and Alpine Rhododrendon Walks to name but a few. There are even trips to "Eldoras" the Lord of the Rings film site at Mt.Sunday

LOCATION:- Situated on S/H77 4kms N/W Methven. From Inland Scenic-Route 72 turn into S/H77 travel 5kms Green Gables Deer Farm is on the right.

Methven *1 km SW of information centre*

B&B Approved

Powderhouse Country Lodge *B&B*

Sue & Alan Lumsden
3 Cameron Street,
Methven, 7730

Tel (03) 302 9105
or 027 341 1242
Fax (03) 3029105
staypowderhouse@gmail.com
www.powderhouse.co.nz

Double/Twin $130-$165
Single $120-$150
(Full breakfast)
Visa MC accepted
Not suitable for children
3 King/Twin (3 bdrm)
Double/twin
Bathrooms: 3 Ensuite

Sue and Alan welcome you to Powderhouse Country Lodge. Set amongst half an acre of lawn and garden in the heart of Methven/Mt Hutt village. We are five minutes walk to the town centre. We offer you fine accommodation with a relaxed atmosphere. Our 3 guest rooms have luxurious superking/twin beds, Ensuites, individual heating, TV/Radio & tea/coffee. Relax in the guest lounge with an open log fire or enjoy a spa with garden views. We have two guest shy cats.

Mt. Hutt - Staveley *20 km SW of Methven*

B&B Approved

Korobahn Lodge *B&B Homestay*

Caroline & John Lartice
Burgess Road,
Staveley

Tel (03) 303 0828
carolinel@slingshot.co.nz
www.korobahnlodge.co.nz

Double/Twin $150-$180
Single $110-$130
(Full breakfast)
Dinner 3 courses with beer or wine, $55 by arrangement
Visa MC accepted
Children welcome
2 Queen 1 Twin (3 bdrm)
large rooms, tastefully and comfortably designed
Bathrooms: 3 Ensuite

Welcome to our unique North American barn style homestead. Korobahn is at the foot of Mt Somers, close to Mt. Hutt, and stands in several acres of gardens, surrounded by farmland. The property offers high quality accommodation and comfort. Korobahn Lodge is on Inland Scenic Highway 72, approximatly 110 kilometres southwest of Christchurch Airport and on the way to Mt Cook and Queenstown. Local activites include bush walking, horse treks, Lord of the Rings film site, jet boating, fishing, and in season skating and skiing.

Staveley - Mt Somers *110 km SW of Christchurch*

Alpine Views Farmstay and B&B *B&B Homestay Farmstay*

Anna & Ken McNally
28 Symes Road,
RD1, Ashburton

Tel (03) 303 0800
or (027) 303 0700
anna@alpineviews.co.nz
http://alpineviews.co.nz

Double/Twin $120-$150
Single $80-$110
(Full breakfast)
Children welcome - pet animals to feed!
Dinner available on request $50
Caravan sites available - $20/night
Visa MC accepted
Children and pets welcome
2 Queen 1 Twin 1 Single (3 bdrm)
All with separate ensuites
Bathrooms: 2 Ensuite

Located in the foothills of Canterbury with panoramic views of the Southern Alps, we are only 15 minutes from Mt Hutt Ski Area and Methven. Situated on the Inland Scenic Route 72, one hour from Christchurch Airport, and en route to Mt Cook and Queenstown destinations. Our homestead is amongst 3 acres of parklike gardens and beyond this we graze cattle and sheep. Feed pet deer and sheep and watch sheep dogs at work! Warm comfortable, quality accommodation and great food.

Rakaia *50 km S of Christchurch*

St Ita's Guesthouse *B&B Guest House*

Miriam & Ken Cutforth
11 Barrhill/Methven Road,
Rakaia Township, Canterbury

Tel (03) 302 7546
or 027 488 8673
Fax (03) 302 7564
stitas@xtra.co.nz
www.stitas.co.nz

Double/Twin $130
Single $90 (Full breakfast)
Children $40
Dinner $30pp
Visa MC accepted
Children welcome
2 Queen 1 Double 4 Single (4 bdrm)
Large, warm rooms with garden views
Bathrooms: 3 Ensuite 1 Private
3 ensuites, 1 private with bath

Relax in our elegant and comfortable historic former convent, 600 metres from SH1 in small town New Zealand. Excellent base for exploring Ashburton District. Excellent first and last stop from Christchurch International Airport. Three bedrooms have ensuites and garden views. The fourth the Chapel has a private bathroom. Walking distance to local shops, great cafes, crafts and winery. Close to golf and salmon fishing, 30 minutes to skiing, jet boating. Wireless available. Dinner by arrangement. Full breakfasts. Share the open fire with our moggie.

Ashburton *1 km N of Ashburton Info Centre*

Carradale Manor *B&B Homestay*

Karen & Jim McIntyre
93 Pages Road, Allenton, Ashburton
Tel (03) 308 6577 Fax (03) 308 6548
jkmcintyre@xtra.co.nz
www.ashburton.co.nz/carradale

Double/Twin $120-$140 Single $80 (Full breakfast)
Children under 12 half price Dinner $40 by arrangement
Visa MC accepted
2 King/Twin 1 Queen (3 bdrm)
Bathrooms: 1 Ensuite 1 Private

We are one hour from Christchurch International Airport. Our sunny spacious home, which is just off State Highway One in Ashburton, is situated in a beautiful, large and sheltered garden by a stream, where you can enjoy peace and tranquility. After offering hospitality for 16 years on Carradale Farm, we have now retired from Carradale Farm in the country to Carradale Manor in the town where we will continue to operate with those same high standards.

We offer either a fully cooked breakfast, or continental breakfast, served with delicious home made jams and preserves. For your convenience tea/coffee making facilities, and electric blankets are for use in all rooms. Internet access available.

As we have both travelled extensively in New Zealand, Australia, United Kingdom, Europe, North America, Zimbabwe, South Africa, Vietnam, Singapore, and Scandinavia we would like to offer hospitality to fellow travellers. Our hobbies include meeting people, travel, reading, photography, gardening, sewing, cake decorating, rugby, cricket, Jim belongs to the Masonic Lodge and Karen is involved in Community Affairs including Probus.

For young children we have a cot and highchair available.Our resident cat 'Lady Jane' is on hand to comfort you.

CARRADALE MANOR, "WHERE PEOPLE COME AS STRANGERS AND LEAVE AS FRIENDS"

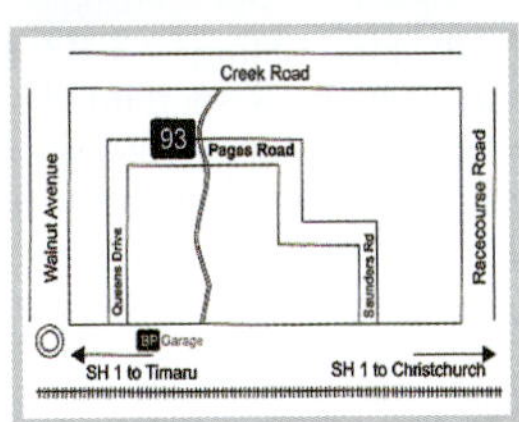

Ashburton *90 km S of Christchurch*

Weir Homestay *B&B Homestay*

B&B Approved

Pat & Dave Weir
2A Sudbury Street,
Ashburton Central

Tel (03) 308 3534
pndweir@clear.net.nz

Double/Twin $100
Single $50
(Breakfast by arrangement)
Dinner $25
Visa MC accepted
1 Double 3 Single (2 bdrm)
Bathrooms: 1 Ensuite
1 Guest share 1 Family share

Our comfortable home is situated in a quiet street with the added pleasure of looking onto a rural scene. We are 10-15 minutes walk from town.Guest rooms have comfortable beds with electric blankets. We welcome the opportunity to meet and greet visitors and wish to make your stay a happy one. Your hosts are retired but active, hobbies general/varied from meeting people to walking etc. Request visitors no smoking inside home. Off-street parking.

~

Ashburton *7 km SE of Ashburton*

Lake Hood Homestay B&B *B&B*

Eric and Eleanor Weir
14 Witney Lane,
Lake Hood,
Ashburton

Tel (03) 302 6914
enquiries@lakehoodhomestay.co.nz
www.lakehoodhomestay.co.nz

Double/Twin $140-$155
(Full breakfast)
Visa MC accepted
Pet free home
Not suitable for children
1 King/Twin 1 Queen (2 bdrm)
Bathrooms: 2 Ensuite

Lake Hood Homestay B&B is part of the exciting, modern development including the Lakehouse Restaurant. The area hosts water sports and is popular for jogging, walking, fishing or relaxing. Lake Hood Homestay B&B, on the attractive, peaceful canal network adjoining Lake Hood, comprises two modern studio suites, each featuring: separate entrance, King or Queen bed (twin by arrangement), own en-suite, TV, tea/coffee making, opening to patio and canal-side garden. Delicious country-style cooked breakfast included. Complimentary use of kayaks and bicycles. See www.lakehoodhomestay.co.nz

South Canterbury & North Otago
80
Lake Tekapo
8
Lake Pukaki
Twizel
8
Lindis Pass
Kimbell
Fairlie
Geraldine
1
79
Winchester
8
Pleasant Point
Timaru
Kurow
82
1
85
Oamaru
Waianakarua
Palmerston
Ealing
0
Kilometres
30
0
Miles
18

Geraldine *0.5 km S of Geraldine*

Victoria Villa *B&B Cottage with Kitchen*

Leigh & Jerry Basinger
55 Cox Street,
Geraldine 7930

Tel (03) 693 8605
or 0800 537 533
or 027 482 1842
Fax (03) 693 8605
gtbasinger@yahoo.com

Double/Twin $100-$125
Single $80-$100
(Full breakfast)
Children $10-$15
Dinner by arrangement
Detached studio unit
Visa MC Amex accepted
3 Queen 2 Double 2 Single (4 bdrm)
Bathrooms: 3 Ensuite 1 Private

Welcome to our historical villa, completely refurbished - spacious bedrooms with ensuites or private bathroom. Off-street parking, private entrance and lounge. Molded ceilings, native woods. Also, separate studio with ensuite and light cooking area; ideal for family. On Highway 79 to Mt Cook and Queenstown. 7 minutes walk to Geraldine Village which has boutique movie theatre, fine restaurants, sports pub,world class glass blower, boutique shops, 2 golf courses. Adjacent to domain. Your hosts will assist to make your stay enjoyable.

~

Geraldine *0.2 km S of Geraldine*

Lilymay *B&B*

Lois & Les Gillum
29 Cox Street,
Geraldine

Tel (03) 693 8838
or 0800 545 9629
lilymay@xtra.co.nz

Double/Twin $95-$100
Single $70-$75
(Full breakfast)
Children $20-$25
Visa MC accepted
Children welcome
2 Queen 1 Double 3 Twin
3 Single (3 bdrm)
Bathrooms: 2 Guest share

Closest B&B to village shops,restaurants & cafes. A charming character home set in a large colourful garden. A friendly, warm welcome is assurred with tea/coffee and Lois' home-baked cookies. Ample off-street parking and separate guest entrance. Teas, coffee, etc. available at all times in the guest lounge with cosy open fire. We are on the main road to Mt Cook, the Southern Lakes and mountains. The ideal stopover from Christchurch (137 km).

Geraldine *3 km N of Geraldine*

B&B Approved

Rivendell *B&B Homestay Apartment with Kitchen*
Erica & Andrew Tedham
Woodbury Road,
RD 21,
Geraldine

Tel (03) 693 8559
or 021 264 1520
rivendellnz@xtra.co.nz
www.rivendellnz.co.nz

Double/Twin $100-$130
Single $85-$95 (Full breakfast)
Self-contained studio unit
with kitchen $100
Not suitable for children
Pets welcome
1 Queen 1 Double 1 Single (3 bdrm)
T.V. & tea/coffee making facilities
in all rooms
Bathrooms: 2 Ensuite 1 Family share
Rose Room has bath and shower

Set in over 3 acres, Rivendell is a traditional New Zealand villa and has beautiful secluded gardens that can be enjoyed relaxing on the large verandah or in the heated spa pool. Our home provides all modern facilities including central heating, internet and laundry. The delightful village of Geraldine with its numerous cafes, restaurants, shops and cinema is only 5 minutes drive. We offer you a truly warm welcome together with our friendly dogs & animals.

Winchester *16 km N of Timaru*

B&B Approved

Stonybanks *B&B*
Chris & Andrew Lush
Stonybanks,
32 Harrisons Rd,
Winchester,
South Canterbury

Tel (03) 615 8385
or 027 661 5888
thegrange@ihug.co.nz

Double/Twin $110
Single $75
(Full breakfast)
Pet free home
Children welcome
2 Queen 2 Single (4 bdrm)
Bathrooms: 1 Ensuite 1 Private
1 Guest share

Stonybanks is a comfortable, well appointed home set in 6 acres of beautiful grounds. We are just off Highway 1 in the village of Winchester, moments from Highway 79 to Mt Cook, Queenstown and Southern Lakes. The area is renowned for its world class salmon and trout fishing. We are within easy driving distance of restaurants, pubs and cafes, and are happy to share our knowledge of the south island with you. We are 200m north of the Winchester village on Harrison Road.

Timaru - Seadown *4.8 km N of Timaru*

Country Homestay *Homestay*
Margaret & Ross Paterson
491 Seadown Road,
Seadown, RD 3,
Timaru

Tel (03) 688 2468
or 021 213 7434
Fax (03) 688 2468

Double/Twin $90
Single $60
(Full breakfast)
Children half price
Dinner $25
Visa MC Diners Amex accepted
1 Double 2 Single (3 bdrm)
Electric blankets on all beds
Bathrooms: 1 Guest share

Our homestay is approximately 10 minutes north of Timaru, situated 4.8km on Seadown Road off State Highway 1 at Washdyke - third house on left past Pharlap Statue. We have hosted on our farm for 11 years - now retired and have a country farmlet with some farm animals, with views of farmland and mountains. Day trips to Mt Cook, Hydro Lakes and ski fields, fishing, golf course few minutes away. Laundry facilities available. Interests are farming, gardening, spinning, embroidery and overseas travel.

Timaru Central *1 km W of timaru*

Jones Homestay *Homestay*
Margaret & Nevis Jones
16 Selwyn Street,
Timaru

Tel (03) 688 1400
Fax (03) 688 1400
nevisjones@xtra.co.nz

Double/Twin $120
Single $70
(Full breakfast)
Children half price
Visa MC accepted
2 Double 1 Twin (3 bdrm)
Bathrooms: 2 Ensuite 1 Guest share

Welcome to our spacious character brick home built in the 1920s and situated in a beautiful garden with a grass tennis court. A secluded property with off-street parking and views of the surrounding sea and mountains. Centrally situated, only 5 minutes from the beach and town with an excellent choice of cafes and restaurants. On arrival tea is served on our sunny verandah. Hosts have lived and worked extensively overseas, namely South Africa, UK and the Middle East, and enjoy music, theatre, tennis and golf.

Timaru *8 km W of Timaru*

Berrillo *Luxury B&B Homestay*

B&B Approved

Owen & Liz Berrill
32 Gladstone Road,
RD 4,
Timaru
Tel (03) 686 1688
or 021 295 2451
Fax (03) 686 1678
oberrill@xtra.co.nz
www.berrillo.co.nz

Double/Twin $145
Single $100
(Full breakfast)
Children $45
Visa MC accepted
1 Queen 2 Twin (2 bdrm)
Bathrooms: 2 Ensuite
Power shower, hair driers, heated towel rails

A Touch of Tuscany in Timaru. A warm welcome and a complimentary glass of wine with hors d'oeurves awaits you on the terrace, overlooking stunning views of Mt Cook. Our award winning Home of the Year 2000 is nestled in an olive grove. We have a purpose-built guest wing with separate antique furnished lounge/library, Sky TV, tea/coffee making facilities.Restaurant 5mins away. A spirit of gracious hospitality sets Berrillo apart.We are well travelled and enjoy music,art and golf. Resident labrador.

~

Timaru Central *0.1 km W of Central Timaru*

Sefton Homestay Bed & Breakfast *B&B Homestay*

@home NEW ZEALAND B&B Approved

Trish & John Blunden
32 Sefton Street,
Seaview, Timaru
Tel (03) 688 0017
or 027 473 7366
or 027 470 0000
Fax (03) 688 0042
trish@seftonhomestay.co.nz
www.seftonhomestay.co.nz

Double/Twin $125
Single $110 (Full breakfast)
Children half price
Visa MC accepted
Children welcome
1 King/Twin 1 Queen
1 Double (3 bdrm)
Bathrooms: 1 Ensuite 1 Private

Relax in our superbly appointed and spacious 2 storey character brick home with sweeping views from the mountains to the sea. Refurbished with the feel of yesteryear, but with ambience and style you will love. All our children have left home with the exception of our labrador Ollie who enjoys meeting people as we do. A genuine 5 minute walk to the nearest restaurants

Pleasant Point - Timaru *17 km W of Timaru*

Longview Bed & Breakfast *B&B Farmstay*

Anita & Alan Blakemore
86 Longview Road,
Pleasant Point,
Timaru 7983

Tel (03) 614 7766
or 027 308 5078
longview86@xtra.co.nz
www.longviewfarmstay.co.nz

Double/Twin $140
Single $80
(Full breakfast)
Children up to $40
Dinner by prior arrangement $40
Visa MC accepted
Children welcome
2 Queen 1 Twin (3 bdrm)
2 Queen & 1 Twin Bedroom
Bathrooms: 1 Guest share

Nestled on 25 acres, Longview has stunning, 'must see to believe', panoramic views of the surrounding farmlands and mountains, just 2 hrs drive from Christchurch and Mt Cook. Two of our guest rooms and the private guest lounge have direct access to the terrace and gardens. Take a stroll through the olive grove (complimentary oil tastings available), meet Becky our Cocker Spaniel, visit our farm animals and soak up the tranquil country atmosphere. 5 minutes from local cafes.

Timaru *1 km S of Information centre*

Blueberry Cottage *B&B Homestay*

Barbara & Rodger Baird
72A High Street, Timaru

Tel (03) 684 3115
or 027 636 4301
Fax (03) 684 3172
relax@blueberrycottage.co.nz
www.blueberrycottage.co.nz

Double/Twin $95-$100
Single $70-$75
(Continental breakfast)
Children negotiable
Visa MC accepted
Pet free home
1 King/Twin 1 Queen (2 bdrm)
Tuscany Double and
Highland Twin/Superking
Bathrooms: 1 Guest share
Bath and Wet shower, separate toilet

Our delightfully upgraded 1950's brick home offers comfort and spectacular closeup views of the ocean and inland to Mt Cook. The tastefully furnished rooms have television, separate patios. Handy to hospital, gardens & beach. Walking distance to shops, cafe/bars, or eating place of your choice. Day trips to lakes, skiing in winter, Mt Cook, fishing rivers, bush walks and towns nearby. Our interests can be detected by our nautical theme, the vintage car in the garage and our choice of music. "Relaxation at its best".

Fairlie *3 km W of Fairlie*

Fontmell *B&B Homestay Farmstay*

B&B Approved

Anne & Norman McConnell
Nixons Road 169,
RD 17,
Fairlie

Tel (03) 685 8379
Fax (03) 685 8379

Double/Twin $100-$120
Single $65
(Full breakfast)
Children $35
Dinner $25
Cottage $150
2 King/Twin 1 Queen 1 Double
2 Twin 1 Single (4 bdrm)
Bathrooms: 1 Private 1 Guest share

Our farm consists of 400 acres producing lambs, cattle and deer. The house is situated in a large English style garden with many mature trees in a tranquil setting. In the area are 2 ski fields, golf courses, walkways and scenic drives. Informative farm tours available. Our interests include golf, gardening and music. New fully self contained 3 bedroom cottage with panoramic views of the Fairlie Basin. Directions: Nixons Road 1km West of Town Centre, Fontmell 2km up Nixons Road.

~

Fairlie - Kimbell *8 km W of Fairlie*

Rivendell Lodge *B&B Homestay Countrystay*

@home New Zealand B&B Approved

Joan Gill
15 Stanton Road, Kimbell,
RD 17, Fairlie

Tel (03) 685 8833
or 027 4819 189
Fax (03) 685 8825
joan@rivendell-lodge.co.nz
www.rivendell-lodge.co.nz

Double/Twin $120-$150
Single $80-$95 (Full breakfast)
Children negotiable
Dinner $45 per person
Visa MC accepted
Pet free home Children welcome
3 Queen 1 Double 2 Single (4 bdrm)
2 queen, 1 queen + sgle, 1 dble+sgle
Bathrooms: 2 Ensuite 2 Private
Separate spa bath available

Quality country comfort and hospitality offered in a peaceful historic village on the Christchurch-Queenstown route. Joan is a well-travelled writer, passionate about mountains, literature and local history. I enjoy cooking and gardening and delight in sharing home grown produce. Take time out for fishing, skiing, walking, golf or water sports. Relax in the garden, complete with stream, or come with us to some of our favourite places. Complimentary refreshments on arrival. Laundry facilities available.

Lake Tekapo *40 km W of Fairlie*

Freda Du Faur House *B&B Homestay*

Dawn & Barry Clark
1 Esther Hope Street,
Lake Tekapo
Tel (03) 680 6513
dawntek@xtra.co.nz
www.fredadufaur.co.nz

Double/Twin $170-$190
Single $100-$110
(Continental or cooked breakfast on request)
Children $95
Visa MC accepted
Children welcome
1 Queen 1 Double 2 Single (3 bdrm)
Bathrooms: 2 Ensuite 1 Private

Experience tranquillity and a touch of mountain magic. A warm and friendly welcome. Comfortable home, mountain and lake views. Rimu panelling, heart timber furniture, attractive decor, blending with the McKenzie Country. Bedrooms in private wing overlooking garden, two opening onto balcony. Refreshments on patio surrounded by roses or view ever changing panorama from lounge. Walkways nearby. Mt Cook one hour away. Views of skifield. Five minutes to shops and restaurants. Call for Directions.Happy hr 6 7. Our new Persian kitten called Bella welcomes you.

~

Lake Pukaki - Mt Cook *7 km N of Twizel*

Rhoborough Downs, Pukaki *Homestay*

Roberta Preston
State Highway 8 Tekapo/Twizel
Tel (03) 435 0509
or 027 621 7941
ra.preston@xtra.co.nz

Double/Twin $130
Single $70
(Continental breakfast)
Children $50
Dinner N/A
1 Double 1 Twin 1 Single (3 bdrm)
Bathrooms: 1 Guest share
Seperate toilets

A quiet place to stop, halfway between Christchurch and Queenstown or Christchurch and Dunedin via Waitaki Valley. 40 minutes to Mt Cook. The 10,000 acre property has been in the family 90 years. Merino sheep graze to 6000 feet, hereford cattle. Views of the southern sky. The homestead is set in tranquil gardens. Twizel has a bank, doctor, shops and several restaurants. Please phone for bookings and directions. Cot available.

Lake Pukaki *27 km W of Lake Tekapo*

Tasman Downs Station *Farmstay*

B&B Approved

Linda Hayman
Tasman Downs Station,
Lake Tekapo 7945

Tel (03) 680 6841
Fax (03) 680 6851
samjane@xtra.co.nz

Double/Twin $120-$130
Single $85-$100
(Full breakfast)
Dinner $45 pp by arrangement
1 Queen 1 Twin (2 bdrm)
Bathrooms: 1 Private 1 Guest share

We welcome you to a place of unsurpassed beauty located on the shores of Lake Pukaki, with magnificent views of the lake, Mount Cook and Southern Alps. Our local stone home blends in with the natural peaceful surroundings. This high country station has been in our family since 1914 and runs mainly Angus cattle. Linda and son Ian enjoy sharing their knowledge of farming with guests. An opportunity to experience farm life with friendly hosts. Dinner by arrangement. Meet our good natured Corgi Charles.

Twizel - Mt Cook *2 km W of Twizel Info Centre*

Artemis B&B *B&B Homestay*

B&B Approved

Jan & Bob Wilson
33 North West Arch,
Twizel

Tel (03) 435 0388
Fax (03) 435 0377
artemistwizel@paradise.net.nz

Double/Twin $125
Single $105
(Special breakfast)
Visa MC Eftpos accepted
Pet free home
Not suitable for children
2 Queen 1 Single (2 bdrm)
Bathrooms: 1 Ensuite 1 Private

Jan and Bob welcome you to the magnificent Mackenzie Basin and the Mount Cook National Park.Our modern home, which is situated on a hectare of land, has stunning mountain views along with space and tranquility.We are a short drive to Mount Cook National Park and a three minutes drive to restaurants.There is a guest sitting room with a balcony and tea/coffee making facilities.We look forward to sharing our home with you and are happy to discuss your New Zealand itineraries and sightseeing.

Twizel - Mt Cook *0.5 km S of Twizel*

Hunters House & Hunters Cottage Self Contained *B&B Cottage with Kitchen*

Anne & Matt Hunter
58 Tekapo Drive,
Twizel

Tel (03) 435 0038
Fax (03) 435 0038
annehunter@xtra.co.nz

Double/Twin $160
Single $110
(Full breakfast)
Visa MC accepted
Not suitable for children
2 King/Twin (2 bdrm)
Bathrooms: 2 Ensuite

Hunters House is architecturally designed for guests and features every comfort in a warm welcoming environment. It overlooks the native tussocks and trees of the Green Belt on the township boundary with the mountains as a backdrop. All rooms are tastefully decorated with all facilities and french doors opening to the peaceful outdoors sited for the sun and views. We also have a self contained cottage fully equiped with all home comforts and same views Situated in its own private setting. "Cead Mile Failte"

Twizel - Mt Cook *1 km N of Twizel*

Pinegrove *B&B Cottage with Kitchen 2 Cottages with kitchens*

Al & Joh Ingram
29 North West Arch,
Twizel 7944
PO Box 88 Twizel

Tel (03) 435 0430
or 021 464 726
aljohpinegrove@xtra.co.nz

Double/Twin $140-$160
Single $100
(Special breakfast)
Children $10-$25
Visa MC Eftpos accepted
Children welcome
2 Queen 1 Double 2 Single (2 bdrm)
2 bedrooms in each cottage
Bathrooms: 2 Private
Walk in showers

Rest a while in the beautiful Mackenzie District with its mountains and lakes. We are only 45 mins from Mt Cook and 2 mins drive to near by restaurants. We welcome you to our sunny cottages situated in an extensive garden with fishpond and tranquil areas to sit in. The cottages are fitted with modern conveniences with your comfort in mind. You can indulge in home baked goodies from the breakfast hamper. We look forward to meeting you and welcoming you to our haven.

Twizel *0.2 km S of Central Twizel*

B&B Approved

Aoraki Lodge *B&B*

Ian & Sandy Darwin
32 Mackenzie Drive,
Twizel

Tel (03) 435 0300
Fax (03) 435 0305
ian.sandy@xtra.co.nz
www.aorakilodge.co.nz

Tariff $150-$190
(Full breakfast)
Children not suitable under 16
Walking distance to restaurants and other facilites
60 kilometres to Mt Cook
Visa MC Eftpos accepted
4 Queen (4 bdrm)
3 Double 1 Twin
Bathrooms: 4 Ensuite

Relax in the informal atmosphere of our Lodge set amongst a rambling "country-style" garden. Aoraki Lodge located in the centre of Twizel at 32 Mackenzie Drive, is a short walk to local restaurants, clubs and facilities, yet offers complete privacy. Ian & Sandy Darwin welcome you and will advise on what to "see" and "do" in this beautiful part of the world. Ian, a member of the NZPFG Association, is a well known Fly-Fishing Guide in this area.

Lindis Pass *17 km W of Omarama*

B&B Approved

Dunstan Downs *Farmstay*

Tim & Geva Innes
Dunstan Downs,
Omarama, 9448

Tel (03) 438 9862
Fax (03) 438 9517
tim.innes@xtra.co.nz

Double/Twin up to $260
Single up to $130
(Full breakfast provisions)
Children half price under 12
Tarrif includes dinner, bed & breakfast
GST will be added to all tariffs
Visa MC accepted
Children and pets welcome
1 Queen 2 Twin 1 Single (3 bdrm)
Bathrooms: 1 Ensuite 1 Guest share
1 Family share

Dunstan Downs is a merino sheep and cattle station in the heart of the South Island high country. Our home is full of country warmth, you are welcome to join us for dinner (wine served) or bed and breakfast. The surrounding mountains and valleys are an adventure playground, tramping, mountain biking, fishing,farming activities or lazing around soaking up the peace and tranquillity.No pets inside.

Kurow *60 km W of Oamaru*

Glenmac Farmstay *Farmstay Campervan facilities*

Kaye & Keith Dennison
RD 7K, Oamaru
Tel (03) 436 0200
Fax (03) 436 0202
glenmac@farmstaynewzealand.co.nz
www.farmstaynewzealand.co.nz

Double/Twin $90-$110
Single $45-$55 (Full breakfast)
Children under 13 half price
Dinner $25
Self-contained price on application
Visa MC accepted
Children and pets welcome
1 Queen 2 Double 2 Twin (5 bdrm)
Bathrooms: 1 Ensuite
1 Guest share 1 Family share

Peaceful location. Enjoy home-cooked meals, a comfortable bed, relax and be treated as one of the family. Explore our 4000 acre high country farm. See merino sheep and beef cattle. On farm enjoy horse riding, take a 4 wheel drive farm tour, walk some of our many tracks. Nearby fly and spinner fishing (guide available), mountain biking, golf or explore the Fossil Trail. Directions: At end of Gards Road which is 10km east of Kurow on right or 13km west of Duntroon on left.

~

Kurow *1 km N of Kurow*

River Valley Cottage *B&B*

Carol Reeves
128 Cattle Valley Road,
Kurow
Tel (03) 436 0668
or 027 207 4861
carolab@clear.net.nz

Double/Twin $80-$100
Single $60
(Full breakfast)
Children half price
Dinner $25
Children welcome
1 Queen 1 Double (2 bdrm)
Bathrooms: 1 Ensuite 1 Family share

Take a breather and relax in the tranquility of our beautiful garden. Listen to the birds and the gentle sound of the brook or go fishing on the Waitaki River which is only minutes away.Our breakfasts include Eggs Benedict, Continental or a full breakfast.We have two friendly dogs, three shy cats and hens.Welcome to our paradise.

Oamaru - Waianakarua *27 km S of Oamaru*

Glen Dendron *B&B Farmstay*
Anne & John Mackay
284 Breakneck Road, Waianakarua, R D 90, Oamaru
Tel (03) 439 5288 or 021 615 227
Fax (03) 439 5288 anne.john.mackay@xtra.co.nz
www.glendendron-farmstay.com

Double/Twin $135-$165
Single $110-$130 (Full breakfast)
Children $50 Dinner $40 with wine
Visa MC accepted Pet free home Children welcome
2 King/Twin 2 Queen (4 bdrm)
Ensuite rooms include TV and tea making facilities
Bathrooms: 2 Ensuite 1 Guest share Spa bath

Award Winning Homestay. Enjoy tranquility and beauty when you stay in our stylish modern home, spectacularly sited on a hilltop overlooking the picturesque Waianakarua River and surrounded by 5 acres of landscaped garden.

After a sumptuous farm-cooked breakfast, feed the sheep and alpacas. Then take a stroll through the forest, native bush complete with waterfalls and birds or beside the river. Play a round on our private golf course. Later, watch the seals and penguins on a beach nearby. Then, complete a perfect day with our gourmet 3 course dinner with fine NZ wine before snuggling down for a peaceful sleep in the fresh country air.

After a lifetime spent in farming and forestry we relish the opportunity to share our home and semi-retired lifestyle with guests. Our adult family lives overseas so we travel frequently and have a great interest in other countries and cultures. We are very keen gardeners, read widely and enjoy antiques. Anne is a floral designer and John is a tree connoisseur.

An overnight stay is not enough to do justice to this lovely area - with so much to see, why not stay awhile!We can plan customised itineraries of the area's many attractions. Oamaru's historic architecture. Garden, heritage and fossil trails. Beaches, fishing, seals and penguins. Famous Moeraki Boulders and other interesting geological features.Use us as a base for day visits to Oamaru, Dunedin, Waitaki Valley and Mt Cook. Christchurch International Airport - 3.5 hours.We dont mind short notice!

Oamaru *3 km S of Oamaru, just off SH1*

Springbank *B&B Apartment with Kitchen Cottage with Kitchen*

Joan & Stan Taylor
60 Weston Road, Oamaru
Tel (03) 434 6602
or 027 403 5410
Fax (03) 434 6602
joan60@clear.net.nz

Double/Twin $110
Single $75 (
Continental breakfast)
Children $10
Visa MC accepted
Pet free home
Children welcome
1 King/Twin 1 Double (1 bdrm)
Twin beds that covert to king DL
Bathrooms: 1 Private
Bathroom has bath and shower

We look forward to sharing our retirement haven with visitors from overseas and New Zealand. Our modern home and separate guest flat are set in a peaceful and private large garden. Feed the goldfish.Our guest flat is sunny, warm, spacious and comfortable. We enjoy helping visitors discover our district's best kept secrets! Penguins, gardens, Moeraki Boulders, beaches, pool, fishing and golf. Our interests are travel, gardening, grandchildren. Stan's are Lions and following sports. Joan's all handcrafts, patchwork, floral design.

~

Oamaru *1.3 km N of Oamaru Centre*

Highway House Boutique B&B *B&B Homestay*

Stephanie & Norman Slater
43 Lynn Street,
(Cnr Thames Highway & Lynn St),
Meadowbank, Oamaru
Tel (03) 437 1066
or 0800 003 319 Fax (03) 437 1066
breakfast@highwayhouse.co.nz
www.highwayhouse.co.nz

Double/Twin $140-$165
Single $120-$145 (Full breakfast)
Children negotiable
Visa MC Amex accepted
Pet free home Children welcome
2 King 1 Twin (3 bdrm)
Thoroughly appointed
Bathrooms: 1 Ensuite 1 Guest share
1 Family share
Large-size showers

Our character residence on Thames Highway, (1.3km north of town centre), has been entirely refurbished to the highest standard. We provide a full cooked breakfast and other refreshments as required. We can assist with tours of historic Oamaru or visits to the nature sites. Our courtesy car can collect or take you to nearby dining establishments. If you appreciate a quality ambiance and particular assistance from Stephanie and Norman who have travelled widely overseas, Highway House will be ideal for you. French also spoken.

Oamaru *0.5 km W of Oamaru centre*

Homestay Oamaru *B&B Homestay*

B&B Approved

Doug Bell
14 Warren Street,
Oamaru

Tel (03) 434 1454
or 027 408 2860
homestayoamaru@paradise.net.nz
www.bellview.co.nz

Double/Twin $80-$100
Single $55-$70
(Full breakfast)
Dinner $25 by arrangement
Pet free home
Not suitable for children
2 Queen 1 Double (3 bdrm)
Warm & relaxing decor, quality beds & great showers
Bathrooms: 2 Ensuite 1 Family share

Sweeping views over the town and harbour. Warm, spacious and comfortable accommodation for the travelling enthusiast, with books, maps, atlases and guides for you perusal. Quiet, private site, close to town centre. (see map on website). Off-street parking. Southern scenic walkway access at property boundary. Some of the area's attractions include sea and river fishing, historic architecture, unique geological features and eco-tourism. Host has detailed local knowledge. Site unsuitable for young children or pets.

Oamaru *8 km S of Oamaru*

Ranui Retreat Bed and Breakfast/Homestay *B&B Homestay*

B&B Approved

Sheryl Laraman and Family
27 Woolshed Road,
Totara,
Oamaru,
8D RD

Tel (03) 439 5241
ranui_retreat@actrix.gen.nz
www.ranui-retreat.co.nz

Double/Twin $130-$160
Single $100
(Full breakfast)
Children negotiable
Dinner 25 pp
Visa MC accepted
Children and pets welcome
2 Queen (2 bdrm)
Bathrooms: 1 Ensuite 1 Private

Welcome to Ranui Retreat. We are close to historic Oamaru and the main highway to Dunedin. Views of Otago rural landscape stretching to the Kakanui Mountains enhance the rural sense of this five acre property of mature oak, elm and ash trees. There is birdsong aplenty. Character rooms include rich, handmade quilts which add to the relaxed ambience. Join the family for the evening or you may like to retire to other spaces with music and a good book from our library selection.

Oamaru *0.5 km S of Oamaru*

Federation House Homestay Inn B&B *B&B Homestay*

Rodger McCaw
60 Tyne Street,
Oamaru, 9400

Tel (03) 434 9537
Fax (03) 434 9537
info@federationhouse.co.nz
www.federationhouse.co.nz

Double/Twin $100-$150
Single $50-$100
(Full breakfast)
Dinner by arrangement
Off Season Rates - special discount from May until October
Visa MC accepted
Pet free home
Children welcome
3 King/Twin 2 Twin (5 bdrm)
Bathrooms: 3 Ensuite 1 Guest share 1 Family share

A large two storied Heritage House with a commanding site in the exclusive suburb of Cape Wanbrow. So very close to Oamaru's Historic Precinct, Harbour and Penguin Colony with views from rooms. Enjoy an era of magnificent building of Australasian Federation architecture.

Palmerston *2 km S of Palmerston*

Mount Royal B&B *B&B*

Jo & Trevor Studholme
Mount Royal,
RD 1
(Just off SH1),
Palmerston,
Otago

Tel (03) 465 1884
or 021 876 880
mt.royal.bandb@clear.net.nz

Double/Twin $130
(Full breakfast)
Private Sitting Room
Pet free home
Not suitable for children
1 King 1 Twin (2 bdrm)
1 Superking
Bathrooms: 1 Private

Our 1930s homestead situated in a quiet rural setting 400m from State Highway 1 and 1km south of Palmerston, the gateway to Central Otago goldfields. As hosts, we enjoy making you welcome and would like you to stay to visit the Moeraki Boulders and coastal walkways, before heading central, perhaps following the gold trail: The Macraes Gold Mine is thought to be the largest open-cast mine in the Southern Hemisphere (tours by appointment).

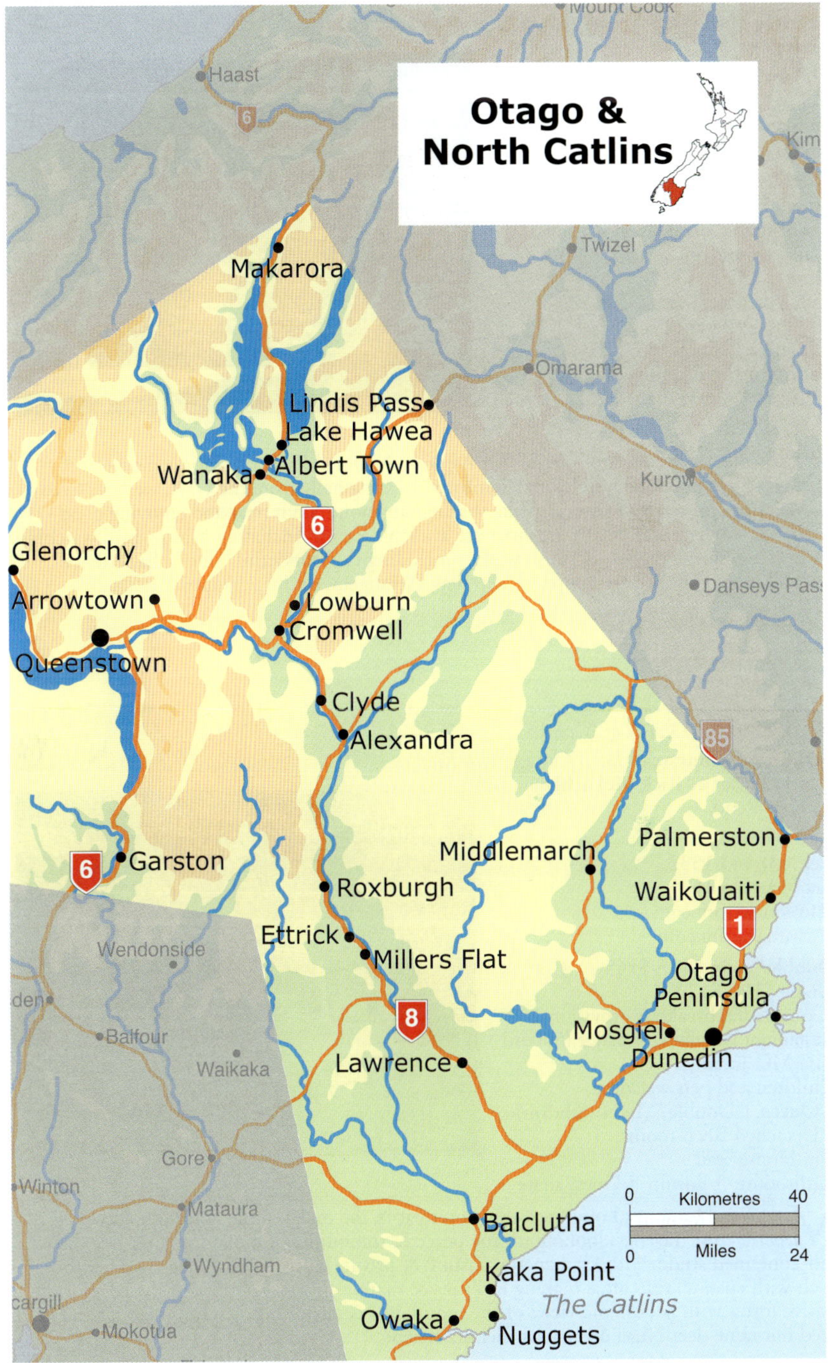
Otago &
North Catlins
Mount Cook
Haast
6
Kim
Twizel
Makarora
Omarama
Lindis Pass
Lake Hawea
Albert Town
Wanaka
Kurow
6
Glenorchy
Danseys Pass
Arrowtown
Lowburn
Cromwell
Queenstown
Clyde
Alexandra
85
Palmerston
Middlemarch
Garston
6
Waikouaiti
Roxburgh
1
Ettrick
Millers Flat
Wendonside
Otago
Peninsula
8
Mosgiel
Balfour
Dunedin
Lawrence
Waikaka
Gore
Winton
Mataura
Kilometres
0
40
Balclutha
0
Miles
24
Wyndham
Kaka Point
The Catlins
Owaka
Mokotua
Nuggets

Makarora *65 km N of Wanaka*

Larrivee Homestay *Homestay Cottage with Kitchen*
Andrea
Makarora, via Wanaka
Tel (03) 443 9177
andilarr@xtra.co.nz
www.larriveehomestay.co.nz

Double/Twin $120
Single $80
(Continental breakfast provisions)
Children under 12 years half price
Dinner $35 BYO
Visa MC accepted
Children welcome
2 Double 2 Single (3 bdrm)
Bathrooms: 1 Ensuite
1 Private 1 Guest share

Nestled in native bush bordering Mt Aspiring National Park, our unique home and cottage are secluded, quiet and comfortable. Originally from the USA, we have lived in Makarora for over 30 years and like sharing our mountain retreat and enjoying good food and conversation. Many activities are available locally, including fishing, bird watching, jet boating, scenic flights and bush walks - including the wonderful 'Siberia Experience', fly/walk/boat trip. We are happy to help make arrangements for activities.

Makarora *65 km N of Wanaka*

Makarora Homestead *B&B Cottage with Kitchen*
Kenna Fraser & Rick McLachlan
53 Rata Road,
Makarora
Tel (03) 443 1532
Fax (03) 443 1525
info@makarora.com
www.makarora.com

Double/Twin $125-$145
Single $100-$120
(Continental breakfast provisions)
Restaurant is walking distance (500 m)
Visa MC accepted
Children and pets welcome
7 Queen 1 Double 7 Twin (8 bdrm)
3 Detached B&B rooms,
5 in Homestead
Bathrooms: 3 Ensuite 3 Guest share

Makarora Homestead offers a secluded retreat in the midst of the Southern Alps & is perfect for travellers looking for the peace & tranquility of the mountains. We offer a self-contained studio with kitchenette, ensuite & private balcony OR 2 detached bedrooms each with ensuite, tea/coffee making facilities & shared sundeck. Nestled at the edge of the native forest with panoramic views of the mountains & surrounding wapiti deer farm. Hand feed our tame deer Nigel & various friendly sheep.

Wanaka *1 km S of Wanaka*

Berryfarm Homestay *B&B Homestay Separate Suite Guest lounge*

B&B Approved

Annette & Bob Menlove
83 Orchard Road,
Wanaka, Central Otago

Tel (03) 443 4248
or CP 021 494 149
or CP 021 344 016
Fax (03) 443 4249
bobannette@menlove.net
www.berryfarmhomestay.co.nz

Double/Twin $150-$170
Single $150
(Full breakfast)
Visa MC accepted
Children welcome
1 King/Twin 1 Double
1 Twin (3 bdrm)
Bathrooms: 2 Ensuite 1 Private
Spa and Bath

We are a Berryfarm growing raspberries, strawberries boysenberries and tomatoes, on the outskirts of Wanaka, just three minutes from town. We are very close to good restaurants, a golf course, ski fields and excellent lake and river fishing. We have two cats and a labrador dog and have just retired from a sheep, cattle and deer farm. Bob and I have been hosting for a number of years and both enjoy meeting people. We have a separate guest area with your own lounge. Bedrooms have their own TV and are very quiet and private.

Wanaka *0.4 km E of Centre Wanaka*

Lake Wanaka Homestay *B&B Homestay*

@ home NEW ZEALAND   B&B Approved

Gailie & Peter Cooke
85 Warren Street, Wanaka

Tel (03) 443 7995
or 0800 443 799
Fax (03) 443 7945
wanakahomestay@xtra.co.nz
www.lakewanakahomestay.co.nz

Double/Twin $130-$140
Single $90-$100
(Full breakfast)
Not suitable for small children
Center of Wanaka
Visa MC accepted
2 Double (2 bdrm)
Double beds, heaters,
electric blankets, dressers, tables
Bathrooms: 1 Guest share
Great shower

Peter & Gailie would love you to join us in our home ideally situated in centre of Wanaka. Just 470 metres walk (5 minutes) to Lake, Restaurants and shops. Relax with us for tea, coffee and homebaking, while enjoying breathtaking views of Lake and mountains. Two comfortable warm, double bedrooms. Safe off street parking. Full cooked breakfast at no extra cost. Interests include fly fishing, golf, skiing, walking, gardening. Kate our Labrador love to meet you. Guest comments "Great hosts, wonderful food and accommodation".

Wanaka *3 km N of Wanaka Shops*

Beacon Point *B&B Homestay Apartment with Kitchen*

Diana & Dan Pinckney
302 Beacon Point Road,
PO Box 6,
Lake Wanaka

Tel (03) 443 1253
or 0272 460 222
or 0274 354 847
Fax (03) 443 1254
dan.di@lakewanaka.co.nz
www.beaconpoint.co.nz

Double/Twin $120
Single $90
(Continental breakfast)
Children $30 Dinner $40
Rolla Beds
Pet free home Children welcome
1 Queen 1 Twin (2 bdrm)
Bathrooms: 1 Ensuite

Beacon Point B&B has an acre of lawn and garden for your enjoyment. Leads to a walking track to the village around the edge of the lake. Private spacious studio with ensuite, queen and single beds (2 rooms), kitchen, TV,DVD, sundeck and BBQ. Studio equipped with every need for perfect stay. We enjoy planning your days with you. Our intrests include farming, forestry, fly fishing, real estate, boating, gardening and grandchildren. Turn right at lake - Lakeside Road - then to Beacon Point Road 302.

Wanaka *1.3 km S of Wanaka*

Harpers *B&B Homestay*

Jo & Ian Harper
95 McDougall Street,
Wanaka

Tel (03) 443 8894
Fax (03) 443 8834
harpers@xtra.co.nz
www.harpers.co.nz

Double/Twin $140
Single $100
(Continental breakfast)
Visa MC accepted
1 King/Twin 2 Single (2 bdrm)
2 in home
Bathrooms: 1 Ensuite 1 Private
Bath and Shower with twin room

We take pride in offering a friendly, comfortable home. Share breakfast and awesome lake and mountain views with us. Also explore our extensive garden, which provides a tranquil environment for relaxing. We offer a drink and muffins on your arrival. This is a smoke-free home. Recent guests' comments: "Wonderful welcoming homestay."Friendly hosts, excellent breakfasts. "Wonderful hospitality, fantastic breakfast." "Excellent hosts, breakfasts to die for." "Very comfortable. Great hosts. Top spot." "Wonderful views. The muffins and pancakes do live up to expectations." "A home from home."

Wanaka *4 km S of Wanaka*

Stonehaven *Homestay*

Deirdre & Dennis
Maxwell Road,
RD 2,
Wanaka

Tel (03) 443 9516
Fax (03) 443 9513
moghul@xtra.co.nz
www.stonehaven.co.nz

Double/Twin $125
Single $95
(Full breakfast)
Children $20 negotiable
Portacots and highchairs available
Visa MC accepted
Children and pets welcome
2 Queen 2 Single (2 bdrm)
Spacious with comfortable beds
Bathrooms: 1 Ensuite 1 Private

Our home is set in two acres about five minutes drive from Wanaka. All beds have electric blankets. Tea and coffee is freely available. We have extensive views of surrounding mountains. Children are welcome and child care by arrangement. Our nearby tree collection has an accent on autumn colour. Local walks a speciality. Organic fruit both in season and preserved. We have a small dog and a cat. No smoking inside please. Please phone for directions.

Wanaka - Albert Town *6 km N of Wanaka*

Riversong *B&B Homestay*

Ann & Ian Horrax
5 Wicklow Terrace,
Albert Town, RD 2,
Wanaka

Tel (03) 443 8567
or 021 113 6397
Fax (03) 443 8564
info@riversongwanaka.co.nz
www.riversongwanaka.co.nz

Double/Twin $150-$170
Single $110
(Continental breakfast)
Children $25
Dinner $55pp by arrangement
Visa MC accepted
1 King/Twin 1 Queen
1 Single (3 bdrm)
Bathrooms: 1 Ensuite 1 Private

Riversong is 5 minutes from Wanaka Township, at Albert Town, on the banks of the majestic Clutha River. At our secluded haven all rooms have river and mountain views, with immediate access to the river. Ann's background is healthcare and Ian's law. We invite you to share the comforts and privacy of our home and garden and Ian's knowledge of the region's fishing and guidance service. We aim to provide a memorable and comfortable stay. We have 1 outside lab dog. Wireless/broadband available.

Wanaka *0.2 km E of Wanaka Central*

Te Wanaka Lodge

B&B Guest House Ski Lodge/Chalet in Winter

Mandy & Wayne Enoka
23 Brownston Street, Wanaka

Tel (03) 443 9224
or FreeCall: 0800 WANAKA (926252)
Fax (03) 443 9246 info@tewanaka.co.nz
www.tewanaka.co.nz

Double/Twin $159-$230
Single $149-$185 (Full breakfast)
Garden cottage room $230 ($250 for 3 persons)
Visa MC Amex Eftpos accepted
9 Queen 4 Twin (13 bdrm)
ensuite with private balconyBathrooms: 13 Ensuite

Owned & run by outdoor enthusiasts, the lodge is a place for active people who want to get out & explore our picturesque town and locale. Get good advice from your hosts about all the local walks and great things to do. Te Wanaka enjoys a reputation as a relaxed, fun and friendly place to stay.

After an adventurous day exploring our mountains, lake & streams, guests can soak in the private garden hot tub/spa, sit back in one of our comfy lounges or enjoy the sun in our pretty courtyard garden.

- All bedrooms with ensuite and private balcony - LCD Flat Screen TV (5 Channels Sky) - Delicious full cooked breakfast included - Vegetarian, gluten & dairy free breakfast options - Guest Lounges with Log Fire & Library - Wireless & High Speed internet available - House Bar specialising in local beers and wines - In-house therapeutic massage - Mountain Bike Hire - Luggage storage - Laundry service - Gear drying room (Ski & other)

Wanaka *0.5 km N of Wanaka*

Criffel Peak View *B&B Apartment with Kitchen*

Caroline Holland
98 Hedditch Street,
Wanaka

Tel (03) 443 5511
Fax (03) 443 5521
stay@criffelpeakview.co.nz
www.criffelpeakview.co.nz

Double/Twin $150-$160
Single $120
(Full breakfast)
Apartment from $200 for 4 people
Visa MC accepted
Children welcome
2 King/Twin 1 King 2 Queen (3 bdrm)
Plus 2 bedroom apartment
Bathrooms: 2 Ensuite 2 Private

A cosy modern cottage situated in a quiet cul-de-sac, just a short walk from the lake and town. Great mountain views, large sunny deck, friendly young hosts and a crazy cat called Splodge. Our 3 guest rooms look out towards the Criffel Range and are equipped with super king or queen sized beds and TVs. The guest lounge has Wireless Internet, guest computer, tea/coffee making and variety of reading material.Our apartment is perfect for larger groups and families.

Wanaka *2.4 km E of Wanaka*

The Cedars *B&B Homestay*

Mary & Graham Dowdall
7 Riverbank Road, RD 2,
Wanaka 9382, Otago

Tel (03) 443 1544
or 021 1208 960
Fax (03) 443 1580
thecedarswanaka@xtra.co.nz
www.thecedars.co.nz

Double/Twin $195-$230
Single $150-$185 (Full breakfast)
Children are very welcome
Highchair and portacot available
Three course dinner/BBQ by arrangement with 24 hours notice
Visa MC accepted
2 Queen 1 Single (2 bdrm)
Spacious, TV, fridge, fluffy bathrobes
Bathrooms: 1 Ensuite 1 Private with Spa Bath

Cead Mile Failte - One hundred thousand welcomes. A warm Irish/Kiwi welcome awaits you at The Cedars, by Mary, Graham, Rough Collie Nessa and cat Cara. Our stone home on 11 acres is close to all of Wanaka's attractions and restaurants,has panoramic mountain views, expansive gardens,paddocks with alpacas and sheep, guest lounge with large open fire. We enjoy travelling, dining, music, literature and sports. Full breakfast is served with fresh and home-made produce. We offer evening meals or BBQ by prior arrangement.

Wanaka *2.5 km W of Wanaka*

Wanaka Jewel *Luxury B&B Homestay Separate Suite*

Pam & Bruce Mayo
7 Foxglove Heights,
Far Horizon Park, Lake Wanaka

Tel (03) 443 5636
or 027 285 6234
or (03) 443 2722
Fax (03) 443 2723
wanakajewel@xtra.co.nz
www.bnb.co.nz/wanakajewel.html

Double/Twin $185-$225
Single $170-$210
(Full breakfast)
Visa MC accepted
Not suitable for children
2 Queen (2 bdrm)
1 larger 1 smaller with lounge
Bathrooms: 1 Ensuite 1 Private
Two persons spa bath

Welcome to Wanaka Jewel - a stay in paradise. 3 minutes from township. Wanaka Jewel is a newly built luxury home with purpose built bed & breakfast suites set on 1 acre surrounded by magestic mountains and superb lake views, close to town. Own private entrance. These suites are beautifully appointed with quality linen. Complimentary pool, spa, tennis courts, gymnasium, BBQ, pitch and putting green available to guests. Complimentary tea, coffee anytime, sumptious breakfast. Be assured of a warm welcome and a memorable stay.

Wanaka *12 km E of Wanaka*

B&B Approved

Kanuka Lodge *B&B*

Heather & Graeme Halliday
110 Shortcut Road,
SH 8A,
Luggate,
RD2,
Wanaka

Tel (03) 443 7448
hallday@es.co.nz

Double/Twin $90-$120
Single $70-$90
(Full breakfast)
Children $20
Visa MC accepted
Children and pets welcome
1 Queen 1 Double 1 Single (3 bdrm)
Bathrooms: 1 Guest share

Our home is near the Clutha river, 10 minutes drive from Wanaka. It features NZ art and books. We welcome you with a glass of fine NZ wine. At breakfast you must try the Central Otago apricots and Heather's wildflower honey. You can admire the alpine landscape with geologist, photographer and fisherman Graeme, and plan your exploration of Wanaka. We have friendly cats and horses. Heather, originally from Bath in England, gives rides in her vintage buggies and grows the exotic spice saffron.

Wanaka *0.2 km E of Wanaka Central*

Renmore House *B&B*

Rosie and Blair Burridge
44 Upton Street,
Wanaka, 9305

Tel (03) 443 6566
or 027 434 2075
Fax (03) 443 6567
info@renmorehouse.co.nz
www.renmore-house.co.nz

Double/Twin $190-$220
Single $170-$190
(Full breakfast)
Children welcome
Visa MC Eftpos accepted
3 King/Twin (3 bdrm)
3 superking/twin
Bathrooms: 3 Ensuite

Blair, Rosie and Sophie the cat extend a warm welcome to Renmore House a luxury, purpose built B&B just 2 minutes walk from Wanaka village and very convenient to most Wanaka activities. We are committed to ensuring your every comfort and privacy in our home including assistance with travel,mountain bikes, wireless internet, laundry facilities, guest lounge and a scrumptious breakfast menu. Sounds of springfed creeks running through our garden create a peaceful ambiance for guests wishing to barbeque or just relax with a book.

Wanaka *12 km N of Wanaka*

Mt Maude Lodge *B&B Homestay*

Russell & Polly Horner
964 Lake Hawea/Albert Town Road,
2RD Wanaka, 9382

Tel (03) 443 6117
or 0272 033 696
Fax (03) 443 6117
stay@mtmaudelodge.co.nz
www.mtmaudelodge.co.nz

Double/Twin $150-$170
Single up to $150
(Continental breakfast)
Dinner by arrangement
Visa MC accepted
Children welcome
2 Queen (2 bdrm)
Queen/single Queen
Bathrooms: 2 Ensuite

We live on 50 acres of private farm land 3kms from Lake Hawea and 12kms from Wanaka. Only a short drive to very good restaurants, golf course, fishing and ski fields. We have 3 cats and a labrador dog.We also have 5 pet sheep running on the property.

Otago North Catlins

Lake Wanaka *1 km N of Post Office*

Black Peak Lodge *B&B Homestay*

Helen and David Rule
38 Kings Drive,
Wanaka

Tel (03) 443 4078
or Mobile 027 457 3539
Fax (03) 443 4038
hellbell@xtra.co.nz
www.blackpeaklodge.co.nz

Double/Twin $180-$220
Single $180-$190
(Full breakfast)
Children gladly welcomed
Visa MC accepted
1 King/Twin 2 Queen (3 bdrm)
Bathrooms: 1 Ensuite 2 Private

Welcome to Black Peak Lodge. Unwind in comfort.... in winter by the log fire, in summer on the open deck in awe of the spectacular view. Relax in the lounge, indulging in fine wines and mouthwatering appetizers.

Recharge and recuperate in the spa amidst the tranquil ambiance that is ....Black Peak Lodge.

Join us in our recreational activities: biking, fishing, boating, water skiing, walking or enjoying time with our gorgeous Golden Retriever, Rosa Bella.

Wanaka *2.5 km W of Wanaka*

Avalanche B & B *B&B Apartment with Kitchen*

@home NEW ZEALAND · B&B Approved

Trish & David Pattison
74 Bill's Way, Wanaka, 9305

Tel (03) 443 6665
or 027 633 2364
or 027 232 2063
Fax (03) 443 6701
davidpattison@xtra.co.nz
www.wanakabedandbreakfast.com

Double/Twin $150-$180
Single $135-$150
(Continental breakfast provisions)
Children negotiable
Visa MC accepted
1 Queen 1 Double 1 Twin
1 Single (3 bdrm)
Studio with queen & single bed
Twin & double rooms
Bathrooms: 1 Ensuite Ensuite or guest share

Avalanche B & B has spectacular views over farmland to the mountains and Avalanche Glacier. We are 2.5 km from the centre of town and 8 minutes walk to the lake and two quality restaurants. Our spacious self contained studio unit with ensuite has a well equipped kitchen. Delicious home made continental breakfast supplies and baking are provided each day.We offer warm hospitality in our comfortable home, set in a lovely, peaceful garden, with our small dog, Roxy, and cat, Tiggy.

~

Wanaka *4 km SE of Wanaka*

The Hayloft *Luxury Self contained apartment with kitchenette*

B&B Approved

Julie Jones & John Wellington
272 Ballantyne Road,
Wanaka, 9382

Tel (03) 443 8183
or 021 027 90039
Fax (03) 443 8882
stay@thehayloft.co.nz
www.thehayloft.co.nz

Double/Twin $180-$200
(Breakfast by arrangement)
See our website for winter specials
Visa MC accepted
Not suitable for children
1 Queen (1 bdrm)
Large room with balcony and walk in wardrobe
Bathrooms: 1 Private

Welcome to our unique, strawbale loft apartment set on 16 acres of rolling farmland, enjoying fantastic views of the Southern Alps. An ideal private haven for couples to relax, the Hayloft has been designed with natural materials and recycled timbers, oozing charm and character. Situated just 4km from Lake Wanaka where you will find a wide selection of shops, cafes, restaurants and activities on offer. John is a tour guide and avid walker and will happily share his local knowledge. Our two cats live downstairs.

Wanaka

Aspiring Lofts *B&B Self Contained Unit*
Don & Lorraine Irvine
42 Manuka Cresent,
Wanaka

Tel (03) 443 7856
or 021 236 1518
info@aspiringlofts.co.nz
www.aspiringlofts.co.nz

Double/Twin $150-$180
Single $150
(Full breakfast)
Visa MC accepted
Children welcome
1 King/Twin 1 Queen (2 bdrm)
Bathrooms: 2 Ensuite

Welcome to Aspiring Lofts - with stunning lake and mountain views. Relax in our new architecturally designed studio apartments. Enjoy luxurious rooms opening onto your own private balcony with outstanding views, an easy walk to lake and cafes and a private entrance. Relax in our contemporary garden. Wireless/broadband available. Don, a retired lawyer and Lorraine, a teacher have extensive local knowledge and can help you plan your day. Wanaka offers untold beauty, tranquility, inspiration and adventure. We invite you to share the experience with us.

Cromwell *1 km S of live in Cromwell*

Stuart's Homestay *B&B Homestay*
Elaine & Ian Stuart
5 Mansor Court,
Cromwell

Tel (03) 445 3636
Fax (03) 445 3617
ian.elaine@xtra.co.nz

Double/Twin $110-$130
Single $70-$80
(Full breakfast)
Dinner $25-$35 by arrangement
Visa MC accepted
Pet free home
Children welcome
2 Queen 2 Single (3 bdrm)
Bathrooms: 1 Ensuite 1 Guest share

Welcome to our home which is situated within walking distance to most of Cromwell's amenities. We are semi-retired Southland farmers who have been hosting for over 15 years. Cromwell is a quiet and relaxed town with historic gold diggings, vineyards, orchards, trout fishing, boating, walks, close to ski fields. 45 minutes to Wanaka or Queenstown. Share dinner with us or just bed & breakfast. Tea and coffee, home-made cookies available. We enjoy sharing our home and garden with visitors and a friendly stay is assured.

Cromwell *1 km N of Cromwell*

B&B Approved

Cottage Gardens *B&B Homestay detached twin studio*

Jill & Colin McColl
80 Neplusultra Street,
Cromwell,
Central Otago

Tel (03) 445 0628
Fax (03) 445 0628
cottage.gardens@ihug.co.nz
www.cromwellbedandbreakfast.co.nz

Double/Twin $100-$110
Single $55-$75
(Continental breakfast)
Dinner $25pp by prior arrangment
Visa MC accepted
Not suitable for children
2 Twin 1 Single (3 bdrm)
Bathrooms: 1 Ensuite 2 Private

Welcome! Hospitality is our specialty. For 15 years we have welcomed travellers, many returning. Our home features local stone and timbers and overlooks an 18 hole Golf course. The spacious Twin studio unit adjoins the garden where Bluebelle the cat plays. The upstairs Twin room has private bathroom, TV, and tea making. Cromwell with vineyards, orchards and Lake has excellent sporting facilities. Members of Lions International and Woolcrafters, Retired Orchardist and Teacher. Queenstown, Wanaka 45 minutes. Fiordland, 2.5 hours. Shops and Restaurants 10 minutes walk. Free laundry.

Cromwell *5 km N of Cromwell*

B&B Approved

Lake Dunstan Lodge *Homestay*

Judy & Bill Thornbury
Northburn,
RD 3, Cromwell

Tel (03) 445 1107
or 027 431 1415
Fax (03) 445 3062
william.t@xtra.co.nz
www.lakedunstanlodge.co.nz

Double/Twin $110-$130
Single $80
(Full breakfast)
Children negotiable
Dinner $25-35 by arrangement
Visa MC accepted
Children welcome
2 Queen 3 Single (3 bdrm)
Bathrooms: 2 Ensuite 1 Guest share

Friendly hospitality awaits you at our home privately situated beside Lake Dunstan. We are ex-Southland farmers and have a cat Ollie. Our interests include Lions, fishing, boating, gardening and crafts. Bedrooms have attached balconies, fridge, tea and coffee facilities. Guests share our living areas, spa pool and laundry. Local attractions: orchards, vineyards, gold diggings, fishing, boating, walks, 4 ski fields nearby. Enjoy dinner with us or just relax in the peaceful surroundings. No smoking indoors please. Directions: 5km north of Cromwell Bridge on SH8.

Cromwell - Lowburn *14 km N of Cromwell*

Smoothwater Haven *Luxury B&B*

Bonnie & Susie Perry
68 Gilmore Road
(Luggate-Cromwell Hwy),
Cromwell, 9383

Tel (03) 445 3231
or 0210 242 3859
Fax (03) 445 3231
info@smoothwaterhaven.co.nz
www.smoothwaterhaven.co.nz

Double/Twin $140-$160
Single $100-$120
(Full breakfast)
Dinner by arrangement $30 pp
European & Asian food
Visa MC accepted
Children and pets welcome
4 Twin (2 bdrm)
Exclusive en suite.
Bathrooms: 2 Ensuite

New lakeside home, overlooking Bendigo Wildlife Reserve, Lake Dunstan. Enjoying uninterrupted 360 degree views of wildlife, lake and mountains, we grow olives, truffles and varieties of nuts. Our large orchard provides fresh fruit and berries. Two large self-contained, purpose-built bedrooms opening onto terraces with expansive views of garden, lake and mountains. Breakfast often served on terrace overlooking the lake. Delightful dog and cat.

Arrowtown *3 km S of Arrowtown*

Peony Gardens *B&B Apartment with Kitchen*

Ian & Margaret Chamberlain
231 Lake Hayes Road,
RD1,
Queenstown

Tel (03) 442 1280
or 0274 361 661
Fax (03) 442 1210
ijchamberlain@xtra.co.nz

Double/Twin $140
Single $120
(Continental breakfast)
Pet free home
Children welcome
1 Queen 1 Double 2 Twin (2 bdrm)
Bathrooms: 1 Guest share

Our garden was the original Peony Gardens situated at Lake Hayes, between Queenstown and Historic Arrowtown. The self-contained flat has two bedrooms, full kitchen facilities, heat pump, and opens onto a balcony which looks over to the lake and our garden. A short walk will take you to the edge of the lake with wonderful views of the mountains. Easy access to four Ski Fields and four very scenic Golf Courses. We enjoy meeting people, will do all we can to make your stay memorable.

Arrowtown *20 km NE of Queenstown*

Arrowtown Heights B&B *Luxury B&B Separate Suite*

B&B Approved

Rae & Winston Wallace
6 May Lane,
Arrowtown

Tel (03) 442 1726
or 027 279 1552
info@arrowtownheights.com
www.arrowtownheights.com

Double/Twin $150-$190
Single $120-$150
(Full breakfast)
Visa MC accepted
Pet free home
1 King/Twin 1 Queen (2 bdrm)
Private luxurious large and sunny
Bathrooms: 1 Ensuite 1 Private

You are always sure of a welcome at Arrowtown Heights. Our contemporary home provides spacious and luxurious accommodation in a separate wing designed especially for guests. Step out of your bedroom to sit and relax in the garden, enjoy the panoramic views or the luxury of the outdoor spa. Join us for coffee and a chat. We are happy to assist or direct you to a wide range of local sights and activities. We look forward to your visit.

Arrowtown *4 km W of Arrowtown*

Willowby Downs *B&B Homestay Farmstay*

B&B Approved

Pam & David Mcnay
792 Malaghans Road,
R D 1,
Queenstown

Tel (03) 442 1714
or 027 222 0964
Fax (03) 442 1887
willowbydowns@xtra.co.nz
www.willowbydowns.co.nz

Double/Twin $150
Single $100
(Continental breakfast)
Children neg
Visa MC accepted
Children and pets welcome
2 Queen 1 Twin 2 Single (3 bdrm)
Double room has 1 queen 1single
Bathrooms: 2 Ensuite 1 Guest share

With Pam & David you are assured of a warm and friendly welcome, ex hoteliers they are passionate and practiced in the art of southern hospitality.With tea and coffee on your arrival you can relax in this warm and sunny home environment. "Willowby Downs" has lovely well appointed guest rooms, electric blankets, T.V, laundry options available with guests welcome to the internet, fax and Telephone facilities. Pam & David are able to arrange any extra tour or special events you may require.

Arrowtown *1 km N of Arrowtown*

Ella's B&B *B&B*

Joyce & Brian Egerton
119 Cotter Ave,
Arrowtown

Tel (03) 442 0266
or 021 071 1313
bj.egerton@xtra.co.nz

Double/Twin $140
Single $100
(Continental breakfast)
Children $20
2 King/Twin (2 bdrm)
Bathrooms: 2 Ensuite

A warm and friendly welcome awaits, when you come to stay at Ella's B&B. Spacious rooms each with their own ensuites and doors onto a sunny balcony. A continental breakfast served either in the dining room or out on the deck. Enjoy the views over Tobins track, the hills above the Arrow River. Your hosts Joyce & Brian await your company at Ella's B&B in beautiful Arrowtown.

Arrowtown *0.5 km S of Central Arrowtown*

B&B Approved

Bernsleigh B&B *B&B Homestay*

David & Linda Peek
21 Bracken Street,
Arrowtown, 9302

Tel (03) 442 1550
or 021 969 610
or 021 969 611
Fax (03) 4421540
lindapeek@xtra.co.nz

Double/Twin $150
Single $120
(Continental breakfast)
Children price negotiable
2 Queen 1 Twin 2 Single (3 bdrm)
Bathrooms: 1 Ensuite 1 Guest share

Welcome to our modern comfortable home situated in a peaceful location overlooking a world-class golf course and panoramic mountain and rural scenes. Private entry leads to your tastefully furnished rooms. enjoy the sunny private courtyard or cosy indoor atmosphere. Facilities available include: email, fax, laundry and BBQ along with assistance in further activity planning. A short walk to a range of cafes and restaurants. Golf courses, ski fields, walking tracks nearby. Come and enjoy the warm hospitality of David & Linda.

Arrowtown - Queenstown *4 km W of Arrowtown*

Willowbrook *B&B Apartment with Kitchen Cottage with Kitchen*

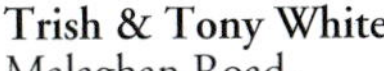

Trish & Tony White
Malaghan Road,
RD 1, Queenstown

Tel (03) 442 1773
or (027) 451 6739
Fax (03) 442 1780
info@willowbrook.net.nz
www.willowbrook.net.nz

Double/Twin $155-$185
Single $125-$145
(Continental breakfast)
Cottage $315 (4 persons)
Visa MC Diners Amex accepted
Children welcome
2 King 2 Queen 3 Twin (7 bdrm)
3 in B&B, 2 in Cottage, 2 in Barn
Bathrooms: 5 Ensuite 1 Private

Willowbrook offers both B&B and self-catering accommodation in an idyllic rural setting below Coronet Peak. Only 15 minutes from Queenstown and 5 minutes from Millbrook Resort and historic Arrowtown, we are close to skifields and golf courses. Our accommodation comprises The Main House (B&B); The Cottage (self-catering) and The Barn (self-catering). All have Sky TV, wireless broadband and own barbeque. The large garden contains a tennis court, luxurious spa pool and some very friendly sheep. Trish & Tony look forward to welcoming you.

Arrowtown - Queenstown *14 km N of Arrowtown*

Crown View *B&B Farmstay*

Caroll & Reg Fraser
457 Littles Road, Dalefield,
Queenstown 9371

Tel (03) 442 9411 or 0274 495 156
or 0274 767 576
Fax (03) 442 9411
info@crownview.co.nz
www.crownview.co.nz

Double/Twin $165-$190
(Full breakfast)
Dinner by arrangement
Barbeque available
Visa MC accepted
Children welcome
3 King (3 bdrm)
Rose Room is large enough
to include roll away bed
Bathrooms: 1 Ensuite 2 Private
Rose Room has spa bath in private bathroom

Peaceful,relaxing rural setting. Fantastic views of Remarkable mountains and Crown Range. 15 minutes from either Queenstown and Arrowtown. 3 double bedrooms two with super king-size beds,1 with king. Rooms have tea & coffee facilities,& TVs. Relax with us and enjoy our rural lifestyle,(A home away from home) along with our west highland dog, Archie, sheep,cows (Issie & Bella)Alpacas (Oscar & Jimmie) and lots of chickens. Come as a guest leave as a friend.

Arrowtown - Queenstown *12 km NE of Queenstown*

The Ferry Bed & Breakfast (circa 1872) *B&B or Cottage*

Glenys & Kevin Reynolds
92 Spence Road, Lower Shotover,
Queenstown, 9371

Tel (03) 442 2194 or 0800 111 804
or 027 235 6104
Fax (03) 442 2190
info@ferry.co.nz
www.ferry.co.nz

Double/Twin $195-$235
Single $195-$235
(Full breakfast)
Children Under 12 free
Whole House Deals -
Contact for further information
Visa MC accepted
Children welcome
1 King 1 Double 1 Twin (3 bdrm)
2 Units, Unit 2 has an addition of Twin Room
Bathrooms: 1 Ensuite 1 Private Dbl with ensuite,Or dbl/Family with Private Bathroom

Unique Historic B&B formerly a popular hotel for over 100 years. Kevin has traced the hotel's history back to 1868 - photos display this throughout. Glenys enjoys helping you to make the most of your stay in Queenstown offering advice & information. Kevin loves to talk Fly Fishing and Buckley our friendly English Springer likes to walk you along our beautiful track by the river. Situated in a delightful rural area, the perfect place to relax after a busy day. Free Wireless Broadband.

Queenstown *0.3 km S of Queenstown Central*

The Stable *B&B Homestay*

Isobel & Gordon McIntyre
17 Brisbane Street,
Queenstown 9300

Tel (03) 442 9251
Fax (03) 442 8293
gimac@queenstown.co.nz
www.thestablebb.co.nz

Double/Twin $200
Single $160
(Full breakfast)
Visa MC accepted
Pet free home
Not suitable for children
1 King 1 Double 2 Single (2 bdrm)
Both our rooms have a double, or twin, plus a single bed
Bathrooms: 1 Ensuite 1 Private

A 135 year old stone stable, shares a private courtyard with our home. The Garden Room is in the house. Our home is in a quiet cul-de-sac less than 100 metres from the beach, shops and restaurants are within easy walking distance. Both rooms are well heated with views of garden, lake or mountains. We are booking agents for all sightseeing tours. We have bred Welsh ponies and now enjoy weaving, cooking, gardening, sailing and the outdoors. We have an interest in a successful vineyard and enjoy drinking and talking about wine. Directions: Please Phone.

Queenstown *1.8 km NE of Queenstown Central*

B&B Approved

Birchall House *B&B*

Joan & John Blomfield
118 Panorama Terrace, Larchwood Heights, Queenstown 9300

Tel (03) 442 9985
Fax (03) 442 9980
birchall.house@xtra.co.nz
www.zqn.co.nz/birchall

Double/Twin $160-$180
Single $130-$145
(Continental breakfast)
Children $50
Visa MC accepted
Pet free home Children welcome
1 Queen 2 Twin (2 bdrm)
Double room has smooth-top, fridge, microwave
Bathrooms: 2 Ensuite

Welcome to our Queenstown home, purpose built for guests in a beautiful setting. Birchall House enjoys a magnificent 200 degree view of lake and mountains within walking distance of town. Guest accommodation is spacious, private, separate entrances, centrally heated, electric blankets,tea/coffee making facilities, smoke-free. From Frankton Road, turn up Hensman Road, left into Sunset Lane. Or, Frankton Road, turn up Suburb Street, right into Panorama Terrace. Access via Hensman & Sunset Lane. Off-street parking. Visit our website: www.zqn.co.nz/birchall.

Queenstown *0.5 km N of Queenstown Central*

B&B Approved

Anna's Cottage & Rose Suite *Cottage with Kitchen Suite with kitchen*

Myrna & Ken Sangster
67 Thompson Street, Queenstown

Tel (03) 442 8994
or 027 693 3025
Fax (03) 441 8994
annas.rose@xtra.co.nz

Double/Twin $125-$155
Single $105
(Breakfast by arrangement)
Visa MC accepted
Children welcome
1 King/Twin 1 Queen (2 bdrm)
Cottage 1b/room, Rose 1b/room
Bathrooms: 2 Ensuite

A warm welcome to Anne's Cottage and Rose Suite. The cottage has fully equipped kitchen, living room, T.V., new ensuite, hairdryer, washing machine, superking bed. Quality towels and linen. Rose Suite attached to the end of our home, self-contained with small kitchen, queen bed with new ensuite, T.V., washing machine. Both serviced daily. Enjoy the peaceful mountain views. Private drive and parking at the Cottage. A few minutes from central Queenstown. Breakfast available at extra charge.

Queenstown *1 km N of Queenstown*

Monaghans *B&B*
Elsie & Pat Monaghan
4 Panorama Terrace,
Queenstown

Tel (03) 442 8690
Fax (03) 442 8620
patmonaghan@xtra.co.nz
www.bandbclub.com/pages/monaghan

Double/Twin $110
Single $90
(Continental breakfast)
1 Queen (1 bdrm)
Bathrooms: 1 Ensuite

Welcome to our home in a quiet location, walking distance to town. Enjoy this panoramic view while you breakfast. 1 couple - personal attention. Spacious comfortable room with separate entrance and garden patio. Queen bed, own bathroom, TV, fridge and tea/coffee biscuits. Interests - music, gardening, sport, travel. We will enjoy your company but respect your privacy. Off-street parking. Directions: turn right up Suburb Street off Frankton Road which is the main road into Queenstown then first right into Panorama Terrace.

Queenstown *0.5 km NE of Town Centre*

Delfshaven *Homestay*
Irene Mertz
11 Salmond Place
(off Kent Street),
Queenstown

Tel (03) 441 1447
irenemertz@xtra.co.nz

Double/Twin $200
Single $150
(Special breakfast)
Visa MC accepted
Pet free home
Not suitable for children
1 Queen (1 bdrm)
Bathrooms: 1 Private
Full Bathroom

Nestled on the lower slopes, close to town and in a quiet street, is my warm, modern 2-storied home offering great hospitality, magnificent views from all rooms over lake, mountains and township. The comfortable guest suite has bath and shower, TV and tea-making facilities and opens to the view and garden. It's a 5 minute downhill walk to the town. I am a retired teacher, widely travelled. I enjoy good food and wine, love art, music and meeting people. My piano waits to be played.

Queenstown *0.8 km NW of Central Queenstown*

Coronet View Apartments & B&B
Luxury B&B Apartment with Kitchen Guest House Private B&B - Hotel

Neil Dempsey
30 Huff Street, Queenstown

Tel (03) 442 6766 or 0800 89 6766
or 027 432 0895 Fax (03) 442 6767
stay@coronetview.com
www.coronetview.com

Double/Twin $165-$250 Single $150-$230
(Continental breakfast)
Children $30 Dinner $35-$70
Apartments from $180-$700
Visa MC Eftpos accepted Children welcome
3 King/Twin 6 King 1 Queen (10 bdrm)
Bathrooms: 9 Ensuite 1 Private

Centrally located just ten minutes walk from town, Coronet View enjoys superb views of Coronet Peak, The Remarkables and Lake Wakatipu.

Beautifully appointed rooms offer every comfort in either hosted accommodation or private apartments. Coronet View offers luxurious guest rooms either B&B or fully self-contained private apartments.

Guest common areas occasionally shared with gorgeous persian cat include elevated and spacious dining and living areas, outdoor decks, a sunny conservatory, outdoor barbeque, pool and jacuzzi area and computers with internet access.

Bed & Breakfast - A home away from home with true kiwi hospitality. Most rooms feature super king beds with lovely quilts, sheepskin electric blankets, tiled ensuites etc.

Your hosts are knowledgeable local people who can recommend and book your activities at no extra cost.

Apartments on site Queenstown. 1-6 bedroomed ensuited apartments. Most configurations feature ensuites, super king beds, generous living areas, fully equipped kitchens and laundries.

Queenstown *1.2 km N of Queenstown*

B&B Approved

Campbells on Earnslaw *B&B*

Aderianne & Bevan Campbell
9 Earnslaw Terrace,
Queenstown

Tel (03) 442 7783
Fax (03) 442 7784
stay@campbells.net.nz
www.campbells.net.nz

Double/Twin $175
Single $135
(Continental breakfast)
Extra person $50
Children welcome
1 Queen 2 Single (2 bdrm)
Bathrooms: 1 Private

We look forward to welcoming you to our home, which has 180 degree spectacular panoramic views of lake, mountains and golf course. Guests own private living room with balcony, TV, fridge, toast, tea & coffee making facilities. Ideal for 2 couples or family, only 1 party at a time. Experienced hosts we can advise and arrange your sightseeing and activities. From Frankton Road turn up Suburb Street, right into Panorama Terrace, right into Earnslaw Terrace. We are only a 10 minute stroll into town centre.

Queenstown *2 km NE of Queenstown*

Lake Vista Bed & Breakfast *Luxury B&B*

Lucille & Graeme Simpson
62 Hensman Road,
Queenstown, 9300

Tel (03) 441 8838
Fax (03) 441 8938
bookings@lakevista.co.nz
www.lakevista.co.nz

Double/Twin $175-$245
Single $130-$195 (Full breakfast)
Dinner By arrangement
Wireless internet available
Visa MC Eftpos accepted
Pet free home Children Welcome
1 King/Twin 2 Queen
2 Twin 1 Single (3 bdrm)
1 full ensuite room and 2 share facilities
Bathrooms: 1 Ensuite 1 Guest share
Large walk-in shower in new private guest share bathroom.

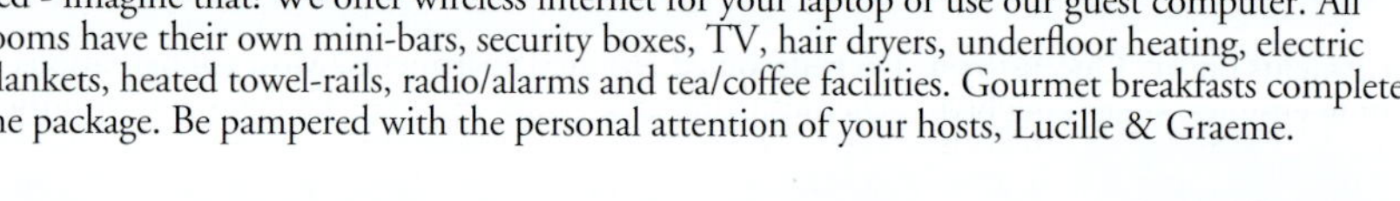

Set high on Queenstown hill, a major feature of Lake Vista is our encompassing views over Lake Wakatipu to the Remarkables mountain range. You can even enjoy the view lying in bed - imagine that! We offer wireless internet for your laptop or use our guest computer. All rooms have their own mini-bars, security boxes, TV, hair dryers, underfloor heating, electric blankets, heated towel-rails, radio/alarms and tea/coffee facilities. Gourmet breakfasts complete the package. Be pampered with the personal attention of your hosts, Lucille & Graeme.

Queenstown *3 km NE of Queenstown centre*

Larch Hill B&B/Homestay

B&B Homestay Apartment with Kitchen

Lesley & Chris Marlow
16 Panners Way, Queenstown

Tel (03) 442 4811 or 027 339 6483 Fax (03) 441 8882
info@larchhill.com www.larchhill.com

Double/Twin $140-$200 Single $120-$160
(Special breakfast)
Apartment (sleeps 4) $230-$320
Visa MC Amex Eftpos accepted Children welcome
2 King 1 Queen 1 Twin 2 Single (4 bdrm)
King; Queen; Twin; S/C Apartment
Bathrooms: 2 Ensuite 2 Private
All rooms have ensuite or private bathroom

Lesley and Chris offer you a warm welcome to Larch Hill B&B in beautiful Queenstown, purpose built on an elevated site overlooking Lake Wakatipu.

As featured in 'National Geographic Traveler' and Cathay Pacific's 'Discovery' magazines, all rooms in our comfortable and relaxing homestay have spectacular lake and mountain views, with tea/coffee making facilities. A restful theme flows through the bedrooms into the dining room with its library, opening onto a sunny courtyard surrounded by cottage gardens.

We are just 3 minutes' drive from the centre of Queenstown and within walking distance of the lake. Public transport passes our street regularly. Breakfasts are generous with homemade bread, freshly baked croissants and pastries, fresh fruit salad, yoghurt, and freshly ground, percolated coffee. Our self-contained apartment is ideal for families or small groups. We can provide pre-arranged complimentary pickups from Queenstown airport. Feel free to use our local knowledge to help plan your itinerary. We are booking agents for Queenstown tours and activities. We have no pets and are non-smokers, but guests are welcome to smoke outdoors. Free wireless internet facilities available.

Directions: from Frankton drive 2.5 kms on State Highway 6A (Frankton Road) towards Queenstown. Turn into Goldfield Heights at Sherwood Manor. Second left is Panners Way. Larch Hill B&B is No. 16 at the end of the accessway, 1/2 way down Panners Way on the left.

Queenstown *1.40 km SE of Queenstown*

Kemnay *B&B*

Heather & Fraser Ronald
57 Panorama Tce,
Queenstown
Tel (03) 442 6270
hfronald@xtra.co.nz

Double/Twin $130-$140
Single $100
(Full breakfast)
Children by arrangement
1 Queen 1 Twin (2 bdrm)
Bathrooms: 1 Private
Bath & Shower

Heather and Fraser warmly welcome you to their Queenstown Home. Wonderful views of lake and mountains, also overlooks golf course. Queen bed, plus twin, private bathroom. Small comfortable seating area with tea and coffee making facilities. One party at a time. Off street parking. 1.4km from town centre.Directions: Approaching Queenstown along Frankton Road, turn right into Hensman Road, then first turn left inot Panorama Tce.

Queenstown *14.5 km SE of Queenstown*

B&B Approved

Bayswater *B&B*

Marie and Angus Buchanan
4 Cedar Drive,
Kelvin Heights,
Queenstown, 9300
Tel (03) 441 2336
or Mobile 027 424 1890
vinnetta@kol.co.nz

Double/Twin $140-$155
Single $90-$110
(Continental breakfast)
2 King/Twin 1 Queen (2 bdrm)
Bathrooms: 2 Ensuite

We would like to welcome you to our warm sunny Kelvin Heights home, with spectacular lake and mountain views. Our rooms have comfortable beds, electric blankets, heaters and own television. Tea/coffee facilities available. We are a 15 minute senic drive to downtown Queenstown. 1/2 hour drive to either Coronet or Remarkables ski fields, 2 minute walk to the beach and amazing walking tracks. A 5 minute drive to the spectacular Kelvin Heights Golf course and less than 1/2 hour to the Arrowtown and Milbrook courses

Queenstown Hill *1 km NW of Queenstown*

B&B Approved

Fine Accommodation *Luxury B&B*

Dale Zimmerman
5 Vancouver Drive,
Queenstown, 9300

Tel (03) 441 8866 or 027 434 7209
zimmermanenterprises@xtra.co.nz
www.fineaccommodation.co.nz

Double/Twin $220-$260
(Continental breakfast)
Dinner by arrangment
Special for Nov $220 per night
including nibbles & wine
Visa MC accepted
3 King (3 bdrm)
Each with own ensuites
Bathrooms: 3 Ensuite
One with spa bath

A luxury bed and breakfast with 3 large bedrooms each with own ensuite,also a private Lounge for the guests to relax in.
Recent comments:
"Wonderful accommodation with magnificent view from every aspect." - Nancy Viner USA.
"Great views, great room and delicious breakfast." - David and Pat U.K.
SPECIAL FOR NOVEMBER AND DECEMBER BOOK AND ON ARRIVAL YOU WILL BE GIVEN A DINNER VOUCHER FOR $30

Garston *50 km S of Queenstown*

B&B Approved

Castle Hill Lodge Bed and Breakfast *B&B*

Mark and Sharon Ford
23 Mcmillan Road, Garston, 9750

Tel (03) 248 8816
markandsharonford@hotmail.com
www.castlehilllodge.co.nz

Double/Twin $150-$220
(Full breakfast)
Children very welcome and
can help us feed our animals
Two course dinner by arrangemrnt
Lighter meals upon request
Visa MC Amex accepted
2 Double 1 Twin (3 bdrm)
1 double en suite,
the other 2 are shared bathroom
Bathrooms: 1 Ensuite 1 Guest share

Nestled within the stunning northern Southland countryside with 9 acres of it's own grounds is the charming Castle Hill Lodge. We will be delighted to offer you a warm welcome, home cooked food and cosy accommodation.The sparkling Upper Mataura river is within walking distance from our home and has some of the best trout fishing in the world. So whether its bustling Queenstown, cruising on the Milford Sounds or just sitting on our deck watching the sun descend. We look forward to your visit

Garston *50 km S of Queenstown*

Menlove Homestay *B&B Homestay Separate Suite*

B&B Approved

Bev & Matt Menlove
17 Blackmore Road,
PO Box 39,
Garston 9750

Tel (03) 248 8516
mattmenlove@slingshot.co.nz

Double/Twin $90
Single $50
(Continental breakfast)
Dinner $25 by arrangement
1 Double 1 Single (1 bdrm)
Bathrooms: 1 Ensuite

We are organic gardeners and our other interests include lawn bowls, sailing, gliding and alternative energy. Garston is New Zealand's most inland village with the Mataura River (famous for its fly fishing) flowing through the valley, surrounded by the Hector Range and the Eyre Mountains. A fishing guide is available with advance notice. For day trips, Garston is central to Queenstown, Te Anau, Milford Sound or Invercargill. We look forward to meeting you.

Garston *50 km S of Queenstown*

Naylor House *Cottage with Kitchen*

John and Avis McIver
33 Naylor Road,
Garston,
Southland

Tel (03) 248 8809
or 027 653 6110
Fax (03) 248 8809
naylorhouse@slingshot.co.nz
www.naylorhouse.co.nz

Double/Twin $150
(Breakfast by arrangement)
Dinner by arrangement
Visa MC accepted
Pet free home
Children welcome
1 King/Twin 1 Queen 2 Twin (3 bdrm)
Bathrooms: 1 Private

Welcome to Historic Naylor House situated in the heart of the beautiful and tranquil Garston Valley. Garston is Central to Queenstown, Te Anau, Milford Sound and Invercargill. The Mataura River which is famed for its fly fishing is on our doorstep. We look forward to sharing all our local knowledge and our beautiful location with you.

Clyde *8 km W of Alexandra*

Argyll Farmstay *B&B Homestay*
Trish & Alan May
1 Annan Street, Clyde,
Central Otago

Tel (03) 449 3268
or 027 431 8241
Fax (03) 449 3268
argyllonclyde@yahoo.co.nz
www.argyllonclyde.co.nz

Double/Twin $130-$160
Single $80-$120
(Full breakfast)
Children negotiable
Dinner $30 by arrangement
Visa MC accepted
Children welcome
2 Queen 1 Twin (3 bdrm)
Comforable beds, quality linen, plush bath towels
Bathrooms: 1 Ensuite 1 Private 1 Guest share
Ensuite includes a bath.

Alan and Trish welcome you to their near new modern home situated in historic gold-mining town of Clyde.They will make your stay a memorable one, pampering you with exquisite accommodation and cuisine. Relax in the spa, enjoy the comforable beds and the delicious cooked breakfast.

Alexandra *3.5 km N of Alexandra*

Duart *B&B Homestay*
Mary & Keith McLean
Bruce's Hill Lane,
356 Manuherikia Road,
No. 3 RD Alexandra, 9393

Tel (03) 448 9190
or 027 316 3569
Fax (03) 448 9190
duart.homestay@xtra.co.nz
www.duarthomestay.co.nz

Double/Twin $110-$110
Single $90-$90
(Continental breakfast)
Children negotiable
Dinner $25 by arrangement
Visa MC accepted
Pet free home Children and pets welcome
1 Double 1 Twin 1 Single (3 bdrm)
Double downstairs, twin and single upstairs
Bathrooms: 1 Ensuite downstairs 1 Guest share upstairs

Your accredited Kiwi Hosts, Mary and Keith, welcome you to our secluded home, 5 minutes from Alexandra. Your privacy is assured, but we enjoy company and conversation if that is your wish. Relish the spectacular views from our extensive stone terraced garden, or relax in the sitting room, library or verandahs. Revel in the myriad activities and experiences Alexandra offers; e.g. the climate, Rail Trail, award winning vineyards, galleries, mountain biking, kayaking etc. Laundry, Sky TV. Complimentary tea, coffee, biscuits, fruit, pre-dinner drink and nibbles.

Roxburgh - Ettrick *17 km SW of Ettrick*

Wilden Station Homestead *B&B Homestay Farmstay*

Sarah & Peter Adam
Wilden School Road,
Wilden,
West Otago

Tel (03) 204 8115
Fax (03) 204 8116
wildenstation@farmside.co.nz

Double/Twin $190
Single $120
(Special breakfast)
Children $20
Dinner $55
Visa MC accepted
Children welcome
2 Queen 2 Single (3 bdrm)
Bathrooms: 1 Ensuite 1 Private

Experience high-country farm life with us, our two boys and two cats. Watch our dogs work the sheep. Stroll through trees to a small lake, explore our historic farm buildings, fish the Pomahaka River, tour the property, or simply relax in our gracious homestead. Enjoy superb meals prepared by your internationally experienced chef/ hostess (all by prior arrangement). Unwind in our tranquil surroundings about 2 hours from Dunedin, Queenstown, Wanaka. Families most welcome. Please telephone for directions.

Roxburgh - Millers Flat *16 km S of Roxburgh*

Quince Cottage *B&B Cottage No Kitchen*

B&B Approved

Wendy Gunn & Cally Johnstone
Rapid No 1581,
Teviot Road,
Millers Flat

Tel (03) 446 6889
thequince@clear.net.nz
www.quincecottage.co.nz

Double/Twin $220
Single $125
(Special breakfast)
Dinner $65pp
Visa MC accepted
1 Queen
Bathrooms: 1 Ensuite

Quince Cottage - half way between Dunedin and Queenstown/Wanaka or a destination in itself. The Cottage is set apart from the house surrounded by a big open garden dotted with trees, and lawn stretching into the distance. It is open plan with a dining table, TV, CD player, fridge, air-con and heating. Meals are served in the main house, however if you wish to dine in the cottage we are happy to deliver your meals. Dinner is $65 pp - 3 courses and complimentary Central Otago wine.

Middlemarch *4 km SW of Middlemarch*

B&B Approved

The Farm *B&B Homestay Farmstay*

Lynley & Glynne Smith
154 Farm Road,
RD 2, Middlemarch

Tel (03) 464 3610
or 027 436 2423
or 021 224 3004
Fax (03) 464 3612
glynley@xtra.co.nz
www.thefarm-homestay.com

Double/Twin $110
Single $90 (Full breakfast)
Dinner $45pp-
3 course meal including wine
Children and pets welcome
1 King 1 Twin (2 bdrm)
Can be altered to 4 singles
Bathrooms: 1 Guest share
Spa available outside

Our charming old stone house and gardens are set amongst mature oaks, with the spectacular Rock and Pillar Range as a backdrop. Lynley & Glynne welcome you to their peaceful relaxed haven which includes a 200 acre farm, sheep, cattle, horses, 1 family cat & a Jack Russell dog. From high country farming background, interested in horses, hunting and a tranquil lifestyle. On the Central Otago Rail Trail, 1 hour from Dunedin, this is a convenient and hospitable stop for exploring this picturesque area.

Lawrence *30 km N of Balclutha*

B&B Approved

The Ark *B&B*

Frieda Betman
8 Harrington Place (Main Road)

Tel (03) 485 9328
the.ark@xtra.co.nz
www.theark.co.nz

Double/Twin $100
Single $60
(Full breakfast)
Children $15
2 Double 1 Twin 1 Single (4 bdrm)
Bathrooms: 1 Family share

My home is on the main road near the picnic ground with its avenue of poplars. The house is 100 years old, has character, charm and a lived in feeling. It's home to Ambrose & Pumpkin, my cats and Holly, a miniature Foxie. Guestrooms are restful with fresh flowers, fruit, and breakfast includes hot bread, croissants, home-made jams. Free-range eggs. There is a lovely peaceful atmosphere in our early gold mining town. Approx. 45 minutes to Dunedin airport, just over an hour to Dunedin.

Palmerston - Waikouaiti *40 km N of Dunedin*

Boutique Bed & Breakfast *Luxury B&B Farmstay Separate Suite*

Barbara & John Morgan
107 Jefferis Road,
Waikouaiti RD 2,
Palmerston South

Tel (03) 465 7239
or 027 224 8212
or 021 161 0243
Fax (03) 465 7239
info@boutiquebedandbreakfast.co.nz
www.boutiquebedandbreakfast.co.nz

Double/Twin $150-$180
Single $130-$150
(Full breakfast)
Visa MC accepted
3 Queen 1 Double (3 bdrm)
Bathrooms: 3 Ensuite

An historic cottage standing in our homestead grounds. Unique private rooms with ensuites designed for your comfort and pleasure. French doors open to wooden verandahs with views of the deer park, garden or tennis court.Enjoy your sumptuous breakfast in our homestead.Experience John's popular deer farm tour with dogs Mildred and George. Allow at least 2 days to explore beautiful coastal Otago. Close to cafes and restaurants. Rated by recent guests the best B&B from 22 other stays.

~

Dunedin *5.5 km E of Dunedin Centre*

Glenrowan Heights *Homestay Separate Suite*

B&B Approved

Sue & Dick Williman
60 Connell Street,
Waverley,
Dunedin

Tel 021 455 874
dick@williman.co.nz
www.bnbdunedin.co.nz

Double/Twin $120-$150
Single $110-$140
(Continental breakfast)
2 Queen 1 Twin (3 bdrm)
Bathrooms: 1 Ensuite 1 Guest share

Our new home offers all the modern conveniences and the most amazing panoramic views of Dunedin and the Otago Harbour, right out to the heads. We are conveniently located not far off the Highcliff road that runs down the Otago Peninsula to Larnach Castle and the Albatross centre. Sue and I have recently retired from operating a motel in the city. We enjoy advising guest on the many opportunities on offer. Our house is at the end of the top section of the private road.

Dunedin *2 km W of Dunedin*

Magnolia House *B&B*

Joan & George Sutherland
18 Grendon Street,
Maori Hill,
Dunedin 9010

Tel (03) 467 5999
mrsuth@xtra.co.nz

Double/Twin $130
Single $100
(Special breakfast)
Not suitable for children
1 Queen 1 Double 2 Single (3 bdrm)
Bathrooms: 1 Private 1 Family share

Our quiet turn-of-the-century villa sits in broad, flower-bordered lawns backed by native bush with beautiful, tuneful birds. All rooms have electric heating, comfortable beds with electric blanket, and antiques, while the queen room has an adjoining balcony. Close by is Moana Pool, the glorious Edwardian house Olveston, and Otago Golf Course. Our special breakfast will set you up for the day. We have a courtesy car, and two burmese cats. It is not suitable for children or smokers.

~

Dunedin *7 km NE of Dunedin*

Harbourside B&B *B&B Homestay*

Shirley & Don Parsons
6 Kiwi Street,
St Leonards,
Dunedin

Tel (03) 471 0690
Fax (03) 471 0063
harboursidebb@xtra.co.nz

Double/Twin $85-$100
Single $70-$100
(Full breakfast)
Children $20
Dinner $30
Visa MC accepted
Pet free home
Children welcome
1 King/Twin 2 Queen 3 Single (3 bdrm)
Bathrooms: 1 Ensuite 1 Guest share

We are situated in a quiet suburb overlooking Otago Harbour and surrounding hills. Within easy reach of all local attractions. Lovely garden or harbour views from all rooms. Children very welcome. Directions: drive into city on one-way system watch for Highway 88 sign follow Anzac Avenue onto Ravensbourne Road. Continue approx 5km to St Leonards turn left at Playcentre opposite Boatshed into Pukeko Street then left into Kaka Road, straight ahead to Kiwi Street turn left into Number 6.

Dunedin *1 km W of Dunedin*

Highbrae Guesthouse *B&B Guest House wireless internet availability*

Fienie & Stephen Clark
376 High Street,
Dunedin 9016
Tel (03) 479 2070
or 027 4328 470
Fax (03) 479 2100
enquiries@highbrae.co.nz
www.highbrae.co.nz

Double/Twin $110-$140
Single $80-$110
(Continental breakfast)
Children $25
if sharing room with parents
Cooked breakfast extra
Visa MC Amex accepted
Pet free home Children welcome
1 King 2 Queen 1 Twin 1 Single (4 bdrm)
Doubles; Queen, King, Queen self contained, Twin singles
Bathrooms: 1 Private 1 Guest share 1 Family share

Experience a taste of early Dunedin. This heritage home was built on the High Street in 1908 to provide first class accommodation to its residents. Today it is still an impressive home with spectacular views of the city and harbour. The upstairs guest rooms and self contained unit are carefully maintained to preserve their character for visitors, who delight in the many features in the home. Wireless internet is available and a courtesy van can meet you at the bus or train if required.

Dunedin *1 km W of Dunedin*

Grandview Bed & Breakfast *B&B Guest House*

Simon, Sarah & Trish Clausen
360 High Street,
Dunedin 9016
Tel (03) 474 9472
or 021 101 9857
or 0800 749 472
Fax (03) 474 9473
nzgrandview@msn.com
www.grandview.co.nz

Double/Twin $100-$195
Single $80-$145
(Continental breakfast)
Extra person or child $20
Visa MC Amex Eftpos accepted
Children welcome
6 Queen 2 Twin 4 Single (7 bdrm)
From Luxury Spa Suites To
Comfy Queen Rooms
Bathrooms: 3 Ensuite 2 Guest share

Grandview is one of Dunedin's oldest listed Mansions dating back to the 1850's. Open to guests for a lovely Bed & Breakfast experience with amazing views and the charm of Dunedin's heritage. Just a short stroll to the City Centre, Cafes, Restaurants and Bars, this makes Grandview a convenient location for guests. We have Bedrooms to suit all budgets, plus Kitchen and Laundry facilities, Sauna and Internet access available.

Dunedin *0.1 km N of Dunedin Central*

B&B Approved

Albatross Inn *B&B*
Glynis Rees
770 George Street, Dunedin,
Tel (03) 477 2727 or 0800 441 441
Fax (03) 477 2108 albatross.inn@xtra.co.nz
www.albatross.inn.co.nz

Double/Twin $110-$160 Single $95-$110
(Special breakfast)
Children $15 Visa MC Diners Amex Eftpos accepted
Pet free home Children welcome
3 King 4 Queen 2 Double 5 Single (8 bdrm)
Bathrooms: 8 Ensuite

Welcome to Dunedin and Albatross Inn! Our beautiful late Victorian house is ideally located on the main street close to the university, gardens, museum, shops and restaurants.

Our attractive rooms have ensuite/private bathrooms, telephone, TV, radio, central heating, tea/coffee, warm duvets and electric blankets on modern beds. Firm beds upon request. Quiet rooms at rear of house. Several rooms have kitchenette and fridge.

Enjoy our sumptious breakfast in our cosy breakfast room. We serve freshly baked bread and muffins, fresh fruit salad, yoghurt, juices, cereals, teas, freshly brewed coffee. We are happy to recommend and book tours for you. All wildlife tours pick up and drop off here. We can recommend many great places to eat, most just a short walk down George Street. Nearby laundry, non-smoking, cot and highchair.

Some comments from our visitors Book! The right balance of everything location, breakfast and lovely room. Delightfully different. Absolutely fantastic as always. Home away from Home. A touch of Class, lovely home beautifully presented. Perfecto!

Homepage: www.albatross.inn.co.nz. Winter special $90 Double - special conditions apply. Complimentary e-mail and wireless internet.

Dunedin *10 km SW of Dunedin*

Grant's Farm *B&B Apartment with Kitchen*

B&B Approved

Tom and Jeanette Grant
151 Old Brighton Road,
Fairfield RD 1,
Dunedin 9076

Tel (03) 488 0336
Fax (03) 488 0364
grantsfarm@xtra.co.nz
www.visit-dunedin.co.nz/grantsfarm.html

Double/Twin $110-$170
Single $90-$120
(Continental breakfast)
Children by arrangement
Dinner not supplied
Visa MC accepted
Pet free home
1 Queen 1 Double 1 Single (2 bdrm)
1 queen,1 double + 1 single
Bathrooms: 1 Ensuite

Our typical NZ woolshed on 20ha is now a unique home with fully self contained guest accommodation with woodfire and wireless internet. Situated on the Kaikorai Estuary we have heaps of bird life sheep cattle and also an airstrip with biplanes. We are in a peaceful rural setting with wonderful views, only 15 minutes from Dunedin Airport and 8 minutes to either Dunedin or Mosgiel. Excellent restaurants and miles of beach walks are minutes away. 1 loving outdoor cat. Guests wish they could stay longer!

~

Dunedin *0.5 km SW of Dunedin*

Deacons Court *B&B*

Jill McDonald & Roger Whitworth
342 High Street,
Dunedin, 9016

Tel (03) 477 9053
or 0800 268 252
Fax (03) 477 9058
info@deaconscourt.com
www.deaconscourt.com

Double/Twin $100-$160
Single $80-$130
(Full breakfast)
Children $20-$50
Visa MC Eftpos accepted
Children welcome
2 King/Twin 2 King
1 Queen 3 Single (4 bdrm)
Extra large and spacious
Bathrooms: 2 Ensuite 1 Private 1 Family share

Deacons Court is a charming superior spacious Victorian villa 1km walking distance from the city centre and is on the city's heritage building register. We are only 500m from cafes, bars and some of Dunedin's unique attractions and offer you friendly but unobtrusive hospitality in a quiet secure haven. Guests can relax in our delightful rose garden and spacious conservatory. Our extra large bedrooms , have ensuite or private bathrooms, TV and comfortable seating. Complimentary broadband, 24 hour tea or coffee, and free parking available.

Dunedin *1km S of City Centre*

City Sanctuary Bed & Breakfast *B&B*

Karen & Paul
165 Maitland Street
City Rise
Dunedin 9016

Tel (03) 474 5002
Fax (03) 474 5006
bnbenquiry@citysanctuary.co.nz
www.citysanctuary.co.nz

Double/Twin $135-$195
Single $115-$160
(Special breakfast)
Children: By arrangement
Visa MC Amex accepted
Not suitable for children
3 Queen (3bdrm)
Bathrooms: 1 Ensuite 2 Private
Ensuite has a double spa bath

Welcome to our attractive restored villa, in an oasis of cottage gardens, yet only 1km to the city centre and all its attractions. Three spacious bedrooms each have; Queen bed with fleecy electric blanket, bath robes, fresh flowers, oil heater, phone, TV, and free broadband internet connection. Relax in the guest living room with home theatre, and free email, or unwind on the deck amidst the organic potager garden. Enjoy a special continental breakfast. Massage available by appointment. 4 cats. Not Suitable Mobility impaired

Otago Peninsula - Broad Bay *16 km E of Dunedin*

Chy-an-Dowr *B&B*

Susan & Herman van Velthoven
687 Portobello Road,
Broad Bay, Dunedin 9014

Tel (03) 478 0306
or 021 156 0715
or 021 036 5190
Fax (03) 478 0306
hermanvv@xtra.co.nz
www.chy-an-dowr.co.nz

Double/Twin $195-$225
(Special breakfast)
Visa MC accepted Pet free home
Not suitable for children
1 King/Twin 1 King 1 Queen (3 bdrm)
1 King ensuite, 1 King/Twin or Queen with private bathroom
Bathrooms: 1 Ensuite 1 Private

Chy-an-Dowr (House by the Water), quality boutique accommodation located midway on scenic Otago Peninsula. Our character 1920's home with its harbourside location has panoramic views and is situated across the road from a small beach and enroute to the Albatross and Penguin colonies. The upstairs guest area is spacious and private with a sunroom and two comfortable suites with bathrobes, tea/coffee, TV, fridge. Enjoy a delicious breakfast at your leisure. Originally from Holland, we enjoy welcoming people and sharing our wonderful location with them.

Otago Peninsula - Macandrew Bay *11 km E of Dunedin*

MacBay Retreat *B&B Cottage with Kitchen*
Jeff & Helen Hall
38 Bayne Terrace,
Macandrew Bay,
Dunedin 9014

Tel (03) 476 1475
Fax (03) 476 1975
jhall9@ihug.co.nz
www.macandrewbay.co.nz/macbayretreat

Double/Twin $135
Single $120
(Continental breakfast)
Extra person $25pp
Visa MC accepted
1 King 1 Double (1 bdrm)
Bathrooms: 1 Ensuite

Mac Bay Retreat - Otago Peninsula. Welcome to your private self-contained smoke-free retreat, 15 minutes from Dunedin centre on the Otago Peninsula. Relax with the spectacular view overlooking the harbour from Dunedin City to Port Chalmers. Your cosy retreat is separate from the host's house and gives you a choice of either a super king or double bed plus an ensuite, modern kitchen and TV. Suitable for 1 couple, possibly 2 couples, travelling together. Only minutes from Dunedin's most popular attractions.

~

Otago Peninsula - Portobello *20 km NE of Dunedin*

Peninsula B&B *B&B*
Toni & Stephen Swabey
4 Allans Beach Road,
Portobello,
Dunedin

Tel 0800 478 090
or (03) 478 0909
Fax (03) 478 0909
toni@peninsula.co.nz
www.peninsula.co.nz

Double/Twin $145-$195
Single $120-$140
(Full breakfast)
Children POA
Free wireless broadband internet
Visa MC accepted
Children welcome
1 King/Twin 1 King 2 Queen 1 Single (4 bdrm)
Bathrooms: 2 Ensuite 1 Guest share

Come and relax in the elegant and romantic Victorian ambience of our beautiful 1880s villa. Situated in peaceful gardens, enjoy wonderful views of the harbour from your ensuite room. Relish your delicious cooked breakfast in the morning, with home baking. Catch up with our complimentary newspaper and make yourself at home with tea/coffee making facilities. Keep in touch with home with our free wireless broadband internet. We are ideally located for wildlife and scenic attractions and just a minute's walk from Portobello's two restaurants.

Otago Peninsula - Portobello *20 km NE of Dunedin*

Captain Eady's Lookout *B&B Homestay*

Richard & Ana Good
2 Moss Street,
Portobello,
Dunedin 9014

Tel (03) 478 0537
or 021 478 785
capteady@earthlight.co.nz
www.capteady.co.nz

Double/Twin $160-$195
Single $150-$185
(Special breakfast)
Children negotiable
Dinner $40 by prior arrangement
Twin Room: $100-$120
Visa MC accepted
Children welcome
2 Queen 1 Twin (3 bdrm)
Bathrooms: 2 Ensuite 1 Family share

Captain Eady's Lookout is a delightful bed and breakfast on the water's edge. This character house, built early last century by Captain Eady, a ferry master, stands on a small bluff overlooking Otago Harbour. One bedroom opens onto a secluded garden, one overlooks the harbour. Breakfast in our conservatory whilst taking in the splendid harbour views. The house has many antiques and on the walls are paintings by local artists. You may sample the large jazz collection. Cats in residence.We are rainbow friendly.

Otago Peninsula - Portobello *20 km NE of Dunedin*

McAuley Glen Bed & Breakfast *Luxury Boutique Bed & Breakfast*

Mary & Pat Curtin
13 McAuley Road,
Portobello, Dunedin

Tel (03) 478 0724
or 021 237 1919
Fax (03) 478 0724
maryandpat@clear.net.nz
www.mcauleyglen.co.nz

Double/Twin $195-$240
Single $165-$195 (Special breakfast)
Children under 10 negotiable
Dinner By arrangement
Visa MC accepted
Children welcome
2 Queen 1 Twin (3 bdrm)
1 bedroom has ajoining twin room
Bathrooms: 2 Ensuite Spacious,walk in shower, heated tile floor.

Magical rural setting, romantic, private, peacfull, 3/4 acre of beautiful gardens with bird song. 5min walk to restaurants, hotel & dairy. 20min drive to Albatross, Penguin & Seal colonies. Suites have: Separate patio garden entrances, TV, CD, DVD, quality furnishings/fittings luxury bedding/bathrobes, Mini kitchen: micro wave,fridge, tea/coffee/baking/chocolates. Complimentery ale/wine, sauna & outdoor jacuzzi spa included. Room service, laundry & internet available. Mary & Pat operate Scenic & Wildlife Tours - sea kayaking & mountain biking. We look forward to sharing our piece of paradise with you.

Otago Peninsula - Broad Bay *15 km N of Dunedin*

Fantail Lodge *2 self-contained cottages with Kitchens*

Vic and Tessa Mills
682 Portobello Road,
Broad Bay, Dunedin

Tel (03) 478 0110
or 0274 156 222
fantail.lodge@xtra.co.nz

Double/Twin $150-$150
Single $100-$120
(Accommodation only)
Extra adults or children $20 each
Continental provisions extra
Visa MC accepted
Pet free home
Children welcome
2 Queen 2 Single (3 bdrm)
Bellbird (Pictured) has queen, Fantail has queen/2 singles
One ensuite in each cottage.

Peacefully situated on the beautiful Otago Peninsula, close to beaches, seals, penguins and albatrosses, our lush, harbourside garden contains two, delightfully rustic, self -contained cottages. Fantail Cottage has queen bed accommodation with two singles on a mezzanine. Bellbird offers a queen bed and an exclusive spa pool. Both are equipped for self catering or continental breakfast hampers by arrangement. Free use of kayaks. An ideal base for touring and a great location for a romantic getaway.

Mosgiel *2 km SW of Mosgiel*

The Trees *B&B*

Jenny Blackgrove & Rex Moore
70 Main South Road,
East Taieri,
Mosgiel 9024

Tel (03) 489 4837
or 021 0244 2839
Fax (03) 477 1479
rex.moore@clear.net.nz

Double/Twin $120
Single $75
(Full breakfast)
Dinner $45 by prior arrangement
Visa MC accepted
Not suitable for children
1 King 1 Twin (2 bdrm)
Large, sunny rooms, TV
Bathrooms: 1 Guest share
Shower and separate bath

Welcome to our quiet, semirural home set on an acre of lawns and trees. We are 15km SW of Dunedin, half-way between Dunedin and the airport. There are 3 golf courses in close proximity. Resident animals are 2 cats and a border collie dog named Dougal. Rex enjoys flying light aircraft and sailing, Jenny is a Cordon Bleu trained cook and besides cooking, Jenny's interests include gardening and reading. We both have travelled extensively. Facilities include off-street parking and make yourself tea, coffee & juice.

Mosgiel *1 km N of Mosgiel*

Marg's Manor *Homestay*

B&B Approved

Margaret
103 Main South Road,
East Taieri,
Mosgiel,
Dunedin

Tel (03) 489 2030
Fax (03) 489 2030
msscott@xtra.co.nz

Double/Twin $100
Single $80
(Continental breakfast)
Dinner $30- by arrangement
Full breakfast by arrangement
Not suitable for children
1 Queen (1 bdrm)
Bathrooms: 1 Ensuite

Haere Mai, welcome to my sunny cottage home situated halfway between Dunedin Airport and Dunedin city, with rural views over the Taieri Plains. Enjoy your own entrance and outdoor table just beside room, or relax up in the back garden spaces amongst the vegetables and herbs that I enjoy cooking with. Dinner and cooked breakfast by arrangement, off street parking available. I enjoy travelling, teach early childhood and I am 5th generation for local knowledge. Resident cat called Fluff.

Balclutha *4 km N of Balclutha/Catlins*

Lesmahagow *Luxury B&B Boutique*

B&B Approved

Noel & Kate O'Malley
146 Benhar Road,
Benhar,
RD 2,
Balclutha 9272

Tel (03) 418 2507
or 0800 301 224 (NZ only)
or 027 457 8465
lesmahagow@xtra.co.nz
www.lesmahagow.co.nz

Double/Twin $160-$190
(Full breakfast)
Dinner $40
Lunches on request
Visa MC Eftpos accepted
Children and pets welcome
2 Queen 1 Double 1 Single (3 bdrm)
Bathrooms: 3 Private

Lesmahagow offers excellent accommodation in an historic homestead and garden setting. Centrally situated, discerning travellers can make Lesmahagow their base to explore the Catlins region, Dunedin and the Otago Penninsula or the historic goldfields of Lawrence. Centrally heated, with delightful bedrooms and gorgeous bathrooms, you can be sure of wonderful hospitality and a truly memorable stay. Evening meals are our speciality and our breakfasts will satisfy all taste buds! Come and discover this hidden paradise! You will love the experience.

Kaka Point - The Catlins *21 km S of Balclutha*

Rata Cottage *B&B Cottage with Kitchen*

Jean Schreuder
31 Rata Street,
Kaka Point,
South Otago
Tel (03) 412 8779

Double/Twin $80
Single $75
(Continental breakfast)
Extra person $15
Children welcome
1 Twin (1 bdrm)
Bathrooms: 1 Ensuite

A fully self-contained sunny bed & breakfast unit in a tranquil bush garden setting, with sea view, bell birds and tuis. Bedroom with twin beds, plus double divan in lounge. Wheelchair facilities. 5 minutes from a beautiful sandy beach for swimming or long walks. Next door to scenic reserve and bush walks. You can have breakfast in the garden with the birds if you wish. Non-smoking. Laundry facilities available. Cooking facilities.

Owaka - The Catlins *15 km S of Owaka*

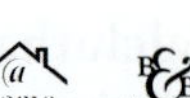

Greenwood Farmstay *B&B Farmstay*

Alan & Helen-May Burgess
739 Purakaunui Falls Road,
Owaka,
The Catlins,
South Otago
Tel (03) 415 8259
or 027 438 4538
Fax (03) 415 8259
greenwoodfarm@xtra.co.nz
www.greenwoodfarmstay.co.nz

Double/Twin $145-$160
Single $120
(Full breakfast)
Children $90 under 10
Dinner $45 per person (3 course)
Children welcome
2 Queen 2 Single (3 bdrm)
3 bedrooms at Greenwood
Bathrooms: 2 Ensuite 1 Private

Welcome ... Within walking distance to beautiful Purakaunui Falls. Alan enjoys taking people around our sheep, cattle and deer farm and you may stand on the cliffs where part of the movie "Narnia" was filmed. We enjoy evening dining with our guests. Our home offers warm, very comfortable accommodation. All guest rooms have ensuite or a private bathroom. Rooms open out to our large garden. Relax and enjoy.Email/phone for directions.

Owaka - The Catlins *1 km N of Owaka*

J T's Catlins B&B *B&B Homestay*
John & Thelma Turnbull
2885 Main Road,
Owaka

Tel (03) 415 8127
or 027 649 7693
jtowaka@xtra.co.nz
www.jtscatlinsbnb.co.nz

Double/Twin up to $120
Single up to $80
(Full breakfast)
Dinner by arrangement
Children welcome
1 Queen 1 Twin (2 bdrm)
Bathrooms: 1 Guest share
Toilet, shower & bathroom,
3 seperate rooms

Welcome to our warm and comfortable home on the Southern Scenic Route, situated on a 25 acre farmlet, surrounded by colourful, peaceful gardens with splendid unspoilt views. Located in the heart of the Catlins, renowned for its wildlife and spectacular scenery, we are within walking distance of Owaka Township with its restaurants, museum and other amenities. Our guests are encouraged to dine with us for the evening meal when we enjoy quality local food and wine. We look forward to meeting you. Travel safely.

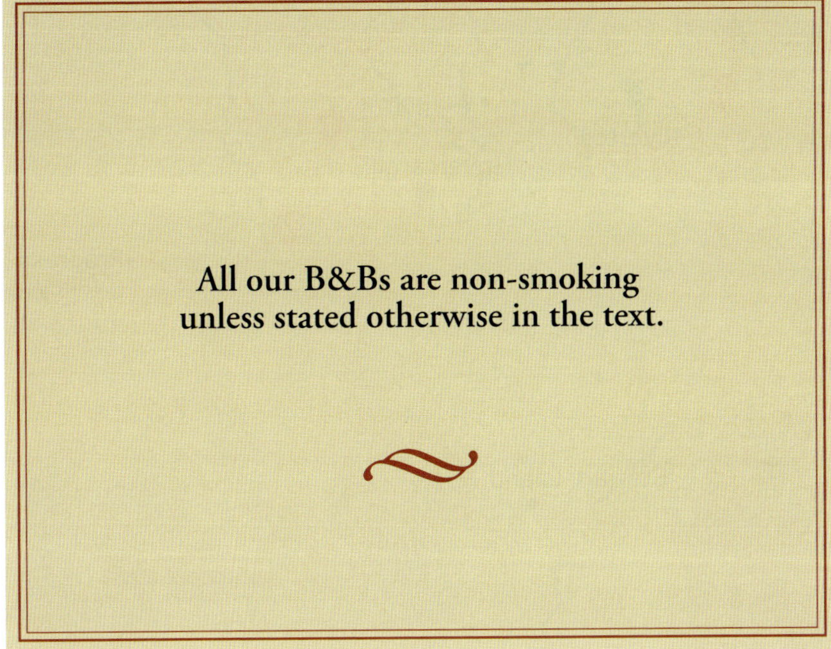

All our B&Bs are non-smoking unless stated otherwise in the text.

Southland,
South Catlins &
Stewart Island
Gibbston
Earnscleugh
Kingston
Garston
Ettrick
Te Anau
Manapouri
94
Mossburn
99
Lumsden
Balfour
96
6
Gore
99
Waianiwa
1
Riverton
Invercargill
92
Progress
Valley
Bluff
Stewart Island
0
Kilometres
30
0
Miles
18

Te Anau - Manapouri *20 km E of Manapouri*

B&B Approved

Crown Lea *Farmstay*

Florence & John Pine
310 Gillespie Road,
RD 1,
Te Anau

Tel (03) 249 8598
or 021 1680 299
Fax (03) 249 8598
crownlea@farmside.co.nz
www.crown-lea.com

Double/Twin $180
Single $180
(Full breakfast)
Dinner $40
1 Queen 1 Twin (3 bdrm)
All with garden views
Bathrooms: 1 Ensuite 2 Private

Our 900 acre sheep, cattle and deer farm offers a farm tour after 6pm, and views of Lake Manapouri, Fiordland mountains, and Te Anau Basin. Day trips to Doubtful and Milford Sounds, visits to Te Anau, glowworm caves, or hikes on the walking tracks in Fiordland all within easy reach. Having travelled in South Africa, UK, Europe, USA, Canada, Hong Kong and Singapore, we look forward to welcoming you to and sharing our home with you.

Te Anau - Manapouri *20 km S of Te Anau*

B&B Approved

The Cottage *B&B Homestay Old-fashioned Homestay B&B*

Don & Joy MacDuff
Waiau Street,
Te Anau - Manapouri

Tel (03) 249 6838
or 021 138 6110
don.joymacduff@xtra.co.nz
www.thecottagefiordland.co.nz

Double/Twin $135-$165
(Special breakfast)
$135.00 is cash discount & booking directly with us
Visa MC accepted
Not suitable for children
1 King 1 Queen (2 bdrm)
Bathrooms: 2 Ensuite
One room has a bath tub

GATEWAY TO DOUBTFUL SOUND & Fiordland. Doubtful Sound Boat only a 2minute walk. Our comfortable home with cottage/decor is a combination of Old/World charm and kiwi ingenuity. Tranquil setting with lovely mountain & water views through the trees. Tea/coffee/fridge in both rooms.Your own private outdoor area. Excellent homemade breakfasts. Enjoy the bird song and our social hour most/evenings. We, with Millie & Archie (Dogs) extend to you a warm Kiwi welcome.

Te Anau *1 km N of Te Anau Centre*

Shakespeare House *B&B Separate Suite*
Marg, Jeff, Kylie & Ray
10 Dusky Street,
PO Box 32,
Te Anau

Tel (03) 249 7349
or 0800 249 349
Fax (03) 249 7629
marg.shakespeare.house@xtra.co.nz
www.shakespearehouse.co.nz

Double/Twin $100-$130
Single $90-$110
(Full breakfast)
Children $5-$15
Self-contained, 2 bedrooms - sleeps 5
Visa MC Eftpos accepted
Pet free home Children welcome
8 King 4 Single (8 bdrm)
Bathrooms: 8 Ensuite No Baths

Shakespeare House is a well established Bed & Breakfast, where we keep a home atmosphere with personal service. We are situated in a quiet residential area yet are within walking distance of shops, lake and restaurants. Our rooms are ground floor and have the choice of king, queen or twin beds. Each room has private facilities, TV, tea/coffee making. Tariff includes continental or delicious cooked breakfast. Guest laundry available, internet and payphone facilities on site. Winter rates May to September.

Te Anau *2 km E of Te Anau*

Rose 'n' Reel *B&B Farmstay Cottage with Kitchen*
Lyn & Lex Lawrence
89 Ben Loch Lane,
RD 2,
Te Anau

Tel (03) 249 7582
or 027 4545 723
Fax (03) 249 7582
rosenreel@xtra.co.nz
www.rosenreel.co.nz

Double/Twin $120-$130
Single $75-$100
(Continental breakfast)
Visa MC accepted
2 Queen 1 Double 1 Single (3 bdrm)
Bathrooms: 1 Private 1 Guest share

Genuine Kiwi hospitality in a magic setting 5 minutes from Te Anau. Hand feed tame fallow deer, meet our friendly cat Ben and dog Meg. Sit on the veranda of our fully self-contained cabin and enjoy watching deer with a lake and mountain view. The 2 room cabin has cooking facilities, fridge, microwave, TV, 1 queen, 1 double plus bathroom. Our 2 storey home is set in an extensive garden. 2 guest bedrooms. Lex is a fishing guide, I love to garden. Directions: please phone.

Te Anau *1.5 km N of Te Anau*

B&B Approved

The Croft *B&B Farmstay Cottage with Kitchen*

Jane & Ross McEwan
153 Te Anau Milford Sound Road,
RD 1,
Te Anau

Tel (03) 249 7393
or 027 682 0061
Fax (03) 249 7393
jane@thecroft.co.nz
www.thecroft.co.nz

Double/Twin $155-$175
(Continental breakfast)
Extra person $25
Visa MC accepted
2 Queen 1 Single (2 bdrm)
Bathrooms: 2 Ensuite

Warm hospitality and quality accommodation are guaranteed at The Croft, a lifestyle farm near Te Anau. Our 2 modern self-contained cottages are set in private gardens and enjoy magnificent lake and mountain views. Timber ceilings, large ensuite bathrooms, window seats and elegant furnishings are highlights. Microwaves, fridges, sinks, TVs, DVDs and CD mini systems. Enjoy breakfast with Jane & Ross or served in your cottage. Pets include Fred the sheep, Mac the Jack Russell, Kitty and Jerry. Lake and river access from our farm.

Te Anau *0.2 km N of Te Anau Central*

B&B Approved

Cosy Kiwi *B&B Guest House*

Eleanor & Derek Cook
186 Milford Road,
Te Anau 9600

Tel 03 249 7475 or 0800 249 700
Fax (03) 249 8471
info@cosykiwi.com
www.cosykiwi.com

Double/Twin $150-$165
Single $140-$150
(Special breakfast)
Children $40
Triple $175-$195
Visa MC Eftpos accepted
Children welcome
4 King 3 Queen 4 Twin
5 Single (7 bdrm) Studio Rooms
Bathrooms: 7 Ensuite

Eleanor Derek and Mia (our miniture schnauzer) welcome you to our Bed & Breakfast (33 years experience in hospitality industry). Privacy with comfort, quiet spacious ensuited bedrooms, quality beds, individual heating and televison. Breakfast buffet of home-made breads, jams, fresh fruits, dessert fruits, yoghurt, brewed coffee, special teas,plus mouthwatering pancakes with maple syrup or ham and cheese. Two minute walk to shops and restaurants, bookings arranged for all tours, pick-up at gate. Guest lounge with internet access,wireless for laptops, laundry, off-street parking and luggage storage.

Te Anau *1 km N of Town Te Anau*

Te Anau Lodge *Luxury B&B*

B&B Approved

Matt Dagger & Chloe Marsden
52 Howden Street,
Te Anau
Tel (03) 249 7477
Fax (03) 249 7487
info@teanaulodge.co.nz
www.teanaulodge.com

Double/Twin $200-$350
Single $170-$270
(Full breakfast)
Visa MC Eftpos accepted
Children welcome
3 King/Twin 3 King 4 Queen 3 Twin
7 Single (7 bedrooms in total)
Bathrooms: 7 Ensuite 1 Private
(7 Bathrooms in total, 2 with spa baths)

Experience the genuine warmth of traditional hospitality in the relaxed and peaceful environment of our 1936 relocated former convent. Set on 2.7 hectares with breathtaking lake and mountain views, Te Anau Lodge has been lovingly restored maintaining its original and delightful charm, with modern facilities. Enjoy our famous cooked breakfasts in the Chapel, spend your evenings relaxing in our library or having a drink in our sunny courtyard. Complimentary laundry facilities, luggage storage and high speed wireless internet access. A unique and special accommodation experience.

Te Anau - Manapouri *8 km S of Manapouri*

Connemara Cottages *B&B Farmstay Cottage with Kitchen*

B&B Approved

Bev & Murray Hagen
415 Weir Road,
Manapouri,
Te Anau
Tel (03) 249 9399
or 027 292 3651
hagen@farmside.co.nz
www.connemarafiordland.co.nz

Double/Twin $140-$200
(Full breakfast provisions)
Children by arrangement
1 Queen 1 Double (1 bdrm)
Bathrooms: 1 Ensuite

Yours exclusively, two cosy self-contained cottages."CONNEMARA FARM COTTAGE", situated on our Deer Farm 8mins from Manapouri GATEWAY to DOUBTFUL/ SOUND Lounge/Kitchenette, ensuite Queen bedroom, sofa/bed in lounge. Lovely mountain and farm views. Our farm bounds two excellent fishing rivers. Farm tour available by arrangement."CONNEMARA ANGLERS ARMS" situated in Manapouri, Two bedroom cottage with Queen beds finest furnishings, open plan living, overlooks the beautiful Waiau River with lovely views of the bush & mountains. Doubtful/Sound Boats only a 2min. Walk. Min stay 2nights. Not suitable children.

Te Anau *0.4 km N of Te Anau Centre*

Antler Lodge *B&B Cottage with Kitchen*

Helen & Chris Whyte
44 Matai Street,
Te Anau

Tel (03) 249 8188
Fax (03) 249 8188
antler.lodge@xtra.co.nz
www.antlerlodgeteanau.co.nz

Double/Twin $130-$155
(Continental breakfast provisions)
Visa MC accepted
1 King 2 Queen (3 bdrm)
Bathrooms: 3 Ensuite

Helen and Chris invite you to enjoy their comfortable bed & breakfast accommodation. Situated in a quiet residential area close to shops, restaurants and within walking distance of the lake. We offer 3 spacious self contained units, each with a private ensuite. The 2 cottages each have kitchen facilities, tv, electric heating and comfortable furnishings. Our third unit is an upstairs suite with private entrance and sunroom dining area. Continental breakfast provisions are provided in this unit. This suite has beautiful mountain views.

~

Te Anau *1 km S of Central Te Anau*

Cat's Whiskers *B&B*

Anne Marie & Lindsay Bernstone
2 Lakefront Drive,
Te Anau 9600

Tel (03) 249 8112
Fax (03) 249 8112
bookings@catswhiskers.co.nz
www.catswhiskers.co.nz

Double/Twin $175-$215
Single $140-$165
(Full breakfast)
Children $40
Visa MC accepted
Children welcome
2 King 2 Queen 4 Single (4 bdrm)
Bathrooms: 4 Ensuite

Our peaceful lakefront home is a comfortable villa with 4 guest rooms all with ensuite bathrooms. Relax while you take in stunning views of Lake Te Anau. Meet fellow guests for a cooked or continental breakfast in our dining room. Opposite Department of Conservation Visitor Centre. Our cat Lucy lives with us. King, Queen or Twin beds. Wireless internet access. TV, fridges, tea and coffee making facilities. Booking service for local trips. Off street parking. Guest laundry and short term luggage storage.

Te Anau *5 km N of Te Anau*

Lochvista B&B *B&B*
Viv Nicholson
454 State Highway 94,
Te Anau

Tel (03) 249 7273
Fax (03) 249 7278
lochvista@xtra.co.nz
www.lochvista.co.nz

Double/Twin $160-$190
Single $150-$160
(Continental breakfast)
Full breakfast by arrangement $15pp
Visa MC accepted
1 King 1 Queen 1 Twin (2 bdrm)
Bathrooms: 2 Ensuite

Welcome to Fiordland. Lochvista is situated on Te Anau Milford Highway 5km from the town centre, overlooking Lake Te Anau and Murchison mountains. 2 rooms one with queen bed and one with king/twin with ensuite, tea/coffee making facilities, fridge, TV & hairdryer. French doors onto the patio where you can sit and take in spectacular views. Fiordland has a great deal to offer and I am more than happy to help guests with any booking to make their stay more relaxing. A cat called Mischief.

Te Anau *.2 km W of central Te Anau*

House of Wood *B&B Homestay*
Merle & Cliff Buchanan
44 Moana Crescent,
Te Anau

Tel (03) 249 8404
or 021 158 6686
Fax (03) 249 7676
houseofwood@xtra.co.nz
www.houseofwood.co.nz

Double/Twin $125-$145
Single $105-$130
(Full breakfast)
Children by arrangement
3 course dinner w/ drinks usually served
Visa MC Eftpos accepted
Pet free home Children welcome
2 King/Twin 1 King 3 Queen (4 bdrm)
Bathrooms: 3 Ensuite 1 Private
1 room with private bath. Separate shower & toilet

A warm welcome is assured when you arrive at our home. We really enjoy meeting guests from overseas (and locals). Our house is a unique architecturally designed home of native and exotic timber. Sit at the outdoor tables and enjoy the beautiful views. Our interests are boating, golf, fishing, rowing, gardening. We can help you plan your activities and book trips, with pick up at door. Two minutes walk from town 5 minutes to Lake. Dinner by arrangement. Wireless internet available. Check-in after 2pm please.

Mossburn *25 km S of Mossburn*

Turner Farmstay *Farmstay*

Joyce & Murray Turner
RD 1,
Otautau,
Southland 9689

Tel (03) 225 7602
Fax (03) 225 7602
murray.joyce@farmside.co.nz
www.innz.co.nz/host/e/etalcreek.html

Double/Twin $100
Single $70
(Full breakfast)
Children under 12 $25
Dinner $35
1 Queen 4 Single (3 bdrm)
Bathrooms: 1 Private 1 Guest share

Our modern home on 301 hectares, farming sheep, is situated half-way between Invercargill and Te Anau, which can be reached in 1 hour. We enjoy meeting people, will provide quality accommodation, farm-fresh food in a welcoming friendly atmosphere. You can join in farm activities, farm tour or just relax. The Aparima River is adjacent to the property. Murray is a keen fly fisherman. Guiding & advice available. Pet Bichon Frise. Evening meal on request. Directions please phone/fax. 24 hours notice to avoid disappointment.

~

Lumsden *12 km S of Lumsden*

Chartlea Park Farmstay *B&B Farmstay Historical*

Ken & Trish MacKenzie
1 Chartlea Park Road, Balfour, 9779

Tel (03) 201 6442
or 027 285 5121
or 027 285 5150
Fax (03) 201 6442
ken.trish.mack@xtra.co.nz
www.chartleaparkfarmstay.co.nz

Double/Twin $145
Single $85
(Full breakfast)
Children $45
Dinner $40pp 2 course NZ with wine
Visa MC accepted
Children welcome
4 King/Twin 1 Queen (3 bdrm)
Large double rooms
Bathrooms: 1 Guest share 1 Family share
Bedrooms have own washstand facilities

Ken, Trish and Jenna MacKenzie welcome you to their 670 acre sheep beef and deer farm in Northern Southland. Enjoy tasty home cooking, a farm tour, meeting and feeding the pets or just relax in the ambience of our historic home. Nearby are excellent fishing rivers, golf courses and spectacular scenery. Our central location to the delights of Invercargill, Queenstown and Te Anau is ideal. We are committed to ensuring your time with us is THE highlight of your travels.

Balfour *3 km N of Balfour*

Hillcrest *Homestay Farmstay*
Liz & Ritchie Clark
206 Old Balfour Road,
RD 1,
Balfour

Tel (03) 201 6165
Fax (03) 201 6165
clarkrl@xtra.co.nz
www.bnb.co.nz/hillcrestbalfour.html

Double/Twin $120-$150
Single $120-$150
(Full breakfast)
Dinner $40pp
Visa MC accepted
Children welcome
2 King/Twin 1 Single (2 bdrm)
Bathrooms: 1 Private 1 Family share

Welcome to our 650 acre sheep and deer farm, 3km from State Highway 94. Relax in our garden, enjoy a farm tour with mountain views or a game of tennis. Trout fishing in the Mataura, Oreti and Waikaia Rivers. Fishing guide can be arranged with notice. Enjoy a relaxing dinner with fine food, wine and conversation. Cooked breakfast is served and enjoy fresh baked bread, yoghurt, muesli, jams and preserves. Interests include handcrafts, tennis, photography and fishing. We have 2 cats. Directions: please phone.

Gore *1 km N of Gore*

Connor Homestay *Homestay*
Dawn & David Connor
29 Aotea Crescent,
Gore,
Southland

Tel (03) 208 3598
or 0800 372 484
027 669 1362
Fax (03) 208 3598
ddconnor@esi.co.nz
www.bnb.co.nz/connororchids.html

Double/Twin $110
Single $90
(Full breakfast)
Visa MC accepted
1 King/Twin 1 Queen
1 Twin (2 bdrm)
Bathrooms: 1 Private 1 Guest share

Dawn & David invite you to enjoy quality accommodation in their modern home, situated in a quiet residential area overlooking the Hokonui Hills & farmland, close to golf course, driving range, bush walks and good fishing rivers including Mataura, well known for its brown trout. Fishing guide or advise available. We enjoy meeting people and sharing travel experiences. Laundry facilities available. Smoke-free accommodation. Please phone for directions.

Gore *3 km NW of Gore*

Hokonui Homestay *Luxury B&B Rural Lifestyle*
Brian & Shona McLennan
258 Reaby Road,
RD 4, Gore

Tel (03) 208 4890
or 0800 70 72 75
or 027 568 4835
Fax (03) 208 4890
bssm@sld.quik.co.nz
www.bnb.co.nz/hokonuihomestay.html

Double/Twin $100-$120
Single $80-$90 (Full breakfast)
Children negotiable
Dinner by arrangement
Visa MC accepted
1 King 1 Queen 1 Twin (3 bdrm)
All bedrooms have bathrooms
and great views
Bathrooms: 2 Ensuite 1 Private

Brian & Shona welcome you to a private, spacious, and modern new home on a 12 acre lifestyle property with spectacular views. Private upstairs unit, underfloor heating and full size snooker table. Close to the Mataura River, 18 hole Golf Course and Native Bush Walks. A perfect base for sightseeing Southland. Gold Guitar Awards and Waimumu Fieldays. Interests- golf,fishing,snooker,horse riding and dog trialing, gardening, music and wine tasting. We have Horses, Sheepdogs and Sheep. Horse and Dog facilities available. Please phone for directions.

~

Gore *2 km N of Gore*

Amble In *B&B*
Richard Preston & Carolyn Moorfoot
74 Wentworth Street,
Gore

Tel (03) 208 5552
Fax (03) 208 5552
moorfoot@xtra.co.nz

Double/Twin $110
Single $60
(Full breakfast)
Children accompanied by adults
Dinner by arrangement
Pet free home
Children welcome
1 King/Twin 1 King
1 Queen 1 Single (3 bdrm)
Bathrooms: 1 Guest share

Richard and Carolyn welcome you to their home, situated amidst farmland overlooking Gore and The Hokonuis. Near by is the Mataura River, famous for Brown trout. Bush walks and art gallery's near by. Fishing guide or advice available with notice. We enjoy meeting new people, talking about New Zealand. Breakfast is served with fresh baked bread and jams and perserves, also with hot cooked bacon and eggs. Three course diners can be as kiwi as you like or perhaps venison or fish may be your choice. Laundry facilities available. Smoke Free accommodation.

Gore *0.5 km S of Gore*

Kowhai Place *B&B*
Helen & John Williams
41 Huron Street,
Gore 9710

Tel (03) 208 8022
or (027) 203 8734
Fax (03) 208 8022
kowhaiplace@xtra.co.nz
www.southland-homestays.co.nz

Double/Twin $130-$150
Single $75-$90
(Full breakfast)
Dinner by arrangement $35
Children welcome
4 King/Twin 1 Queen (3 bdrm)
Queen bedroom has ensuite,
lounge sofa bed and kitchen
Bathrooms: 1 Ensuite 1 Guest share

We are right on the banks of the Mataura River, so famous for it's fly-fishing. Our place the ideal base if you wish to make day trips to many places including The Catlins, Invercargill, Bluff and Queenstown. Te Anau and the World Heritage Fiordland National Park are all within a two-hour drive from Gore.We will be happy to advise you on places to visit and things to do during your stay here and we know you will enjoy our typical southern hospitality!

Progress Valley - South Catlins *6 km N of Waikawa*

Catlins Farmstay B&B *B&B Farmstay*
June & Murray Stratford
174 Progress Valley Road,
South Catlins,
Southland

Tel (03) 246 8843
Fax (03) 246 8844
catlinsfarmstay@xtra.co.nz
www.catlinsfarmstay.co.nz

Double/Twin $180-$260
Single $130-$160
(Full breakfast)
Children negotiable
Visa MC accepted
Children welcome
1 King 2 Queen 1 Twin (4 bdrm)
Bathrooms: 3 Ensuite 1 Private

Ours is a great location close to fossil forest at Curio Bay. Spacious guest rooms plus king self-contained suite available with private entrances. We farm 1000 acres running, 2500 sheep, 500 deer, 150 cattle with 3 sheepdogs. Farm tours by arrangement. Directions: turn off at Niagara Falls into Manse Road, drive 2km. Ask about our new Waterside s/c cottage at Waikawa . Dinner available at Niagara Falls Cafe. Licensened Restaurant 2km drive from our house.

Invercargill *5 km N of Invercargill city*

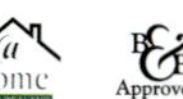

Glenroy Park Homestay *B&B Homestay*

Margaret & Alan Thomson
23 Glenroy Park Drive,
Invercargill

Tel (03) 215 8464
or 027 376 2228
Fax (03) 215 8464
home_hosp@actrix.co.nz
www.bnb.co.nz/glenroypark.html

Double/Twin $110-$120
Single $75-$85
(Full breakfast)
Children up to 12 years $12
3 course dinner $35
Children welcome
1 Queen 1 Twin 1 Single (3 bdrm)
Bathrooms: 1 Private 1 Guest share
Heated tile floors

Exclusively yours, in a quiet retreat near restaurants and parks. Be our special guests and share an evening of relaxation and friendship. Our interests are golfing, meeting people, travel and cooking. We look forward to your visit. Invercargill is the gateway to Queenstown, Fiordland, Catlins and Stewart Island. Directions: from Queenstown turn left second lights (Bainfield Road), take first left, third house on left. From Dunedin turn right second set of lights (Queens Drive), travel to end, turn left, first street right, third house left.

~

Invercargill *5 km W of Invercargill*

B&B Approved

The Oak Door *B&B*

Lisa & Bill Stuart
22 Taiepa Road,
Otatara,
RD 9,
Invercargill 9879

Tel (03) 213 0633
Fax (03) 213 0633
blstuart@xtra.co.nz

Double/Twin $100
Single $80
(Full breakfast)
Children POA
Pet free home
2 Queen 2 Twin (3 bdrm)
Bathrooms: 1 Guest share
1 Family share

Bill (Kiwi) & Lisa (Canadian) welcome you to their warm, self-built, unique home. Enjoy attractive gardens and native bush setting; minutes from: Invercargill CBD, Scenic route amenities, airport. Coffee/tea awaits you on arrival at The Oak Door. Guests comment on a warm comfortable visit, where beds, breakfast and hospitality are quality plus! A Warm Welcome! (Nonsmoking/no pets). Directions: Drive past the airport entrance. Take first left (Marama Avenue South). Take first right Taiepa Road second drive on right (#22).

Invercargill *3 km N of Invercargill City Centre*

Gimblett Place *B&B*

Alex & Eileen Henderson
122 Gimblett Place,
Kildare,
Invercargill

Tel (03) 215 6888
Fax (03) 215 6888
the_grove@xtra.co.nz
www.bnb.co.nz/hosts/gimblettplace

Double/Twin $95
Single $65
(Full breakfast)
Children negotiable
Dinner by arrangement
Visa MC accepted
Pet free home
1 Queen 2 Single (2 bdrm)
Bathrooms: 1 Private

Eileen & Alex are experienced hosts who are ex-farmers and offer comfortable accommodation in a quiet cul-de-sac close to city amenities, golf, parks, restaurants. We are pleased to assist with local and tourist information and can guide if required (ie Catlins). Alex is a vintage car and machinery enthusiast and can arrange good viewing. Close to famous trout fishing rivers. Directions: find Queens Drive, Gimblett Street is first left north of Thomsons Bush, fourth right into Gimblett Place (cul-de-sac)

~

Invercargill - Waianiwa *18 km W of Invercargill*

Annfield Flowers *B&B Homestay*

Margaret & Mike Cockeram
126 Argyle-Otahuti Road,
Waianiwa,
RD 4,
Invercargill 9874

Tel (03) 235 2690
or 021 385 134
Fax (03) 235 2745
annfield@woosh.co.nz

Double/Twin $110-$120
(Full breakfast)
Dinner $25 to $30
Visa MC accepted
1 King/Twin 1 Double (2 bdrm)
Only 1 group of guests at a time
Bathrooms: 1 Ensuite

We are 1km from the Southern Scenic Route (signposted Waianiwa/Drummond). Annfield has modern facilities but retains 1860's character. Our sunny guest room opens into the garden. We only host one party at a time. We are semi-retired, and keep coloured sheep and alpacas. We enjoy meeting people and sharing dinner or a light meal, including our own produce. Our dog, Meg, will greet you and she and two cats have limited access to the house. Complimentary laundry facilities.

Invercargill *10 km E of Invercargill on Southern Scenic Rte*

Long Acres Farmstay *Farmstay Self-contained & B&B*

Helen & Graeme Spain
Waimatua, RD 11, Invercargill

Tel (03) 216 4470
or 027 228 1308
Fax (03) 216 4470
longacres@woosh.co.nz
www.longacres.co.nz

Double/Twin $150
Single $100-$120 (Full breakfast)
Children negotiable Dinner $45
Self-contained $160-$200
Visa MC accepted
Children welcome
2 Queen 1 Twin 1 Single (4 bdrm)
Self-Contained 1 Queen, 1 Twin
Homestead 1 Queen, 1 Single
Bathrooms: 1 Queen Ensuite
1 Queen Private 1 Single guests share

Long Acres Farmstay retreat offers quality warm accommodation, Superb Hospitality and a 1500 acre working farm with cows, sheep, lambs, beef cattle, dogs and hens. A free farm tour with Graeme. Amazing native bush/bird walk. Ideal stopover for Stewart Island, Catlins, Te Anau, Queenstown and Dunedin. Hearty breakfasts provided and evening meals available from home grown produce. A peaceful relaxed farmstay for the length of time you choose. Directions. From Invercargill, east on Southern Scenic Route 10kms.Farmstay Sign on left.

Invercargill *4 km N of Invercargill Central*

Stoneleigh Homestay *B&B Homestay*

Joan & Neville Milne
15 Stoneleigh Lane,
Invercargill

Tel (03) 215 8921
joan@stoneleighhomestay.co.nz
www.stoneleighhomestay.co.nz

Double/Twin $110-$125
Single $80-$90
(Full breakfast)
Dinner $35
Visa MC accepted
Pet free home
1 Queen 3 Single (3 bdrm)
Bathrooms: 1 Private 1 Guest share

We welcome guests to share our modern home in a quiet lane 5 minutes from the main centre, and just off the main road to TeAnau and Queenstown. We have underfloor heating, electric blankets and guests have their own TV. We are keen golfers and members of the Invercargill club, a championship course rated in the top 10 in N.Z. Our interests are golf, travel, gardening, cooking, wine and meeting people. Enjoy our hospitality, share an evening meal with us. Pick ups can be arranged.

Invercargill *6 km NE of Invercargill*

The Manor *B&B Homestay*

Pat & Frank Forde
9 Drysdale Road 9872,
Myross Bush 2 RD, Invercargill

Tel (03) 230 4788
or 027 667 0904
Fax (03) 230 4788
the.manor@xtra.co.nz
www.manorbb.co.nz

Double/Twin $110-$150
Single $75-$90 (Full breakfast)
Children negotiable
Dinner by arrangement
Visa MC accepted
Pet free home Children welcome
3 Queen 2 Single (3 bdrm)
Very comfortable beds
Bathrooms: 1 Ensuite 1 Private 1 Guest share

Relax, enjoy our warm, comfortable home, underfloor-heating, a sheltered garden setting, 10 acre farmlet (sheep, lambs, horses, hens). Private guest area, television, wireless internet, refrigerator, tea/coffee making facilities. We are retired farmers, golfers, enjoy gardening, harness racing, travel, meeting people. Pleasant outdoor areas, meals of fresh home-grown produce, cooked/continental breakfasts. Courtesy pick up. A stop on your way to Stewart Island, Southern Scenic Route, Queenstown or Te Anau. We would enjoy having you stay with us. 5 minutes drive north east Invercargill along State Highway 1.

Invercargill *0.01 km NW of Invercargill City Centre*

Victoria Railway Hotel *Hotel*

Trudy & Eian Read
3 Leven Street,
off Picadilly Lane,
Invercargill

Tel (03) 218 1281
Fax (03) 218 1283
vrhotel@xtra.co.nz
www.vrhotel.info

Double/Twin $145-$180
Single $117-$130
(Full breakfast)
Children $15
Dinner Mains $26-$32 pp
Breakfast $10-$20 pp
Visa MC Diners Amex
Eftpos accepted
5 Queen 4 Double 2 Twin (11 bdrm)
Bathrooms: 11 Ensuite

Come and enjoy old world charm and southern hospitality in a boutique hotel in the heart of the city. This Invercargill Landmark built in 1896 is a Class 1 heritage building. Architecturally designed upgrade completed May 2004. City Council Environment Award recipient May 2007. Variety of accommodation options including Executive and VIP, plus two Ground floor Accessible units. Come relax in our lounge bar before dining in and enjoy traditional home cooked meals and a selection of fine NZ wines and local Invercargill Beers.

Invercargill *15 km N of Invercargill*

Tudor Park Country Stay and Garden *B&B Homestay Country Stay and Garden&Beach House*

B&B Approved

Joyce & John Robins
RD 6, Invercargill, 9876
Tel (03) 221 7150
or 027 431 0031
Fax (03) 221 7150
tudorparksouth@hotmail.com
www.tudorpark.co.nz

Double/Twin $140-$225
Single $100-$130 (Full breakfast)
Children are welcome
with parent supervision
Dinner by arrangement from $50
Cottage at Riverton from $130
per night, min 2 nights
Visa MC accepted
1 King/Twin 3 Queen 1 Twin (5 bdrm)
All rooms have good views and private facilities
Bathrooms: 2 Ensuite 1 Private 1 Guest share in cottage

Tudor Park has been tastefully decorated and furnished with antiques and quality linens. All rooms have their own facilities and garden views. Guests privacy is respected whilst enjoying quality accommodation with friendly persoalised service.You are welcome to relax, enjoy the large garden, animals & attractions of the area.We enjoy travel, overseas & in NZ, walking & people. We also have a house 20mtres from the beach at Riverton. Please enquire.

Bluff *25 km S of Invercargill*

The Lazy Fish *Separate Suite Cottage with Kitchen*

@home New Zealand — B&B Approved

Robyn & Roy Horwell
35 Burrows Street,
Bluff, 9814
Tel (03) 212 7245
or 021 211 7424
Fax (03) 212 8868
horwell@thelazyfish.co.nz
www.thelazyfish.co.nz

Double/Twin $100-$120
(Breakfast by arrangement)
Continental breakfast $10 pp
Children welcome
2 Double (2 bdrm)
Bathrooms: 2 Ensuite

Very homely fully self-contained unit attached to our home, in a peacefull garden setting. Sleeps 4, double bed in bedroom and sofa bed in lounge. Also double bedroom attached to house, tea & coffee making facilities and microwave. Sunny shelterd courtyard. Friendly labrador in residence. Gateway to Stewart Island and Southern Scenic Route. Take a break and absorb our Coastal and native bush walks, maritime museum, restaurants and supermarket all within walking distance. 5 minutes walk to Stewart Island ferry. Continental breakfast by arrangement.

Riverton *45 km W of Invercargill*

Reo Moana *B&B*

Jean Broomfield
192 Rocks Highway,
Riverton,
Southland

Tel (03) 234 9044
alanb@orcon.net.nz

Double/Twin $150
Single $100 (Full breakfast)
Children negotiable
Extra roll away bed and cot available
Pet free home
Children welcome
1 King 1 Twin (2 bdrm)
Well appointed spacious rooms with sea views
Bathrooms: 2 Ensuite
Excellent Showers & heated tile floors

Reo Moana overlooks a beautiful secluded swimming and surfing beach with extended views to the open sea beyond, and northward to the mountains and hills of Southland. Tastefully decorated, the warm and spacious guest rooms each have ensuite bathrooms and sea views. Your host Jean has many years experience in the tourism industry. I welcome you to Riverton, on the Southern Scenic Route and just 45 minutes from Tuatapere and the Humpridge track.

~

Stewart Island *1 km S of Oban*

Glendaruel Bed & Breakfast *B&B*

Raylene & Ronnie Waddell
38 Golden Bay Road,
Oban, Stewart Island

Tel (03) 219 1092
Fax (03) 219 1092
glendaruel@xtra.co.nz
www.glendaruel.co.nz

Double/Twin $220
Single $110-$160
(Full breakfast)
Children by arrangement
Dinner $50 by arrangement
Visa MC accepted
1 King/Twin 1 Queen
1 Single (3 bdrm)
1 King / Twin 1 Queen 1 Single
Bathrooms: 3 Ensuite

Peaceful bush setting, 10 minutes walk from village, 3 minutes from Golden Bay on beautiful Paterson Inlet. Handy for water taxis, kayak hire, sandy beaches and bush walks. Large guest lounge and three balconies with bush and sea views. Colourful garden - bird lovers' paradise. Central heating. Courtesy transfers. Advice and assistance with local activities. We have travelled widely and love welcoming guests from around the world. We do our best to provide traditional Scottish and Kiwi hospitality. "A Hundred Thousand Welcomes!"

Stewart Island *0.2 km W of Oban township*

Sails Ashore Luxury B&B & Kowhai Lane Self Catering Holiday Home and Apartment *Luxury B&B Apartment with Kitchen Holiday Home & Self-catering Flat*

Iris and Peter Tait
11 View Street & 6 Kowhai Lane, Stewart Island
Tel (03) 219 1151 or 0800 783 9278 (0800 Stewart)
tait@sailsashore.co.nz
www.sailsashore.co.nz

Double/Twin $160-$425 (Breakfast by arrangement)
Restaurants nearby for dinner
Please Note Photos are of Sails Ashore
Visa MC Eftpos accepted
Pet free home
Not suitable for children
5 King/Twin 1 Queen 2 Single (7 bdrm)
2 in Sails Ashore 5 at Kowhai Lane
Bathrooms: 7 Ensuite

Sails Ashore is everything discerning guests would expect from a Qualmark 4 Star plus hosted boutique accommodation. Kowhai Lane Holiday Home is 4 star self catering and available on either a room or whole of house basis. Both are situated within 4 or 5 minutes stroll of the village centre, overlook the harbour and are packaged with a Sails guided exploration of Ulva Island.

All rooms are centrally heated. Facilities include an extensive library of books and local interest DVDs to enjoy on lazy evenings.

Stewart Island *0.2 km W of Stewart Island*

B&B Approved

Stewart Island Lodge *B&B*

Jo Leask and Wayne Skerrett
14 Nichol Road,
Halfmoon Bay, Stewart Island

Tel (03) 219 1085 or 0800 65 65 01
Fax (03) 219 1085
info@stewartislandlodge.co.nz
www.stewartislandlodge.co.nz

Double/Twin $390
Single $390 (Full breakfast)
Children $390
$290 during Apr, May, Sep, Oct.
Closed June-August
Visa MC Diners Amex Eftpos accepted
Pet free home
5 King/Twin (5 bdrm)
All bedrooms open to a large balconyBathrooms: 5 Ensuite

Stewart Island Lodge is an up-market bed & breakfast nestled in native bush on Stewart Island. Located just five minutes walk from Oban village, the lodge has commanding views across Halfmoon Bay and Foveaux Strait.The lodge's grounds are home to many native birds, including kaka (native parrots) which may be viewed from the terrace.Each evening guests are invited to enjoy a pre-dinner drink and appetisers in the guest lounge with their hosts. Restaurants are available for evening dining in the township of Oban (at guests expense).

Happy Travels!

Index

A

Abel Tasman National Park 291, 292
Acacia Bay 148, 152-153
Ahipara 10, 11
Akaroa 352-357
Akaroa Harbour 354
Albany 63
Albert Town 385
Alexandra 407
Anakiwa 256
Aro Valley 240
Arrowtown 394-398
Ashburton 363-364
Atawhai 269, 274, 276
Auckland 67-77
Auckland Airport 76
Avondale 338
Avonhead 332

B

Balclutha 419
Balfour 430
Banks Peninsula 351
Barry's Bay 355
Barrytown 301
Bay of Islands 12-29
Bay View 180-182
Bell Block 168
Belmont 227
Bethells Beach 59
Blenheim 258-265
Bluff 437
Bream Bay 40
Brightwater 280
Brixton 164
Broad Bay 415, 418
Burnside 333
Burwood 337

C

Cambridge 90, 91
Cape Foulwind 298
Carters Beach 299, 300
Carterton 212
Castle Hill 357
Charleston 300
Christchurch 330-349
Clyde 407
Coatesville 63
Collingwood 294
Cooks Beach 107
Coopers Beach 9
Coroglen 108
Coromandel 102-104
Cromwell 392-394
Culverden 326

D

Darfield 358
Dargaville 32-33
Days Bay 229, 231
Devonport 64-67
Drury 79
Dunedin 410-415

E

Eastbourne 228-231
Egmont Nat. Park 169
Eketahuna 209
Ellerslie 72
Enner Glynn 277
Ettrick 408

F

Fairlie 371
Feilding 201-202
Fendalton 335
Fernside 327
Fox Glacier 311-313
Franz Josef 311
French Farm 354
French Pass 266-267

G

Garston 405-406
Geraldine 366-367
Gisborne 161-162
Glen Murray 83
Gore 430-432
Greenmeadows 190
Greymouth 302-305

H

Hahei 109
Hamilton 84-90
Hamurana 147
Hanmer Springs 323-325
Harbourview 225
Harewood 330-331
Hastings 191-193
Havelock North 193-196
Herne Bay 67
Hobsonville 58-59
Hokitika 306-309
Hot Water Beach 110
Houhora 9
Howick 75
Huntly 83

I

Ilam 334
Invercargill 433-437
Island Bay 246-249

J

Johnsonville 231-232

K

Kaiapoi 329-330
Kaikoura 316-323
Kaitaia 10, 11
Kaiteriteri 289-291
Kaka Point 420
Kamo 39
Karamea 298
Karangahake 97
Karori 237, 238
Katikati 117-119
Kelburn 239
Kenepuru Sounds 252
Kerikeri 12-13
Khandallah 233
Kimbell 371
Kuaotunu 105-106
Kumeu 57-58
Kurow 376

L

Lake Pukaki 372-373
Lake Rotoiti 143
Lake Tekapo 372
Lake Wanaka 390
Lawrence 409
Levin 206-207
Lindis Pass 375
Lowburn 394
Lower Hutt 224-227
Lowry Bay 229
Lumsden 429
Lyttelton 350
Lyttelton Harbour 350

M

Macandrew Bay 416
Mahanga Beach 179
Mahau Sound 253
Mahia Peninsula 179
Makarora 382
Manapouri 423, 426
Mandeville 330
Mangamaunu 322
Mangatarata 82
Mangawhai Heads 45
Mangere 76
Mangere Bridge 76
Manukau 77
Manurewa 77
Mapua 281, 282
Marahau 291
Marine Parade 185
Martinborough 213-214
Marton 177
Masterton 209-211
Matakohe 33
Matangi 90
Matata 126-127
Matauwhi Bay 24
Matua 121
Merivale 336
Methven 358-361
Middlemarch 409
Millers Flat 408
Mission Bay 73
Moores Valley 228
Mosgiel 418, 419
Mossburn 429
Motueka 286-288
Motueka Valley 284-286
Motuoapa 156
Mt. Hutt 361
Mt Cook 240, 372-374
Mt Eden 71
Mt Hutt 358-360
Mt Maunganui 123-125
Mt Pleasant 347
Mt Somers 362
Mt Victoria 242-243
Murchison 295
Murray Aynsley 346

N

Napier 180-190
Napier Hill 186, 191
Nelson 269-277
Nelson Lakes 295
New Plymouth 164-168
Ngaio 234
Ngakuru 135
Ngongotaha 139, 146
Ninety Mile Beach 10
North Shore 62

O

Oamaru 377-380
Oaro 317
Ohakune 173-174
Ohaupo 86-87
Ohoka 329
Ohope 132
Ohope Beach 130-132
Okahu Bay 72
Okains Bay 351
Okiato 23, 27
Okuku 327
Okura 62
Omapere 31
Omokoroa 119-120, 122
Onerahi 37
Opawa 345
Opito Bay 106
Opononi 30
Opotiki 133
Opua 21, 22
Orakei 72
Orewa 53, 54
Oriental Bay 241
Oropi 122
Otago Peninsula 415-418
Otane 197
Otorohanga 92
Owaka 420-421
Owhango 172
Oxford 328

P

Paeroa 97
Paihia 14-22
Pakaraka 29
Pakawau 294
Palmerston 380, 410
Palmerston North 202-205
Pamapuria 10
Papakura 78
Papamoa 124
Papanui 334
Paparoa 34
Parapara 293
Paremata 222
Parua Bay 38
Patons Rock Beach 292
Paua Bay 352
Pelorus 253
Pelorus Sounds 266
Picton 251-258
Pikowai 127
Pio Pio 95
Pleasant Point 370
Plimmerton 221
Plummers Pt 123
Ponsonby 68-69
Portobello 416-417
Progress Valley 432
Puhoi 51-52
Puketapu 187
Punakaiki 301-302

Q

Queen Charlotte Sound 253-254, 256
Queenstown 397-404
Queenstown Hill 405

R

Raetihi 173
Raglan 84
Rakaia 362
Ramarama 80
Rangiora 326-327
Rangitikei 175
Ranui 61
Rapaura 258
Raumati Beach 221
Red Beach 53
Redcliffs 346
Reefton 297
Remuera 70-71
Renwick 265-266
Rerewhakaaitu 147
Riccarton 335-336
Richmond 278-279, 337
Riverhead 63
Riverlands 265
Riverton 438
Roseneath 243-245
Rotorua 134-147
Roxburgh 408
Ruakaka 40
Ruatapu 309
Ruby Bay 282-283
Russell 22-28

S

Sandspit 47, 49, 51
Seadown 368
Silverdale 56
Snells Beach 50
South Bay 323
South Catlins 432
St Arnaud 295
Staveley 361, 362
Stewart Island 438-440
St Heliers 73-74
St Martins 345
Stokes Valley 226-227
Stratford 169
Sumner 348-349
Sumner Beach 348
Swanson 60
Sydenham 344

T

Tahunanui 273
Taihape 174-176
Taiharuru 37
Tairua 110
Takaka 292-293
Tamahere 87
Tapu Bay 290
Taradale 184
Tata Beach 293
Taumarunui 172
Taupo 148-155
Tauranga 120-123
Tawa 223
Te Anau 423-428
Te Awamutu 92
Teddington 350
Te Hana 46
Te Horo 217
Te Kauwhata 82-83
Te Kouma 103
Te Kuiti 94
Templeton 343
Te Pahu 89
Te Puke 125, 126
Te Puru 102
Te Wahapu 27
Thames 97-101
Thames Coast 102
The Catlins 420-421
The Redwoods 145
Timaru 368-370
Tirau 91
Titirangi 75
Tolaga Bay 160
Totara 101
Turangi 155-158
Twizel 373-375

U

Upper Hutt 223
Upper Kokatahi 307
Upper Moutere 284

V

Vogeltown 246

W

Wadestown 235-236
Waianakarua 377
Waianiwa 434
Waihau Bay 133
Waihi 112, 113
Waihi Beach 114-115
Waikanae 217, 219-220
Waikanae Beach 218-219
Waikouaiti 410
Wainuiomata 228
Waipaoa 160
Waipapa 13
Waipawa 197-198
Waipu Cove 41, 42
Waipukurau 198-199
Waitakere Ranges 60
Waitarere Beach 205
Waitoki 56
Waitomo Caves 93
Waitomo District 92, 94-95
Waitotara 170
Waiwera 52
Wakefield 280
Wanaka 383-392
Wanganui 170-171
Warkworth 47-51
Wellington 231-249
Wellsford 46
Westhaven 342
Westport 298-300
Westshore 189
Whakatane 128-129
Whangamata 111
Whangaparaoa 54-56
Whangarei 35-39
Whataroa 310
Whatawhata 89
Whitianga 107-109
Winchester 367

Y

Yaldhurst 331
York Bay 228

The New Zealand
Bed & Breakfast Book

Please help us to keep our standards high

To help maintain the high reputation of **The New Zealand Bed & Breakfast Book** we ask for your comments about your stay.
You can simply stick a stamp on this form or save all your comment forms and return them in an envelope.

Alternatively, leave your comment at our website
www.bnb.co.nz

Name of Host or B&B____________________________________

Address ____________________________________
____

Considering things such as breakfast, meals, beds, cleanliness, hospitality and value for money, what is your overall satisfaction rating, with 1 being the lowest and 10 being the highest rating?

1 2 3 4 5 6 7 8 9 10

Do you have any comments?

We may display your comments on our website. The rating will be confidential and will be kept for administration purposes.
Fill in your details to go into our regular prize draws!
Your details will not be passed on to anyone else. If you do not have email we suggest you use a friend's email address.

Your name ____________________________________

Your Town/city
and country ____________________________________

Email ____________________________________

Please Post this form to:
The New Zealand B&B Book,
PO Box 6843, Wellington, New Zealand

Place stamp
here or send
forms in one
envelope

Moonshine Press
PO Box 6843
Wellington
New Zealand